HOUGHTON MIFFLIN COMPANY
EDITORIAL ADVISORY COMMITTEE
IN EDUCATION

Herold C. Hunt, Harvard University
C. Gilbert Wrenn, Arizona State University
Van Cleve Morris, University of Illinois at Chicago Circle
Samuel A. Kirk, University of Illinois
William Van Til, New York University
Paul R. Hanna, Stanford University

Reading
Instruction

DIMENSIONS AND ISSUES

Edited by WILLIAM K. DURR

Michigan State University

72844

HOUGHTON MIFFLIN COMPANY • BOSTON

New York • Atlanta • Geneva, ILL. • Dallas • Palo Alto

LIBRARY

Copyright © 1967 by William K. Durr.
All rights reserved. The selections in this book
are used by permission of and special arrangement
with the proprietors of their respective copyrights.
Printed in the U.S.A.

LB
1050
D85

✣ INTRODUCTION ✣

4/13/72, alandar 5.95

I am grateful for the confidence and friendliness William Durr expressed when he asked me to write a brief introductory statement for this volume. His point of view about the teaching of reading, his devotion to and patience with children, and his ways of working are more than a little familiar to me. Also, for quite a number of years the undersigned himself has been concerned with the improvement of instruction in reading. It is only natural, therefore, that I am glad to comply with Dr. Durr's request.

The purpose of this book is to provide a readily accessible collection of writings on certain topics that are introduced to students in many collegiate courses in the teaching of reading and that are also of great concern to teachers now in service. No single textbook available does or could treat these topics — and the various related viewpoints and issues — with the detail that the student or teacher needs. That is why this book should be a valuable supplement for use in conjunction with almost any textbook on instruction in reading.

The fourteen topics the book discusses were chosen with considerable care by Dr. Durr and can be identified easily by a brief perusal of the chapter titles as listed in the table of contents. Dr. Durr's opening statement at the beginning of each chapter introduces the topic with which the chapter deals, contributes to the reader's understanding of that topic, and sets the scene for the selections which follow. The bibliographies provided by Dr. Durr at the end of each chapter (as well as those provided by some of the authors of the selections themselves) should be helpful to anyone who wishes to read further on the particular topic with which a given chapter is concerned.

Taken together, the fifty-four selections contained in the book explain a variety of viewpoints and issues, supply reports of research, describe instructional programs now in use, provide statements of what should be taught, and offer suggestions pertaining to specific instructional techniques. Although some of the selections were written by recognized specialists in the teaching of reading, Dr. Durr's chief criterion in deciding whether or not to include a given selection was his judgment of its merit and its elucidation of the topic with which it is concerned.

The fifty-four selections offer answers to many questions with which the student or teacher should be acquainted. Among these questions are the following:

What changes have taken place in the teaching of reading since 1910?

What should be included in instruction which is intended to prepare pupils for beginning reading?

What different approaches are used in teaching beginning reading?

At what age should instruction in reading begin? What should be included in this instruction?

What are the advantages of i/t/a or other special orthographies proposed for use in teaching beginning reading?

What can be done to help pupils develop the power to unlock independently words that are strange to them only in print? What are the advantages and disadvantages of each proposal?

What can be done to improve pupils' comprehension of what they attempt to read?

What is critical reading? What can be done to teach pupils to react critically to what they read?

What are the characteristics of disadvantaged pupils? What adjustments should be made in teaching reading to such pupils?

What characterizes gifted pupils? What special provisions should be made for such pupils in the teaching or reading?

What types of organization for instruction in reading are used? What are the advantages of grouping pupils?

What types of materials are needed for providing adequate instruction in reading?

What is linguistics? What contribution can it make to the teaching of reading?

What should be done to evaluate the reading that pupils do and the progress that they make?

What are reading disorders? What can be done to alleviate or remove them?

As Dr. Durr states or infers more than once, the pupil's level of achievement at any given time and the progress he makes in learning to read during his school days are dependent upon a number of different factors. Among these factors are (1) the motivation and the intellectual equipment the pupil brings to his task of learning to read; (2) the quality of the instructional materials used; (3) the teacher's understanding of what instruction in reading is, the extent to which he uses effective materials and methods as they are intended to be used, his awareness of just what he is trying to do by means of any piece of teaching he undertakes, his acquaintance with the pupil's weaknesses, strengths, and potential growth, and his attention to individual differences among pupils; and (4) the standards of achievement set by the teacher.

This fourth factor deserves more emphasis than it usually receives. Any student or teacher of reading should keep in mind that at any level boys and girls have a strong tendency to be fully satisfied with meeting whatever standards of achievement the teacher sets. If these standards are vague or low, as most certainly they are in many cases, it is idle to expect pupils to learn as much as they could under more stimulating conditions or to achieve as much as their present ability permits. But when the standards are clear-cut and actually challenge the pupils, both the quality and quantity of learning is likely to be much greater than what is considered satisfactory today at almost any level in most schools. This latter is true of the great majority of pupils, but particularly of those who happen to be even a little bright. Fortunate indeed is the pupil who has each and every year of his school life a teacher who sets standards of achievement which he can understand and which challenge him to do the very best he can. For him, reading can become the most effective means of continuing to educate himself long after his school days have passed and of obtaining the pleasures literature offers.

Paul McKee
Greeley, Colorado

✦ PREFACE ✦

Although the school's responsibilities continue to grow year by year, and although there are wide swings in the intensity of emphasis on different areas of learning, the improvement of reading ability consistently maintains a top spot among the goals of the school. Good teachers strive to improve their methods, materials, and organizational procedures so that every single child will develop to a point where he *can* and *will* read at the level of his individual capacity. There is no academic goal that is more important.

The materials in this book have been selected to help teachers achieve this goal.

Each of the selections and the articles and books included in the suggested readings at the end of each chapter have been published since 1960. This criterion for selection — recency of publication — does not deny the value of the many articles published before 1960, but the editor of a book of readings has the unique opportunity to bring together samples of the most recent thinking on a particular subject — thinking which has been influenced and honed by that which has gone before.

No instructional innovation in reading should be adopted blindly merely because it is classified as "new," however. Underlying the question continually confronting those who work in this field — "What's new in reading instruction?" — is the implication of the value of change just for the sake of change. Yet nothing could be more unfair to the children we teach. Certainly new knowledge should lead to improvements in reading instruction, but the words *change* and *improvement* are not synonyms. We should search for and examine innovations, but the only question that can be professionally sound is, "What is the best in reading instruction?" In seeking an answer to this question, we must analyze the tried as well as the new, then reject, modify, or adopt according to our judgment of what is best.

Some of the articles in this collection have been selected to reflect a diversity of opinions on certain controversial issues: early versus later reading instruction, artificial orthography versus traditional orthography, the instructional versus the neurological view of the problem of reading retardation, to mention a few. The aim has been to present both sides of such issues so that the reader may have a better basis for reaching his own conclusions.

The primary criterion for the inclusion of an article, however, was that it should provide information of immediate, practical value to those who teach reading. Teachers frequently are, and should be, interested in the theoretical questions undergirding reading instruction. But their most pressing concerns often revolve around such problems as how to help the slow-learning child, how to provide challenges for the gifted, how to organize a class for effective instruction, what kind of pre-reading program to provide, how to evaluate each child's reading level, when to begin reading instruction, and what kinds of instructional materials to select. These problems and many others are explored here by reading experts occupying a wide diversity of positions on practices and procedures for the teaching of reading.

I am grateful to all those authors who have consented to have their articles reprinted here. Their concern and mine is that our pupils should receive the very best instruction that can be provided, and we share the hope that this collection may, in some small measure, improve the teaching of reading. I am also grateful to the many teachers throughout the country whose views and provocative questions provide a continuing stimulation in the search for more effective teaching. And I am deeply indebted to Dr. Paul McKee, whose life-long concern has been the improvement of reading instruction and who remains a dedicated and gracious leader in this endeavor.

William K. Durr
East Lansing, Michigan

❖ CONTENTS ❖

Reading Instruction

DIMENSIONS AND ISSUES

1

Reading in Our Schools

The reading programs in today's schools represent a spectrum of approaches which defy generalization. In one classroom we see all of the children taking turns reading orally from the same book, while the others follow along in hesitant anticipation of their turns under the watchful eye of a teacher who has not yet learned the meaning of "reading-skill development" or "individual differences." In another room we see a competent teacher providing instruction in reading skills for one group of children while the rest of the class is busily engaged in valuable, independent activities. In still a third room we see children reading quietly alone as the teacher works individually with those who need his help.

Our classroom visits could extend indefinitely and, although we could place our teachers in certain broad categories according to the teaching methods used, the differences in specific techniques used could also extend indefinitely.

How, then, can we describe current reading programs in our schools without describing each and every teacher of reading? We can do so only in the broadest way and with the repeated admonition that the descriptions may include more differences than similarities.

The main ingredients in our reading programs are the children, our teaching techniques, and the materials we use. In our continuing efforts to improve our instructional programs, we must never lose sight of any one of these ingredients; our classification schemes, however, sometimes unintentionally lead us to concentrate on one of these ingredients and to ignore the others. For example, some approaches to reading are classified according to the organizational scheme used for placing children into classrooms or for grouping them after they are placed. Hence, there are reading programs categorized as cluster-grouping approaches or the "Joplin Plan" approach. Some approaches are classified according to the order of skill development, and here we may speak of the phonics approach or the whole-word approach. Still others may be classified according to the kinds of materials used, and here we may speak of the basal-reader approach, the language-arts approach, or the i/t/a approach.

In discussing these various approaches, it is not essential that we examine each minute variable for all classifications at once to determine which should be used with certain children in certain situations; however, it is essential that we do not concentrate on one to the exclusion of all the others. For example, we may cognitively explore the pros and cons of a certain procedure for grouping children, but we must not myopically conclude that any one grouping pro-

1

cedure will develop good readers without also paying close attention to the materials and teaching techniques used.

As Olson, using one system of classification, points out in one of the selections in this chapter, the most common approach today centers around the use of a basic-reading series. But, though this approach calls to mind the materials used, it must not lead us to envision a stereotyped design of teaching which does not vary from classroom to classroom. The variables associated with teacher competency and pupil attributes may lead to markedly different uses of these tools from room to room. In fact, any given teacher will probably change his ways of using these materials from year to year even with children who are much alike.

All of us who teach must sometimes long for magic solutions to our instructional problems. This semi-latent desire for an easy method of "instant learning" may lead us to dash wildly from one promised panacea to another, only to find that we have exchanged one kind of educational problem for two others. The good reading teacher, however, has learned to distrust the extravagant claims of those who promise effortless success for all children, just as the intelligent consumer has long since learned to distrust the patent medicine which professes to remove warts, grow hair, or cure ulcers. Progress in teaching reading has evolved over the years through the experimentation and research of reading specialists with the dedicated cooperation of classroom teachers.

A knowledge of history does not guarantee a better understanding of our current actions and attitudes, but it can provide a dimension which enables us to view them in proper perspective. This vertical view of reading programs may provide a greater appreciation for the programs in today's schools and an understanding of how our present practices have evolved. It also may lessen our susceptibility to the blandishments of the educational Pied Pipers who promise miracles. In the first selection in this chapter, Nila Banton Smith, probably our foremost reading historian, presents an overview of reading developments. which should entice the reader to explore this fascinating area more fully.

In the following articles, current practices are described from two perspectives. Arthur V. Olson classifies modern reading approaches into six major categories and briefly describes each one, while Dorothy Prince describes the important characteristics of a successful reading program in one school district.

What Have We Accomplished in Reading?
A Review of the Past Fifty Years

❖ NILA BANTON SMITH

This last half-century stands out as a truly golden period in the progress of reading instruction. More innovations have been effected in reading during the last fifty years than during the entire three hundred years antedating this period of American history. I am sure that progress has been equally notable in the other phases of the language arts constellation. It is most appropriate that accomplishments in all of the language art areas be reviewed upon this momentous occasion — the Golden Anniversary of The National Council of Teachers of English!

Progress in reading instruction has been marked by a succession of turning points. For a period of years reading methods and materials all over the country are quite similar — so similar, in fact, that an unbiased examiner might arrive at the conclusion that all had been turned out of the same mold, with just a slightly different crimp here and there in the contour of the pan. Then, rather suddenly, a new plan becomes popular, and we teach reading in this manner until another turning point arrives. Thus, epoch after epoch of reading instruction passes (26).

Fortunately printed records are available to which we can turn in delineating these epochs and ascertaining their characteristics. In attempting to obtain information to bring to you about reading epochs during our recent half century the following source materials, published between 1910 and 1960, were explored: prominent educational magazines that usually contain reading articles, yearbooks of learned societies, summaries of published investigations in reading, lists of unpublished master's and doctoral researches completed or under way. More than three hundred pieces of materials were surveyed for the purpose of picking up the sequence of events and trends which marked the pilgrimage of reading in its upward march from 1910 to the present time. This information will be presented to you by decades.

Accomplishments from 1910 to 1920

The dramatic decade beginning with 1910 ushered in the first truly great breakthrough in reading progress. This was the birth of the scientific movement in education. In 1909 Thorndike made the initial presentation of his handwriting scale before a meeting of the American Association for the Advancement of Science, and in 1910 it was published (29). Generally speaking, the publication of the Thorndike scale has been recognized as the beginning of the contemporary movement for measuring educational products scientifically. In

From *Elementary English*, 38: 141–150; March, 1961. Reprinted with permission of the National Council of Teachers of English and Nila Banton Smith, Distinguished Service Professor, Glassboro State College, Glassboro, New Jersey.

3

the immediately ensuing years scales and tests appeared rapidly: Courtis arithmetic tests, Hilligas' Composition Scale, Buckingham Spelling Scale — and then a reading test — The Gray Standardized Oral Reading Paragraphs (13). This test was published in 1915. Other reading tests followed shortly.

As a result of the strong new surge of interest in placing education on a scientific basis together with its correlative motives for developing instruments of measurement, we would naturally expect that the scientific study of reading problems would take a vigorous spurt. And this it did.

Through all the years up to 1910 only thirty-four studies had been reported in reading. During the 1910–20 decade, two hundred accounts appeared, about six times as many as had been reported during the entire history of reading preceding this time. These studies had to do mostly with tests and school surveys as would be expected.

As for the method: the most revolutionary thing happened that had happened since clergy began to teach reading in churches, and dames began to teach reading in kitchens. "For hundreds of years oral reading had maintained a supreme and undisputed claim on teaching methods" (25). During this decade, however, the concept of teaching *silent* reading burst into our slumbering complacency like a bombshell. It came suddenly and in the midst of a period in which school people were serenely content in the use of sentence-story methods applied to the oral reading of selections in literary readers. For the most part they continued to use these practices to the end of the decade but the startling new idea was at least launched. Discussions of the advantages of silent reading appeared for the first time in the Sixteenth (16) and in the Eighteenth (17) Yearbooks of the National Society for the Study of Education. Speakers at educational conventions began to talk about it, magazine articles began to discuss it. The idea had been born.

To sum up: developing the concept of applying scientific techniques to the study of reading, devising standardized instruments to measure reading achievement, increasing the number of studies tremendously, initiating the silent reading idea. These seem to have been the major accomplishments from 1910 to 1920.

Accomplishments from 1920 to 1930

The period extending from 1920 to 1930 is perhaps the most golden decade in this golden era of progress in so far as fundamental changes in reading practices are concerned. These changes were largely due to the scientific movement which had shaped up during the preceding period and which now was opening up fresh wells of information with improved and extended applications.

The new studies conducted during this decade carried with them three distinct earmarks of progress: the number increased tremendously; they covered a wider scope of problems; many of them were conducted in classrooms by teachers and other school personnel, rather than being confined to the laboratory.

As to the number of investigations: Gray's summaries reveal that 763 were reported as compared with 200 during the preceding decade. This unprecedented increase reflected the zeal and enthusiasm with which school people were searching for more information about the important subject of reading.

The studies of this period probed a variety of problems, but there were three problem areas which were most highly significant. They were significant because they resulted in sweeping changes in practice. These three areas were (a) silent reading, (b) individual differences, and (c) remedial reading.

The first half of this decade might well be called "The Age of Silent Reading." "These years were marked with an exaggerated, often exclusive emphasis on silent reading as opposed to the traditional oral reading techniques" (25). As previously mentioned, the concept of teaching silent reading was initiated during the latter part of the preceding period, but it didn't really take hold as a nationwide classroom practice until during the years of 1920 to 1925. This sudden and widespread reversal in practice was largely due to two influences: the development of tests which revealed that silent reading was superior to oral reading in speed and comprehension; and the publication of The Yearbooks of the National Society for the Study of Education. As already indicated, one article each appeared in the Sixteenth (16) and the Eighteenth (17) Yearbooks. The climax, however, came with the publication of the Twentieth Yearbook, Part II (19) of which was devoted entirely to the report of the "Society's Committee on Silent Reading." Following the appearance of this Yearbook, "textbook writers began to produce readers based on silent reading procedures; other authors prepared professional books on silent reading; teachers busied themselves in preparing exercises that would check comprehension of silent reading by means of drawings, true-false statements or completion sentences and so forth. The whole country for a time seemed to be obsessed with the idea of teaching silent reading" (25).

This extreme emphasis, however, was soon balanced with other factors. By 1925 the novelty of the new idea had worn off, somewhat; investigations revealed some unique uses of oral reading, school people discovered that there still were some special needs for oral reading in the school program. Perhaps, the culminating influence came with the publication of the Twenty-Fourth Yearbook, Part I (20), which appeared in 1925. This Yearbook advocated a broader program of reading instruction which among other things recognized both oral and silent reading. New courses of study, professional books and readers immediately reflected the broadened objectives of this Yearbook and methods during the years 1925-1930 were shaped largely by its contents. So during the first two decades of the last fifty years we progressed from extreme oral reading to extreme silent reading to a broader program which recognized both. In my opinion, this was an indication of real accomplishment.

As for individual differences: with the administration of the newly developed tests, a very great fundamental truth became apparent with a violent impact — the realization that there were wide individual differences in the reading achievement of children, in the same grade and in the same classroom. This discovery spurred school people to experiment with a variety of adjustments in classroom organization and instruction, designed to cope with this newly revealed variation in the learning rate of children.

There were reports of adjustments made in classrooms which maintained the regular organization such as ability grouping, flexible promotions, and differentiated assignments. But the pulsating new idea was that of breaking up class organization entirely to permit of individual progression. This plan of organization received as much attention at this time as it is receiving at the present moment. Speeches, articles, and yearbooks dealt with the subject. San Francisco; Los Angeles; Detroit; Winnetka; Madison, Wisconsin; and other school systems reported (21) results they had obtained by individual instruction. The states of Connecticut and Illinois reported (21) experiments in individualizing instruction in rural schools.

The various plans, on the whole, were patterned after the Winnetka or the Dalton ideas, in both of which individual progression in reading and other subjects was made possible by means of assignments in which the child worked through subject material that increased in small increments of difficulty. The important point to note is that attention to individual differences in reading received its first great impetus during this decade of remarkable progress.

The concept of *remedial* reading was launched from its small island of study during this period and sent out over unexplored seas in quest of answers to disability problems. The movement was spurred on by the use of standardized tests. These tests revealed that thousands of boys and girls were failing each year to make normal progress in reading. Published reports of work in the reading disability field indicate that the chief interest at this time was in diagnosing individual cases. As for method, it was during this period that Fernald evolved her kinesthetic method, and that Orton expounded his theory on mixed dominance and the treatment that accompanied it. Remedial reading did get under way during this period.

In beginning reading there also were innovations. Experience charts first came into use. The Nineteenth Yearbook (18), published in 1920, dealt with reading materials. In it examples were given of charts based on children's experiences, and the practice of introducing children to beginning reading through the use of such material was advocated. This practice was not widely accepted until much later, but progress had been made in evolving the idea.

And last but not least, mention must be made of another mark of progress which clearly stamped itself into the later annals of this decade. The reading readiness concept began to take shape at this time.

In 1926 the International Kindergarten Union in cooperation with the United States Bureau of Education conducted an investigation on "Pupils' Readiness for Reading Instruction upon Entrance to First Grade." The first articles on the subject were published in *Childhood Education* in January, 1927. Two of these articles used the term "reading readiness." In so far as I am aware, this was the first time that this phrase crept into our reading vocabulary (27). In Gray's summaries published in 1928, he reported for the first time three studies on reading readiness. A few master's theses and a trickling of articles on this subject also appeared before the close of the decade. The new concept, however, was still in the formative stage, and little was done about it in a practical way until the following period, but the movement was on its way.

Much more could be said about the accomplishments made during this unprecedented period. I should like to dwell longer on the accumulation of information gathered about reading and the auspicious innovations in classroom practice that were inaugurated at this time, but I must pass on to other conquests and other days.

Accomplishments from 1930 to 1940

This period may be characterized largely as one of extension and application rather than one of revelation and initiation.

Investigations continued at an accelerated pace. In round figures about twelve hundred studies were reported between 1930 and 1940. Not only were these studies greater in number, but they were superior in isolation of problems, in designs, and in controls.

Some of the embryo ideas that had sprouted in the preceding decade came into full bloom and fruited profusely at this time. For example: the reading readiness interest reached its zenith in this period (27). Published investigations on this topic increased steadily during each successive year of this decade (9), reaching their climax of frequency in 1940 when Gray reported twenty-two studies relating to this topic in one year. Since that time the number has decreased steadily.

Turning to unpublished research, this was the hey-day of aspiring masters and doctors in finding problems for research in the readiness area. The first doctoral dissertation on readiness was reported in 1927. From that time on, the number of master and doctoral studies increased, reaching its peak in the years 1937 to 1940. Fourteen such studies were completed in 1937, fifteen in 1938, fourteen in 1939, and twelve in 1940. Since that time only two or three academic studies on readiness have been reported each year.

A similar trend is seen in published articles on reading readiness. Periodicals abounded with discussions on readiness topics from 1930 to 1940. Articles on this subject rarely appear in present-day literature.

In the light of this evidence, it may be concluded that this was the period of most vigorous emphasis, both on investigations of reading readiness and applications of the readiness theory. The concept has been accepted now and we hear little about it at the present time.

Remedial reading, which had experienced a touch-and-go recognition during the preceding period, now became established and gained stature. Many significant studies were conducted in the remedial reading areas: causes of difficulties, diagnosis, and corrective procedures. Professional books devoted exclusively to remedial reading were first published. Some laboratory studies were still made but the majority of studies now were conducted in schools. Remedial reading, which had started in laboratories, now became a topic for practical experimentation in the public schools themselves.

A new trend that began to emerge was that of giving beginning attention to high school, college, and adult reading. Studies made at these levels, however, were mostly concerned with interests in, and uses of reading, rather than with reading achievement and teaching procedure.

Every decade reviewed so far has been characterized by one or two events of great distinction. In the 1910-1920 decade, it was the application of scientific measurement and investigation to reading, in the 1920-'30 era, it was the startling innovation of silent reading and of individual progression. What was the spectacular event in the nineteen-thirties?

The Activity Movement swept the country during these years, and the startling new idea in reading was to teach this skill as a part of the Activity Program. In such a program children worked freely and spontaneously and actively in following their own interests; and teachers were intrigued with the new "game" of trying to get all of their subject matter across through "Units of Work."

In so far as reading was concerned, pupils had access to a considerable number of books bearing largely on the topic of their "Unit of Work." This was the first big impetus for bringing a quantity of books into the classroom for reading. There was a profusion of charts and school-made booklets growing out of children's interests. Pupils read functionally from their co-operatively prepared materials and out of many books in doing research in connection with their Units. In a word, this was how reading proceeded in the Activity Program in the thirties.

We no longer hear of the Activity Program at this time nor of the teaching of reading in connection with this program. The Activity Movement, however, made a vigorous impact on the teaching of reading and other subjects at this time — an impact so strong that its influence still continues. The Activity Movement distracted the school public from its age-old concept of schools centered almost exclusively on subject-matter goals to schools in which consideration is given to the child, himself, his stage of development, his interests, his activities, his choices and his decisions.

In summary, we may say that progress in this decade was characterized by continuing investigations, greater in number, higher in quality than in the preceeding decade; intensive application of the readiness concept; transfer of remedial activities from laboratory to classroom; beginning attention to reading at higher levels; and wide-spread interest in teaching reading as an integral part of the Activity Program.

Accomplishments from 1940 to 1950

An event resulting from progress in science overshadowed all other indications of progress during this period. The "birthday of the atomic age" is officially set as December 2, 1942, when Dr. Enrico Fermi turned on the first successful nuclear energy machine in Chicago. The first atomic bomb destroyed Hiroshima on August 6, 1945. On the face of things, this terrifying discovery with its possibilities for good or for evil reduced to comparative insignificance our little scientific achievements in reading. Yet, could this achievement have been possible without reading? Can we cope adequately with its future destructive or beneficent effects, as the case may be, without more efficient reading skill and a wider reading citizenry? The atomic age and reading immediately become interactive.

But we didn't realize this at the time. We were too close to this earth-shaking event to sense its import for reading instruction. The war probably only had two *immediate* effects on reading. One of these was a diminution in the number of reading investigations. This was probably due to the fact that many of the psychologists and educators who conducted research in reading, or stimulated others to do so, were in the armed services.

The other major effect of the war was the shocking discovery that at this day and age thousands of young men in the military service could not read well enough to follow the simple printed instructions for camp life. Coupled with this discovery was the revelation that reading could be taught to these young men in army camps in an amazingly short time. Concurrently, several new investigations disclosed reading deficiencies in large numbers of high school and college students. These several influences combined to produce a spurt in attention to reading at these higher levels. Immediately following the war, a great deal of professional literature on reading emerged and among these publications several bulletins and one yearbook appeared dealing with high school and college reading. Chief among these publications was a bulletin of the National Education Association titled *Reading Instruction in Secondary*

Schools (15), and the Forty-Eighth Yearbook, Part II of The National Society for the Study of Education, titled *Reading in High School and College* (24). The actual teaching of reading at these levels had not progressed far at this time but the idea was vigorously expanding.

During this period, reading in the content subjects also became a matter of wide discussion and the subject of a few investigations. The studies at this time pointed to the general conclusion that while good readers can read well in all subject fields, special practice in reading in particular subject areas is helpful to average and poor readers.

In the forties, wide recognition was given to the interrelationships amongst the language arts. Studies, articles, speeches were concerned with the relationship of reading to spelling, handwriting, vocabulary, and composition. As a result we came to recognize that reading was not an isolated skill independent of other skills used in the interchange of ideas, but that it was just one aspect of the total language arts constellation mutually dependent upon and interactive with all other skills in the communication dimension.

A strong new concern also sprang up in regard to the effects of three of the newer media for mass communication: comics, movies, and radio. Television did not come in for much attention until the next decade but during this period wide dissemination of entertainment through the first named agencies stirred up worry on the part of school people and parents. They feared that interest in listening to radio, looking at comics, viewing movies would reduce interest in reading and thus decrease the amount of reading done. Numerous popular articles bemoaned the situation and pointed out its dangers. Several studies were conducted directed toward the exploration of students' interests in this area and finding out how much time they devoted to the offerings of these types. Thus initial steps were taken in obtaining information to combat what was thought to be the first threat to reading.

Remedial diagnosis and treatment continued to claim a large segment of the spotlight. Mechanical instruments and devices which had been introduced during the preceding period increased in numbers and use. There were fewer studies reported on psychological factors such as dominance, handedness, eyedness, and reversals. An increasing number were devoted to personal factors as related to reading: personal interests and attitudes, personal status in social, emotional, and experiential maturity. This attention to other growth and development factors as related to reading was certainly one of the most notable advances made during this period.

To sum up: the chief points of progress during this decade were: increased attention to teaching reading at the higher levels; growing attention to reading in the content subjects; concerns about mass communications; attempts to find relationships between reading and handwriting, spelling, vocabulary and composition; and, perhaps most important of all, a growing consciousness of the profound truth that reading doesn't develop in a vacuum by itself, but that it is part and parcel of general child development and is affected by all other aspects of child growth.

Accomplishments from 1950 to 1960

A most exciting decade! For one thing, interest in reading instruction became almost universal during this period. There was a time when primary teachers were the only people interested in the teaching of reading. Now teachers of all subjects and at all levels want to know more about reading. Parents are asking questions, pursuing books and articles on reading. Students at high-school and college levels and adults beyond college are flocking to reading centers. Slick magazines and laymen are discussing reading freely. A great conflagration of interest has been ignited amongst teachers and students, and more especially amongst the lay public. And this is good.

During this period, however, for the first time in history, reading instruction in American schools underwent harsh and severe criticism by laymen. School people maintained that the criticisms were unfair and rose to the defense of their methods through articles, speeches, discussions, and investigations. Several comparative studies of "Then and Now" were made. These studies, on the whole, showed that we were teaching reading as well as or better than in preceding years.

Insofar as progress is concerned the criticism by laymen probably had three good effects: it caused school people to examine their present methods more carefully; it stimulated the interest of parents and other laymen in reading instruction; it offered motives and opportunities to school people to explain the research, psychology, and philosophy on which present methods are based. So in this situation, as is often the case in other situations, even criticism caused reading to move forward.

Perhaps as an off-shoot of interest and criticism, coupled with a growing awareness of the complexity of the reading process, there has been a spurt of activity in the re-instatement and increase of reading courses in the curriculums of teacher-training institutions. Concurrently with this interest in adding more courses, standards are being raised in regard to the qualifications of teachers of reading and of reading specialists. This movement toward better-trained teachers in reading is a big step forward.

As for the number of investigations: studies during this period reached incredible proportions. Gray reported over one thousand studies in his 1960 summary, but in his introduction he said for the first time in his thirty-five years of annual summarizing, "The number of studies are increasing so rapidly that it is no longer possible to report all of them in this annual summary. Those referred to this year represent either a new or distinctive approach to a problem or suggest significant issues in need of further study." Not only was this increase apparent in the published reports of reading investigations, but it also was reflected in the reports of dissertations completed or in progress which soared to new numerical heights, the number reported averaging about ninety per year as compared with about fifty in the preceding decade.

Advance is shown in the subjects of investigation. Reading in the content fields, adult reading deficiencies, and television as related to reading came in for strong additional attention. The most gratifying trend revealed, however, is that we are at present delving more deeply into the reading process and more broadly into the factors that affect it. The former popular topic of phonics now seems to have been replaced with studies of perception. Comprehension is no longer treated as a lump sum; the emphasis at present is upon the higher thinking processes of interpretation and critical reading. The old readiness studies are replaced with investigations of predictions and expectancy. Remedial reading is not so much concerned now with studies of gadgets and specific teaching remedies as it is with organismic and personality factors. Parental personality, attitudes, and interactions with the child as related to reading entered the research scene for the first time during this period, and many reading investigations concerned with parents and their children are now being reported. Studies are made in regard to the climate of the classroom and its effect on reading. This mere glimpse at some of the subjects of the most recent studies is indicative of a trend toward probing to greater depths and in wider breadths than was evident in most of the studies preceding this period.

Special mention should be made of a clearly discernible advance in regard to reading and the other language arts. In the preceding decade we became strongly concerned about the relationships of reading to the subjects of spelling, handwriting, vocabulary, and composition. During this decade we have moved on to a concern about aspects of the language arts which perhaps are less tangible than the subject matter areas but more inclusive in their application to the entire block of communication skills. Listening studies have increased by leaps and bounds. Some of the most recent dissertation topics have to do with semantic studies of reading content, multiple meanings, figures of speech in reading, and the linguistic approach to reading. Is it not an accomplishment to have moved on from subject interrelationships to relationships dealing with listening and the various aspects of linguistics?

The innovation in reading method which has loomed large on the horizon of late is the plan known as *individualized instruction.* The amount of attention given to this plan in this decade is comparable to that given to individual instruction in the nineteen-twenties. It probably is the most popular topic of discussion at present in educational magazines and often at teacher gatherings.

This individualized plan of the present is different from individual instruction which was popular in the twenties. The earlier plan was subject-matter oriented. Each child was given subject matter assignments divided into small increments of difficulty and he was permitted to progress as fast as he, personally, could complete each successive increment. The present plan is child-psychology oriented utilizing particularly Dr. Willard Olsen's theory of *seeking, self-election,* and *pacing* in that the child seeks that which stimulates him, selects the book he desires to read, and proceeds at his own rate.

This plan has been used too recently for research reports to have crept into published summaries of investigations. Most of the research on this topic at present falls into the unpublished category of theses, dissertations, or mimeographed reports of experiments carried on in certain school systems. An examination of the most recent sources listing dissertations completed or under way indicates that a quantity of research is now taking place in regard to this topic. Much of it will undoubtedly find its way into print in the near future.

Much more could be said about this period, but because of lack of time we now shall let the curtain fall over the last scene in fifty years of reading accomplishment. As we review the stirring events of the past, we have a right to feel cheered, grateful, proud. In looking back in retrospect we might wonder whether another fifty years could possibly bring about so many changes. This was the first period in which experimentation could be conducted scientifically. In consideration of the newly developed tools, our eagerness to learn, and studies conducted, we might reason that practically all facets of reading instruction have been explored and thus another era could never be so great as this.

If we do reason to this conclusion, we probably are wrong. We pioneered during the period in unexplored territory. We chopped down and cleared away the large virgin trees, but perhaps some of the humble shrubs or creeping vines or fragile mosses may hold even more significance for us than the strikingly obvious, first-sight timbers. But these more obscure growths won't yield their significance with the use of heavy saws and axes. We shall need fresh, piercing insights in choosing which of these to select for dislodgment, and then we shall need unique, delicate tools to pry them loose from their tangled environment and to test the potency of their effect.

What I am trying to say is that while our accomplishments have been very great, indeed, it may be that we have only penetrated the first layer, the troposphere, so to speak. Undoubtedly, brilliant new insights will be revealed, ingenious new techniques of experimentation will be evolved. Possibilities of such developments portend opportunities for unlimited achievement in the future.

Most assuredly, we shall not rest complacently in the glory of achievement during this past golden age. Rather shall we look forward to still greater accomplishments in reading. Let us push on and on with more and more vigor in the next decade and the next decade, and in all of the other decades ahead!

References

This bibliography would be too voluminous if each separate piece of material examined were listed. In case of educational journals, yearbooks, and summaries of investigations, each successive issue or publication was examined during the period of years indicated by dates accompanying the general reference. In cases in which a specific reference was made, or a quotation was stated from one particular publication, that publication is listed. Professional books on reading were examined but the titles are too numerous to include in this list.

1. Betts, Emmett Albert, and Thelma Marshall Betts. *An Index of Professional Literature on Reading and Topics.* New York: American Book Company, 1945.
2. *Childhood Education,* 1–37, 1924–1960.
3. *College English,* 1–22, 1939–1960.
4. *Doctoral Dissertations Accepted by American Universities.* New York: H. W. Wilson Co., 1934, 1955.
5. *Educational Index,* 1–31. New York: H. W. Wilson Co., 1930–1960.
6. *Elementary School Journal,* 10–60, 1910–1960.
7. *Elementary English,* 1–37, 1924–1960.
8. *English Journal,* 1–49, 1911–1960.
9. Good, Carter V. "Doctoral Studies Completed or Under Way," *Phi Delta Kappan,* 1923–1953; (Separate publications) Lyda, Mary Louise; Jenson, Glenn; Brown, Stanley; Anderson, Harold, Phi Delta Kappa, Bloomington, Ind. 1954–1959.
10. Gray, William S. *Summary of Investigations Relating to Reading.* University of Chicago Supplementary Monograph, No. 28. Chicago: 1925.
11. ———. "Summary of Investigations Relating to Reading," *Elementary School Journal,* 26–32, 1925–1932.
12. ———. "Summary of Investigations Relating to Reading," *Journal of Educational Research,* 5-54, 1932-1960.
13. ———. *Oral Reading Paragraphs Test.* Bloomington, Indiana: Public School Publishing Co., 1915.

14. National Education Association. "Newer Practices in Reading in the Elementary School," *The National Elementary Principal,* Seventeenth Yearbook, 1938.
15. ———. *Reading Instruction in Secondary Schools,* Research Bulletin, Vol. 22, No. 1, 1942.
16. National Society for the Study of Education. Sixteenth Yearbook, Part I, 1917.
17. ———. Eighteenth Yearbook, Part II, 1919.
18. ———. Nineteenth Yearbook, Part I, 1920.
19. ———. Twentieth Yearbook, Part II, 1921.
20. ———. Twenty-Fourth Yearbook, Part I, 1925.
21. ———. Twenty-Fourth Yearbook, Part II, 1925.
22. ———. Thirty-Sixth Yearbook, Part I, 1937.
23. ———. Forty-Eighth Yearbook, Part I, 1949.
24. ———. Forty-Eighth Yearbook, Part II, 1949.
25. Smith, Nila Banton. *American Reading Instruction.* New York: Silver Burdett, 1937.
26. ———. "Historical Turning Points in Reading," *NEA Journal,* 280–282; May, 1952.
27. ———. *Readiness for Reading and Related Language Arts.* National Council of Teachers of English, 1950.
28. *The Reading Teacher,* 1–14, 1947–1960. International Reading Association.
29. Thorndike, E. L. *The Thorndike Scale for Handwriting of Children.* New York: Bureau of Publications, Teachers College, Columbia University, 1910.
30. Traxler, Arthur E. *Ten Years of Research in Reading* (with Seder, Margaret), 1941. *Another Five Years of Research in Reading* (with Townsend), 1946. *Eight More Years of Research in Reading* (with Townsend), 1955, *Research in Reading During Another Four Years* (with Jungeblut). New York: Educational Records Bureau.
31. U. S. Library of Congress, Catalog Division, *American Doctoral Dissertations Lists.* Washington: Government Printing Office, 1913–1940.

Reading: The Approaches We Use

✤ ARTHUR V. OLSON

Never before has there been such a profusion of materials for teaching reading. With the advent of the "space race" and the resulting emphasis upon education, the public has placed the entire educational system under careful scrutiny. Since reading skills are the key to knowledge, it is obvious why the public has such an interest in the way reading is taught and the outcomes of progress in that field.

From *The Clearing House,* 39: 259–264; January, 1965. Reprinted by permission. Arthur V. Olson is Associate Professor of Education, University of Georgia, Athens.

Without the skill of reading, a child cannot make satisfactory progress in our schools. Not all of our children learn to read. We know that this is true, but the failure of some children is not easily explained. It may be because of low intelligence, emotional problems, poor teaching, physical problems, moving from town to town continuously without establishing roots, or poor home environment — any one or a combination of these factors. Because of the inability to point to a single factor for reading failure, many approaches and panaceas have been offered to educators within the last few years. As a result of the interest by the general public and the misunderstandings concerning the teaching of reading, it is important that those directly responsible for the curriculum be as informed as possible.

The reading controversy centers, not on any claim that we are not teaching the reading skills, but on the question of how we can teach the reading skills so that more children will be able to find success in school. Several approaches are in use. The most common is the basal reading approach; second is the basal reading approach used in conjunction with experience charts; third is phonics programs; fourth is reading programs based upon the language experience of the child.[1] These four approaches are the ones which have the greatest frequency of use in our public schools. Two others, however, are worth mentioning: the initial teaching alphabet and the linguistic approach.

The Basal Reading Approach

This approach is the one most commonly used throughout the United States at the present time. There are several series of readers on the market, each of which provides textbook material, workbooks and supplementary materials for the students, and manuals and guides for the teacher. Usually the basal readers provide instruction from reading readiness up through Grade 6, and in many cases through Grade 8.

The vocabulary is carefully controlled from book to book, primarily in Grades 1 through 3, with careful development of a sequential program and balanced skills. Within the last few years the basal readers have come through many an extensive change. The vocabulary has been enriched in many cases to meet the individual needs, the content has been changed somewhat by the introduction of stories written by well-known children's authors and authors of adult material. Much supplementary material for classroom use has also been introduced.

The basal readers are used by thousands of teachers throughout the United States with a great deal of success. Until a new teacher becomes thoroughly acquainted with the reading program, it is inadvisable for her to try to develop a reading program on her own. The material which is in the basal reader has been developed through years of study and many years of experience by classroom teachers. Because most of the material has been experimented with in many types of situations, the teacher's guide provides a valuable resource for the teacher in providing interest and productive activities for her class. Even for the teacher who has a great many years of experience and a good grasp of the skills which make up reading, the basal reader still offers a

---

[1] Mary C. Austin and Coleman Marrison, *The First R* (New York: The Macmillan Company, 1963).

valuable source of material for devising a skills program. The teacher may feel that she wants to use the material in a variety of ways. She may want it used as a part of an enrichment program or an individualized reading program, or to supplement other basal readers. In any case, it should be useful to the teacher as a guide for checking on the skill to be developed.

In some cases the basal reader has not been used as it was intended. The basal reader is not a total and complete program by itself. It is merely a part of the total program. It is impossible to teach through the basal reader all of the skills which are needed. Most of the content is story material. Since this is true, many of the skills that we teach, such as finding main ideas, organization, sequence, study skills, and others, must be taught in the content area as well. The basal reader, although it does have a number on the outside cover, is intended to meet the different instructional levels of all the children in every class. Because of the wide range of ability which we have in our classrooms, it is impossible to take care of all of the instructional needs through one book. A teacher must use other books within the same series for the children below and above the instructional level of the grade, or she may use a co-basal series.

Since reading is a sequential development of skills, there is no such thing as having children cover all pages in a certain reader by the end of the year. The statement has been made by some experts in the field of reading that as many as 30 per cent of our children are reading at the frustration level. If this is true, we are not doing our job.

The teacher's guide was never meant as a detailed prescription to be followed exactly in all aspects for all children. We know full well that some children are going to need more development in some skills than in others. There are also going to be some children who do not need the drills or some of the skills which are taught.

One of the most important criticisms that have come out of the basal reading program is directed against the teacher's use of the workbooks. If workbooks are used indiscriminately with all children, they have little value in developing needed skills. If the teacher fails to check the workbook activities with the children so they know the progress they are making and the errors they are making, the material is being grossly misused. The value of the material lies in the information it can give the teacher about the application of the skills. It has never been intended as a testing situation or as a busy-work activity.

In many of the activities involving the basal reader, directions must be given to the children. As this is to be a learning situation, the experience that a child is going to need to bring to the reading must be developed before, and the teacher's guidance through the material is mandatory.

The basal reading programs which are most commonly used in our public schools are as follows:

Alice and Jerry Basic Readers. Mabel O'Donnel and others. New York: Harper & Row, Publishers.

Betts Basic Readers. Emmett Betts and others. New York: American Book Co.

Developmental Reading Series. Guy Bond and others. Chicago: Lyons and Carnahan.

Ginn Basic Readers. David Russell and others. Boston: Ginn and Company.

Macmillan Readers. Arthur Gates and others. New York: The Macmillan Company.

New Basic Readers, Curriculum Foundation Series. Marion Monroe and others. Chicago: Scott, Foresman & Co.

Reading for Interest Series. Paul Witty and others. Boston: D. C. Heath & Co.

Reading for Meaning Series. Paul McKee and others. Boston: Houghton Mifflin Company.

Sheldon Basic Readers. William D. Sheldon and others. Boston: Allyn and Bacon, Inc.

Winston Basic Readers. Russell G. Stauffer and others. New York: Holt, Rinehart and Winston, Inc.

The Basal Reading Approach Used in Conjunction with Experience Charts

Charts based upon the real experiences of children provide available reading material for the beginning stages of reading instruction and for later development. The preparation of the charts involves very specific techniques which can be mastered easily by any interested teacher. The charts can usually be divided into two general categories: (1) charts made by the teacher from the dictation of the students, and (2) practice charts made by the children with the aid of the teacher.

The function of the first type of chart is to give the children the experience of seeing their own spoken words converted into printed symbols. The emphasis is not upon reading the chart but upon noticing the fact that words can be written down and the process by which we do write words — primarily left to right, return sweep to the next line, and left to right again.

There will be some children who have advanced in reading maturity and who will probably be able to read some of the words just from seeing the material written. There may be some children who will even want to learn to read the whole chart by themselves.

The second kind of chart, the practice chart, is prepared primarily to give actual practice in reading and writing. In developing this, the teacher will try to guide the children into making simple sentences, with the vocabulary load closely related to those they will find in their reading material. Because these charts will be ones in which the children have a direct and immediate interest, the material will often provide a welcome change from that which they find in their basal reader.

Even as the children progress through the grades, the experience charts will be of value in helping them to summarize their ideas of materials that they have read in the content areas. It will also afford them the opportunity of having more experiences with the vocabulary that they are trying to learn.

The Phonics Approach

Of all the issues in reading instruction, none has received more attention or aroused more discussion and misunderstanding than phonics. Not only are teachers interested in the role of phonics, but parents have looked upon it as an answer to all the reading problems.

The advocates of this approach believe that phonics (sounds as they apply to reading) should be introduced either before a sight vocabulary is established or on a parallel with the beginning basal reader. They reject the "whole-word" approach, because they believe the child first sees the word as individual letters and then the larger unit of the word as a whole.

Among the proponents of the "phonics-first approach" there is little consensus of opinion regarding the proper method of teaching. Each approach establishes a step-by-step sequence which the authors warn must be followed if the child is to read. They emphasize that learning phonics is a memorization process that can only be mastered by repetitive drill. Their material consists of workbooks containing page after page of isolated words and phonic elements.

One phonic system calls for learning the names of all twenty-six letters of the alphabet on the first day of instruction. Another emphasizes a letter-by-letter approach to reading, with the emphasis upon the sound of each separate letter. Others teach all of the vowel sounds first (long and short), followed by the consonants, while some teach only the long or short vowel sounds first. The teaching of blends, vowels or consonant digraphs, and dipthongs varies to a greater extent even than some of the other elements in the various materials. In some cases, only selected elements are taught, and others are ignored. In most of the material, there is little, if any, effort to help children evolve or understand phonic principles or to aid them in arriving at useful generalizations.

There is no evidence as to the value of many of the phonics programs now available to our schools except the opinions and prejudices of their authors. There is little consensus of opinion as to appropriate methods in the phonics approach, and serious doubts should be raised about the use of most phonics materials either in isolation or in conjunction with basal readers.

If the school is pressured into using a phonics program, it should be used on a very limited basis, rather than school-wide, and it should be evaluated under the best research conditions possible. Wholesale adoption can only result in confusion, more problems, and no indication as to the worth of the material.

The Language Experience Approach[2]

The language experience approach was developed in San Diego County, California, under the direction of R. Van Allen, curriculum director for the county school system. This approach attempts to integrate the communication skills of speaking, writing, reading, and listening.

In simplest terms, the approach can be thought of in the following manner. What a child thinks about he can talk about; what he can talk about he can write, or the teacher can write for him. What he writes he can read; he can read what he writes and what others write. What he has to say and write is as important to him as what other people have written for him to read.

From the very beginning of the school year, the children are encouraged to express themselves through speaking, writing, painting, and so forth. The teacher works with individual children and with small groups of children, helping them to write down "talk." Reading skills are taught informally by the teacher's talking to the children about the words, names of letters, beginning sounds, ending sounds, sounds in between.

The language experience approach seems to have some merit for beginning

[2] Doris May Lee and R. Van Allen, *Learning to Read Through Experience* (New York: Appleton-Century-Crofts, Inc., 1963).

reading instruction. It does seem to develop an interest in reading, there is an integration of the language arts and other communication skills, the children understand that reading is an important form of communication, and the approach does encourage creative expression.

Certain aspects of the approach are open to careful questioning. A teacher using this approach would have to be well aware of the development of reading skills, to be sure that the children were getting a balanced and sound program. There would be some danger of continual misspelling, poor expression, and punctuation errors if the teacher, fearing to hamper creativity, failed to correct errors. It is also possible that memorization of written material may be mistaken for reading.

The Initial Teaching Alphabet[3]

The i/t/a was developed in England by Sir James Pitman for use in teaching beginning readers. In this alphabet, there are forty-four symbols instead of our twenty-six letter alphabet. These symbols represent all of the sounds in the English language and are consistent in that a given symbol represents the same sound each time it is encountered. In traditional orthography, the twenty-six letters, individually or in combination, can represent upwards of 2,000 sounds.

The i/t/a, derived from the Augmented Roman Alphabet, is not designed as a continuing method. It is devised for use during the first 15 months of formal reading instruction. This method is in its fourth year of a five-year research study in England, with concurrent research projects in the United States. The largest of these involves forty-six first-grade classrooms in Bethlehem, Pennsylvania, and is sponsored by a research grant from the Ford Foundation and directed by Dr. Albert J. Mazurkiewicz of the i/t/a study center at Lehigh University.

Supporters of i/t/a claim that a child using it can learn to read in much less time than those using traditional orthography. The studies have not been in progress for a sufficient length of time, however, to determine if wholesale adoption is justified. There is still the unanswered question of transition to regular print after the initial teaching period and the possible affect upon later spelling and speed of reading.

Sir James Pitman is more than aware of these problems, and warns that the i/t/a method is only in the first stage of a long-term research investigation.

The Linguistics Approach[4]

The science of linguistics has aroused much interest in the last few years as a possible aid in improving reading competencies. Linguistics, because it is a complicated science, has resulted in misunderstanding, confusion, and hastily constructed material when applied to reading. The fact remains, however, that its application to reading is evolving.

The contribution of the science of linguistics to reading has come primarily from the descriptive linguists. They believe that, in reading, the child must

[3] John Downing, *The Initial Teaching Alphabet*. New York: The Macmillan Company, 1964.

[4] Carl E. Lefevre, *Linguistics and the Teaching of Reading*. New York: McGraw-Hill Book Company, 1964.

be able to respond to the language signals as represented by written symbols (words) in the same way that he responds to the patterns of auditory shapes. The key to an understanding of descriptive linguistics is in the concept of "pattern." It is argued that some of our reading failures are due to the obvious differences between the patterns of speech of children and the patterns we ask them to read. Much of the child's reading material is in a pattern that is unreal to him. It is imperative that a child have sentence sense, that is, that he should possess a knowledge of word arrangement and corresponding word function.

At the present time, there is some confusion regarding where to start beginning readers. Some would have the child begin with the smaller units in structural analysis, such as the phoneme (elemental speech sound), morpheme (the smallest unit with a meaning), word, and grapheme (letter symbol for a phoneme). Others would have us start with the simple sentence first. At the present time the concepts in linguistics, as they apply to the development of reading skills, are not well enough defined or established to arouse more than curiosity and a "wait-and-see" attitude.

Summary

The approaches used in teaching reading are many, and the problem of selecting the approach that will be most successful with all of our children is still solved by an educated trial-and-error method. There is probably no one approach that meets the needs of all. For most students, the basal reader has to be supplemented with more work in study skills, word recognition skills, comprehension skills, or other skill development areas. None of the approaches mentioned solves all the reading problems. The one thing we are sure of, however, is that an eclectic approach, taught by an intelligent teacher, supported by knowledgeable administration, is a prerequisite to good reading instruction.

Step by Step We Grow in Reading

✤ DOROTHY PRINCE

When one of the young fathers in our community started out to do some errands on a recent Saturday he found himself accompanied by his three youngsters. As he guided the car through the traffic, Molly, the two-year-old, picked up the words *tomato* and *potato* from the conversation. So far from correct was her pronunciation that her father proceeded to try to clarify the words. Over and over he patiently repeated the words and over and over

From *Elementary English,* 40: 436–439; April, 1963. Reprinted with the permission of the National Council of Teachers of English and Dorothy Prince, Coordinator of Elementary Instruction, Ector County Independent School District, Odessa, Texas.

Molly mispronounced them. Finally, seven-year-old Marty, one of our second-graders, could stand it no longer. "Daddy," he said analytically, "I think that if you would stress the consonants she could say them."

Late in January of this year I received an intriguing invitation from one of our second grade classes. "We enjoy reading so much," the note said. "Won't you please come and read with us next Wednesday morning?" Who was I to turn down an invitation like that! Never have I seen children enjoy reading more than these. Each group read from its basic reader. Since I was "new" and hadn't heard the previous stories, they brought me up-to-date on the characters, plots, motive, and outcomes. Surely there were some prospects for book reviewers and Broadway critics in this group. After each group had read, the teacher asked if the children would like to tell me how many library books they had read this year. As various ones showed their lists of books (the reading of each certified by both parent and teacher) we decided to total the number. We discovered that the twenty children present in that classroom that day had read a total of 680 books since September. Each at his own rate — each on his own level.

Last fall our local newspaper carried an article reviewing a current book critical of the public-school reading program. The book implied among other things that American children have a much more limited reading vocabulary than Russian children. Fortunately, or unfortunately, our children had read the newspaper item. Of course, no group of red-blooded American sixth-graders is going to let a statement like that by without proof. One of our sixth-grade classes decided to spend its spare time for one week checking on the size of their reading vocabularies. These students worked in pairs. Each pair took certain letters of the alphabet. They listed only those words that they could read and define. At the end of the week they had a total of 39,998 different words. If the Friday-afternoon bell had been five minutes late, they would probably have been well over forty thousand.

Illustrations such as these, plus a steady and consistent year-by-year gain in reading on standardized achievement tests, cause us to review our program with pride and challenge us to work toward greater goals in the future. In spite of the problems of rapid growth (our school population has more than doubled in the past ten years) our teaching and administrative staff have worked tirelessly for a strong reading program. Amidst the confusion brought about by the advocates of a "phonics-or-else" program, the saviours of reading through speed, the groupers, the individualizers, and others, I pass on our story in the hope that it may be of help to others.

If I were to use one word to describe the reading program in our school system I might select the word "eclectic." (This was a good word when McGuffey used it and it's still a good word today.) Our experience leads us to believe that three factors are essential in attaining and maintaining an effective program: (1) a dedicated, efficient, and hard working teaching staff, (2) adequate materials, (3) an interested community.

Teaching and Administrative Staff

Although there might be disagreements on techniques or materials, on philosophies or practices, I am sure there is one factor on which all else depends — a good teacher. And what is a good teacher of reading? Although many have tried to describe one, all have found words inadequate. As I visit in classrooms I am reminded that many, many things are involved in good teaching and that in no one classroom do we find them all. (Wouldn't school be dull for children and supervisors if all good teachers were exactly alike?) If I were characterizing our teachers, however, I believe I could say they are teachers who understand children, who can give and take ideas and suggestions from other teachers, who know and can use effectively a variety of sound techniques and materials, who share the hopes and concerns of parents, and who are willing to give extra time and effort to help children, but not to the extent that they fail to have some time and energy for themselves.

But teachers cannot do this big job alone. Administrators need to be ready to lend all assistance needed through their aid, guidance, support, and encouragement. Through their leadership the teacher's job becomes more effective and the total program stronger.

As I work with our teaching and administrative staff I constantly marvel at the consistency, yet flexibility, with which they work. Here are almost six hundred teachers and administrators in grades one through eight scattered in thirty buildings. As a total staff they are working toward system-wide overall goals in reading, yet each has enriched the program with his or her own personality and techniques.

Adequate Materials

As a foundation for our program we have relied very heavily on a series of basic readers. I am somewhat amazed when I hear or read criticism of basic readers. Frankly, I wonder if the critics have tried them, or, more pointedly, if they have used them as they are meant to be used. Surely no faculty who has ever used them efficiently would question their use, but for those who may have missed this valuable aid here are a few of the reasons why I feel so strongly about them.

1. A basic reading program sets up guidelines for a sequential program of skills. Learning is based on past experience — it is a step-by-step process. Skills taught at one grade level prepare children for skills taught at the next grade level. A skills program should be a program woven in with the warp of comprehension and interpretation and the woof of word recognition.

2. Basic readers provide the best in reading research to the teacher through the accompanying guide-books. So clearly do today's reading guidebooks outline and suggest effective teaching techniques that the teacher cannot fail to profit from their use. Certainly, I would not want to see teachers rely on them to the extent that they did no planning on their own, or that they read rather than taught from the guidebook. This, however, is never a problem to a good teacher. She uses the guidebook to "guide" her planning and teaching.

3. Children like the basic readers. This statement may come as quite a shock to the critics, but I can show you "living proof" in classrooms all over our system. The only children that I have ever encountered anywhere who didn't *enjoy* and *like* the stories in basic readers have been a few who have gotten the idea that they shouldn't from some thoughtless adult.

A few weeks ago some first-grade children from one of our elementary schools dramatized eight stories from their first-grade basic readers. Never have we seen actors even on Broadway put themselves so wholeheartedly into their performance. Only children who enjoyed and understood these stories could have done it with so much ease and naturalness. Of equal interest to adults present on this occasion was the obvious interest and delight of the first-grade audience. The stories they had read in their readers had come to life.

Far from bored was a group of sixth-grade students whom I dropped in on one morning recently. They had just finished reading a story about crop dusters and the discussion that followed was both lively and thought-provoking. Stories of early American heroes, tales that have become classics, accounts of scientific progress, legends, myths, poetry — uninteresting? Our children don't think so.

4. Basic readers teach more than skills. One has only to scan a series of good readers to find much informational material to supplement other areas of the curriculum. But — there is more. One of our fourth-grade teachers asked a group to take the unit they had just completed in the basic reader and list all of the "lessons," including thoughtfulness, ambition, loyalty, courage. They placed each of these on a little construction paper banner and mounted it on a dowel in stair-step arrangement. Here was evidence of moral and spiritual values that children identified in basic readers.

5. Basic readers can serve as the foundation for a reading program that extends and expands to meet the needs of all — the intellectually gifted, the educationally accelerated, the plodder, the emotionally disturbed, the leader, the follower, the enthusiastic, the indifferent, the slow learner. Through the multiple teaching suggestions, the thorough, yet flexible, presentation of skills, and the challenging variety of enrichment activities teachers find answers to meeting individual needs. Perhaps no other single source offers so many possibilities for enrichment activities. Last month in a system-wide fourth-grade exhibit our children displayed activities made in connection with every unit in their basic readers. Each group selected the story or stories they wished to illustrate. It was a marvelous display — crayon drawings, murals, dioramas, notebooks, bulletin boards, log cabins, dressed dolls, patchwork quilt tops, puppets — yes, and even the home of the Musicians of Bremen electrically lighted! To those of us who saw it, it was more than a beautiful exhibit; it was a panorama of the creative activities stimulated by reading.

For these reasons and many more I never underestimate the values of basic readers. Truly, I believe that when the history of education of the mid-twentieth century is written — Dick and Jane, Tom and Susan, Alice and Jerry will be featured among the greatest contributions.

But, our reading program is much more than just a series of basic readers. I sometimes illustrate our concept of a well-balanced reading program with a drawing of a tree. The basic reading program is the trunk of the tree, well rooted in skills. The limbs of the tree are the extensions — reading in other curriculum areas, research, current reading, fiction, biography. Through these extensions each child can branch out in various areas as far as his abilities and interests will permit.

Our extended reading program leads our children from the books and materials in the classroom to the school library. We now have a well-stocked library with a full-time, trained librarian in every elementary school. In addition to the extensive use that children and teachers make of reference and current materials our total circulation of library books during last school year was 509,665. The number read by individual children varied. Some read as few as five during the entire year, while one second-grader read seventy-five during one semester. Essential to an effective reading program are the facilities of a library.

An Interested Community

As I was leaving one of our elementary schools one morning last week I met the father of one of our fourth-graders rushing into the building. "I'm supposed to be on the job," he said, "but I helped whittle the sticks for the log cabin in the pioneer unit display in my son's classroom and I want to see how the whole thing turned out."

A community that is interested in and willing to support the reading program is one of the greatest assets any school system can have. In this we have been most fortunate. During Public School Week this spring over twelve thousand patrons visited in our schools. Hundreds of them arranged their visits at a time when they could observe their children reading. A mother excused herself early from a PTA committee meeting last fall. "I'm sorry to leave," she said, "but I'm invited to a reading party in the first grade. I wouldn't miss it!" Another mother said to us recently, "There's just one thing that bothers me; we're just finishing second grade and already Kathy knows more phonics than I do."

To supplement books and reading materials furnished by state and local school budgets, PTA's and parent clubs have purchased dictionaries, supplementary readers and library books. Fathers have manned booths at Halloween carnivals and mothers have served literally barrels of chili and spaghetti at school suppers to provide the necessary funds. Time and effort have proved the depth of their interest.

Reading — the skill that underlies all areas of the school curriculum, that opens doors to success in professions and vocations, that fills with pleasure leisure hours, that is almost essential to our very existence — demands our best. It is a skill that cannot be learned overnight, but requires day after day, year after year consistent, intensive work on the part of children and teachers. No one set of cards, or album of records, or phonics workbook, or teaching machine will do the job, but rather a planned program using as many effective teaching aids as are necessary. Remember, the "proof of the pudding" is children who *can* and *do* read.

Further Reading for Chapter 1

Botel, Morton. "We Need a Total Approach to Reading," *The Reading Teacher,* 13: 254–257; April, 1960.

Clymer, Theodore. "Approaches to Reading Instruction," *The National Elementary Principal,* 45: 47–55; November, 1965.

Dawson, Mildred A., and Henry A. Bamman. *Fundamentals of Basic Reading Instruction.* New York: David McKay Co., Inc., 1963. Chapter 1.

DeBoer, John J., and Martha Dallman. *The Teaching of Reading.* New York: Holt, Rinehart & Winston, Inc., 1964. Chapter 2.

Gray, Lillian. *Teaching Children to Read.* New York: The Ronald Press Company, 1963. Chapters 2 and 3.

Harris, Albert J. "Progressive Education and Reading Instruction," *The Reading Teacher,* 18: 128–138; November, 1964.

Homze, Alma Cross. "Reading and the Self-Concept," *Elementary English,* 39: 210–215; March, 1962.

Keshian, Jerry G. "The Characteristics and Experiences of Children Who Learn to Read Successfully," *Elementary English,* 40: 615–617; October, 1963.

McKee, Paul. *Reading: A Program of Instruction for the Elementary School.* Boston: Houghton Mifflin Company, 1966. Chapters 1, 2, and 7.

McKim, Margaret G., and Helen Caskey. *Guiding Growth in Reading in the Modern Elementary School.* New York: The Macmillan Co., 1963. Chapter 2.

Moore, Walter J. "Reading in the K-12 Language Arts Program," *Elementary English,* 41: 207–210; March, 1964.

Robinson, Helen M. "Teaching Reading Today," *The Instructor,* 74: 56; March, 1965.

Ross, Ramon, and Margaret LaPray. "Two Iconoclasts Re-View Reading," *Elementary English,* 41: 530–531; May, 1964.

Russell, David H. "Reading Research That Makes a Difference," *Elementary English,* 38: 74–78; February, 1961.

Tinker, Miles A., and Constance M. McCullough. *Teaching Elementary Reading.* New York: Appleton-Century-Crofts, Inc., 1962. Chapter 17.

Weiss, B. J. "Reading: Blind Alleys and Fruitful Byways," *Education,* 84: 529–532; May, 1964.

Witty, Paul A. "Guiding Principles in Reading Instruction," *Education,* 85: 474–480; April, 1965.

————, Alma Moore Freeland, and Edith H. Grotberg. *The Teaching of Reading: A Developmental Process.* Boston: D. C. Heath & Company, 1966. Chapters 1 and 2.

✤ **2** ✤

Readiness and Beginning Reading

When the phrase *reading readiness* was initially coined, it served a useful purpose. It represented a sound idea — the idea that not all children who enter school are prepared at the same time to profit from the same introduction to reading. This idea had two basic implications: first, that the child's total development influences his ability to profit from instruction, and, second, that before the child can efficiently profit from reading instruction, he must have certain knowledges and abilities, such as knowledge of word meaning and the ability to see differences and similarities among words.

Although these implications are as sound today as they were several decades ago, their application to the classroom has sometimes become so distorted that they stand in the way of good instruction. First, although there is no evidence that any specific mental, emotional, social, and physical age is essential for success in initial reading, many children must wait until they are mentally, emotionally, socially, and physically older before they are taught to read — no matter how "ready" they may actually be. Second, the implications have sometimes led to repetitious exercises which, although they are assigned to pupils in the name of reading readiness, are not prerequisites for reading instruction. For example, in an effort to help children build meaning vocabularies, teachers sometimes require all the pupils in a classroom to discuss pictures endlessly before they allow them to begin reading such words as *come, go, stop,* and *see,* which are already familiar in their oral forms to all but the most disadvantaged pupils. Or, to take another example, in the name of building skill in visual discrimination for reading, teachers sometimes assign page after page of exercises designed to teach the ability to discriminate between objects in pictures to children who already know how to distinguish the similarities and differences among words and letters.

Perhaps we need another term to replace *reading readiness.* Many of the concepts this term now calls to mind are merely *learning* readiness — which is important, but no more a part of *reading* readiness than any other kind of readiness. In addition, many authorities no longer reserve the term for the prereading period but also use it to reflect the developmental nature of a reading-skill program. That is, at any stage of the reading program the pupil is expected to master skills he will use during later stages. Although this sequential nature certainly characterizes a reading-skill program, using the term *reading readiness* to denote it does much to detract from the clarity of the term.

Probably the most significant misuse of the concept of reading readiness is

25

the practice by many schools of instituting and maintaining "reading readiness" programs that do not directly prepare the child for success in his first reading experiences. The child brings many abilities to school with him. He has the ability to understand the meanings of thousands of words and to use these words in oral communication. He usually has a knowledge of sounds in words and the ability to see differences and similarities between words and letters, which, at most, only needs refining. A sound prereading program builds on what the child has and builds directly toward the skills which will enable him to help himself most effectively as he begins to read.

The question of when to begin direct instruction in reading cannot be separated from the issue of what constitutes reading readiness. Certainly in a broad, vague, and somewhat indirect way, all of the school's earliest experiences for the child might be called *reading readiness*. In this sense, when reading readiness is considered a part of the total reading program, then it can loosely be said to begin for all children when they first enter school.

The current concern with the most appropriate time to initiate reading instruction, however, usually centers on those activities which are most directly related to the act of reading. Should kindergarten teachers limit their reading program to the kinds of activities which promote a general readiness for learning? Or should they provide prereading activities which will develop skills that the child can directly apply when he begins to read, such as knowledge of letter-sound associations? Although there are arguments which can be forcefully advanced on all sides of this issue, there are studies which provide us with something more than conjecture as a basis for our decisions.

In this chapter, Helen Huus explores the factors associated with a general reading-readiness program, such as general language development, as well as some of the aspects of a more specific prereading program, such as teaching the names of the letters. James Hymes, Jr. presents what he sees as the extreme dangers involved in an early reading program and concludes that, although the opportunity to read should not be completely removed from the child, the more direct prereading and reading experiences should not be a part of the regular kindergarten program.

In the next three articles, the merits of early reading experiences are described as they occurred in California, Illinois, and Colorado. Dolores Durkin was not concerned with providing early direct instruction in reading and then noting its results. Instead, she selected beginning first-grade children who had learned to read and then examined them longitudinally. Despite the fact that no school curriculum revisions are indicated, after three years these pupils still maintained a marked superiority.

One important question that Dr. Durkin raises in this selection as well as in some of her other works is the question of when to begin reading instruction for children whose intelligence quotients indicate less than average academic potential. It has usually been assumed that instruction for such students should be postponed until they have attained higher mental ages. The provocative question, however, is whether, since these pupils may develop reading skills at a less-than-average rate, they should not begin the development of these skills sooner, to partially compensate for the slower rate of growth to follow.

The studies by Joseph E. Brzeinski in Denver and Robert L. Hillerich in Glenview, Illinois, are two more examples of the growing body of information which supports early reading instruction. The evidence in these studies shows that such instruction provides an initial superiority which is maintained, and that the undesirable side effects which some predict do not occur.

In the last study in this chapter, William W. Wattenberg and Clare Clifford explore a different dimension of success in beginning reading. This study may help remind us that there are many factors vital for success in beginning reading, and that one of these factors is the way in which the child views himself.

Developing Reading Readiness

❖ Helen Huus

The term *reading readiness* came into the vocabulary of most primary teachers with the publication of Harrison's book in 1936 (3). Until very recently, the basic considerations presented in that volume had not been challenged. However, the advent of television, the academic pressure following in the wake of Sputnik I, subsequent "new" curriculums for elementary schools, and recent studies of children who come to school already reading have influenced thoughtful teachers to reevaluate the role of readiness in the total program of teaching children to read.

Prerequisites for Reading

Some prerequisites for reading are common to all learning — such factors as health, mental alertness, emotional adjustment, and having parents who give love and support. However, the discussion here is limited to aspects more specifically related to the act of reading itself.

Visual Factors. It stands to reason that if a child's vision is impaired, he is likely to have difficulty in differentiating between symbols that are similar in shape and detail. Those of you with faulty vision can understand this, for if you try to read without your glasses, you soon realize the strain and guesswork that result. Consider, too, that you have had experience with reading and even a faint outline can give you a clue.

Adequate checks must be made of children's vision — more than just the Snellen test at twenty feet. Tests at reading distance and checks on muscle balance and bifocal fusion are also needed. Even with vision corrected some children have problems of recognizing differences between *a, c,* and *e; b, d, p,* and *q;* or *u, n,* and *m.* Until children see such symbols as different, they are not ready to read. Activities such as fitting puzzles together, matching pictures or symbols with successively finer differentiations, locating like and different letters in groups, and matching two like words in a set of three, give children practice.

Some newer methods for beginning reading emphasize teaching first the letters of the alphabet, both lower case and capitals. Other methods emphasize the importance of combining initial teaching of reading with the child's writing of the words. In both instances, one of the purposes is to call the child's attention to the distinctive features of letters. This visual discrimination requires not only the ability to "see" differences and likenesses, but also to recognize and remember them.

Auditory Factors. Before children come to school, most of them have learned to speak the language they will be reading. In learning this language, they

From *The Instructor*, 74: 59–60; March, 1965. Reprinted by permission. Helen Huus is Associate Professor of Education, University of Pennsylvania, Philadelphia.

repeat what they hear others around them say. Although a child's hearing may be good, he may say "chimley," "breakthast," or "wiver," partly because he has not listened to finer distinctions and partly because he has not learned to say some sounds in certain positions.

He must hear differences between such like words as *pig, dig, wig; than, that; white, right;* and *which, witch.* Saying words that begin or end the same way, *Peter Piper,* for example, and noting alliteration in Mother Goose rhymes, finding rhyming words, then thinking of additional ones, help to establish auditory distinctions.

Children delight in the sound of words, and they will, without invitation, chime in on the refrain of "hundreds of cats, thousands of cats, millions and billions and trillions of cats" (2). So capitalize upon this and let them say poetry together without the formality of labeling it "choral speaking." Singing, too, helps develop auditory discrimination, and it is always a wonder that some children who cannot speak words correctly seem to have little difficulty when singing. Perhaps you may play a game where sounds like pouring water or sharpening a pencil are made behind a screen, with the children trying to figure out what is happening. In any case, point out to them sounds that need careful attention.

Language Factors. Facility with language is one indication of readiness for reading. Just as the child's pronunciation indicates his ability to hear and mimic, so do his vocabulary range and sentence structure indicate his level of maturity. Compare the language of a child who says, "Me go too," with one who asks, "If you go to the library, may I go with you?" The difference is obvious, but teachers need to know the various levels of language development so that they recognize sophisticated and immature patterns.

Teachers can provide a speech model for children to emulate; they can engage children in conversation — really listen to them, answer their questions, and encourage them to speak freely. "Show and Tell" has become so firmly entrenched in primary grades that traveling fathers are on the lookout for appropriate objects to bring back for Junior. Still, the exercise does provide children a means to present ideas and to discuss.

Retelling stories, particularly folktales with their definite sequence, telling original stories, or engaging in dramatic play are other activities that encourage children to talk. Sometimes a picture or a series or related pictures serves as the stimulus; sometimes the naming and classifying of objects; and sometimes the playing of a game such as "I went to Denver and took my ———," with each child in turn adding his bit.

Experience Factors. One of the most striking characteristics of children with preschool years barren of ordinary childhood experiences, and meager exposure to language and books, is deficient language development. In fact, such children usually lack many of the very qualities that make for readiness to read: speaking and understanding language, the ability to form concepts, visual and auditory discrimination, attention and memory, motor coordination, good relationship to adults, order in living, and self and group image (1). The provision of interesting experiences during the readiness period aids in bridging this gap, for these not only will provide children with the content of what to say, but will build the vocabulary with which to say it.

Take a trip around the school if you cannot get a bus or make other arrangements to take the children off the school grounds. Let the principal or supervisor tell what he does, what he thinks the school should do, and how the children can cooperate. Visit the librarian, the custodian, or another class, or take a walk around the grounds. Be alert to possibilities of extending the children's vocabulary: Talk about the maple tree, the oak, the elm, rather than just "trees," or say "corridor" instead of "hall," and notice how quickly the children follow suit.

When you are back in the classroom, make a chart of each visit using these later to call attention to such details as the first sentence, "Mary's sentence," to capital letters and their uses, to letters that look alike, to words that are identical or similar, and to the elements that make a story interesting. Illustrate the chart by drawing or making models.

The activity of making the chart lets the children see the language arts as an integrated whole, for they *tell* the story, the teacher *writes* it down, someone *reads* what it says, and the rest *listen*. Reading becomes a part of the day's activities, and children come to understand, like the six-year-old reported by Monroe, that it is "just *talk* wrote down!" (4).

Children's books — those wonderfully illustrated stories, enchanting tales, and singing verses — provide endless pleasure besides being instructive. Think of the concepts gained from Jack and Jill "fetching" water, from Dr. Foster going to Gloucester, or from the ride to Banbury Cross. Add the sensory images of the fairy tales, the humor of Dr. Seuss, and the warm relationships of Little Bear and his family and friends, and you get a glimpse of what books can do.

When to Start Teaching Reading

One of the pressing questions of the moment is when to start reading instruction. The pat answer is, of course, "When children are *ready*." The word itself connotes a certain tentativeness, for when a child has acquired the abilities that send him into reading, its usefulness is outlived, only to spring forth again at a higher level as readiness for the new task. Needlessly prolonging the stage of readiness is as foolish as ignoring it altogether, for some fives are advanced socially, physically, and mentally over some six-year-olds.

A sensible and realistic approach includes a recognition of learning as a continuum and of reading as having its own sequence. Since each child progresses at a pace that is his own, teachers who know the sequence of teaching reading can accept these children and accommodate to them. It may mean letting some who are in kindergarten go "up" to first grade for their reading; it may mean letting some use their ability by reading to others in the kindergarten and then giving them individual help on their own reading needs; it may mean letting kindergarten teachers keep a group two or three years in order that children can make an easy transition into reading without paying much attention to grade designations.

And so teachers provide environmental experiences through trips and excursions; fact and fancy through stories and poetry; skills and habits through lessons in discrimination; and opportunities for expression through art, music, and the manipulation of materials. While children are enjoying these interesting, varied activities, they are all the while readying themselves for learning that which most of them came to school to do — learn to read for themselves.

References

1. Clark, Kenneth. "Discrimination and the Disadvantaged," *College Admissions 7: The Search for Talent.* New York: College Entrance Examination Board, 1960. Pp. 12–18.
2. Gag, Wanda. *Millions of Cats.* New York: Coward-McCann, 1928.
3. Harrison, M. Lucille. *Reading Readiness.* Boston: Houghton Mifflin Co., 1936.
4. Monroe, Marion. *Growing Into Reading.* Chicago: Scott, Foresman and Co., 1951. P. 68.

Early Reading Is Very Risky Business ❧ James L. Hymes, Jr.

There is nothing wrong at all when individual children become accomplished readers at an early age, because they are fully ready for the achievement. But this is *not* what the current drive for early reading is all about.

Nor is there anything wrong when young children in groups — kindergarten youngsters, even children in nursery schools — have experiences with reading that are appropriate to their stage of development. But this, too, is *not* what the current drive for early reading is all about.

In today's early reading programs, individual differences are ignored. And while there is a plethora of new gimmicks — new phonetic approaches, a new alphabet, machines, TV, words in color, letters in sandpaper — the gimmicks are only skin-deep variations on the old inappropriate formal workbook-textbook approaches. This kind of formal early reading has so many things wrong with it.

It makes learning to read a sterile un-intellectual act, with baby-like content.

It isolates reading from the ongoing life of a group, turning it into a function-less process.

It deranges the kindergarten program and turns kindergarten into a sit-down place.

It turns teachers into quizmasters, drillers.

But, most significant of all, formal early reading is a very risky business.

A child pressured into achievement before he is ready — a child manipulated by adults — a child straining — a child buying love and approval at the expense of his own developmental urges — runs the risk of becoming a less sturdy, a less sure, a less sound and healthy personality.

From *Grade Teacher,* 82: 88, 90–91; March, 1965. Reprinted from *Grade Teacher* magazine by permission of the publishers. Copyright March 1965 by Teachers Publishing Corporation. James L. Hymes, Jr. is Professor of Education, University of Maryland, College Park.

A child pressured into achievement before he is ready runs the risk of resisting and rejecting, when he is a free agent, the learning that has been forced on him.

Frightening Hazards

These are two frightening hazards. Everyone loses if we produce early readers but in the process weaken humans. Everyone loses if we produce early readers but in the process kill the joy of reading.

The sad fact is that today's pressure for formal early reading is a re-hash of a pathetic old tale. Advocates of early reading programs cite their successes as if forced early achievement was news: "Eighteen-month-olds learn to read!" . . . "Two-year-olds learn to read!" . . . "Four- and five-year-olds learn to read!" Do they forget? Or did they never know? All through the years some mothers have always pushed for early achievement and "succeeded." Their children were weaned too early. They were toilet-trained too early. They were made to share too early, and to hold in their tears too early. They were made polite too early. The claim for this kind of "success" is ages old. Only the awareness of the degree of risk involved is new.

Today more and more mothers have become aware of the hazards of this "success" in infancy and in very early childhood. As professionals, we certainly ought to be aware of the dangers in the areas we guide.

Those who push early reading say: "The children love it." Doubtless some children do. Not every child is harmed, but every child is *exposed* to harm and it is difficult, if not impossible, to predict for sure on whom the blows will fall. But it is good at least to hear the claim that "the children love it." This is at least recognition of the need children have to accept learnings as their own, not imposed. Today the most authoritarian approaches use the sweetest words.

Why do we so blithely plunge into so risky a business? When there is such reason to believe that the real need is to take the heat off many of our Sixes, why do we pressure-cook our Fives?

The children may or may not really love formal early reading — but a great many adults do. Some have very dubious motives. Some parents love formal early reading because early reading is a new status symbol.

For the Wrong Reasons

Some teachers love this reading in the kindergarten. The children sit — thank God! The children are more manageable. Through all the years there have been people who simply have never liked Fives in the public school. They have never liked Fives' noise and activity. They have never liked their imagination. They have taught Fives, but they have never felt comfortable setting a stage so that children could learn; they wanted to be the center of the stage themselves. They feel comfortable only when they hold all the right answers in their own hands.

These selfish adult reasons are a realistic part of the whole early-reading push. But other reasons also lead some to favor the idea. Formal early reading can look like the solution to some of the kindergarten's pressing problems. It is the wrong solution, or people have chosen the wrong problem.

In many an overcrowded kindergarten, movement and choice or activity or firsthand experiencing are impossible. A program of structured learning that keeps children seated can seem like the answer. But the basic problem isn't how to adjust ourselves or the children to the mess we are in. The real task is to reduce class size, to allow Fives to be up and about, in action.

The anxiety of many parents is another legitimate cause for concern. Parents are frightened today. They are frightened by the scarcity of colleges; they are frightened by the bombardment of scare magazine articles. Everyone with sensitivity will agree: no parent should have to suffer today's anxieties about whether his child will learn to read. A program of formal early reading can seem like a solution to these unpleasant worries. But giving in to anxiety is hardly a sound approach. Working with parents intensively is a much better alternative than working prematurely with children. Schools today have a wonderful chance to build on what Spock has already taught parents about individual differences, about readiness, about the developmental significance of stages of growth, about the wholeness of humans. We ought to be doing much more than any school is now doing to strengthen and deepen parent understanding. We do parents no favor, and their children no favor, when we turn to answers that stem from fear.

So Different?

Many people are persuaded that today's Five is different. He has looked at TV. He has been all around in the family car. He has had stories at home, and sometimes has been to nursery school. Youngsters today seem "brighter," so the reports go; they seem to "know so much more."

This observation has curriculum implications, but it does not necessarily lead specifically to programs of formal early reading. Do these childhood experiences actually speed up total maturation? Do they argue for less firsthand learning for today's children, or for more? Do they in any way change the basic style of a five-year-old: a social, active, talking, playing, imaginative youngster, immersed in the task of finding himself and finding for himself his way in this world? Kindergarten must be challenging, but there are alternatives more stimulating than sitting today's children down with a workbook.

Perhaps our lack of imagination about alternatives is the heart of the difficulty. We act as if we had only two choices: formal reading or no reading at all for Fives. We act as if we either had to wait . . . wait . . . wait until children are ready, doing nothing with reading in the meantime — or plunge into formal programs, ready or not.

The fact is, *children at all ages are always ready for significant experiences in reading.* Given decent class size — this we *do* have to work for — it is no superhuman task to create a kindergarten life that taps the varying readiness of a whole wide range of Fives.

Reading does not begin suddenly (in kindergarten now, or in first grade, or nowhere suddenly) once a book is put in a child's hand or once the child is sat in a circle.

Reading is no one single, isolated activity.

Reading involves no single skill alone.

Many of the old-fashioned experiences, truly beloved by Fives through all the years, teach reading. When a child has the chance to hear one good story after another, day after day, he is being taught to read. When his kindergarten year is a series of mind-stretching, eye-filling trips, helping him know more solidly his world, he is being taught to read. When a child hears good adult language, and when he has the fullest freest chance to use his own language, he is being taught to read. When he creates with blocks, when he communicates with paint, when he uses his body freely as a means of expression, he is being taught to read. When a child stares, fascinated, at a picture — when he looks ever so carefully at the scale in his store or at the life in his aquarium, he is being taught to read. When he hammers ever so carefully at the workbench, fashioning his battleship, this too teaches him to read. When he uses his whole body — two eyes, two hands, two arms, two legs and knees and feet — to pull himself up a scary slanted climbing board, he is being taught to read.

You can build into all of this natural, vigorous child-life as many of the symbols associated with reading as any of the children can make use of. Labels can be written on their dramatic play construction: *Garage . . . Firehouse . . . Gas Station . . . Grocery Store.* Letters can be written in connection with trips, recipes can be written in connection with cooking, plans can be written in connection with construction. And the more that children do, the more there is that can be written down: stories, reports, humorous incidents. . . .

In the good kindergarten, life doesn't *stop* so that the children can be taught to read. The *life goes on so* that the children can be taught to read. The chance to read is ever-present, but never in a coercive or artificial or teacher-dominated way. The chance is always there, built into a total on-going program, for any child to become an accomplished reader at an early age, if he is fully ready for the achievement. The chance is always there, too, for every child for those experiences with reading that are appropriate to his own stage in development.

There is an alternative to formal early reading programs that is not a risky business. The alternative suffers from having too simple a name: *Kindergarten . . . a place for Fives.* It has no gimmicks, but it does have life going on, with busy children engrossed in a variety of work, compelled by their interests rather than the teacher's commands. In such a setting each child is strengthened, regardless of where he is on a long developmental line of readiness. And learning is exciting — regardless of where the child is on the line of readiness. This is not only the safer alternative, it is the sound way of living with humans.

An Earlier Start in Reading?

❧ Dolores Durkin

Today the subject of reading and the preschool child is attracting much attention. It is provoking controversy too — or at least differences of opinion. Reactions of kindergarten teachers, for example, tend to fall into three categories. Some spurn any kind of reading instruction for the five-year-old. Others seem too eager to rush to a workbook curriculum. Somewhere in the middle is another group that recognizes the inadequacy of typical kindergarten programs for some five-year-olds and does not interpret the asking of questions about these programs as a prelude to inevitable and unfriendly criticism.

Parents of young children show other differences in reaction. At one extreme are the Harvard-conscious parents who seriously believe that three years of age is none too soon to develop good study habits and at least a small amount of achievement in reading. At the other extreme are those parents who conscientiously heed educators who continue to maintain that preschool help with reading results in confusion and leads to problems when a child enters first grade.

Meanwhile, nationwide publicity is being given to the Denver schools as they attempt to develop TV programs on reading for parents of preschool children. Attention is also being focused on Omar Moore, at Yale University, who is using complicated machinery to introduce pre-first-grade children to written language. Whitby School in Connecticut, too, is attracting attention as it demonstrates the learnings of three- and four-year-olds when a Montessori curriculum is followed.

Many different groups, then, are examining, proposing, and opposing the idea that children start to learn to read before the age of six. Consequently, it becomes important to step outside the controversy to look carefully at the questions that are being raised and at those that ought to be raised.

Among the important questions, certainly, is that of the future value of an early start in reading. (If a child gets a head start in reading, will he remain ahead? If a child enters first grade with the reading ability of an average second- or third-grader will he, over the years, continue to remain ahead of children who are of equal mental ability but could not read when they started first grade?)

This article is directed to these questions. It is a report on one part of a longitudinal study of children who could read when they entered first grade.[1]

From *The Elementary School Journal*, 63: 146–151; December, 1962. Reprinted from "An Earlier Start in Reading?" in *The Elementary School Journal* by Dolores Durkin by permission of The University of Chicago Press. Copyright © 1962 by The University of Chicago. Dolores Durkin is Professor of Education, University of Illinois, Urbana. The research on which this article is based is described in her book, *Children Who Read Early* (New York: Bureau of Publications, Teachers College, Columbia University, 1966).

[1] This article is based on a paper read at a meeting of the American Educational Research Association in Atlantic City, February, 1962.

In September, 1958, all the beginning first-graders in a California public school system were individually tested to identify those who had learned to read at home.[2] From this group of 5,103 children, forty-nine were found to have some ability in reading. At the time of the first testing, their reading achievement ranged from 1.5 to 4.5, according to grade-level norms. The median grade level was 1.9. Intelligence quotients derived from the Revised Stanford-Binet Scale ranged from 91 to 161, with a median quotient of 121. The coefficient of correlation for intelligence and reading achievement was +0.40.

(To examine the future value of an early start in reading, the plan was to compare, at the end of third grade, the reading achievement of the forty-nine early readers with the reading achievement of children who had started school with them, who had had the same teachers as they for the first three grades, and who were of comparable mental ability but who were not able to read when they started first grade. Mental ability was to be assessed in terms of intelligence quotients derived from the Kuhlmann-Anderson Intelligence test, which was administered by the school system when the children were in second grade)

As it turned out, even a cursory look at these intelligence quotients showed that they were anything but realistic. (There was no apparent relationship, for example, between a child's intelligence, as measured by the Kuhlmann-Anderson Intelligence test, and his achievement score in reading.)

For the children who were not early readers, the intelligence quotients hovered narrowly around 100. For the early readers the Kuhlmann-Anderson scores consistently underestimated the intelligence of the brighter children, as it had been measured by the Revised Stanford-Binet Scale.

It was decided, therefore, to include in the control group only those children who had been given the Revised Stanford-Binet Scale by a school psychometrist. This decision necessitated other changes and, in a sense, compromises in the research plan. These will be noted indirectly in the description of what finally constituted the experimental group and the control group.

The experimental group included twenty-five of the forty-nine early readers. The remaining twenty-four had either transferred to other schools or had been double-promoted during the three-year period. Although the experimental group was reduced to twenty-five children, the intelligence quotients based on results of the Revised Stanford-Binet Scale still ranged from 91 to 161. The median intelligence quotient for the group was 114.8. Reading scores based on tests administered by the schools towards the end of Grade 3 showed grade levels ranging from 4.4 to 6.0, with a median of 5.0.

The control group was made up of 201 children who had entered first grade with the twenty-five preschool readers but who could not read when they started school. They had remained in the same schools as these early readers for Grades 1, 2, and 3. They had also been given the Revised Stanford-Binet Scale. For this control group, intelligence quotients ranged from 70 to 191, with a median of 110.2. Reading achievement scores based on school-administered tests ranged from 2.0 to 6.0, with a median grade level of 4.3.

A scatter diagram, in which reading scores for both the experimental and the control groups were plotted, revealed the inadequacy of the school-administered

[2] Dolores Durkin, "Children Who Learned to Read at Home," *Elementary School Journal,* 62: 15–18; October, 1961.

reading tests in establishing upper limits of achievement for the brighter children.[3] Consequently, a twofold comparison was made between the achievement of the early readers and the achievement of children who were not early readers. The first comparison focused on children who had intelligence quotients of 120 or less. The second comparison considered children who had intelligence quotients of 121 or higher.

Of the children who were not early readers 129 had intelligence quotients of 120 or less. A first step in examining the value of a head start in reading was to calculate the coefficient of correlation between the intelligence as measured by the Revised Stanford-Binet Scale and the reading achievement of these children who were not early readers. The coefficient of correlation was found to be +0.61.

Next, the regression equation for predicting reading achievement on the basis of intelligence was formulated. The equation was then used to calculate predicted reading scores for each of the fifteen early readers who also had intelligence quotients of 120 or less.

When these predicted scores were calculated, it was found that for all the children who were early readers actual scores in reading were greater than would have been predicted for them on the basis of their intelligence, as measured by the Revised Stanford-Binet Scale. The greatest single difference, in terms of years of reading achievement, was 1.3. The smallest single difference was 0.2. Group differences, according to intelligence tests, are shown in Table I.

**TABLE I. Deviation of Achievement of Early Readers
from Expected Achievement on the Basis
of Intelligence Quotients**

Intelligence Quotient	Number of Pupils	Average Deviation in Years
91–100	5	+0.92
101–110	6	+0.68
111–120	4	+0.35
121–130	3	+0.30
131–140	4	−0.33
141–161	3	+0.43

Because the groups were small, no statement can be made at this time about children who are early readers in general. Two observations can be made concerning these fifteen early readers who had intelligence quotients of 120 or less. First, they appear to have profited from their early start. Second, the lower the child's intelligence quotient, the greater seems to be the advantage of starting early.

What can be said about the children who had intelligence quotients higher than 120? As I pointed out earlier, the school-administered reading tests were

[3] A carefully planned testing procedure has been followed for all the forty-nine early readers. In this particular part of the study, data from school-administered reading tests had to be used because these were the only data available for the control group.

not difficult enough to establish the upper limits of achievement for the brighter children in either the control group or the experimental group. As a result, the coefficient of correlation between the intelligence quotients of the seventy-two children who were not early readers and their reading scores was only $+0.17$.

With such a low coefficient of correlation it is not too meaningful to ask: As derived from the relationship between reading achievement and intelligence, what would be the predicted reading score for each of the early readers who had intelligence quotients of 121 or more? Nonetheless the question was asked, and the answer appears in Table I.

Probably the most appropriate comment to make at this point is to express the hope that when more appropriate reading tests are used with the control and the experimental groups at the end of Grade 6, more meaningful and more significant findings will be available, especially for the brighter children in both groups.

Meanwhile, it seems appropriate to attempt some kind of summary of conclusions or, to be more accurate, some kind of summary of ideas and feelings that resulted from this longitudinal study of precocious readers.

Certainly, one persistent feeling is that many parents of preschool children are confused and uncertain about their role, or lack of it, in the matter of their child's learning to read. Frequent contacts with parents, through interviews and correspondence, repeatedly point to the need for home-school communication that gives parents, first, at least a general understanding of their role as educators of the preschool child and, second, specific help on how they, as parents, can advance the language skills of young children without putting uncomfortable pressures on them.

These same contacts with parents also suggest that educators have been encouraging parents, perhaps unintentionally, to put a child's questions about words into a do-not-touch category on the assumption that what a child learns about reading before he enters school interferes with subsequent school instruction. This study of early readers does not verify this assumption.

In fact, what is tentatively suggested is that children of relatively lower intelligence especially benefit from an early start. Should this finding be duplicated in a second study recently begun in another school system, it might well mean that slower children need contact with learning to read that is spread out over time. Instead of a postponement of reading instruction, they need an earlier start with it. This thinking, to be sure, is in contrast to much current thinking on reading readiness. But it is a possibility that deserves attention.

One final comment on kindergarten children and kindergarten programs. I urge that the schools pay some attention to the five-year-olds who are already reading and to those who are so close to it that even less than mediocre help would turn them into readers. If we really believe that good education begins where the child is, then kindergarten teachers ought to feel obligated to give certain children help with reading.

Out of this new concern might eventually come not only achievement in reading but, in addition, a really fresh approach to the teaching of beginning reading. It might well be that those of us who are interested in teaching methods and materials have for too long been greasing a squeaky wheel when we should have been looking for a genuinely new one.

Beginning Reading in Denver

✣ JOSEPH E. BRZEINSKI

For many years some children have been coming to the first grade already able to read. In some cases this deviation from the norm has been viewed with mixed feelings by the teacher. Readers of *To Kill a Mockingbird* will recall the plight of Scout who had been taught to read by her beloved father and who was, therefore, admonished because she did not fit readily into the mold desired by the teacher.

Now, greater numbers of children able to read are beginning school. Recognition of this trend led to consideration of what positive action the Denver Public Schools should take. If children were coming to school able to read before being taught in first grade, could a planned program of beginning reading instruction produce greater numbers of children who could learn to read successfully in the home or in the kindergarten?

Review of the first grade reading program revealed that a primary aim of the early teaching efforts was the development of language and listening skills. First grade teachers provided a wealth of experiences so that words would have meaning for the pupils. Trips about the neighborhood, excursions to the zoo, visits to the museums, introduction to rhymes, stories, and books were used so that the printed words the child was to read would have meaning and association with people, places, and things. A large part of the initial teaching was devoted to providing these kinds of activities, which were at one time almost uniquely within the province of the school.

Almost without exception today, however, children from all segments of our affluent society have rich experiences that in the past were limited to a relatively few individuals. Children today have many educational experiences provided by the family. They live in a world of words, seeing them in books, magazines, newspapers, on TV, and on signs. Many children have attended nursery school. Even among the very poor, television and all the experiences it presents have been part of their lives from their earliest memories. Firsthand experiences have been provided by trips about the community, the state, and the nation. All of these experiences have contributed to the development of a kindergarten-age speaking vocabulary which has been estimated to contain typically five to ten thousand or more words.

This enriched environment seemed to affirm that children could be taught to read at early ages. At this stage, it seemed well to review research related to teaching young children to read.

Review of the literature appeared to indicate that reading readiness has been rather narrowly interpreted and often applied to justify delay in reading instruction. Perhaps a more tenable position was voiced at the 1959 Woods Hole

From *The Reading Teacher*, 18: 16–21; October, 1964. Reprinted with permission of Joseph E. Brzeinski and the International Reading Association. Joseph E. Brzeinski is Administrative Director, General Curriculum Services, Denver Public Schools, Denver, Colorado.

Conference: "Readiness, that is, is a function not so much of maturation as it is of our intentions and our skill in transplanting ideas into the language and concepts of the age level we are teaching."[1]

In summary, available evidence appeared to warrant testing the following points of view:

1. No one mental age is a guarantee of beginning reading success. Equally important are the methods and materials of instruction.

2. Difficulties of young children in auditory perception or visual discrimination may be overcome by providing specific training.

3. Success in beginning reading achievement in first grade is highly correlated to children's previous opportunities for reading at home, in the community, or in the kindergarten.

4. Children can be taught to read at earlier ages than they presently are being taught in most public school systems. Many investigations have established this point. Additional research is needed in which the time of beginning the teaching of reading is systematically varied, using a method of teaching specially designed for the age level at which it is to be employed and paying special attention to the effects of the time of beginning on the later development of the child.

A great deal of time during our first year was spent in constructing a research design and in planning appropriate instructional materials.

(Seven groups of beginning reading activities were developed by Dr. Paul McKee and Miss M. Lucile Harrison of the Colorado State College) These activities provided practice in using beginning consonant sounds with contextual or meaning clues to identify a printed word. (The rationale for the system is based on the fact that kindergarten children know the sounds and meanings of many thousands of words. However, children do need to be taught that the sounds they know are represented by the particular letters and letter combinations in printed words.) These skills, in connection with contextual clues, provide early steps toward independent reading. The reading materials developed were tried in a preliminary study for the purpose of testing the research design and to discover what problems might arise.

In the fall of 1960 the Denver Public Schools, with the aid of a grant from the Cooperative Research Branch of the United States Office of Education, began a longitudinal research study to determine the effectiveness of beginning the teaching of reading in kindergarten.[2] Pupils in the research project are to be studied through the fifth grade.

When the main study began, the Denver Public Schools had about nine thousand kindergarten children divided into three hundred classes. This study involved 122 classes randomly assigned by school to control and research groups. (This assignment resulted in sixty-one classes in the control group and sixty-one classes in the research group) Thus, approximately four thousand pupils were divided equally into control and pilot groups for kindergarten instruction. (Children in the control classes followed the regular kindergarten program. Children in the research classes received instruction in the beginning

[1] Jerome S. Bruner, *On Knowing — Essays for the Left Hand* (Cambridge: Harvard University Press, 1962), p. 108.
[2] The executive director of elementary education in the Denver schools is Mr. Lloid B. Jones.

reading activities for approximately twenty minutes per day. The remaining two hours and ten minutes of the kindergarten session were devoted to established kindergarten procedures.)

When the children in the study entered first grade, the research and control groups were in turn divided into two groups. This division provided four first grade groups:

Group I: Regular program in kindergarten
   Regular program in the first and later grades
Group II: Regular program in kindergarten
   Research and adjusted program in the first and later grades
Group III: Research program in kindergarten
   Regular program in the first and later grades
Group IV: Research program in kindergarten
   Adjusted program in the first and later grades

Group I provided the necessary basis for comparison with the research groups. Group II permitted a comparison between groups who received the same instruction introduced at different times. Group III made possible the assessment of the effect of early reading followed thereafter by the regular reading program. Group IV was established to test the full effect — beginning reading in the kindergarten followed by a program accelerated to take continuing advantage of any gains made.

Pupils in the study were tested periodically, using standardized reading tests and other appropriate measures, including specially devised tests, the quantity and quality of reading, rating for reading disabilities, and other similar indicators.)

Results

Appropriate evaluative techniques have been included in the research design. The pre- and post-tests given in kindergarten were specially designed to measure progress in the skills being taught. Analysis of the data gathered in kindergarten was made to determine the suitability of the trial method and materials for that age level.

Data obtained were analyzed by the covariance technique, which adjusts scores to account for initial differences between groups on variables related to performance, such as intelligence and age. In this way groups are, in effect, statistically equated or matched.

Kindergarten Results. (At the end of the first year of study, the data indicated that kindergarten-age children were able to recognize letter form and to learn letter names and associated letter sounds. The pilot program of systematic instruction in beginning reading skills appeared to be more effective than the regular kindergarten program, which incidentally provided opportunity for the development of reading readiness.)

Children taught the beginning reading skills in kindergarten did not forget them during the summer intermission. The possibility was tested that since the pilot classes seemed to learn more than did the control classes they would also forget more during the summer months when less actively engaged in learning activities. This did not prove to be the case.

First-Grade Results. The Gates Primary Reading Test and the Gates Advanced Primary Reading Test were used to gather data in the first grade. Analysis of the adjusted test scores suggests that the pilot groups of children who had the beginning reading activities in kindergarten scored significantly better at the end of first grade than did the control groups of children who had the regular kindergarten program. Optimum reading achievement was obtained when adjustments were made in the first grade program to take advantage of gains made in kindergarten. Those children who were taught the pilot materials in kindergarten were significantly better readers than those children who began the same method in first grade. The differences reported for the first grade are significant beyond the .001 level of confidence.

The possibility that the early teaching of reading might cause an increased incidence of problems related to vision, hearing, or social and academic adjustment was checked. Each of the four groups in the study had virtually the same percentage of children who showed (1) difficulties necessitating the wearing of glasses, (2) a hearing loss, and (3) adjustment problems. This would seem to indicate that the early introduction to reading did not affect the number of pupils exhibiting physical disabilities or adjustment problems. It appeared that teaching beginning reading in kindergarten neither created nor prevented problems in these areas, since the differences found between groups were not statistically significant.

As an outgrowth of the previous research, the Denver Public Schools, with the aid of a grant from the Carnegie Corporation of New York, began a parallel study to determine how effectively parents could prepare their preschool children for reading.

Parents have for years carried on informal activities which contribute to their children's early and effective reading. The present study was designed to find out whether parents with suitable professional assistance and direction, could systematize and accentuate such activities to their children's benefit.

Three research groups were established. The first was called Group X. Parents of the children in this group received no instruction in teaching the basic reading skills. They were encouraged to continue with the types of activities normally carried on within their family. However, the children in this group took the same test as those in the other groups so that it would be possible to distinguish between reading development which might occur as a result of maturation and normal family life. In Group Y the parents were provided instruction in teaching the skills which are basic to beginning reading. They taught their children at home using a specially prepared guidebook and programs presented on educational television. The parents of children in Group Z were provided instruction in teaching the basic skills to their children at home by use of the guidebook, along with the guidance of experienced teachers, using kinescopes of the television programs in small parent-discussion groups.

The guidebook for parents entitled *Preparing Your Child for Reading* presented the basic instructional plan. The book contains the necessary special materials normally not found in the home. The suggestions and materials were organized in sixteen chapters or sections designed to enable parents to follow the sixteen television programs. Instructional content of the television programs and films was geared to the lessons in the guidebook. To determine the values for parents of this adult education program, the amount and kind of instruction given to children, and parent judgment about the worth of these activities, several evaluative instruments were administered during the period when the children were being tested. Included among these were an individual Stanford-Binet test for each child, Tests 3 and 5 of the Tests of Skills Basic to Beginning Reading, published by the Houghton Mifflin Company, and a special questionnaire.

The study raised several important questions, and analysis of data collected from all sources provided some answers. Parents involved in the project have given it a strong vote of confidence. Eighty-five per cent of them indicated that they felt this was a good method for teaching the beginning reading skills. More than 80 per cent thought that the instruction they received was helpful, and about the same number felt that the instruction was important to their children. About 75 per cent said they would like more help of this kind and stated an intention to continue practicing the beginning reading activities.

The study indicated that a preschool child can be taught certain beginning reading skills provided he has a mental age of at least four and a half years. The amount a child learned was related directly to the amount of time someone practiced the beginning of reading activities with him. The minimum amount of practice established as necessary was thirty minutes per week. Statistically significant gains in achievement were made by those who practiced thirty minutes or more per week. Reading to the child was also found to have a significant effect, whether or not the child was in one of the groups who practiced the beginning reading activities. In fact, many parents in the control group read to their children and produced an increase in test scores. The best performance on the test was made by children who had both practiced the beginning reading activities more than thirty minutes per week and who had been read to more than sixty minutes per week. It appeared that reading to the child should be recommended along with the program of beginning reading activities.

The information obtained from the parent education study appeared to indicate that parents are eager to teach their children beginning reading skills. Thus, in this area of learning, as in all learning, parent interest, concern, and participation are invaluable ingredients.

The television lessons and accompanying guidebook which were developed for this study are presently available from the National Educational Television Center in New York City. These lessons are presently being shown by a number of educational television stations throughout the nation.[3]

Conclusion

Because the present study is of a longitudinal nature, final evaluation must await the end of the research project. Interim results, however, appear to indicate that (1) parents can help their children begin to read, (2) many boys and girls in a large public school system can be taught beginning reading successfully, and (3) such early reading instruction has a measurable, positive, continuing effect.

[3] See "The Denver Prereading Project Conducted by WENH-TV," by Anastasia McManus [*The Reading Teacher,* Vol. 18, October, 1964].

Kindergarteners Are Ready!
Are We? ✤ Robert L. Hillerich

Change has become a by-word in our society. Many are the changes that have taken place in elementary schools: methods and materials have been improved; the level of development has been raised; subject areas have been added. Yet, "reading readiness" in most kindergartens remains unaffected.

The Traditional Approach

Traditionally, in kindergarten, reading readiness has been a matter of providing general experiences. The program has emphasized expansion of vocabulary and knowledge through trips and discussions; it has included practice in gross visual and auditory discrimination; it has aimed toward development of interest in reading through listening to good stories and looking at good books. Obviously these activities are important preliminaries to a more formal program. They are not to be discarded or replaced completely. The question to be asked is: how much of the kindergarten year should be spent in this generalized kind of readiness? In kindergarten today, *some* children may need all of these activities, but others are ready to go much further than the traditional kindergarten program has allowed them to go.

Professional journals have devoted considerable space to this area of "early reading instruction" or a more formalized kindergarten program. Opinions pro and con have been discussed elsewhere (5); however, typical of the statements supporting the status quo is one made by Sheldon:

There is no body of research or evidence which proves conclusively that early reading instruction will be both effective and free from physical and mental health hazards. (13)

This statement is true, of course, but it implies that we must close our eyes to change around us and refuse to look at new approaches. Then, too, one might ask, where is the "body of research or evidence which proves conclusively" that reading instruction should begin as it now does in first grade?

What has kept us from moving forward? Primarily it has been tradition. Formal reading began in first grade historically when there was no kindergarten. Then, as educators learned more about children, reading instruction was delayed to provide time for readiness activities, still in first grade. Morphett and Washburne's report (8) reinforced this position. They found that a mental age of six and a half was optimum for beginning reading. Many people further justify the first grade placement of beginning reading from the standpoint of children's visual maturity and experience; five-year-olds supposedly are not

From *Elementary English*, 42: 569–573; May, 1965. Reprinted with the permission of the National Council of Teachers of English and Robert L. Hillerich, Assistant Superintendent, Glenview Public Schools, Glenview, Illinois. This article is based on an address given at Lesley College in 1963.

capable visually of reading print, and they do not have a sufficient listening vocabulary to enable them to get meaning from reading.

Basis for Change

Many things have been happening in recent years to make us question these views. While the mental age of six and a half is often referred to, we know there is not the relationship between mental age or I.Q. and reading that this implies. Durkin (3), in her study of children who could read before they started to school, reported a correlation of only .40 between Binet I.Q. and reading. The Kuhlman-Anderson, with which she also tested, showed no relationship at all between I.Q. and reading achievement. Along these same lines, Newton (10) reported that correlations between mental age and beginning reading ranged from .60 down to .00.

We must remember, too, that Washburne's study was based on the children, the methods, and the materials of the 1930's. All have changed considerably. Children today come to school with larger vocabularies and broader experiences: they have seen and listened to TV; they have traveled; in general, they have profited from parents whose education and standard of living is higher than was true in 1930.

An interesting note on this subject is provided by students of comparative education. In the United States today, most children begin to read successfully at about six and a half years of age. In Scotland they begin at about five and a half, while in the Scandinavian countries the age is about seven. A common factor among these various children is the experience of about half a year of formal instruction.

The question of visual maturity has been investigated by Dr. Thomas Eames (4) of the Harvard Psycho-Educational Clinic. Dr. Eames, in reporting on the vision of five-year-olds, stated:

Children five years of age were found to have *more* accommodative power than at any subsequent age. The poorest *near* visual acuity found among the pupils studied was quite sufficient for reading the usual texts.

Thus far we have been destructive and negative. Perhaps we can now take a new approach and rebuild in specifics. We know that the kindergarten teacher does not initiate readiness to read. In the broadest sense, this begins when the child is born, or even conceived. Parents more specifically help later in the life of the preschool child by providing him with experiences in speaking, listening, looking at books, and so on. The kindergarten teacher is the first to provide an environment designed for intensive and specific instruction. If she goes no further than merely to continue the general experience — important though this may be — she is holding many children back.

Evidence has been accumulating rapidly in recent years to show what kindergarten children can do. The most pertinent research evidence is the preliminary report from Denver (2). In a large-scale study, using an experimental form of the McKee program, the Denver schools investigated the success of the program in terms of scores at the end of first grade on the Gates Reading Battery. Of four approaches, and significantly better than the next best, was the use of the McKee materials in kindergarten.

Other studies, while not always on this specific program, support the approach. Alice Nicholson (11), in her doctoral dissertation under Durrell, studied 2,188 first graders to determine the background abilities that might be related to reading success in first grade. She found that few children began first grade with any knowledge of letter sounds, but that the traditional matching of pictures and geometric forms was a "waste of time."

Her conclusion was verified in the study by Arthur Olson (12). He found that most of the 1,172 first-grade children tested could match letter forms and could identify capital letters prior to instruction in school.

Morrone (9) reported that children can profit from phonics before a mental age of seven. This was a gross understatement compared with Anderson's findings (1) two years later. She used the McKee program and found that a group of kindergarteners with mental ages ranging from fifty-two to sixty-five months benefited equally as well as a group with mental ages of seventy-nine to ninety-one months.

Such studies certainly add strength to McKee's statements and are verified in our own experience. Children *can* do more than the gross kinds of discrimination we usually ask of them. Why give them practice in distinguishing a picture of a car from one of a wagon? Most five-year-olds can already distinguish the Ford like theirs from one of a different year. They are ready and able to do much more. Most of them can learn very easily to distinguish one letter form from another.

Why try to *teach* children to hear such a gross difference as that between the sound of a bell and that of a horn? Most *four*-year-olds already hear the differences in beginnings of words. Try calling four-year-old Donnie "Lonnie" or "Connie" or "Bonnie" and see his reaction. If the youngster could not *hear* these differences he would not have learned to speak intelligibly. Some people talk about beginning reading as if they believe we are trying to teach the child a foreign language. The typical five-year-old has been speaking this language for several years and understanding it for even longer. What we really need to teach the five-year-old is what we *mean* by "the beginning" of a spoken word.

Let's not err in the other direction, however, and assume knowledge that does not exist. Of course the typical five-year-old sees a meaningless jumble when he looks at a printed word. He does not even know the part of the page on which he must start to read. He needs to be taught that he can use context in reading just as he already uses it in listening. He needs to distinguish letter forms and to associate certain sounds with the proper letters. He needs to be *taught* these skills and their application in reading, along with certain mechanics such as left to right, top to bottom, and so on.

What then should the program be? It must be a program which will provide the basic skills preliminary to beginning reading, a program which will encourage interest in reading, and also one that recognizes and utilizes the inquiring mind, boundless energy, and short attention span of the five-year-old. In brief, it must develop skill and interest while working within the capabilities of the kindergartener. And let's not underestimate these capabilities!

The Glenview Study

In Glenview, we began investigating just such a program in 1961. When McKee's *Getting Ready to Read* (6) became available in January, 1963, all of our kindergarten teachers had decided they wanted to be included in the trial use of the program. This decision was neither quick nor easy. Most of the eleven kindergarten teachers had over ten years of experience. It was a considered and considerable step to depart from what was known to be good in order to incorporate what was unknown. We maintained the view that the program was to be developed informally; it was to be taught as an exposure rather than for mastery of the skills by all children. Each step was developed as provided in the manuals, with activities which the children could enjoy, such as "games" — each gaining as much as he was capable of handling.

Essentially, in this study, we set out to answer four questions: (1) Can kindergarten children adequately develop specific pre-reading skills? (2) Do they forget what they have learned over the summer? (3) Are they better readers by the end of grade one? (4) Are they more interested in reading by the middle grades?

Procedures

Ten sections of children experienced the program with the Houghton Mifflin workbooks; twelve sections used all of the materials except the workbooks for children. This divided approach was in recognition of a concern some teachers had about having kindergarteners use workbooks. It enabled us to expand our first question to include a comparison of the effectiveness of the program both with and without workbooks.

Prereading skills were tested at the end of kindergarten (June 3–7, 1963). Part Two of "A Prereading Inventory of Skills Basic to Beginning Reading" (7) was administered by the kindergarten teacher. The same test was administered by the first-grade teacher during the week of September 9–13, 1963.

To establish a criterion group in terms of reading achievement, all first-grade children (N = 449) were administered Level One of "Primary Reading Profiles" (14) by the Primary Consultant and Assistant Superintendent in May, 1963. All children who exceeded the system mean of 92.9 were administered Level Two of the test by the classroom teacher. This same procedure will be followed with the experimental group in May, 1964. Comparisons will be made to determine what differences in reading skill may exist between the groups.

An instrument to measure degree of interest in reading is now being developed. This will be administered to control groups (Grades 3 and 4) in February, 1965, and to the experimental group (Grade 3) in February, 1966.

Statistical significance of results will be determined by t-test in the case of all hypotheses except the first. Since no criterion group was available against which to compare the experimental group in terms of skill development in kindergarten, "adequately" was arbitrarily defined as a score approaching the point recommended by the test authors as adequate for beginning reading instruction.

Results

Despite the fact that no group completed the program, the mean for the total group of 402 kindergarten children was 48 points out of a possible 58. The authors recommend 45 as the point at which children have sufficient skill to begin reading instruction. The mean score for the group with workbooks was 52, compared with a mean of 44 for those without workbooks. This difference in favor of the use of workbooks was significant at the .01 level (Table I).

Comparison of the kindergarten mean with the grade one mean for the total test indicates a loss of less than three points over the summer. While this was statistically significant (.01 level), for all practical purposes it removed any concern about kindergarten children's ability to retain these skills over the summer.

The loss for the non-workbook group was less than for the workbook group, and it was not significant. The fact that many children in the workbook group received perfect scores on the initial test (in kindergarten) made it impossible for them to improve. This regression toward the mean seemed to account for the greater loss in the workbook group. Scores of individual pupils exhibited this same statistical tendency: some children actually gained as much as 14 points, while others lost that much.

Subjective evaluations based on reactions of children, teachers, and parents verified the objective measures. First-grade teachers reported that their children initially were more settled and were developing reading skills more efficiently than had classes in previous years. Library books were used earlier in the year and in greater numbers.

A "bonus" in the program was the report of the speech therapists. In screening first-grade pupils this year, speech therapists reported that a considerable reduction (36 per cent) had occurred in the number of children with minor speech problems as well as in the variety of those problems. We had wondered if the earlier awareness of sounds and "beginnings" of spoken words might make children more conscious of language as they experienced it in their daily lives. Apparently they have been helped to overcome such substitutions as *w* for *l*, *f* for *th*, *s* for *th*, and *b* for *v*.

As a result of findings to date, the prereading program is underway with workbooks in all kindergartens in Glenview for the 1963-64 school year. Results of reading-skill testing at the end of first grade will be available in the summer of 1964.

TABLE I. Mean Scores in Kindergarten and Grade One

	N	1	2	3	4	Total	F	t
Workbook:	205							
Kindergarten		7.6	16.7	12.6	15.4	52.3		
							1.5715*	5.7719*
Grade One		7.0	16.2	11.9	13.1	48.1		
Non-Workbook:	197							
Kindergarten		6.4	15.5	10.4	11.4	43.6		
							1.0010	1.0565
Grade One		6.2	15.1	10.4	10.8	42.6		
Total Group:	402							
Kindergarten		7.0	16.1	11.5	13.4	48.0		
							1.0120	4.0284*
Grade One		6.7	15.6	11.1	12.0	45.4		

Sub-Tests span over columns 1-4.

* = significant at .01 level

Summary

Methods, materials, and children have been changing through the years. Investigations need to be made to improve the programs offered in kindergarten. Such a view does not imply that kindergarten should become a "young first grade." We all recognize that the good teacher, even with a very limited program, is far better than a poor teacher with the best program. But let's also recognize that the good kindergarten teacher can carry out a formal program *in an informal manner* just as easily as the poor teacher can make a party *formal*. The goal is really a good teacher with an organized program, developing that program in terms of the individuals in her class.

References

1. Anderson, Dorothy. "A Study to Determine if Children Need a Mental Age of Six Years and Six Months to Learn to Identify Strange Printed Word Forms When They Are Taught to Use Oral Context and the Initial Sound of the Word," unpublished doctoral dissertation, Colorado State College, 1960.
2. Denver Public Schools. "Reading Instruction in the Kindergarten." Denver Public Schools Bulletin, 1962.
3. Durkin, Dolores. "An Earlier Start in Reading?" *Elementary School Journal,* 63: 147–151; December, 1962.
4. Eames, Thomas. "Physical Factors in Reading," *The Reading Teacher,* 15: 432; May, 1962.
5. Hillerich, R. L. "Dare We Evaluate Paradise?" *Illinois Education,* 51: 326–345; April, 1963.
6. McKee, Paul, and Lucille Harrison. *Getting Ready to Read.* Boston: Houghton Mifflin, 1962.
7. ———. *Pre-Reading Inventory of Skills Basic to Beginning Reading.* Boston: Houghton Mifflin, 1963.
8. Morphett, Mable, and Carleton Washburne. "When Should Children Begin to Read?" *Elementary School Journal,* 31: 496–503; 1931.
9. Morrone, Victor. "A Critical Analysis of Scientific Research in Phonics," unpublished doctoral dissertation, University of Pittsburgh, 1958.
10. Newton, Eunice Shaed. Unpublished speech presented at the Science Research Associates Conference in Chicago, 1960.
11. Nicholson, Alice. "Background Abilities Related to Reading Success in First Grade," unpublished doctoral dissertation, Boston University, 1957.
12. Olson, Arthur, Jr. "Growth in Word Perception as It Related to Success in Beginning Reading," unpublished doctoral dissertation, Boston University, 1957.
13. Sheldon, William. "Should the Very Young Be Taught to Read?" *NEA Journal,* 52: 20; November, 1963.
14. Stroud-Hieronymous-McKee, *Primary Reading Profile.* Boston: Houghton Mifflin, 1957.

Relation of Self-Concepts to Beginning Achievement in Reading

✤ WILLIAM W. WATTENBERG
AND CLARE CLIFFORD

For some time there has existed evidence that among children severely retarded in reading there are many who also have low self-regard. For example, when Barber (1) examined the school records of twenty-three pupils accepted into a remedial reading class, she found that all displayed anxiety about self and relationships with people to a marked degree. Lumpkin (6) compared twenty-four overachievers in reading with twenty-four underachievers matched for chronological age, mental age, sex, and home background at the fifth-grade level. The overachievers revealed significantly more positive concepts. Bodwin (2) studied one hundred pupils with reading disability, one hundred with arithmetic disability, and one hundred with no educational disability, and found relations between immature self-concepts and reading disability giving correlations of .72 at the third-grade level and .62 at the sixth-grade level.

It would appear that this relation between self-concept and academic achievement is not limited to extreme cases. Bruck (3) obtained self-concept measures for three hundred pupils from the third to sixth grades of three public elementary schools and from the eleventh grade of a senior high school in Flint, Michigan. He found positive and significant relations between self-concept measures and grade-point averages at all grade levels. Hamachek (5) found high achievement and intellectual self-images related to reading age among one hundred children who had attended the University of Michigan School for three or more years. Coopersmith (4) found a partial correlation of .30 between Iowa Achievement Test scores and self-esteem measures in fifth- and sixth-grade children when socioeconomic status was held constant.

That the relation is not accidental is indicated by a study which Seay (7) made of the relation between changes in reading skills and self-concepts accompanying a remedial program for boys with low reading ability and reasonably normal intelligence. The seventy-two boys in the program were matched with a control group having no reading problems on the basis of age, grade, and language ability. He found that changes in self-concept were positively associated with experiences in the remedial reading program.

The purpose of the study to be presented in this article[1] was exploratory in nature, to gather data as to the direction of causality in the relation reported by such studies as those cited above.

From *Child Development*, 35: 461–467; June, 1964. Reprinted by permission. © Society for Research in Child Development, Inc., 1964. William W. Wattenberg is Professor of Educational Psychology, Wayne State University, Detroit, Michigan.

[1] This study was performed under a research contract with the Office of Education, as Cooperative Research Project No. 377, United States Office of Education, Department of Health, Education, and Welfare.

The basic design called for obtaining measures of mental ability and self-concept for a group of children shortly after their entrance into kindergarten. At the conclusion of the second grade, measures of self-concept and reading ability would again be obtained. If the early measures of self-concept were predictive of later reading achievement, and had a predictive efficiency beyond that of intelligence tests, then one could surmise that self-concepts had a causal relation to reading achievement. If, on the other hand, there was a strong relation between reading achievement and changes in self-concept, one would be inclined to believe that the experiences in reading influenced the self-concept.

In order to have some partial control on socioeconomic factors and also the influence of reading methods, it was decided to draw the population for the study from two elementary schools in Detroit, one with a working-class parental occupational level and one with a middle-class clientele. Both schools were in districts where parents sent their children to kindergarten in the public school, but half in each case transferred to a Catholic school in the first grade; different methods of teaching reading were used in the public and in the Catholic schools.

Although complete data at the kindergarten level were obtained on 185 children, the N on follow-up was reduced to 128. Of these, twenty-five were in the middle-class public school; thirty-four, in the middle-class Catholic school; thirty-two, in the working-class public school; and thirty-seven, in the working-class Catholic school.

As a measure of intellectual ability, scores recorded on the Detroit Beginning First Grade Intelligence Test, when routinely given near the close of the second semester of kindergarten, were used. For the measure of reading achievement at the close of the second grade, because of the differences in reading method and vocabulary used in the two textbook series, the tests distributed by the textbook series publishers were employed.

In order to secure a quantified measure of self-concept, tape recordings were made of the remarks of the children while drawing a picture of their families and responding to an incomplete sentences test devised for the purpose. Typescripts were prepared from the tape-recordings. Two independent raters divided the recordings into thought units. The thought units were classified as to whether or not they constituted self-references. The self-references were further classified as to whether they dealt with competence, personal worth, or some other issue. Those which dealt with competence and personal worth were further rated as to whether they were positive, negative, or neutral. In each case the ratio of positive to total references was calculated. Respectively, these will be termed Quantified Self-Concept (Competence) and Quantified Self-Concept (Good-Bad). For the typescripts of the kindergarten interviews, the product-moment correlations for the two raters were .89 for the competence ratios and .75 for the good-bad; at the second grade level, these were .82 and .71.

In addition to the quantified measures, the classroom teachers and a clinically trained interviewer were asked to rate the children as to their feelings of competence and worth. Additional ratings were secured on ego-strength, defined as follows: "A strong ego is shown by a child who seems to act on a fairly good estimate of reality, who exercises good self-control, who is able to stick with a task, and who can use spontaneous imagination."

Hypotheses

For purposes of proper employment of statistical measures, the following hypotheses were set up:

1. Measures of self-concept and ratings of self-concept taken in the first semester of kindergarten will be predictive of later achievement in reading.
2. The correlation between measures and ratings of self-concept on the one hand and a mental test score on the other will be low. (In effect, the measures of self-concept will add significantly to the predictive efficiency of an intelligence test.)
3. The association between reading achievement and changes in measures of self-concept from kindergarten to second grade will be positive but low. (In effect, the self-concept is more important as a determinant of learning efficiency than learning experiences are in the formation of the self-concept.)
4. Ratings of ego-strength will show a high positive correlation with achievement in reading.
5. There are different aspects to the self-concept which can be measured separately and which will show only moderate intercorrelation. (Specifically, for kindergarten children, self-concept as to competence will be more related to success in academic achievement than is self-concept as to goodness versus naughtiness.)
6. The self-concept will display some characteristics of defensive reactions. (Specifically, children verbalizing a high ratio of self-references will show lower success in reading than those not evidencing a preoccupation with self-characteristics.)

Findings

It was recognized from the start that the problem of obtaining adequate tests of the hypotheses would be complicated by the well-known facts that early achievement in reading is linked to sex and to socioeconomic class. Also, at the second grade level differences in the vocabulary content of the readers employed in series of textbooks used in different methods might also affect scores on tests.

It was decided to order the data in two distinctive ways. First, in an attempt to get at global relations, the entire population was dichotomized on second-grade reading according to whether at the end of the second grade a child was reading in the book appropriate to his grade level or in a book lower in the series. They were also dichotomized on the other variables. A series of four-cell tables were prepared and tested for significance of differences by the *chi square* test; since direction of relations has been established by the hypotheses, one-tailed tests of significance were used.

In the second ordering of data, the population was divided into subgroups homogeneous as to sex, socioeconomic class, and textbook in which they were reading at the time. Each subgroup was rank ordered on each pair of variables, and the rank-order correlations were calculated by the Spearman *rho* technique. The level of significance was calculated for one-tailed tests.

In general, the results on the dichotomized ordering of the data were inconclusive. Only one table produced results where the level of confidence was at the .05 level; this table showed that success in reading was linked to an improvement in the self-concept as to competence.

However, when the rank-order correlations among the variables for the subgroups were examined, substantial support of the hypotheses was apparent.

Of the fourteen subgroup correlations between second-grade reading-test scores and quantified self-concept (competence) measures, ten were positive; two, at the .05 level. For the quantified self-concept (good-bad), the comparable figures showed that, of fourteen correlations, eleven were positive, with three at the .05 level and an additional one at the .01 level.

The ratings as to self-concept by the teachers and the clinician gave an equally impressive performance. Of the twenty-eight correlations between reading achievement and the ratings of self-concept (competence) in the kindergarten, nineteen were positive; three held at the .05 level and an additional one at the .01 level. For the ratings of the self-concept (good-bad) there were twenty-two positive, with three at the .05 level and an additional one at the .01 level.

Examination of the detailed tables showed no concentration of effect for either sex, for socioeconomic level, or for reading series. The phenomena appear to have been general.

By contrast, the correlations for those scores with the mental test scores were close to chance expectations. Of the fourteen correlations between the mental test scores and the quantified self-concept (competence) measures, only six were positive, and none strongly enough to show even a .05 level of confidence; for the quantified self-concept (good-bad) measure there were seven positive correlations; one at a .05 level.

For the ratings of self-concept, the expected halo effect was clearly operating. Of the twenty-eight correlations between mental test scores and self-concept (competence) ratings, there were nineteen positive; four at the .05 level. For the self-concept (good-bad) ratings there were twenty-one positive, with five at the .05 level and an additional one at the .01 level.

As for the third hypothesis, that which dealt with the possibility that experience in reading might be a determinant of the self-concept, the rank-order correlations showed a pattern which at first sight seemed puzzling. On the whole, the correlations between reading test scores and changes in quantified measures of self-concept were slightly inclined to be negative. Of the twenty-eight correlations, only ten were positive and not one of these reached an acceptable level of significance. However, in view of the decided correlations between reading achievement and the kindergarten self-concept scores, this was not surprising. After all, in a rank ordering, high ranks have no place to go but down and low ratings, by chance alone, would move upward. The tendency, then, for the faintly negative results would support the hypothesis that the self-concept in kindergarten has greater influence in the development of reading skill than the reading experience has upon the self-concept.

For the hypothesis as to the effect of ego-strength, the only evidence comes from the ratings by the teachers and the clinical interviewer. The rank-order correlations strongly supported the hypothesis. Of the twenty-eight correlations, twenty-two were positive; three at the .05 level and an additional one at the .01 level.

A matter of theoretical interest for workers interested in self-concept phenomena was raised by the fifth hypothesis that, far from being a unitary attribute, the self-concept has at least two aspects which vary somewhat independently of each other. When correlations were calculated between the quantified measures of self-concept (competence) and self-concept (good-bad), of the fourteen subgroups, positive results were found for nine, but none at the .05 level.

The last hypothesis to be tested was related to the possibility that in some cases at least a child's apparent self-concept might be a psychological defense. To get at this, use was made of the assumption that a child who had a need for this type of defense would show some evidence of preoccupation with self. If this were the case, then we would expect that the larger the proportion of comments which were self-references, the stronger was the need for defense. It could be surmised that children with such needs and preoccupations would do less well in learning to read than those with milder defensiveness. Accordingly, for each child ratios were calculated of the proportion of all thought units in the testing situation protocols which were self-references, and the proportion of these which were related to competence on the one hand or personal worth on the other. These ratios were correlated for all subgroups with the scores on reading tests at the end of the second grade. The presumed indices of defensiveness behaved as predicted as far as the ratios of self-reference and of competence mentions were concerned. Here, of the twenty-eight correlations, eighteen were negative (the predicted direction); three at the .05 level and one additional at the .01 level. However, for the proportion of good-bad mentions, contrary to hypothesis, ten out of fourteen correlations were positive. When correlations were run between the "defensiveness" measures and the two quantified measures of self-concept, similar trends appeared. Of these, the most intriguing and possibly most revealing was the series of correlations between the quantified self-concept (good-bad) scores and the proportion of good-bad references in the protocols. Contrary to hypothesis, eleven of these were positive. The strength of the correlations was such that had the contrary hypothesis been set up the one-tailed test of significance would have shown four at the .05 level and an additional one at the .01 level.

Conclusions

Although the levels of significance were far from overwhelming, the consistency in results was striking. In general, the measures of self-concept and of ego strength taken at the kindergarten were predictive of reading achievement two and one-half years later. The association between these measures and intelligence test scores was so low that one can say with some assurance that measures of the self-concept as to competence and personal worth if taken early in kindergarten would add significantly to the predictive efficiency now attainable through tests of mental ability.

One of the questions which led to the present exploratory study had to do with whether the association previously reported between self-concept and academic achievement had its origin in self-concepts being causal to achievement or, by contrast, the experiences of academic success or failure playing a part in the formation of the self-concept. The findings previously reported earlier in this article would appear to be definite: even as early as kindergarten, self-concept phenomena are antecedent to and predictive of reading accomplishment at the least.

It would also appear that there is more than one dimension to the self-concept in children. In this study it was possible to obtain measures of at least two relatively distinctive aspects: feelings of competence and feelings of personal worth (goodness versus badness). The correlations between these two, while positive, were rather low, and the two measures behaved differently.

Finally, it must be pointed out that, because the findings seem to have far-reaching import, it is essential that they be checked with a variety of techniques and research designs. Efforts should be made to develop speedier and less costly ways of measuring self-concepts in their several dimensions, to study the phenomena at other age levels and with respect to other areas of academic competence, and, finally, to seek experimentally to change self-concepts in order to discover whether such changes affect academic achievement.

References

1. Barber, L. "Immature Ego Development as a Factor in Retarded Ability to Read," unpublished doctoral dissertation, University of Michigan, 1952.
2. Bodwin, R. F. "The Relationship Between Immature Self-Concept and Certain Educational Disabilities," *Dissertation Abstracts,* 19: 1645–1946; 1959.
3. Bruck, M. "A Study of Age Differences and Sex Differences in the Relationship Between Self-Concept and Grade-Point Average," unpublished doctoral dissertation, Michigan State University, 1957.
4. Coopersmith, S. "A Method of Determining Types of Self-Esteem," *Journal of Abnormal Social Psychology*, 59: 87–94; 1959.
5. Hamachek, D. E. "A Study of the Relationship Between Certain Measures of Growth and the Self-Images of Elementary School Children," unpublished doctoral dissertation, University of Michigan, 1960.
6. Lumpkin, D. D. "Relationship of Self-Concept to Achievement in Reading," unpublished doctoral dissertation, University of Southern California, 1959.
7. Seay, L. C. "A Study to Determine Some Relations Between Changes in Reading Skills and Self-Concepts Accompanying a Remedial Program for Boys with Low Reading Ability and Reasonably Normal Intelligence," unpublished doctoral dissertation, North Texas State College, 1960.

Further Reading for Chapter 2

Ames, Wilbur. "The Understanding Vocabulary of First Grade Pupils," *Elementary English*, 41: 64–68; January, 1964.

Barrett, Thomas C. "The Relationship Between Measures of Pre-Reading Visual Discrimination and First Grade Reading Achievement: A Review of the Literature," *Reading Research Quarterly*, 1: 51–76; Fall, 1965.

———. "Visual Discrimination Tasks as Predictors of First-Grade Reading Achievement," *The Reading Teacher*, 18: 276–282; January, 1964.

Bond, Guy L., and Eva Bond Wagner. *Teaching the Child to Read.* New York: The Macmillan Co., 1966. Chapters 2 and 3.

Davis, David. "Phonemic Structural Approach to Initial Instruction in Reading," *Elementary English*, 41: 218–223; March, 1964.

Dawson, Mildred A., and Henry A. Bamman. *Fundamentals of Basic Reading Instruction.* New York: David McKay Co., Inc., 1963. Chapters 4 and 5.

DeBoer, John J., and Martha Dallmann. *The Teaching of Reading.* New York: Holt, Rinehart & Winston, Inc., 1964. Chapter 5.

Doman, G. J. "Little Children Can Learn to Read," *P.T.A. Magazine,* 59: 30–32; January, 1965.

Durkin, Dolores. "Children Who Read Before Grade I: A Second Study," *Elementary School Journal,* 64: 143–148; December, 1963.

————. "Early Readers — Reflections After Six Years of Research," *The Reading Teacher,* 18: 3–7; October, 1964.

————. "Kindergarten and Reading," *Elementary English,* 39: 274–276; March, 1962.

Dykstra, Robert. "Auditory Discrimination Abilities and Beginning Reading Achievement," *Reading Research Quarterly,* 1: 5–34; Spring, 1966.

Fowler, W. "Structural Dimensions of the Learning Process in Early Reading," *Child Development,* 35: 1093–1104; December, 1964.

Gray, Lillian. *Teaching Children to Read.* New York: The Ronald Press Company, 1963. Chapters 5, 6, and 8.

Harris, Albert J. *How to Increase Reading Ability.* New York: David McKay Co., Inc., 1961. Chapters 2 and 3.

Heilman, Arthur W. *Principles and Practices of Teaching Reading.* Columbus, Ohio: Charles E. Merrill Books, Inc., 1961. Chapters 2, 3, and 4.

Hillerich, Robert L. "Pre-Reading Skills in Kindergarten: A Second Report," *Elementary School Journal,* 65: 312–317; March, 1965.

Kelley, Marjorie L. "When Are Children Ready to Read?" *Saturday Review,* July 20, 1962, p. 58.

Lynn, R. "Reading Readiness and the Perceptual Abilities of Young Children," *Educational Research,* 6: 15–19; November, 1963.

Martin, J. H. "Using the Computerized Typewriter for Early Reading Instruction: Edison Responsive Environment Instrument," *Audiovisual Instruction,* 10: 309–310; April, 1965.

McKee, Paul. *Reading: A Program of Instruction for the Elementary School.* Boston: Houghton Mifflin Company, 1966. Chapters 3, 5, and 6.

McKim, Margaret G., and Helen Caskey. *Guiding Growth in Reading in the Modern Elementary School.* New York: The Macmillan Co., 1963. Chapters 3, 4, and 5.

McNeil, John D., and Evan R. Keislar. "Value of the Oral Response in Beginning Reading," *The British Journal of Educational Psychology,* 33: 162–167; February, 1963.

Muehl, Siegmar. "The Effects of Visual Discrimination Pretraining on Learning to Read a Vocabulary List in Kindergarten Children," *Journal of Educational Psychology,* 51: 217–221; August, 1960.

Olson, Arthur V. "Phonics and Success in Beginning Reading," *Journal of Reading,* 6: 256–60; Summer, 1963.

Plessas, Gus, and Clifton Oakes. "Prereading Experiences of Early Selected Readers," *The Reading Teacher,* 17: 241–245; January, 1964.

Schoephoerster, Hugh; Richard Barnhart; and Walter M. Loomer. "The Teaching of Prereading Skills in Kindergarten," *The Reading Teacher,* 19: 352–357; February, 1966.

Smith, Henry P., and Emerald V. Dechant. *Psychology in Teaching Reading.* Englewood Cliffs, N. J.: Prentice-Hall, Inc., 1961. Chapter 4.

Smith, Nila Banton. "Early Reading: Viewpoints," *Childhood Education*, 42: 229–232, 241; December, 1965.

————. *Reading Instruction for Today's Children.* Englewood Cliffs, N.J.: Prentice-Hall, Inc., 1963. Chapters 15 and 17.

Spache, George D. *Reading in the Elementary School.* Boston: Allyn and Bacon, Inc., 1964. Chapters 2, 7, and 8.

Sutton, Marjorie Hunt. "Attitudes of Young Children Toward Reading," *Education*, 85: 238–241; December, 1964.

————. "First-Grade Children Who Learned to Read in Kindergarten," *The Reading Teacher*, 19: 192–196; December, 1965.

Thackray, D. V. "Relationship Between Reading Readiness and Reading Progress," *British Journal of Educational Psychology,* 35: 252–254; June, 1965.

Tinker, Miles A., and Constance M. McCullough. *Teaching Elementary Reading.* New York: Appleton-Century-Crofts, Inc., 1962. Chapters 3, 4, 5, 19, and 20.

Weintraub, Samuel, and Terry P. Denny. "What Do Beginning First Graders Say About Reading?" *Childhood Education*, 41: 326–327; February, 1965.

Witty, Paul A.; Alma Moore Freeland; and Edith H. Grotbert. *The Teaching of Reading: A Developmental Process.* Boston: D. C. Heath & Company, 1966. Chapters 5 and 9.

3

Artificial Orthographies

The term *artificial orthography* is something of a misnomer, since so-called correct spelling has become so through usage and is no more "natural" or "artificial" than any other spelling method. Those who advocate change, however, have sometimes referred to the generally accepted spelling patterns as traditional orthography, or "T.O.," as they compare it with the different orthography which they recommend. Since there are a number of such orthographies which have been suggested, it is necessary to have some term to encompass them all; hence, the term *artificial orthographies*.

These artificial orthographies are all based on the premise that the inconsistencies of spelling as we know them today are unnecessary barriers to learning to read English. Although their proponents do not promise that all reading problems will become non-existent when their alphabetic reforms are adopted, they all do indicate that the vagaries of English spelling are a major cause of reading difficulties and that the adoption of their alphabetic systems will remove a majority of the difficulties by removing their cause.

There have been, of course, many attempts to provide more consistency in English spelling. Although these attempts have generally received scant acceptance, reading teachers in recent years have sometimes listened attentively to the promises of great growth in reading ability, if a particular orthography is adopted.

The most widely publicized of these has been the Initial Teaching Alphabet, which began in England as the Augmented Roman Alphabet. There are, however, several other methods which have been vigorously proposed by their backers for classroom use. These include Words in Color, The TV Alphabet, the Diacritical Marking System, and the "Single-Sound" or Unifon System. Because these latter methods have received less notice than i/t/a, teachers searching for another method of beginning reading instruction sometimes ask the wrong question about changing orthographies. The question most often asked in relation to this issue is, "Should i/t/a be used?" There are, instead, at least two very pertinent questions which should be asked before we consider the relative merits of i/t/a. First, should we use an artificial orthography at all, at least for beginning reading instruction? Second, which artificial orthography shows the greatest promise? There are certainly other points to raise, but unless we first seek answers to both of these questions, we run the grave risk of changing directions without examining all of the paths which are open to us.

The proponents of i/t/a, in particular, stress that their alphabet represents a "means, not a method." That is, they hold that the alphabet is a system of spelling which does not dictate, for example, whether a teacher uses a whole-word approach or a phonic approach. Though there is nothing in the nature of these artificial orthographies which *requires* the teacher to use a certain method, it must certainly be true that they imply that the child will use a certain method to identify words — that is, the method of single symbol-sound relationships. If a child were merely going to memorize words without paying particular attention to the sound that each letter symbol represented, it would make no difference whether there was a high degree of correspondence between symbol-sound relationships or not. There is, then, a strong implication that the child would learn to use single-letter phonics, since a single symbol-sound relationship is the basic strength of these systems.

In this chapter, several different artificial orthographies are examined by their most persuasive proponents, each stating the case for his particular program.

John R. Malone presents an orthographic system which he recommends as a spelling reform for all reading matter for both children and adults. This spelling reform is recommended for a number of reasons, one of the most important of which is its adaptability to language-using machines. Mr. Malone does more than merely extol the virtues of his system, however; he also lists thirteen different reasons why he believes that his symbols are superior to those of two other competing systems.

In the second article, Edward Fry discusses the Diacritical Marking System. This system does not represent a complete spelling reform but, like i/t/a and Words in Color, it is a system recommended only for the early stages of English reading instruction. In this system, unlike the other two discussed in Chapter 3, we find the regular alphabetic symbols as we know them, together with diacritical marks which can be made on any standard typewriter.

The remaining three articles deal with i/t/a. In the first of these, Albert J. Mazurkiewicz makes a strong plea for the use of i/t/a in beginning reading instruction. In the next, Thomas C. Barrett examines some of the uncontrolled variables which may have influenced research results with i/t/a, and suggests reserved judgment. The last article, a strong criticism of i/t/a by William B. Gillooly, with rebuttals by Theodore B. Dolmatch and Dr. Mazurkiewicz, examines more minutely some of the i/t/a research and shows most clearly some of the sharp disagreements which have arisen in this area.

The Larger Aspects of Spelling

Reform ✤ John R. Malone

For a hundred years and more, a variety of movements and individuals have sought to revise the spelling of English, in the direction of system, a phonetic or phonemic relationship, and away from the conventions frozen by a series of orthographic accidents from about the time of Caxton (the first printer of English) to the time of the King James Bible.

In spite of the power of the personalities involved and the utter rationality of their cause, the movement has gotten virtually no place. Highly competent scholars like Dr. Godfrey Dewey of Harvard (now Emeritus), and Dr. Ralph Owen of Temple, and effective gadflies like George Bernard Shaw, the late Colonel R. R. McCormick of the *Chicago Tribune,* and Thorstein Veblen, have contributed their attentions for long years, to little avail.

As is obvious, there are two great restraints on change: the very bulk of printed materials and size of the publication industry in the English-using portions of the world on the one hand, and the cost of changing type patterns and typesetting machinery on the other. These are very real deterrents. Until a few years ago, it was estimated that it would cost several hundred thousand dollars to change the pattern molds and matrices for one character in a single family of type, when all its sizes, in roman, bold face, italic, and small caps were considered, because the basic first mold for each size in each style had to be hand-tooled.

Today, for the first time since Gutenberg, it has become feasible for change in the alphabet, in terms of the equipment for setting type. A variety of new typesetting methods, some photographic (relying on optics to diminish or enlarge the size), and some typewriter-like, permit a change for an entire font to be made for a few hundred or a few thousand dollars in artwork.

There have also been changes in the form of printing plates, due to the economics of offset lithography (multilith-like systems) and high speed engraving of type from typewriters or photographically composed originals. The Photon, the Fotosetter, and many more devices have been put on the market; type-matter for plates, books, newspapers, and magazines is being produced from these machines.

Thus one of the objections to change has been reduced in importance by the changes in technology. The second objection, that of bulk of materials printed in traditional spelling or orthography, and the very size of the ongoing printing industry, still must be reckoned with.

The objection of existing practices and accumulation requires that any change be one that will be reasonably consistent with past practices, or else tied by mnemonics to past practices, so for several generations a person might be expected to know two systems for writing and reading English, with the exception that the traditional, unsystematic, and diseconomic system would slowly wither away.

From *Elementary English,* 39: 435–445; May, 1962. Reprinted with the permission of the National Council of Teachers of English and John R. Malone, Executive Director, Unifon Alphabet Foundation, Park Forest, Illinois.

In general, however, the orthography for a language has one powerful and overriding need, that of isomorphism. In classic concept, the alphabet of a language should be such that there is one unique symbol for each phoneme, and one unique phoneme for each symbol; this quality is the means by which a language is made readily accessible to others, and enables a child to learn to spell, or read, in a few weeks. German and Russian have this characteristic quality, with a few small exceptions. Turkish, Japanese (Romaji literation), Spanish, and most Scandinavian and central European languages are so written. To a slightly lesser extent is Italian and Portuguese written isomorphically, French is not isomorphic, but its irregularities are systematic. As a consequence, English is perhaps the hardest language to learn from written materials, although inherently it is a language as nearly easy as any of the Oriental languages, in terms of structure. On the other hand, most other languages are relatively easy for English users to learn, because of the systematic quality of spelling. We are abstracting from inflections, idioms, vocabulary and structure, of course.

Now we get to the crux of the matter.

Today, English is the *lingua franca* of the modern world, with far wider currency than Greek or Latin ever had. Literally millions of people around the world want to learn English, the language of technology, science, and commerce. It is the language of international air navigation and operation. It is a required course in the schools of about 90 of the 115 nations of the earth. But English-teaching, because of the unsystematic spelling and inadequate alphabet, is a costly, frustrating matter. It is frequently said that most non-English vernacular users never learn *both* the literate and spoken forms of the English language in one generation unless they are rare minds, and are given much costly training.

This apparent perversity of the English-using peoples stems from the fact that English is a pot-pourri of many languages, and the users of the language have had no Goethe, or Academy, to standardize and systematize spelling. It stems also from the fact that the range of sounds or phonemes for English approximates forty, the largest of any European language. And to write these with only twenty-six letters, requires conventions, digraphs, silent *e*'s to indicate a "long" sound, and so forth.

Over the seven or eight hundred years English orthography has been developing, a number of scribes, printers, and users, of varying intelligence, background knowledge, and insight have striven to devise "make-do's" for this task, each time using the inadequate Latin alphabet. In many cases they have only succeeded in confusing the issue, reflecting a local dialect, or using an unnecessary device.

To provide an adequate system for doing this, the World Spelling System of the Simpler Spelling Association was devised and has been pushed for many years. But this requires rules, too. For instance, the word *chaotic* is spelled *kaeaatik*. Is it possible to look at this word and arrive at pronounciation more easily than the old way?

Thus it would seem that any scheme short of a new forty-character letter system should be unacceptable, lest we get tangled in battles for rules and conventions as the users of the language and the writers of dictionaries have been for several hundred years.

But there is even a more important aspect of spelling reform, namely the irrefutable logic of language-using machines. Sound-discriminating typewriters which type as they are dictated to are being developed. [There are] about a

Figure 1: Current Orthographic Treatment of the Forty Common English Phonemes

The Sixteen Vowels and Vowel-Diphthongs

h*a*t **A**
A: add   EA: pear
A-E: care
AI: plaid

f*a*te **△** 
A: favor   A-E: ale
AU: gauge   AIG: campaign
AG-E: champagne   AY: stray
E: cafe   E-E: suede
EE: matinee   EA: steak
EI: veil   EIG: reign
EIGH: weigh   EY: they
ET: bouquet

b*a*ll **Λ**
AW: law   O: orb   A: call
O: ought   AUGH: caught

b*e*t **E**
E: let   IE: friend
EA: feather   AE: aesthetic

see **I**
E-E: eve   E: event
IE: machine   EA: stream
EE: see   AE: Caesar
IE: yield   OE: phoenix
EY: key   AY: quay
EI: seize   EO: people

h*er* **Ǝ**
I: fir   E: her   U: hurt
OE: Goethe   O: Shön
EU: jeu

b*i*t **Ⱶ**
I: ill   Y: pretty
EIG: foreign   E-E: here
EI: weird   EA: fear
AI: captain   UI: build
O: women

b*i*te **⟠** 
I-E: wife   IGH: nigh
EYE: eye   Y: my   YE: lye
I: bicycle   HY: rhyme
IG: sign   AI: Cairo
AY: bayou   AYE: aye
EI: Eifel   EIGH: height
IE: tie   UI: guise   UY: buy
IS-E: isle   AIS-E: aisle
Y-E: style

p*o*t **O**
O: odd   EA: heart   A: dance
ER: sergeant   UA: guard

c*o*ld **Ω**
O: old   O-E: note   OW: low
OUGH: though   OWE: owe
EAU: eau   EW: sew
OE: hoe   OA: foam
AU: chauffeur   EO: yeoman
OO: door   OU: soul
OS: apropos   OT: depot

f*oo*t **⟠** 
OO: foot
U: pull

h*ow* **⊕** 
OU: out
OW: cow
AO: lao
AU: frau

b*oy* **Ɠ**
OI: oil
OY: boy

c*u*t **U**
U: up   A: account
A (article)   E: the
OE: does   OU: tough
EOU: gorgeous   O: love
E: silent

b*oo*t **⊔** 
U: rumor   OO: food
IEU: lieu   WO: two
EW: grew   O: who
UE: due   OUGH: through
OO-E: ooze   U-E: rule
HEU: rheumatism   OE: shoe
OU: soup   UI-E: bruise
UO: buoy   IOUX: Sioux

*u*se **Ⱳ**
U: human   U-E: cube
U: menu   EU: feud
YOU: you   UG: impugn
UGH: Hugh   EAU: beauty
YEW: yew   IEW: view
UU: vacuum   EUE: queue

TOTAL:
139 Ways of Spelling, 16 Vowel and Vowel Diphthong Sounds or Phonemes, an average of more than 8.5 spellings per sound.

Figure 1, Continued

Consonants: Twenty-Four Identifiable Ones

*b*est	**B**	B: as in bee, bit
*c*ell	**C**	C: as in cell S: as in sit SS: as in hiss SC: as in scene PS: pseudo
*ch*est	**Ɔ**	CH: chair TCH: match TI: question TE: righteous TU: nature
*d*o	**D**	D: day ED: bobbed
*f*at	**F**	F: fan GH: cough PH: phantom
*g*et	**G**	G: get GG: egg GH: ghost GU: guard GUE: plague
*h*at	**H**	H: hat WH: who W: what (inversion)
*j*et	**J**	J: just DI: soldier G: gem DGE: edge GI: religion
*k*ill	**K**	K: kick CH: epoch QU: conquer QUE: pique CK: pack C: cube X(*s*): expect
*l*et	**L**	L: late LL: holly
*m*et	**M**	M: man MM: hammer MB: lamb MN: hymn
*n*et	**N**	N: nod GN: sign, gnat KN: knob PN: pneumonia MN: mnemonic
si*ng*	**И**	NG: sing N: think NC: junction NGUE: tongue
*p*en	**P**	P: pen
*r*un	**R**	R: rat RH: rhomboid WR: wrap
*sh*oot or *s*ure	**S**	S: sure SH: shop CH: machine SSI: mission CI: social TI: nation SCI: conscious SS: issue CE: ocean SE: nauseous
*t*o	**T**	T: talk ED: baked TH: Thomas
*th*in	**θ**	TH: thin (voiceless) PTH: pthalic
*th*ere	**Ɵ**	TH: the (voiced)
*v*an	**V**	V: van F: of
*w*ell	**W**	W: want U: persuade O: choir
*y*et	**Y**	Y: yet DU: verdure E: grandeur I: onion
*z*oo	**Z**	Z: zone S: is X: xylophone
lei*s*ure	**Ƶ**	Z: azure SI: vision ZI: glazier GE: rouge S: pleasure

TOTAL: 87 ways of spelling 24 consonant sounds, an average of 3.6 spellings per sound.

GRAND TOTAL: 40 vowel and consonant sounds—226 ways of spelling them.

Copyright © 1962 The Foundation for a Compatible and Consistent Alphabet. By permission.

dozen in this country and abroad. To make them work with English as it is written is not impossible, but so costly that it would be cheaper to have five or six secretaries. To make them work with only twenty-five or twenty-six letters and the usages of the World Spelling System would not be quite so hard, but still a costly task. To make a dictatable or phonetic typewriter, similar to that recently patented by the Radio Corporation of America, work in English at a reasonable price (under a thousand dollars, say), requires that we extend our alphabet so that we have *one letter for each sound*. Otherwise, the rest of the world, particularly Europe and Russia, can use their dictatable typewriters freely, having the keys thump out letters as they speak into the circuitry and microphone. It is doubtful if we want to keep ourselves for long at such a disadvantage with respect to the rest of the industrialized world, which lies now only a few hours by air from any city in our nation.

But more than these two items, is our problem of teaching our young today: our youngsters go to work with vocabularies of from ten thousand to twenty-five thousand words, learned in urban surroundings, on radio and TV, and in the stepped-up pace of twentieth century industrialized life. At present I'm in the midst of listing the vocabulary of a four-year-old child in my own household. She can manipulate more than two thousand words orally. Her six-year-old sister can easily handle fifteen thousand. It will be three or four years of customary school before she can write and read these words, because of the irregularities of spelling. In four to six weeks, her Latin, Russian, or German cousins can spell nearly everything they can handle orally. There are no frustrations, no boresome "Run, Dick, Run."

The result is that European schools are easily two and three years ahead of American schools. The classic and academic *Gymnasium* or *Lycée* courses have youngsters taught through integral and differential calculus and are using several languages freely at the end of high-school terms.

The key to knowledge is reading; the key to science is mathematics. These two areas of school are essentially the keys to our survival as a nation, and to the success of our public school system. We are at work on the mathematics; but for the moment there is a forced lagging in the teaching of reading and writing, not because of the schools, but because of an irrational spelling, which must be learned not by letters but much like Chinese ideographs, a word at a time.

There are other aspects to the design of an alphabet; adoption of characters which will easily encode themselves into binary codes for fast transmission by wire, for typesetting, for computer use and storage, all of which must now be tediously hand-punched from a keyboard. The system of letters must be as closely concurrent with the Latin usages of Europe and elsewhere as possible, so ultimately the same keyboard could be used to type a multiplicity of languages. It ought to have the greatest possible legibility, because in the long run the world's shortest supply resource is paper. Today, for instance, the neutrality of Indian public opinion is controlled by Russian-controlled supplies of newsprint into her ports and newspapers. The Single-Sound Alphabet with its all-capitals (much like Russian) is designed so that about 2.5 times as much legible print can be put in the same space that this material is being upper-and-lower-case typeset in, and at the same legibility level.

Although studies have shown that reading speed is controlled by the use of ascenders and descenders, narrow letters and wide, this generalization does not

Figure 2: The New Single-Sound Alphabet

A — at	Δ — ate	Λ — all	B — bow	C — cell say
Ɔ — chair	D — dip	E — hen	Ⅎ — he	Ǝ — her
F — fast	G — goat	H — hat	ⵖ — bit	ⵗ — bite
J — jaw	K — kiss	L — low	M — music	N — no
Ŋ — king	O — lot	Ω — old	Ⓞ — look	Ⓠ — out
Ɠ — boy	P — pipe	R — run	S — sure	T — table
θ — thirst	⊥ — there	U — up	∪ — due	⨆ — you
V — vest	W — wig	Ƶ — azure	Y — yes	Z — zebra

⊥U L+TL RED HEN

WUNC UPΛN U TΔM L+TL RED HEN L+VD
+N U BORN W+θ HƎR FΛV Ɔ+KC. U P+G
U KAT AND U DUK MΔD ⊥ER HΩM
+N ⊥U CΛM BORN. IƆ DΛ L+TL RED
HEN LED HƎR Ɔ+KC OT TƆ LⓄK FΛR
FⓄD. BUT ⊥U P+G, ⊥U KAT, AND ⊥U
DUK WⓄD NOT LⓄK FΛR FⓄD.

The Rules: How Method Would Be Used

Following are the English spelling rules for use of the 40-phoneme alphabet:

1 Spell each word exactly as it sounds: i.e., alfubet, kat, kup, Jon, met, etc.
2 No silent letters; no double letters.
3 Each sound symbolized the same way, exactly, each time it is used.
4 Diphthongs and sounds represented by Latin consonant pairs use new symbols.
5 "Short" vowel sounds utilize customary Latin-English symbol; new "long" vowels have a prominent, added, full-width horizontal member plus Latin symbol.
6 No digraphs or smybols having both consonant and vowel usage are used.
7 All words sounding the same are spelled the same way; context determines meaning as in the normal spoken tongue.
8 Diphthongs and combination sounds made standard with separate symbols: ai, ch, ng, ou or ow, oi or oy, sh, th (voiced), th (unvoiced), yu, and zh.
9 Forty phonemes are made conventional but where local dialects or sharper inflection is used, the nearest approximation shall be used for writing. If necessary, accent marks, diacritical marks, etc., can be used for precision in drama work, speech training.

Copyright © 1962 The Foundation for a Compatible and Consistent Alphabet. By permission.

Figure 3: The Augmented Roman Alphabet

A Transitional Literation as proposed for beginning readers by Sir James Pitman, M.P., London, England

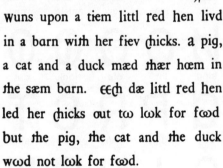

ſhe littl red hen

wuns upon a tiem littl red hen livd in a barn wiſh her fiev ᴄhicks. a pig, a cat and a duck mæd ſhær hœm in ſhe sæm barn. ᴇᴄh dæ littl red hen led her ᴄhicks out tω lωk for fωd but ſhe pig, ſhe cat and ſhe duck wωd not lωk for fωd.

Courtesy *Parents' Magazine*. By permission.

Figure 4: World English Spelling Alphabet

a	**aa**	**ae**	**au**	**b**
at	father	main	cause	back

ch	**d**	**dh**	**e**	**ee**
cheap	do	this	bet	meet

Permanent Revision of English spelling proposed by Simpler Spelling Associations of England and the United States using twenty-six letters

f	**g**	**h**	**i**	**ie**	**j**
for	get	had	it	time	just

k	**l**	**m**	**n**	**ng**
can	light	met	net	thing

nk	**o**	**oe**	**oi**	**oo**
think	not	note	point	good

dhe litl red hen

wuns upon a tiem litl red hen livd in a barn widh hur fiev chiks. a pig, a kat and a duk maed dhaer hoem in dhe saem barn. eech dae litl red hen led hur chiks out too look for fuud. but dhe pig, dhe kat and dhe duk wood not look for fuud.

ou	**p**	**r**	**s**	**sh**	**t**
pound	pack	right	see	shall	to

th	**u**	**ue**	**uu**	**v**
thin	but	few	food	very

w	**wh**	**y**	**z**	**zh**
with	which	yet	please	pleasure

Courtesy *Parents' Magazine*. By permission.

consider the matter of paper price. Remember: the three-mil sheet of newsprint tablet is an expensive item in Latin America, India, Africa, or the Far East. And English, today, is the world's language, not just America's or Great Britain's.

To reduce by 90 per cent the time it requires to teach one of our youngsters to read, or to reduce by 95 per cent the time it requires a Congolese or Puerto Rican to learn English, it seems to me would justify change. These are things we have seen happen. Dr. Margaret Ratz in the summer of 1961, in a test by the Foundation for a Compatible and Consistent Alphabet and the American Broadcasting Company, taught a small group of children to read at third- and fourth-grade levels, in both literations, after about eighteen hours of teaching over eighteen days. Today, larger tests in the Chicago City Schools, the St. Louis City Schools and the Principia lower school in St. Louis are testing this program on a much extended basis. For other schools in reasonably stable neighborhoods who may want to test this program, materials can be obtained at moderate costs.

Why "Single-Sound" is Preferable to the World English or Augmented Roman Alphabets as a General Reform

1. It is the only one of the three shown which is completely isomorphic: it alone has one letter or configuration for each phoneme or sound, which is the basic requirement for an English-compatible alphabet. It is, as a result, the most economic by about 14 per cent in number of characters. To spell the phoneme range, World English needs sixty-one letters, Augmented Roman, fifty-five letters or configurations, Single-Sound only forty.

2. It is the only alphabet designed for both machine- and human-reading; each letter is designed in a standard 5 x 7 proportion module with a matching set of arabic numbers for simple encoding or scansion into a seven-bit or seven-channel binary code for machine operation, computer use, or data-phone transmission.

3. It is the only one of the three designed for simple manual lettering by very young children; since kinesthetic experience is an important part of learning at preschool ages, this must be considered.

4. It is the only alphabet purposely devised with mnemonic devices designed into the structure of the letters. For instance, all the "long" vowels have a built-in, added, full-width horizontal member.

5. It is very nearly fully consistent with the Latin conventions of most European spelling: Polish, Czech, Spanish, Italian, Turkish, German, while still being consistent with 80 per cent of English, in terms of frequency of appearance in the language.

6. It is designed for maximum legibility. In the *Parents' Magazine* display (pp. 66–67) all are in approximately the same font-type size determined by measurement from bottom of the lowest descender to top of highest ascender, i.e., *p* and *b*. Where the World Alphabet can be read at ten feet and the Augmented Roman at eight feet, the "Single-Sound" can be read at eighteen to twenty feet.

7. It can be read by an English speaker with less than an hour of re-training, with the mnemonic devices explained to him at the same time.

8. Although it can be used immediately as a transitional spelling for teach-

ing literate English to the young, and both forms, oral and literate, to non-vernacular learners, it is designed for permanent adoption for both man and machine. Augmented Roman is to be used only as a transitional device.

9. It is the only alphabet set up with a supporting Foundation and commercial instrumentality with sufficient adjunct devices to provide support, and change cost, for the long period of transition. Transliteration standards, teaching programs, and the like can be properly financed along with type redesign, translation programs for computers, etc.

10. It is immediately useful for a variety of purposes, and can be accepted at any desired speed, socially, and conversion can take place at a rapid or leisurely fashion, as policy may decree.

11. It is consistent with other international conventions for such devices as computers, weather typewriters, teletype machines, and the like.

12. It requires no rules for conversion, breaking compound vowel pairs, as World English spelling needs; for example, chaotic, kaeaatik vs. KΔOTⱧK.

13. It is designed to stand on its own merits as a synthetic adjunct spelling of English and seven other languages including Russian, adopted or not.

Why the Choice of Letters and Phoneme Conventions for the "Single Sound" Alphabet

1. The basic common Latin-English sound representations were adopted for: *B, D, F, G, H, K, L, M, N, P, R, T, V, W, Z.*

2. For sounds having two letters, one was made conventional; or if two sounds, one made conventional:

C was given to the sibilant hiss sound, since the hard *C* sound had been preempted by *K* which had only one sound commonly accorded to it.

J was given to the soft *g* of *gesture* or *John;* the hard *G* of *get* going to the ordinary *G*.

S now without its customary "hiss" representation was given to its secondary sound the *sh* of *sugar*, ordinarily spelled *SH*.

Y was given only its consonant sound as in *yet;* the vowel sound being retained by the long or short *i* symbols.

3. The sixteen vowels of English were given the following values and symbols. The basic five short Latin vowels were given their old symbols, but the *I* was crossed to bring the character to full character width:

A as in *bat*	*O* as in *pot*	*I* as in *pit*
E as in *get*	*U* as in *but*	

Their customary long sounds retained the basic letter configuration, but with a full width horizontal member integrated into the letter to assist as a mnemonic in transitional learning:

A as in *gate*	*O* as in *toe*
EE or *I* as in *feel, machine*	*OO* as in *boot*
I as in *pie*	or *U* as in *lute*

Additionally there were some vowel diphthongs and related sounds which required memory ties:

A as in *awe*   U as in *use*
E as in *her*   OW as in *how*
OO as in *look*   OY as in *boy*

4. The six sounds normally spelled with digraphs in English as consonants are as follows:

sh, ch, ng, th (voiceless), *th* (voiced), *zh* (or sometimes, *z, s*) are represented as

$$(\text{S}. \text{Ɔ}. \text{И}. \Theta. \bot. \text{ and } \text{Ƨ}.)$$

the first of which was explained. The reversed C suggests a *c*-like sound, systematic with the Italian; the *ng* configuration is suggested in the N and *tail;* the Greek Theta and upside-down *t* suggest these basic sounds. The backward *z* suggests the French J and the *z*-like sound already in use.

5. All of these choices were indicated by an earlier mini-max program, which indicated that for eight major industrial languages, a literation with this convention set would minimize the spelling changes, when measured and weighted with both frequency of appearance in the language and population using the language pattern.

A Diacritical Marking System to Aid Beginning Reading Instruction

❖ EDWARD FRY

By definition an alphabet is a set of symbols which represent speech sounds. The problems inherent in this system are that (1) speech tends to be a continuous flow of sound, and letters are discrete, and (2) spoken language changes relatively rapidly over the decades while the alphabet and orthography have become extremely resilient to change.

The problem of changing an alphabet or a spelling system is largely political. Certainly any scholar could single-handedly propose changes in the present system which would greatly improve our present system but the people who have the power to change it have a vested interest in the present system while the people who need the change the most, illiterate adults and children, have virtually no political power.

However, renewed interest in the beginning reading problem has opened up the historical problem of inadequate alphabet and spelling rules. The purpose of this paper is not to survey the history of alphabet and spelling reform which is indeed long and noble and largely fruitless. Rather the purpose is to present a system of adding diacritical marks to the regular alphabet for the purpose of largely regularizing the phoneme-grapheme relationship for the use of beginning readers.

For sake of convenience we will refer to this as DMS for Diacritical Marking System. These marks are to be of a temporary nature and after the reading habit has been established they are to be vanished. The principle of holding one variable constant while others are being learned is sound pedagogy.

The goal of this system is to help children and illiterate adults learn to read easier, faster, and possibly in the case of children, at an earlier age.

All alphabets are a compromise. Even the illustrious International Phonetic Alphabet is considered considerably less than perfect by many scholars, though virtually everyone would admit that it is a far superior system for representing speech sounds than the inadequate twenty-six letters we now use. The chief trouble with the IPA for our purpose is that the visual form of the word is so different from our traditional alphabet that transfer would be difficult. Hence, we see another goal emerge, that of facility in transfer to traditional alphabet.

Other modified alphabets, most notably Pitman's Initial Teaching Alphabet (the Augmented Roman) have attempted to compromise letter form between the IPA and our regular letters. It is my contention that the phoneme-grapheme relationship, while improved, is not regular enough nor is the word form near

From *Elementary English,* 41: 526–529, 537; May, 1964. Reprinted with the permission of the National Council of Teachers of English and Edward Fry, Director, Reading Center, and Professor of Education, Rutgers, The State University, New Brunswick, New Jersey.

enough for maximum ease in transferability. Pitman's alphabet also poses problems in the teaching of writing and spelling as well as teacher resistance.

There are a number of systems for making diacritical marks. Virtually every major dictionary has its own. The chief difficulty with them is that most of them are far too complicated for beginning readers. Not only are the sound differentiations too complicated but the marks themselves are numerous and varied. Furthermore, they lack consistency from dictionary to dictionary which tends to depreciate any value of learning a dictionary system of diacritical marks as a valuable bit of knowledge in itself. Though this is not to deny that learning any set of diacritical marks, including the DMS, will have strong transferability to any other set of marks.

A further consideration is the ease with which the marks can be perceived and written. Young children need to be able to recognize them easily and they may need to write them as well. Often initial reading is wisely combined with initial writing. Teachers often prepare reading material so the systems should be easy for the teacher as well. All the diacritical marks in this system can be made on the standard typewriter.

Finally, the DMS can be used with or without special phonics instruction. Educators have often noted that even in school systems where there is very little, one might almost say no regular phonics instruction, the children still have some knowledge of the sounds of letters. For example, many of them could correctly sound out nonsense syllables. Why is this? It is my contention that they learn phonics in spite of their teachers. They learn much of the regular phoneme-grapheme correspondence because it is inherent in the system just as a child learns grammar rules without grammar lessons, or social class without a sociology text. What this system should do then is to greatly facilitate that incidental phoneme-grapheme learning.

A teacher may use a book or reading materials printed with DMS with no reference to the marks — in brief, she may use only the "sight or word method." Of course, if the teacher wishes to teach phonics then her lessons are immeasurably easier and more applicable. Incidentally, some studies have shown that the teacher's knowledge of phonics is not too satisfactory and the use of this system of diacritical marks would help to familiarize her with this aspect of the basic structure of our language.

Publishers also should find the DMS easy to apply to their standard reading texts with simply an overprinting or other methods retaining exactly the same page composition. It is also possible that publishers will have some useful vanishing techniques of a mechanical sort, such as printing the diacritical marks in successively lighter shades of gray or in thinner lines.

A minor possible side effect of importance, especially with young children and foreigners, is the speech correction aspects of the use of DMS. As the learner is presented a more accurate graphic representation of speech, he is more apt to question his own departures and it will be easier for the classroom teacher to point out why a word is being mispronounced.

DMS — The Diacritical Marking System

The purpose of the Diacritical Marking System is to regularize orthography for beginning reading instruction by adding marks to regular letters. The marks are used because basic word form is preserved. They can later be vanished as the reading habit is established. The DMS can be used with or without any special phonic instruction.

Basic Rules

1. Regular consonants and short vowels are unchanged.
2. Silent letters have a slash mark. (w̸rit̸e rig̸h̸t)
3. Long vowels have a bar over mark. (mād̸e māi̸d)
4. Schwa vowels have a dot over mark. (ȧgo lemȯn)
5. Other consistent sounds than those above are indicated by the bar under. (i̲s̲ au̸tō)
6. Digraphs have a bar under both letters. (s̲h̲ut c̲h̲at)
7. Exceptions to the above stated basic rules have an asterisk above the letter. (o*f onc*e̸)

The **R** Problem

The letter *R* is temporarily raised to the status of a vowel which permits one to do the following: f̸i̸r f̸u̸r he̸r acre̸. Note that *R* maintains the same sound as in *red*.

The two sounds of the *AR* digraph are made by a bar under the *AR* as in a̲rm and by treating *A* as long in vāry.

The *OR* digraph is made by a bar under the *OR* as in f̲o̲r.

The **Y** Problem

By far the commonest use of the letter *Y* is at the end of a polysyllabic word such as *funny,* hence its use for making that sound does not have a diacritical mark. Dictionaries say that this is a short *I* sound and I say that it is a long *E* sound but it doesn't matter as long as the teacher is consistent.

The next commonest use of *Y* is the long *I* sound in the middle of a word or at the end of a single syllable word, and this sound is shown by putting a bar over the *Y* as in mȳ and cȳclōne̸.

Finally, the least common use of *Y* is to make its beginning sound and for this a bar under the *Y* is used, as in y̲es.

Consonant Digraphs

Consonant digraphs are all indicated by the bar under both letters to show that they make a unique sound not a blend of the regular letter sounds.

SH	s̲h̲ut	T̵H̲	t̲h̲ing (voiceless)
CH	c̲h̲at	TH	t̲h̲is (voiced)
WH	w̲h̲it̸e̸	PH	p̲h̲ōne̸ (F sound)
		NG	sin̲g̲

Figure 1: The DMS Alphabet

Sound	Letter	Mark	Example
Short A		No change	cat
Long A	Ā	Bar over	mādҿ māȝd dāy
Schwa	Ȧ	Dot over	ȧgo
Broad A	A̱	Bar under	a̱utō a̱wful al̸
AR Digraph	A̱R	Bar under	a̱rm
AR Digraph	ĀR	Bar over A	vāry āȝr
	B	No change	bat
K sound	C	No change	cat
S sound	C̱	Bar under	c̱ity
	D	No change	dog
Short E	E	No change	
Long E	Ē	Bar over	mēȿt mēҿt
Schwa	Ė	Dot over	
Silent	E̸	Slash	comҿ
ER Digraph	E̸R	Slash E	hҿr
	F	No change	fat
Regular (soft)	G	No change	got
J sound (soft)	G̱	Bar under	g̱em
	H	No change	hat
Consonant	using H		
Digraphs	at end		
Short I	I	No change	it
Long I	Ī	Bar over	pīe
IR Digraph	I̸R	Slash I	fi̸r
	J	No change	jack
	K	No change	kiss
	L	No change	lip
	M	No change	man
	N	No change	not
Short O	O	No change	not
Schwa O	Ȯ	Dot over	lemȯn
Long O	Ō	Bar over	nō
Broad O	O̱	Bar under	o̱ff
OI Diphthong	O̱I	Bar under	bo̱il
OY Diphthong	O̱Y	Bar under	bo̱y
OW Diphthong	O̱W	Bar under	o̱wl
Long OO	ŌO	Bar over	fŌOd
Short OO	O̱O	Bar under	lo̱ok
OR Digraph	O̱R	Bar under	fo̱r
	P	No change	pin

Figure 1, Continued

Sound	Letter	Mark	Example
QU Digraph	QU	Bar under	q<u>u</u>een
	R	asterisk	
	R	No change	rat
Regular	S	No change	sat
Z sound	S	Bar under	ha<u>s</u>
	T	No change	tat
Short U	U	No change	hut
Long U	Ū	Bar over	ūse
TWO Dot U	U	Bar under	rul∅
UR Digraph	∅R	Slash U	f∅r
	V	No change	very
	W	No change	we
KS sound	X	No change	fox
Long E sound (or short I sound)	Y	No change	funny
Long I sound	Ȳ	Bar over	mȳ
	Y	Bar under	<u>y</u>es

DMS Specimen

Thė Littl∅ Red Hen

Önce upon a̓ tīm∅ Littl∅ Red Hen liv∅d in a̓ ba<u>r</u>n wit<u>h</u> h∅r fīv∅ chi∅ks. A̓ pig, a̓ cat, and a̓ du∅k mād∅ the*r hōm∅ in thė sām∅ ba<u>r</u>n. E∅ch dāy <u>the</u> littl∅ red hen led h∅r chi∅ks <u>ou</u>t to l<u>oo</u>k f<u>or</u> fōōd. But thė pig, thė cat, and <u>the</u> du∅k wo∅ld not l<u>oo</u>k f<u>or</u> fōōd.

Bibliography

Bloomfield, Leonard. *Language*. New York: Henry Holt and Company, 1933.

Fry, Edward. "A Frequency Approach to Phonics," *Elementary English,* accepted for publication, Winter, 1964.

Kenyon, John. "A Guide to Pronunciation," in *Webster's New International Dictionary*, 2nd Ed. Springfield, Mass.: G. & C. Merriam Company, 1943.

Moore, James T. "Phonetic Elements Appearing in a Three Thousand Word Spelling Vocabulary," unpublished dissertation, Stanford University, 1950.

Thorndike, E. L., and Clarence Barnhart. *Thorndike-Barnhart Beginning Dictionary*. Chicago: Scott, Foresman and Co.

The Initial Teaching Alphabet for Reading? Yes! ✣ ALBERT J. MAZURKIEWICZ

All of us involved in the teaching of reading and the preparation of teachers to teach reading have followed various trails over the years. We have been searching for more acceptable solutions to the problems involved in teaching beginning reading. We have recognized that every existing program for teaching reading does in fact teach children to read. The question has always been: How well?

The National Council of Teachers of English estimates that four million elementary school pupils have reading disabilities. Other reports indicate that reading is a handicap for 25 to 35 per cent of all high school students and that our nation has a minimum of eight million adult functional illiterates. We have recognized, too, that we are required to introduce remedial reading instruction in the elementary school, beginning in the second grade generally, and to continue it through high school and college and university.

What appears to be wrong? Our methods have been of proven excellence, for we do develop a high degree of reading skill in the population. While no single factor can be isolated which limits learning, current studies show the spelling of our language to be a significant fact. These studies may be interpreted as bringing to an end the greatest longitudinal study in history. Since we all admit to the need for longitudinal studies to inform us about long-range effects, it is unfortunate that it has taken us some three hundred years in American education to draw conclusions about traditional orthography and its negative implications for reading instruction.

Sound and Symbol

Tardy though we may be, we have in recent years begun to agree that there are many irregularities in the relationship between sound and symbol in English. We have begun to agree that almost every phonic rule children can be taught, or can be led to discover, has exceptions. We have come to agree that this makes the teaching and learning of English phonics considerably more difficult than it would be if each letter represented just one sound, as is true or nearly true of several European languages.

Current research evidence points out that the normal learning curve (which we had seen to exist in virtually every facet of the curriculum as a reflection of the normal distribution of learning potential) also exists in that aspect of reading called word recognition when the medium has been modified to a more regular system. We can conclude, therefore, that if English were regularly spelled (not necessarily perfectly encoded) that learning to read and write

From *Educational Leadership,* 22: 390–393, 437–438; March, 1965. Reprinted with permission of the Association for Supervision and Curriculum Development and Albert J. Mazurkiewicz. Copyright © 1965 by the Association for Supervision and Curriculum Development. Albert J. Mazurkiewicz is Chairman, Department of Education, and Professor of Reading, Newark State College, Newark, New Jersey.

would be essentially a simple process, that the mean of word recognition ability for a normal population would be at the fifth grade or a fifth grade reader level by the end of the first grade, and that it would be a simple process to isolate those children who are having significant learning — not necessarily *reading* — difficulties, problems of learning related to intellectual potential, emotional or neurological disturbances, etc.

Few, if any, educational leaders see a complete reform in our orthography as practical in the foreseeable future. We can, therefore, ask whether we should keep trying for a simplified orthography if a temporary i/t/a, such as Pitman has constructed, can be used successfully to introduce the child to the complex world of English orthography. Thus, the design of i/t/a is *not* a design for spelling reform; rather, the initial teaching alphabet is what its name implies. In this context, it seems to be the most serviceable pattern that has up to now been proven workable in introducing the child to the reading and writing process. i/t/a design was intended to encourage early reading as much as possible on a frustration free basis. When the child develops his reading skills (somewhere around the third reader level), he makes an effective transition from i/t/a to traditional orthography. This usually occurs in the first grade.

Studies of Transition

An examination of i/t/a's use shows it to epitomize a psychologically valid principle which we follow in other areas of life: that learning proceeds from the simple to the complex. It parallels our treatment of another familiar area of the curriculum: handwriting. In our present writing system we go from manuscript to cursive, and we demand a transition which seems to be more difficult for a normal child in a traditional alphabet than the transition in reading which moves from i/t/a to T.O. (traditional orthography).

Research in the United States confirmed the findings of the earlier research in England and added data such as the following:

At the ten-week mark, the top groups of the population were capable of reading and dealing effectively with a vocabulary of 320 words. This compared with the third pre-primer status achieved by the same percentage of population using the traditional alphabet. Under the T.O. procedure, children could read sixty-six words on a purely sight basis at the end of this period.

At the beginning of the fifth month of instruction, significant differences in the i/t/a population were observable:

For the i/t/a population, the reading program could be structured to follow the various rates of learning of children. The skills portion of the program was found to be embodied in the initial tasks the child had — learning to make, fix and use associations between the sounds of his spoken language and the i/t/a symbols used to represent them. For the bright child, this word recognition program appeared to become a program of two to three months and about four to five months for the average child.

Statistics in the eighth month indicated that the instructional levels of the i/t/a-taught children were as follows: 24 per cent of these first-grade children were instructionally placed in third-reader materials, 51 per cent were reading second-reader materials, 15 per cent were reading first-reader materials, and 11 per cent were reading at or below primer level. In contrast, only six per cent of the children taught using the traditional alphabet (T.O.) were found at second-reader levels.

Standardized tests in their T.O. form given in May to document the status of both populations indicated that no differences existed between the populations. though most of the experimental population children were still in i/t/a instruction. As noted by the children, this type of procedure was unfair since they commented: "We'll take this test if the other kids take a test printed in our alphabet." Since the question always arises concerning the child's ability to read in T.O. though he is given i/t/a instruction, and since earlier American research on this question has been largely ignored, it was important to test and report such data.

At the post-transition period, however, differences between the populations begin to point to a superiority in favor of the i/t/a-taught child. On the standardized tests given, some 91 per cent of the i/t/a population achieved at second grade or above point, compared with 67.4 per cent of the T.O. population at this early point in instruction. Better than 29 per cent of the i/t/a population achieved third-reader or above grade levels, compared with 10.8 per cent of the T.O. population. These results when tested for significance indicated that the i/t/a population was generally superior in word recognition and comprehension as well as total reading. Again, when tested in terms of a measure of spelling achievement (Stanford Achievement in its T.O. form), no significant differences between the spelling ability of the populations were noted.

The follow-up into the second year indicates that further improvement in reading ability on a T.O. basis exists in an i/t/a population, whereas the T.O. population's results indicate a drift toward the mean achievement of the population.

Conclusions such as the following can be drawn from the bare statistics of the studies:

1. Traditional spelling of English is a significant source of difficulty in beginning reading, though not the only factor in reading instruction.

2. Children can learn to read more rapidly (with less observable frustration) when the beginning reading program is printed in i/t/a.

3. Children can learn to encode sound and to communicate through writing with a high degree of facility when taught using i/t/a. i/t/a seems to have a releasing effect on a child's ability to communicate through writing.

4. The first-grade classroom, according to teacher reports, is more easily controlled, fewer organizational problems occur, and more individualized teaching is accomplished within a grouping structure. These reports indicate the child develops independent work habits much earlier than usual, appears to have a better test-taking ability because of his improved work habits, has a greater capacity for work, and appears to be more self-motivated in learning situations.

5. Through the use of i/t/a, the sentence structure and vocabulary of first grade materials can more closely approximate the vocabulary and sentence structure of the child at an early point in the first year of school. His wide interests can be more readily met in such reading material.

6. Post-transition reading performances in T.O. of i/t/a-taught children as measured by standardized tests in the ninth month and then in September fol-

lowing the summer hiatus appear to be much better than that developed by children taught by similar procedures in T.O.

7. T.O. spelling achievement post-transition for the i/t/a child in the ninth month of school is no different from that developed by children taught only T.O. spellings. Spelling achievement in an ongoing program during the second year for i/t/a children seems to be improving markedly.

Advantages of i/t/a

As with any application of a new idea, many observations have been made independent of statistics which further point up the desirability of the use of i/t/a as it is presently conceived. Observers note that improvement of speech defects is a natural by-product; reading failures are greatly reduced; advanced children are sped to high reading levels. The most dramatic flowering of all is evident in the large numbers of free, self-expressive six-year-old writers. They write more abundantly and about many more subjects than do children learning the traditional alphabet. They write alone, without help or editing from teachers, sounding out their own spellings and using any words they feel like using in any sentence pattern that occurs to them.

Other observations indicate that the first-grade teacher's complaint about "what to do with the other children when working with one group" seems no longer to be a problem in i/t/a classes. While learning may start with whole-class activity, this disappears in a short time in favor of individualized activity based on the rates of learning of individual children. The range of ability in a given classroom begins to show itself and the teacher finds himself working with individuals within groups. It is noted that the teacher with many years' experience in first grade feels that an i/t/a approach answers the first-grade teacher's cry: "There must be an easier way of teaching reading."

Based on the language and experiences of children, the earliest reading material in i/t/a is centered on the child's world; yet soon textbooks begin to expand his interests and abilities. Basic texts serve as a nucleus for a reading program but in no way are a limitation of the program; wide personal reading in i/t/a and T.O. is encouraged from the outset. This is true, since 40 to 65 per cent of the words in an i/t/a program are regularly spelled (or quite similar) to a T.O. procedure.

Other observers note that the normally strong teacher is permitted a freedom to teach under an i/t/a procedure — a freedom very often inhibited by the T.O. medium — and that the weaker teacher is supported by i/t/a. Some observers now conclude that the weaker teacher no longer exists in this educational situation because i/t/a, being a simple medium, encourages the child to engage in self-teaching.

All of the above might cause the uninitiated to think of i/t/a as *the panacea* which seemingly no one has been looking for. However, i/t/a's purpose is not to show dramatic differences in achievement at the end of the first, second, or third grade; its purpose is not to suggest that all learning problems may now be eliminated and that no attention to individual rates and ways of learning need be emphasized. Its purpose, as a simple alphabetic medium approximating the traditional, is to insure that the beginning stages of reading are as natural as possible, that reading can begin without frustration, that the child will learn

Figure 1: Pitman's Initial Teaching Alphabet, with Its Forty-Four Symbols and Words Illustrating the Sounds These Symbols Represent

Initial Teaching Alphabet Publications, Inc.

20 East 46 St., New York, N. Y. 10017

Courtesy i/t/a Publs., Inc., N.Y. Reprinted by permission.

readily, learn reading and writing easily, and that, after he has developed his decoding skills to an efficient level, his transfer to traditional print will be as simple and effective as possible. These purposes are met. As suggested by various observations on concomitant effects, these purposes are exceeded.

Shall we encourage wide use of i/t/a for beginning reading instruction? The research evidence, the observations of teachers, supervisors, and specialists, and I say "Yes!"

i/t/a: A Step Forward or Sideways?

✣ THOMAS C. BARRETT

Among the more recent and more unique innovations in reading instruction is the Initial Teaching Alphabet (i/t/a) created by Sir James Pitman. Briefly, the i/t/a is an augmented Roman alphabet utilizing twenty-four of the original letter symbols and twenty new symbols which generally look like combinations of the original letters. By adding the twenty new symbols, Pitman's i/t/a makes it possible for each phoneme or sound in the spoken language to be represented by a single symbol or grapheme.

This article, however, is not designed to discuss the features of the i/t/a, for these have been ably described by John A. Downing (1, 2). Rather, its purpose is to take an objective look at the status of the i/t/a, with a major emphasis on the Lehigh-Bethlehem investigation presently being conducted in the United States.

The i/t/a in England

The first large scale research into the merits of the i/t/a as a medium for teaching beginning reading began in England in September, 1961, under the direction of John Downing. Since i/t/a is a two-stage approach which requires children to begin in i/t/a and eventually to transfer to the traditional orthography (T.O.), Downing's study was originally scheduled to take place over several years. But the longitudinal nature of the investigation, as well as the great interest it generated, prompted Downing to make periodic progress reports (1, 3, 4). The most recent findings reported in these sources indicated that, on the basis of standardized tests printed in T.O., 146 children taught with i/t/a were significantly superior in reading comprehension and accuracy, to a group of 190 children taught with T.O. eighteen months after instruction began, and that a group of 318 children taught with i/t/a spelled T.O. words

From *Educational Leadership,* 22: 394–397; March, 1965. Reprinted with permission of the Association for Supervision and Curriculum Development and Thomas C. Barrett. Copyright © 1965 by the Association for Supervision and Curriculum Development. Thomas C. Barrett is Assistant Professor of Curriculum and Instruction, University of Wisconsin, Madison.

significantly better than a group of 602 children taught with T.O. two-and-one-half years after the experiment began (3, 4).

What these interim results from the investigations in England mean for the teaching of reading in the United States appears to be clear at the present time. First, it seems appropriate to observe, on the basis of what is known, that the findings in England cannot be generalized across the Atlantic Ocean for a number of reasons: (a) the number of children upon which the interim results are based is quite small; (b) the children in the study began to read at the ages of four and five, while children in the United States generally begin reading at the age of six; (c) Downing's investigation in England will not be completed until 1974, and, on the basis of the principal investigator's statements, the interim results are still tentative.

The second implication that the i/t/a experiment in England holds for reading instruction in the United States is that it is a way of teaching reading which warrants objective evaluation in the context of the classrooms in this country.

The Lehigh-Bethlehem i/t/a Study

Several worthwhile investigations[1] on this subject are presently under way in this country, as a result of the work in England. However, the one which has progressed farthest is the Lehigh-Bethlehem i/t/a study conducted by Albert J. Mazurkiewicz. The purposes of this study, which is designed to last three years, are: (a) to demonstrate how i/t/a may be inducted into a school system over a period of time; and (b) to evaluate the long term differences in achievement that may occur when some children are taught to read with i/t/a while others are taught to read with T.O.

Until recently, only bits and pieces about the Lehigh-Bethlehem study were available; however, Professor Mazurkiewicz corrected this situation by publishing a progress report in November, 1964 (5).

The most important findings appearing in this report were those obtained during May, 1964, nine months after the study was initiated. At this point, 114 i/t/a students, who made the transition from i/t/a to T.O. and who had been reading only T.O. materials for at least one week, were selected from the total sample of 454 i/t/a students and matched with 114 of the 874 T.O. students on the basis of I.Q., sex, age, and socioeconomic status. These two groups were compared on their mean achievements in reading and spelling based on the results from the California Reading Test, Lower Primary (CRTLP), California Reading Test, Upper Primary (CRTUP), and Stanford Achievement Spelling Test, Primary (SAST). The results indicated that the i/t/a students were significantly superior to the T.O. students in word recognition and total reading on the CRTLP and in word recognition, comprehension, and total reading on the CRTUP. No significant differences were found between the two groups on the CRTLP comprehension subtest or on the SAST.

On the basis of these results, Mazurkiewicz tentatively concluded that i/t/a children who made the transfer to T.O. by the ninth month of the first year

---

[1] See the U.S. Office of Education, Cooperative Research Program, First-Grade Reading Project, discussed in this issue [*Educational Leadership*, Vol. 22, March, 1965] in the "Research in Review" column edited by James Macdonald (p. 441).

were significantly better readers of T.O. than a comparable group of children who had been taught by similar procedures but who had been taught with T.O. from the start.

Evaluation of the Study

How can one evaluate the Lehigh-Bethlehem Study as described in the progress report? Since the main hypothesis of the Lehigh-Bethlehem study is that differences in achievement in reading between the i/t/a group and T.O. group can be attributed to the differences in the alphabets used, the study itself should rule out factors, other than the differences between the two alphabets, which might account for any differences in achievement. However, the first interim report leaves a number of possible influencing factors open to question.

First, no mention is made of the comparability of the i/t/a teachers and the T.O. teachers. How were the teachers selected for their roles in the investigation? Did they volunteer? Were the teachers in both groups comparable in terms of education, experience, and enthusiasm for their parts in the experiment?

The answers to these questions were not made clear in the Lehigh-Bethlehem progress report and, as a result, the effect teachers had on the results is open to question.

Second, although the report indicated that the two programs emphasized a language-arts approach and that the two programs were comparable, the fact remains that the T.O. children were exposed to a co-basal program, while the i/t/a children were exposed to the i/t/a Early-to-Read Series. A cursory look suggests that T.O. basal series differ markedly from the Early-to-Read Series, particularly in terms of their pacing of instruction in word analysis. For example, the report indicated that the i/t/a word recognition program placed primary emphasis on relating the sounds of English to the forty-four i/t/a symbols. Furthermore, it was stated that the capable i/t/a children completed this part of the word recognition program in three or four months, while the average i/t/a children completed it in five or six months. In contrast to this, most basal series do not work on vowels until the end of first grade or the beginning of second grade. Assuming that the T.O. teachers followed their manuals, this difference between the two programs could mean that the majority of the i/t/a students were far ahead of their T.O. counterparts by the sixth month of the experiment in their understanding and use of sound-to-symbol relationships, when decoding an alphabetic language.

The point here is, if the purpose of the study was to compare the efficacy of i/t/a with T.O. as a medium for teaching beginning reading, the two programs should have been as nearly alike as possible, particularly in word analysis. It appears that this was not attempted in the Lehigh-Bethlehem study and that it may have had an effect on the first year results.

A third factor, which may have influenced the first year results of the Lehigh-Bethlehem study, was the amount of time devoted to reading instruction in the two groups. It is not clear in the research report whether all the children in both groups started to learn to read at the same time.

The fact that the T.O. children were exposed to a co-basal program suggests that actual reading instruction may have been delayed for some children in this group. On the other hand, the use of a single series with the i/t/a children implies that all of the children in this group may have started actual reading at the same time.

If a difference in instructional time did occur, and this is not clear, the comparison made in the ninth month of the experiment may have matched some T.O. children with i/t/a children in terms of sex, age, I.Q., and socioeconomic status, but not in terms of the amount of actual reading instruction they received. Such an arrangement would put the T.O. group at a disadvantage.

Finally, it can be hypothesized that the ninth month results favoring the 114 i/t/a children, who had made the transition to T.O., might have been different, if the eleven best readers in the T.O. group had been used for the comparison. This is not intended to detract from the thorough approach used by Professor Mazurkiewicz in this portion of his study, for he carefully matched the children on the important independent variables of I.Q., sex, age, and socioeconomic status. However, since these variables have less than a perfect correlation with reading achievement, individually or in combination, the ninth month comparison very possibly pitted the best 114 i/t/a students against 114 T.O. students who undoubtedly were not the best readers in their group, although they matched the i/t/a group on the important variables. The fact that the standard deviations of the scores on the tests used in the ninth month, indicated a greater variability for the T.O. group than for the i/t/a group makes this hypothesis plausible.

Since the four factors just discussed may have influenced the ninth month results, the hypothesis that any differences which occurred in achievement in the first year of the Lehigh-Bethlehem study were a result of the differences between i/t/a and T.O., alone, is untenable. Until these factors are satisfactorily accounted for, this position seems to be a reasonable one. Hopefully, the next Lehigh-Bethlehem report will clarify some of these questions.

Research Needed

Is i/t/a *a* way or *the* way to teach beginning reading? On the basis of the work done in England and the first year of the Lehigh-Bethlehem study, it is apparent that i/t/a can be utilized as a medium to teach some youngsters to read T.O. very well. Whether i/t/a is the only reason for these youngsters' success is a moot question at the moment.

On the other hand, the only way to determine whether i/t/a is the way for all children to learn to read is through carefully designed research which will provide reliable and valid answers to a number of questions, such as: What long-term effects will i/t/a have on reading and spelling? How will i/t/a affect children who have already begun to read? Is it necessary for all children to go through i/t/a and the transition before moving to T.O.? Will the transition to T.O. be overly frustrating and confusing for some children? What will happen to children who begin in i/t/a and move to a T.O. school before the transition has been completed? How will i/t/a compare with T.O. when similar word recognition programs are utilized with both?

Since these questions and others require answers, it is too early to take sides for or against i/t/a on an all or none basis. Therefore, the consumer of research on this topic must be objective and must reserve judgment until all the cards are dealt or at least until the cards are reshuffled and dealt again.

References

1. Downing, John A. "The Augmented Roman Alphabet for Learning to Read." *The Reading Teacher,* 16: 325–336; March, 1963.
2. ———. *The Initial Teaching Alphabet Explained and Illustrated.* New York: Macmillan, 1964.
3. ———. "Teaching Reading with i/t/a in Britain," *Phi Delta Kappan,* 45: 322–329; April, 1964.
4. ———. "The i/t/a (Initial Teaching Alphabet) Reading Experiment," *The Reading Teacher,* 18: 105–110; November, 1964.
5. Mazurkiewicz, Albert J. "Teaching Reading in America Using i/t/a." *Elementary English,* 41: 766–772; November, 1964.

The Promise of i/t/a Is a Delusion:

YES! ✣ William B. Gillooly

NO! ✣ Theodore B. Dolmatch and
Albert J. Mazurkiewicz

1. By William B. Gillooly

If the grapheme-phoneme (symbol-sound) correspondences of our writing system were regular (that is, if each sound was represented by one letter), children would only need to learn the sounds for which the letters of the alphabet stand before they could read. However, since English uses twenty-six symbols to encode forty-odd sounds, the result is an irregular writing system which, at present, uses about two thousand or so ways of representing the sounds of the language. Consequently readers face such inconsistencies in the sounds represented by symbols as exhibited by the letters *ough* in the following words: *cough, furlough, ought, plough, thorough, though, through,* and *tough.* Another frequently encountered example of inconsistency is the sound *eye,* which is spelled in about twenty different ways.

One of the prices we seem to pay for such inconsistency is a relatively high rate of failure among beginning readers. Another is the ubiquitous spelling error. By comparison, the children of countries which use more regular writing systems seem to have little difficulty learning to read and spell.[1] It has been reasoned that if the writing of our language could be altered so as to correspond

From *Phi Delta Kappan,* 47: 545–550, 552–553; June, 1966. Reprinted by permission. William B. Gillooly is Assistant Professor of Education, Johns Hopkins University, Theodore B. Dolmatch is President, Pitman Publishing Corporation, New York City, and Albert J. Mazurkiewicz is Chairman, Department of Education and Professor of Reading, Newark State College, Newark, New Jersey.

[1] Roger Brown, *Words and Things* (New York: The Free Press, 1958), p. 66.

more closely with the spoken form, the learning of reading and writing skills in this country would be facilitated.

Since the possibility of spelling reform is quite remote, proponents have suggested that its benefits may be derived, nevertheless, from beginning reading instruction with a more regular writing system.[2] After developing sufficient competence in this system, they would presumably be in a better position to deal with the traditional orthography (T.O.) and all its inconsistencies. The result should be better readers and spellers in T.O.

The writing system proposed to bring this innovation about is the Initial Teaching Alphabet (i/t/a), which shares twenty-four symbols with our conventional alphabet and augments these with twenty additional symbols. By means of these forty-four symbols, the sounds of English are represented in approximately eighty-eight ways.

The investigation of this issue has led to several experiments and a considerable amount of controversy. It is the goal of this paper to review these experiments and to ascertain the benefits, if any, which derive from the use of i/t/a.

Another system for increasing grapheme-phoneme correspondences is Edward B. Fry's Diacritical Marking System (DMS).[3] We will have an opportunity to view the results of a comparison of this system with i/t/a as well as with T.O.

The criteria used in selecting studies for review in this paper (in addition to their availability) are as follows:

1. Only those studies which report the results of investigations conducted in this country will be included. The number of these studies is such that we do not have to depend upon data collected abroad, with the attendant concern about generalizing these findings.

2. Because there is an insufficiency of data beyond the first grade, only data collected to this point is treated.

3. Only reading achievement data in the form of test results (not, for example, the instructional level of the most recently completed reading book) are reported.

4. Only the results of tests administered in the conventional alphabet are included.

5. Insofar as possible, only data on the total sample groups will be considered. That is, data collected on subsamples of the experimental and control conditions will be avoided. This restriction seems necessary in the light of the finding from an early analysis that at least one researcher has reported data on an unrepresentative subsample of the total experimental group.[4]

The Control Condition in i/t/a Research

In evaluating the effectiveness of any particular factor (such as i/t/a) in an educational setting, there are a host of other factors which must be taken into consideration and controlled or else their effects will be confounded with those

---

[2] For an interesting treatment of this whole issue, the reader should consult Maurice Harrison, *The Story of the Initial Teaching Alphabet* (New York: Pitman Publishing Corporation, 1964).

[3] Edward B. Fry, "A Diacritical Marking System To Aid Beginning Reading Instruction," *Elementary English,* 1964, pp. 526–30.

[4] William B. Gillooly, "A Critical Analysis of the i/t/a Interim Reports," 1966, unpublished.

of the experimental (the to-be-evaluated) variable. These extraneous factors include: the students (their intelligence, cognitive factors associated with sex, etc.), the teachers (their age, experience, level of training, competence, etc.), the teaching methods, the materials of instruction, and novelty (the so-called Hawthorne effects). The manner and degree of control exerted over these factors varies from study to study but the following treatment will provide a flavor of the kind of controls used in the research on i/t/a. Of course, it goes without saying nowadays that there will be control groups; therefore our concern is for the way in which these groups are formed and treated.

Student Factors. The most frequently, explicitly stated practice was to assign the pupils to classrooms according to the usual administrative practice and to assign these "intact classes" to the i/t/a or T.O. condition in random fashion.[5] The pre-experimental equivalence of the groups was evaluated by means of a variety of measures. In three studies, the pretests showed significant differences favoring one or the other group: i/t/a in one case[6] and T.O. in the other two cases.[7] In two of these situations, the magnitude of the difference was 2.7 points[8] and 2.3 points,[9] both on the Pintner-Cunningham General Ability Test.

Teacher Variables. Usually, the teachers (who were most often volunteers, by the way) were assigned randomly to the two conditions[10] or they were matched on some measure of competence and then randomly assigned.[11] However, in Chasnoff's study one teacher taught reading and related language activities to both groups (i/t/a and T.O.) in the same school and another teacher taught the other activities.

Teaching Method. Chasnoff and Mazurkiewicz seem to have done the best job of controlling this factor, with the edge going to Mazurkiewicz. He provided specific training for his T.O. teachers in the methods to be used by the i/t/a teachers in developing reading, writing, speaking, and listening skills with instructions for them to use the same methods. Other studies left the decision to the teacher (therefore, for those studies, this factor is confounded with the teacher variables discussed above).

[5] Robert E. Chasnoff, *Comparison of the Initial Teaching Alphabet with the Traditional Alphabet in First-Grade Reading.* Report of Cooperative Research Project No. S-210 of the U.S. Office of Education, 1965; Edward B. Fry, *First Grade Reading Instruction Using a Diacritical Marking System, the Initial Teaching Alphabet, and a Basal Reading System.* Report of Cooperative Research Project No. 2745 of the U.S. Office of Education, 1965.

[6] H. J. Tanyzer, H. Alpert, and L. Sandel, *Beginning Reading — The Effectiveness of Different Media.* Report of the Nassau School Development Council, Mineola, New York, 1965.

[7] Albert J. Mazurkiewicz, *First Grade Reading Using Modified Co-Basal Versus the Initial Teaching Alphabet.* Report of Cooperative Research Project No. 2676 of the U.S. Office of Education, 1965; H. Tanyzer and H. Alpert, *Effectiveness of Three Different Basal Reading Systems on First-Grade Reading Achievement.* Report of Cooperative Research Project No. 2720 of the U.S. Office of Education, 1965, a summary.

[8] Tanyzer, Alpert, and Sandel, *op. cit.*

[9] Mazurkiewicz, *op. cit.*

[10] Fry, *op. cit.,* Tanyzer and Alpert, *op. cit.*

[11] Tanyzer, Alpert, and Sandel, *op. cit.*

All studies introduced some measure of control over the amount of time spent on reading instruction; however, Tanyzer, Alpert, and Sandel tested the significance of the difference between their groups on this factor. The difference was not significant (at the P = .05 level). Evidence that reading and related language skills were not pursued to the detriment of other skills is reported by Chasnoff in the form of data from the arithmetic section of the Stanford Achievement Test administered on the 160th day of instruction. Not only was there no difference between the i/t/a and T.O. groups but both scored approximately at the expected grade level (2.01, to be exact).

Materials. Most of the reported studies did not attempt any control over this factor and, as a result, the effects due to the materials themselves have been confounded with the writing medium (i/t/a or T.O.). Strictly speaking, therefore, these studies did not compare i/t/a with T.O. More precisely, they compared different reading systems which employ a different alphabet in addition to different stories, etc. In some of Chasnoff's schools, however, the materials were controlled. That is, the i/t/a children used transliterated editions of the T.O. readers. And, in addition, Fry was able to introduce a considerable degree of control between the DMS and the T.O. groups. The DMS children used a reprinted form of the Allyn and Bacon Sheldon Readers which, in addition to the added diacritical marks, differed only with respect to the pictures, which were black and white in the DMS edition.

The reading series used by the control groups in other studies include the Lippincott *Basic Reading* series and the Scott, Foresman *New Basic Readers.* The most often used i/t/a materials were Albert J. Mazurkiewicz and Harold J. Tanyzer's *Early-To-Read* series. All researchers exerted a considerable amount of effort to provide the i/t/a groups with supplementary reading materials. In some cases, this was accomplished by transliterating T.O. materials into i/t/a.

Hawthorne Effects. All studies provided some control for Hawthorne effects, but the most effective control was exercised in the study by Edward Fry. There, two experimental groups were used (i/t/a and DMS). Since both methods are equally novel, comparisons between them are free of novelty effects. Further, the number of visitors and the duration of teacher training were equalized for all groups (as they were in other studies as well).

The sample size of these studies ranged from 338 in Chasnoff's study to 926 in Mazurkiewicz's. The mean number of subjects was 630 and the total was 3,147.

Some Thoughts About Criteria for Evaluating i/t/a

In recent correspondence with this writer, Albert J. Mazurkiewicz stated that the comparison of i/t/a with T.O. using a test of reading comprehension (such as the Paragraph Meaning subtest of the Stanford Achievement Test) is inappropriate in evaluating i/t/a because comprehension does not reflect simply the alphabetic aspects of the reading program. For this reason, he believes that the word-attack skills developed by experience with i/t/a are better assessed with other tests — the Detroit Word Recognition Test or the Word Reading subtest of the Stanford, perhaps.

To give the reader some idea of the extent of disagreement on this important issue, we will turn to the words of another researcher: "We feel that probably the Paragraph Meaning subtest (of the Stanford) is the most important as this represents a true complex reading task."[12]

It is true that word recognition skills are important, but they are so only to the extent that they influence comprehension. Comprehension is, after all, the purpose of reading. Further, in the studies reported here, as has already been pointed out, comparisons have been made between reading systems — programs which have differed in several respects. Only in Chasnoff's study has there been a concerted effort to control the effects due to the materials themselves (the actual stories employed, etc.) and even there, although one can state that control has been approximated, the author himself does not claim it has been attained.

Consequently, we must employ measures which do in fact provide us with a total assessment of the effectiveness of the reading programs. Most of the studies reported in this paper have used the Stanford Achievement Test[13] and some have, in addition, collected data with the California Reading Test and the Detroit Word Recognition Test on their total sample group. If there are relevant differences between the reading systems under consideration, these tests should be sensitive to those differences.

Nor does this writer agree with Mazurkiewicz when he states, "Further, a truer test of a child's spelling ability is not that of standardized tests but rather that found in his written expression in daily activity."[14] Examining the written work of children may be quite deceptive, due to the possibility that children will mask their deficiencies by choosing only those words they believe they can spell correctly. Because the inferior spellers would seem to have more opportunity to learn the set to mask spelling deficiencies, they might be mistaken for the better spellers in a free-writing situation. Moreover, this writer considers that the standardized spelling tests (such as the spelling subtest of the Stanford) are not inappropriate (subject to the limitations of spelling tests in general in evaluating competence in this area[15]).

What the Data Show

We turn now to an examination of the evidence which has accumulated with respect to children's achievement of three skills: reading, writing, and spelling.

Reading. When the i/t/a and T.O. groups' reading in the traditional alphabet is compared on the Stanford Achievement Test, there is no statistically significant difference between them. The result is the same whether the groups are compared in terms of (1) the total score on the Stanford,[16] (2) a composite of

[12] Fry, *op. cit.,* p. 4.

[13] The relevant subsections of this test are: Word Reading, Paragraph Meaning, Word Study Skills, and Spelling.

[14] Albert Mazurkiewicz, "Lehigh-Bethlehem i/t/a Study," Interim Report Ten, *Journal for the Reading Specialist,* March, 1966, p. 119.

[15] William B. Gillooly, *op. cit.* There is reason to believe that error rates for i/t/a children spelling in T.O. vary according to the class of word (regular or irregular) involved, with fewer errors being made on the regular words (those spelled identically in the two systems). Such a state of affairs prevents our use of test results as a basis for making inferences about the i/t/a group's general spelling proficiency in English until an analysis of the composition of our language by word class determines whether those tests include the correct proportions of the two word classes.

[16] Chasnoff, *op. cit.*

several reading subtests of the Stanford,[17] or (3) each separate subtest.[18] In addition, the Diacritical Marking System is not significantly different from either i/t/a or T.O.

Further, there is concurrence with the data collected from other reading tests. No significant i/t/a-T.O. differences have been found at the end of the first grade on the total raw scores of the California Reading Test, or on the mean grade scores of the Reading Vocabulary and Comprehension subsections of that test.[19] Finally, the Detroit Word Recognition Test shows no differences among i/t/a, T.O., and DMS.[20]

This finding is stable enough to withstand the small but significant pre-experimental differences in the intelligence of the i/t/a and T.O. groups in three of the studies.[21]

Spelling. The spelling data tell a different story. Analysis of the results obtained on the Spelling subtest of the Stanford Achievement Test shows that the T.O.-trained children are significantly better spellers (in T.O.) than the i/t/a-trained. Chasnoff's data indicate that the difference may be as great as three and one-half months at the end of first grade.[22]

Fry has found that when i/t/a spelling is scored as correct there is no significant difference between the i/t/a and T.O. groups. Therefore, as one would expect, the i/t/a group's spelling deficiency is the result of the group's having learned inappropriate spellings. The DMS group, by the way, spells equally as well as the T.O. controls in the conventional alphabet.

Writing. Our ignorance of the effects of using i/t/a are, perhaps, greatest in this area. In Chasnoff's study, 616 writing samples were collected after 120 days of instruction. The samples were transformed so that the four judges could not tell in which group they originated. They were then rated for "communication of meaning." A significant difference favored the i/t/a group.

Fry collected writing data from a random sub-sample of forty youngsters from each of his three conditions. There it was found that although the i/t/a children wrote longer stories, they were significantly inferior in writing mechanics (punctuation, capitalization, indentation). He attributed the differences to the different training given the children, not the use of a different alphabet. The i/t/a teachers had been urged throughout the year to encourage their children to write.

There are two studies whose data do not agree with the above treatment. The

---

[17] Tanyzer, Alpert, and Sandel, *op. cit.* For Tanyzer and Alpert, *op. cit.*, the finding holds only for the comparison of the i/t/a group with the Lippincott controls. Both of these groups (i/t/a and Lippincott T.O.) were significantly superior to the Scott, Foresman (T.O.) controls.

[18] Fry, *op. cit.;* Mazurkiewicz, *op. cit.;* Tanyzer, Alpert, and Sandel, *op. cit.;* and Tanyzer and Alpert, *op. cit.*, with the exception that Lippincott T.O. is superior to i/t/a on the Vocabulary subtest. However, I believe this is due to the pre-experimental differences in intelligence which favored the Lippincott group in this study. Vocabulary tests are highly related to general intelligence in children.

[19] Chasnoff, *op. cit.*

[20] Fry, *op. cit.*

[21] See footnotes 6 and 7.

[22] However, Fry has collected data in the middle of the second year which indicate that although the i/t/a children are still inferior, they are no longer significantly so.

i/t/a program receives strong support from both Shapiro[23] and Dunn and Mueller.[24] However, neither of these studies employs as stringent control over extraneous variables as do the studies cited above. For example, the post-tests in the Dunn and Mueller study were administered over a seven-week period. That this in itself could account for most of the post-test differences is not taken into account.

In the study reported by Shapiro, in addition to the fact that there was no attempt to control Hawthorne effects, there is small reason to believe that the student factors are controlled. Starting with a sample of 3,600 pupils in twenty-three school districts, final analyses were made on 1,018 pupils in ten districts. The latter group was quite atypical, since both i/t/a and T.O. pupils averaged five months ahead of grade placement on the Stanford Achievement Test at the end of the first grade. That the final comparison groups were not equivalent is indicated by the fact that reported significance levels are based on an analysis of covariance, a technique used for adjusting the scores of non-equivalent groups. However, in this writer's judgment the assumptions on which the use of analysis of covariance depends seem risky here.

In the light of this analysis, it was decided to discount the findings of these two studies.

The Results of a Questionnaire. It will be informative to determine if the conclusions about i/t/a will be the same if we radically alter our evaluative techniques. What would be the outcome if, instead of examining test data, we asked teachers for their opinions about i/t/a? Tanyzer *et al.* administered a questionnaire to their teachers and some of their findings will be summarized here.

Ninety-four per cent of the i/t/a teachers agreed that their bright, average, and slow pupils made more progress in i/t/a than previous youngsters had made by using the conventional alphabet. Further, 88 per cent of the teachers stated that they preferred to continue teaching with i/t/a.

However, only 41 per cent of the i/t/a teachers thought all first-grade children should be i/t/a taught. The major reservation concerned those who already could read T.O. when they came to school. These, it was often stated, should be spared i/t/a.

Fifty-three per cent of the teachers reported that they had received complaints from parents about the i/t/a program. The reasons for complaining were varied, but spelling was mentioned quite often. In commenting, teachers often mentioned the beneficial effects of i/t/a on children's creative writing.

In general, teachers' responses do not lead to the same conclusions as the data. The use of i/t/a seems to have generated considerable enthusiasm among

[23] Bernard J. Shapiro, *A Comparison of the Reading Achievement of i.t.a. and t.o. Groups in the First Grade, 1964–65: A Report for Classroom Teachers and School Administrators,* Evaluation and Testing Department of the Educational Research Council of Greater Cleveland, February, 1966.

[24] Lloyd M. Dunn and Max W. Mueller, *PLDK and ITA in Nashville — After One Year:* An Interim Report on the Efficacy of the Initial Teaching Alphabet and the Peabody Language Development Kit with Grade One Disadvantaged Children. Report of the Institute on Mental Retardation and Intellectual Development, George Peabody College for Teachers, Nashville, Tennessee, 1965. (In collaboration with M. D. Neely, Nashville Metropolitan Public Schools.)

the teaching staff. This disparity should alert those educational administrators who depend upon their competent teachers' impressions to forecast end-of-year test results.

Is i/t/a Better for the Dull Children?

So far, we have been examining the performance of children without regard for their individuality. However, one could suppose that using i/t/a might not affect all children in the same way. In fact, i/t/a might be beneficial only for slower children. We turn now to evidence which bears on this question.

None of the studies which have investigated the issue have found any evidence that i/t/a is better than T.O. for the dull or for the average — or for the bright child, for that matter.[25] In other words, i/t/a affects all children in a consistent way — it is no better than widely available T.O. reading programs for any sub-group.

Will Weaning Children from i/t/a Be Difficult?

To this writer's knowledge, no detailed treatment of the difficulties some children experience in making the transition to T.O. is yet available. That sizeable numbers do have trouble is indicated by the following figures from Mazur-kiewicz's study: Thirty-five per cent of the i/t/a children had not transferred to T.O. by the tenth week of the second grade and 5.5 per cent still clung to i/t/a on April 15, 1965 (approximately thirty weeks into the second grade).[26] It should become an important part of longitudinal studies to tell us more about these children.

In responding to the Tanyzer, Alpert, and Sandel questionnaire, one teacher indicated that the transition to T.O. may produce undesirable emotional effects in some children.[27] These, too, ought to be investigated further.

Concluding Remarks

The call for more data is indeed, as Roger Brown states, "a stale tune."[28] Psychologists are obliged to advise educators concerning procedures which are justified by the available data. But before doing so we will draw some conclusions from the data.

There is no reason yet to believe that i/t/a is more effective in teaching children to read the traditional alphabet than other widely used conventional reading programs. There is, however, evidence which strongly supports the conclusion that the i/t/a children are inferior spellers, although these effects may be surprisingly transient. The possibility that some children experience difficulty in making the transfer to T.O. deserves investigation, as do the effects of i/t/a on writing. It is difficult to tell yet whether it is i/t/a or other aspects of the training situation (such as the instructions used in the Fry study, "Don't worry about your spelling, go ahead and write") which have led the

[25] Chasnoff, *op. cit.;* Fry, *op. cit.;* Tanyzer, Alpert, and Sandel, *op. cit.;* and Tanyzer and Alpert, *op. cit.*

[26] Albert J. Mazurkiewicz, *Second Annual Report on the Lehigh University-Bethlehem Area Joint School System Demonstration and Evaluation Project:* Use of the Initial Teaching Alphabet in Reading Instruction, unpublished, undated.

[27] Tanyzer, Alpert, and Sandel, *op. cit.,* p. 34.

[28] Roger Brown, *op. cit.,* p. 78.

i/t/a group to write longer, more effective (at communicating meaning) stories.[29]

The present situation certainly does not justify the widespread adoption of reading materials which use the Initial Teaching Alphabet. Their continued use on a limited scale ought to be undertaken with all of the caution which should accompany any experimental innovation in such an important academic area.

In addition to his responsibilities to professional educators, the educational psychologist has a responsibility to speak to the researchers. It would seem that there is no longer any need to conduct additional research with the same level of control as exerted in these studies. There is need now for longitudinal studies using more and tighter controls so that the effects due to i/t/a alone can be evaluated. Perhaps some American researchers can learn about controlling the effects due to the materials from their British counterparts.[30] For the purposes of their research, the British transliterated their most widely used reading series into i/t/a.[31]

Greater control over the materials and other extraneous aspects of reading programs, coupled with a policy of collecting data with more and varied post-tests, will eventually lead to precise knowledge of the role played by grapheme-phoneme correspondences in beginning reading instruction.[32]

2. Comments on Mr. Gillooly's Review
by Theodore B. Dolmatch

In terms of his criteria, which Mr. Gillooly very explicitly presents to the reader, his review is unexceptionable. Unfortunately, these criteria — which are both his privilege and his responsibility — make his conclusions less useful than they might otherwise be. This is a vital point, lest the reader accept his conclusions as being really relevant to an evaluation of i/t/a.

Analyses of i/t/a research that are more comprehensive than Mr. Gillooly's are now in preparation; one of them which I have seen reviews scores of research projects, as compared to Mr. Gillooly's rather small and selective sample. When these and other analyses appear, they will undoubtedly be useful.

---

[29] Fry believes that the instructions are the responsible factor. If it is the instructions producing the effect, there seems to be no reason why we can't exploit the phenomenon, if we wish, using T.O. Edmund H. Henderson (University of Delaware), for one, has undertaken the investigation of this possibility.

[30] That the effect of the materials is considerable is indicated by the finding from the Tanyzer and Alpert study that differences between T.O. reading programs are as great as those which exist between i/t/a and T.O. reading programs.

[31] John Downing, *The i.t.a. Reading Experiment.* London: Evans Brothers, Ltd., 1964, p. 26.

[32] Another study was received too late to be given detailed treatment in this paper. It is Robert B. Hayes and Joseph S. Nemeth, *An Attempt To Secure Additional Evidence Concerning Factors Affecting Learning To Read,* Report of Cooperative Research Project No. 2697, U.S. Office of Education, 1966. The results of this study add support to the findings of Chasnoff, Fry, Mazurkiewicz, Tanyzer *et al.,* and Tanyzer and Alpert. The i/t/a group's reading is not significantly different from the Lippincott T.O. or the Scott, Foresman T.O. program supplemented by a phonics and a word power program. However, the i/t/a children are inferior spellers (in T.O.).

In this response I must confine myself to just a few remarks on Mr. Gillooly's criteria:

1. The results of British research just cannot be disregarded, particularly since the British experience with i/t/a has extended longer than that in the United States. In addition, since there are scores of U.S. research studies on i/t/a available (as Mr. Gillooly himself points out), why he selected only three is a reasonable question.

2. Two of the projects on which Mr. Gillooly reports were one-year projects with relatively small populations. Mazurkiewicz's and others are both larger and have extended longer. Most of the researchers recognize the inadequacy of their one-year studies and have requested extensions. Although most children in the U.S. have transferred to the conventional alphabet by the end of the first year, perhaps 20 per cent have not. It might be reasonable to assume that testing children as a group at an arbitrary point of time in a writing system with which they have insufficient familiarity might be misleading, particularly if an evaluation of i/t/a's worth confines itself to this kind of testing. And what about the teacher whose work is evaluated after one year and one year only in a completely new program?

3. Most of us have so many reservations about reading tests generally that Mr. Gillooly might have mentioned a few that are particularly germane here. Thus, all the tests to which he refers are conventional measures with content validity determined in terms of the basal readers conventionally used. But most of the experimental groups used i/t/a materials which departed significantly from those by which these tests were validated — the same tests that were used in one form or another by the T.O. population. Also, most populations were matched before testing in "intelligence" (comprehension?) and finally tested for "comprehension" (intelligence?). The differences were slight, and only a few of us were surprised. I'll not deal with the fact that i/t/a is measured here only as a reading vehicle when its implications reach far beyond the decoding process.

4. This point is covered above. It's a pity that no one thought to install a control by testing the T.O. populations with i/t/a versions of the tests used. Something might be learned from this procedure.

5. Mr. Gillooly cites his own findings to justify his eliminating the available data on subsamples. But he later departs from this principle to cite one lone teacher who had something negative to say about i/t/a. It is in just these subsamples of the three research projects selected by Mr. Gillooly and others — all larger than one teacher — that one can see so many positive aspects of i/t/a.

If Mr. Gillooly's criteria are so structured that they limit the usefulness of his study, one might wonder why they were selected. It cannot be that Mr. Gillooly was unaware of other research. Even we have most studies available for examination. Had Mr. Gillooly identified his purpose on his only visit to our office, we would have been pleased to spend the time and provide the detailed information that we freely offer to professional visitors. Two of the questions that he asked, only of our sales representative — "You can tell me, isn't there anything wrong with i/t/a?" and "How are the i/t/a books selling?" — might have been answered with more authority by me or another available executive. However, let me answer them now:

1. None of the data show that i/t/a is less effective than T.O. Most of the data show that i/t/a is significantly better than T.O. as a medium for beginning reading. Tens of thousands of children in hundreds of schools in forty-seven states and countries around the world demonstrate this better than I can. I wonder whether Mr. Gillooly has visited any i/t/a classrooms.

2. Our own books are selling very well. There are almost forty publishers in England and at least a dozen others here now producing i/t/a books. I assume that theirs are selling well too.

Let me place one final question in the researcher's mouth: Why do *I* take issue here, in this "educator's domain"? The answer is that we, as publishers of educational materials, take our responsibilities at least as seriously as some educators do, and that we must protect ourselves against irrelevancy and bias in order to do so.

3. Comments by Alfred J. Mazurkiewicz

Mr. Gillooly's report suffers from bias, selective reporting, and quoting out of context. There is deliberate non-use of data which would negate the position taken.

Harris, Sheldon, and others, in their first-grade studies, all note the weakness of the outcome-variable testing. Harris[33] states, "Available reading tests, including those prescribed for the cooperating studies, tend to be inherently biased for or against particular teaching procedures." He notes that the vocabulary section of the Stanford test, for example, "seems to emphasize the words commonly taught in basal reader series for the primary grades," and cautions against generalizing from such results. Mr. Gillooly apparently cares nothing about this, since he accepts unquestioned such outcome variables as the *only* basis for his analysis and even rejects any other view as unthinkable.

Mr. Gillooly quotes selectively a statement on spelling, which, out of context, does not show that second-grade spelling was first tested on the Stanford Achievement Spelling Test and that the i/t/a children's results were significantly better than their T.O. counterparts whether the raw (and most unequivalent) or the matched-pair sample results were used. He ignores the data because they don't support his position, and further rejects the view that spelling in creative writing may be more meaningful than that found on biased standardized tests.

Mr. Gillooly states that "there is an insufficiency of data beyond the first-grade level," hence he deals only with data from the first grade. Yet it seems peculiar that he quotes Fry in a personal conversation about his second-grade findings and selectively quotes from my Second Annual Report to justify his position.

Later, Gillooly notes that there is no statistically significant difference between the i/t/a and T.O. groups and neglects to mention that in every one of the studies a large segment of the i/t/a population had not had any school experience with the T.O. medium on which they were tested (they had not transferred). He neglects to point out the remarkable fact that despite this the raw

[33] Albert J. Harris, *Comparison of Reading Approaches in First Grade Reading with Disadvantaged Children,* Cooperative Project No. 2677, p. 98.

populations' results were as good as the results with T.O. children who had been taught only in that medium. We might conclude that there is something drastically wrong with our T.O. programs under these circumstances, but Gillooly avoids the obvious in order to justify his position.

Still later, Mr. Gillooly seems to ignore the fact that children are different and learn at different rates. He quotes my statement that by the tenth week of the second grade (my second-year report, by the way) 35 per cent of the population had not transferred to T.O., and apparently believes that all children should have stopped reading i/t/a material in the first grade. He forgets that an educator's first concerns are the child's security and ego-strength, acceptance of the laws of learning, and the effects of intelligence on learning (in this population I.Q.'s range from 55 to 146). The well-grounded educator would not presume to think that all children should accomplish the same amount of work in the same length of time. The view that transition to T.O. is a difficulty is wholly incorrect; Mr. Gillooly appears to discount the rates of learning or the learning difficulties of the mentally slow and the effects of cultural deprivation on language learning. He should note that when the slowest children made the transition to T.O., in May and June, 1965, they were effectively reading second-grade material. For a child with an I.Q. of 55 to 75, such achievement is remarkable. No one, to my knowledge at least, has presumed to say that all children will leave i/t/a at the same time. Rather, every analogist has, from the outset, assumed that in i/t/a (even though it is vastly easier), as in T.O., children will learn at different rates and gain confidence and security in their command of the reading process at different rates. Transition should not be pushed but may be expected when that point of confidence is reached.

Mr. Gillooly's offhand dismissal of the interesting findings of Nemeth and Hayes is curious, since I made these results available to him at the same time he acquired much of the other data. His interpretation of the Nemeth-Hayes study is contrary to their statements.

The most glaring faults in this review, however, appear to be a result of his predetermined view to accept uncritically *only* data from unequivalent populations. Apparently, equivalency may be disregarded in research — a most peculiar view and one which effectively cuts off any consideration of the positive results in favor of the i/t/a populations when covariance or matched-pair studies are done.

4. Mr. Gillooly Replies

The Messrs. Dolmatch and Mazurkiewicz hold two contradictory positions at the same time. The first is that I have been too selective in collecting studies, and the second is that none of the present studies are of much use anyway, since they have employed currently available reading tests which are inappropriate for evaluating i/t/a. If the second is true, the first is irrelevant.

The decision concerning whether or not a test is suitable for the task assigned it ought to be made before the results of its use are known. Otherwise, researchers could reject, as inappropriate, test results which do not conform to their expectation — a very unsatisfactory condition indeed. It is relevant to note that the tests used for evaluating i/t/a were selected by twenty-seven recipients of U.S. Office of Education grants. The group included Jeanne Chall, Edward Fry, William Sheldon, George Spache, Harold Tanyzer, and *Albert*

Mazurkiewicz. Whatever misgivings Mr. Mazurkiewicz entertains should have been voiced to the other researchers at that time. To quarrel about the tests after the results start going against i/t/a is out of order.

In this writer's judgment, the most effective defense of the Pitman Publishing Corporation and Mr. Mazurkiewicz's interests would be for them to cite the studies which support their views on the matter. Each of them had the opportunity to do so this spring when I visited with them in their home offices. Again, I invite them to produce those studies. After they are produced, we can discuss each on its merits. But let it be known now that the studies will have to be quite good to be of a caliber equal to the six studies (not three, as Mr. Dolmatch reports) which support the position expressed in my review. The Hayes and Nemeth study, by the way, was received by this writer on April 7, 1966 — five days before my manuscript had to leave to meet the publication deadline. Hence, it could be treated only in a footnote. Mr. Mazurkiewicz seems to be under the impression that I should have included their findings (which, by the way, do agree with the five others in support of the position taken in my review) because he told me about them when we talked in Bethlehem. I must comment here that it is not my policy to report and comment on research results obtained in conversation with a third party. All of the data I reported were treated only after I received a *written* copy of the researcher's formal report. To proceed on hearsay in such an important matter would have been inexcusable.

The charge of bias against me is a curious one, unsupported by the inclusion of a motive. But for the record, let me state now that I stand to gain nothing material from the success or failure of i/t/a. My concern is for the discovery of the facts in this issue and my bias, if any, is toward careful, well-controlled research — regardless of its outcome. I am disturbed by the thought of large numbers of children using a new writing medium, the claims for which are not supported by presently available, carefully designed studies. I wonder if my accusers are prepared to make an equally frank evaluation of their motives.

Further Reading for Chapter 3

Bentley, Harriett. "Words in Color," *Elementary English*, 43: 515–517; May, 1966.

Boutwell, William D. "Learning to Read With ITA," *Scholastic Teacher*, 10: 10; March, 1965.

Downing, John. "Teaching Reading with i.t.a in Britain," *Phi Delta Kappan*, 45: 323–329; April, 1964.

Goodman, Harriet. "Words in Color," *Wilson Library Bulletin*, 40: 61; September, 1965.

Harrison, Maurice. *Instant Reading: The Story of the Initial Teaching Alphabet.* London: Sir Isaac Pitman and Sons Ltd., 1964.

Hodges, Richard E. "Short History of Spelling Reform in the United States," *Phi Delta Kappan*, 45: 330–332; April, 1964.

Malone, John R. "The Unifon System," *Wilson Library Bulletin*, 40: 63–65; September, 1965.

Riemer, G. "Bizarre Alphabet Teaches Johnny to Read," *Ladies Home Journal,* 81: 70–71, 137–140; October, 1964.

Sebesta, Sam Leaton. "Artificial Orthography as a Transitional Device in First-Grade Reading Instruction," *Journal of Educational Psychology,* 55: 253–257; October, 1964.

Sheldon, William, and Roma Gans. "ITA," *Grade Teacher,* 82: 34–35; October, 1964.

Southgate, Vera. "Approaching i.t.a Results with Caution," *Educational Research,* 7: 83–96; February, 1965.

Stewart, Rebecca W. "I.T.A. — After Two Years," *Elementary English,* 42: 660–665; October, 1965.

❖ *4* *❖*

Word Attack

A vital element in successful reading — perhaps *the* vital element if any can be so classified — is the ability to translate printed word symbols into meaningful word sounds or thoughts. For the beginning reader, this task essentially involves translating an unknown word symbol into a sound and meaning which are already known. For example, when the young child sees the unknown printed form *street* in the sentence, *The dog ran into the street,* he must use some procedure for changing that unknown word form into the known sound and meaning which it represents, if he is to read the sentence. That is, he must use some procedure to unlock the sound and meaning which he already knows and which is represented by a group of symbols on paper.

Word attack at later stages of reading becomes more complex. Here the child is likely to come across words which are strange to him in additional ways, that is, he may come to words which he has never seen before and which are also unknown to him in sound and meaning. For example, when he meets the word *adduce* in a story for the first time, unless the word sound that those symbols represent has meaning for him, it does him no good to learn that word sound, since he will still be unable to read it with understanding.

In Chapter 4, the emphasis is on unlocking words — translating unknown word forms into known sounds and meanings — since most of the word-attack problems which the child will encounter fall into this category. It is vital, however, that we continually realize that applying phonics or any other procedure for translating word forms into word-sounds is ineffectual unless meaning is also involved.

Proponents of all recognized procedures for teaching reading now recognize that some method of word attack is essential. The variabilities arise in determining specifically *how* and *when* it will take place. The "how" recommendations vary from a highly formalized program, involving hundreds of rules to be memorized, to a self-discovery kind of approach where the child is expected to inductively determine needed generalizations for himself. The "when" recommendations vary from a complete program of word analysis which precedes the introduction of any story materials to a program that involves generalizations which only come through words that the child has already memorized.

Some implied suggestions on these two points were made in the studies by Brzeinski and Hillerich in Chapter 2. In their studies, the greatest success was attained by children who had been given some assistance in unlocking words before their introduction to story material.

In the first selection in this chapter, the editor of this volume recommends a procedure which most directly builds on the abilities that the child already has, and develops a technique of unlocking words which he can use to help himself, even in his first reading experiences. This technique involves the child's ability to use context together with the letter-sound associations for consonants.

Although the procedure recommended above does not involve rules for sounding out words, support for the importance of consonants can be found in the second article, by Theodore Clymer, which emphasizes the inconsistency of rules for determining vowel sounds, consonant sounds, accents, and syllabication. Although there were many cases of low utility for rules in the other three areas, only one of the ten consonant rules Clymer explored (20 through 29) fell below a 95-per-cent utility in the materials examined.

In the last article Arthur J. and Elsa M. Bronstein present a historical review of the status of phonics instruction in our schools and an examination of the contributions that linguists can make to phonics instruction today. The knowledgeable teacher will find that some reading programs have already incorporated some of the linguist's findings without labeling them as linguistics, and he may want to critically analyze which of the others should most profitably be adapted to the classroom.

Developing Reading Independence in the Primary Grades

❖ William K. Durr

Approaches to initial reading instruction are now undergoing much-needed analysis. Wise teachers no longer unthinkingly accept the dictates of research which was conducted even before the parents of today's first graders were born. Our methods have progressed and certainly children have changed over the years. The procedures we use must take account of these differences.

Most of us would like to have a magic pill which would instantly change today's young children into mature readers. Unfortunately, however, the "get-educated-quick" schemes seem to have the same results as most "get-rich-quick" schemes. The followers are left with little to show for their dreams. The suggestions I offer today do not come as magic elixirs. They come as methods of teaching, methods which *will* work when applied by teachers who want to help children grow in reading ability.

First, though, let's look at the task of reading for the primary child. At its very simplest level, reading a word involves looking at a group of marks, thinking the word-sound that those marks stand for, and recognizing the meaning for that word-sound. This does not deny all of the background experiences nor all of the inter-relationships that are involved in reading, nor does it deny the various kinds of reading such as critical and creative reading. It does, however, give us a common understanding at its very simplest level of the task involved in primary reading where the child's initial job is to translate word and sentence symbols into word and sentence sounds and meanings.

If this is the goal of the beginning reader, how can we best help him to reach that goal? This answer lies in an examination of three questions. First, what does the child have when he comes to us that he can use to become a good reader? Second, in light of what he already has, what does he need? And, third, how can we help him develop what he needs?

First, what does the child already have when he comes to us? Actually, he has a great deal. He has familiarity with two of the three aspects of a word. That is, he has familiarity with the word sound, he has familiarity with the word meaning, and he lacks only familiarity with the particular symbols which stand for the sound and meaning that he already knows.

For example, the young child has heard the word-sound *dog* many times before he comes to school. This is a sound that is familiar to him. In addition, he has, over the years, developed an understanding of what that particular sound stands for. Consequently, when he hears the sound *dog,* he has a concept of "dogness" which that particular sound triggers in his mind.

From *Today's Challenges in the Teaching of Reading,* SCIRA Conference Proceedings, 1965 (New York: Scholastic Magazines, Inc., 1965), pp. 75–80. Reprinted by permission. William K. Durr is Professor of Education, Michigan State University, East Lansing.

Similarly, he is familiar with the sounds and meanings for many other words. *No, don't,* and *stop hitting your sister* are all sounds which many children are extremely familiar with. Research doesn't give us a definitive answer on the exact number, but we know that for most children this vocabulary competency runs well into the thousands.

His job, then, is to translate word forms into familiar word sounds. But even here he has some abilities which can be refined to aid in that translation. He has the knowledge that word-sounds together are supposed to make sense. For example, if you say to him, "I like to eat candles," he will conclude that there is something wrong with you because those particular sounds are not sounds which he would expect to come together. That is, people just don't eat things that he has come to know as *candles. Candy,* yes, but not *candles.*

In addition to this knowledge that word-sounds together are supposed to make sense, he also has some knowledge of sounds in words. To verify his ability, try this with almost any kindergarten child you know. Ask him his name and, when he tells you, repeat it for him, changing just one of the sounds. For example, if he says that his name is Bill, ask him, "Did you say hill?" He knows that he did not say "hill," he said "Bill," and he has enough familiarity with letter sounds in words to know that the two are not the same.

To summarize, then, what is it that he brings to school which can help him become a good reader? First, he has a knowledge of word-sounds. Second, he has a knowledge of word-meanings. Third, he has the knowledge that words together are expected to make sense. And, fourth, he is able to recognize some sounds within words.

Let's look at the second question, then. What skill does the child need initially to read? The obvious answer is that he needs to know how to associate word form — which he doesn't know for any given word — with the sound and meaning which he does know. That is, he needs to have some simple procedure for translating the squiggly marks on paper into word-sounds which stand for meanings that he already has.

This obvious truth is sometimes overlooked by those of us who have lengthy, readiness activities to teach boys and girls information which is basically not essential for beginning reading. For example, we sometimes go to great lengths to build meaning vocabulary as a prerequisite for initial reading experiences. There can be no question that children should have lots of valuable experiences which will help them develop meaning vocabulary. There can be a serious question, however, about making these experiences a prerequisite for reading such words as *look, see, come,* and all of the other controlled vocabulary words which appear in most children's initial reading experiences.

Yes, children should have many experiences to build meaning. No, these experiences are not essential before we will help the child begin to read. They can, in fact, profitably take place concurrently with initial reading instruction.

Now let's look at our third question. We have looked at what the child has and at what he needs and does not need in order to learn how to read effectively. How, then, can we help him develop what he needs? That is, how can we help him develop the ability to decode — to unlock — that printed form?

Traditionally educators have fluctuated from one extreme to the other in searching for an efficient procedure. This seems to be a common fault of education in many fields besides the field of reading. At one extreme we find the position that children should start with the rote memory of a word. That is, the word is presented to them in printed form, they are told what it is, and they are then brought into contact with it frequently so it will become automatically known.

There are certain inherent dangers in this procedure. First, it obviously does not teach the child self-help methods of reading from his very first reading experiences. Such children often initially develop one method of unlocking a word. It is known as the arm-waving method and consists of waving the arm until the teacher's attention is attracted and then asking her what the word is. Although many children have started with this method, it seems that a procedure of self-help would more quickly develop the habits of self-reliance that our children are capable of developing. Second, this procedure does not adequately stress meaning. No child would say, "Mother and Daddy went into the horse," but many children read *horse* for *house* and go blithely on, if they have not been taught to demand meaning from their reading throughout all of their reading experiences.

At the other extreme is the position that children should be taught a long list of phonic rules before they are introduced to stories. This, too, fails to build on the child's natural tendency to look for meaning in sentences and, instead, places the greatest importance on the rules for puzzling out words. The child who develops the habit of puzzling out each new word letter by letter is neither building on what he has nor developing the most efficient word attack skills. If we take into account what the child already has when he comes to us and try to make full use of this knowledge in our initial reading instruction, we should be able to do a more efficient job of helping him develop reading independence easily and early.

Since the child already has some ability to hear letter-sounds in words, we can refine this ability and help him make limited associations between consonants and the sounds they stand for before he reads. When these letter-sounds are clearly made only an *aid* to reading, the child will not develop the habit of puzzling out a word letter by letter but he can use the necessary consonant sounds to help him when he needs help.

Why consonants? Consonants are important for two reasons. First, they are consistent and, as a result, are less likely to lead to confusion when the child tries to make the association between a symbol and a sound. Second, they are also most useful in unlocking words. To prove this to yourself, make up two different sentences. In one sentence leave out all of the vowels and substitute in their places blank dashes. In the other sentences, leave out all of the consonants and substitute in their places blank dashes. Ask someone to read these sentences for you and note how much more easily he can read the sentence in which only the consonants appear.

There are many ways to build these consonant-letter sound associations. Good teachers frequently start by having children associate sounds as they relate these sounds to pictures. For example, children can put the pictures of a ball, a bat, a bee, and a bun together, because all of these pictures stand for words which have the same sound at the beginning. Children can be encouraged to bring pictures from home and to mount these on separate newsprint charts with all of the words starting with one sound on one chart, all of the words starting with another sound on a second chart, etc. One kindergarten teacher I know who used this then merely added the appropriate letter to each chart — one chart per day. The letters *B* and *b* were put at the top of the chart with the *b* pictures, the letters *M* and *m* were put at the top of the chart with the *m* pictures, etc.

There are many ways in which you may provide such interesting associations between the letter and the sound it represents for your children.

It is important, however, that children do not learn to rely entirely on these letter-sounds as a basis for unlocking words if we are to promote meaning and combat overanalysis. They bring with them another ability which can be refined and used with consonant sounds to help unlock words — this is the ability to use context. They can refine the ability and develop the habit of using the sense of a sentence or paragraph to help determine what a word might be.

You can help sharpen this ability in many of your daily activities. For example, when you are reading a story to your children, stop momentarily at an appropriate place and see if they can tell you what words could come next in the story and make sense. Or, have them play one word riddles with each other. One child says a sentence such as, *I like to eat* ——, and the child who guesses the correct word gets to be the next sentence-maker. The important thing is that they continually select words which could make sense because refining the ability to look for sense in such sentences can aid in later word attack and help sharpen subsequent reading comprehension as well.

These two skills, the ability to use context and the ability to make consonant letter-sound associations, can help the child help himself from his first reading experiences. As he reads, he expects to get sense from his reading and he expects any unknown word he meets to make sense with the other words. When he uses this knowledge — this expectation — with his knowledge of consonant-letter sounds, he can learn to read effectively without waiting for the teacher to tell him every new word or without having to memorize long lists of rules for sounding-out words. If teachers would use these two facets of word attack to help the child with all new words that he meets in his basal reading program, the child could soon develop his own ability to apply these skills independent of the teacher.

This, obviously, is not the entirety of reading. There are many things he must learn, such as vowel sound associations, since he will occasionally meet words out of context which will require this knowledge. He will also have to build meanings for new words as he goes upward through the grades and meets strange words in print that would also be strange in word-sound. In his initial reading experiences, however, the child is basically called upon to decode marks on paper which stand for sounds and meanings that he knows. If he is taught to use context plus consonant letter-sounds before he is required to read words, his initial reading experiences can be more successful and he can be developing proper habits of self-help from the very beginning.

The Utility of Phonic Generalizations
in the Primary Grades ❖ Theodore Clymer

The origins of this study go back to Kenneth, an extraordinary elementary pupil. Prior to my encounter with Kenneth I had completed a reading methods course in a small teachers college which provided a background in the principles of teaching reading as well as a good introduction to techniques. Among these techniques were procedures to develop phonic generalizations and also *the* list (not *a* list) of the most valuable generalizations to develop. (To those of you who might like copies of the list, I am sad to report that somehow through the years it has been lost.)

Difficulties with Kenneth began as the class reviewed phonic generalizations at the start of the school year. Our procedures were like those used in many classrooms: Groups of words were presented, and the class analyzed their likenesses and differences with a view toward deriving a generalization about relationships between certain letters and sounds or the position and pronunciation of vowels.

Throughout these exercises, following the dictum of my reading methods teacher, we were careful not to call the generalizations "rules," for all our statements had a number of exceptions. As the class finally formulated a generalization regarding the relationships of letters, letter position, and sounds, such defensive phrasing as "most of the time," "usually," and "often" appeared as protective measures. We also spent time listing some of the exceptions to our generalizations.

At this point Kenneth entered the discussion. While the class was busily engaged in developing the generalization, Kenneth had skimmed his dictionary, locating long lists of exceptions to the generalization. In fact, he often located more exceptions than I could list applications. When I protested — somewhat weakly — that the dictionary contained many unusual words, Kenneth continued his role as an educational scientist. He turned to the basic reader word list in the back of his text and produced nearly similar results. Today, of course, Kenneth's behavior would be rated as "gifted," "talented," or "creative" — although I remember discussing him in other terms as I sat in the teachers' lounge.

As Kenneth had provided a memorable and even a "rich" learning experience for me, he furnished the impetus for a series of studies which will attempt to answer three questions: (1) What phonic generalizations are being taught in basic reading programs for the primary grades? (2) To what extent are these generalizations useful in having a "reasonable" degree of application to

From *The Reading Teacher*, 16: 252–258; January, 1963. Reprinted with permission of Theodore Clymer and the International Reading Association. Theodore Clymer is Professor of Education, University of Minnesota, Minneapolis. This paper is an extension of a report given at a joint meeting of the International Reading Association and the National Conference of Research in English, May, 1961. Thomas Barrett, Harriette Anderson, Joan Hanson, and David Palmer provided invaluable assistance in various phases of the study.

words commonly met in primary grade material? (3) Which of the generalizations that stand the test of question 2 can be learned and successfully applied to unknown words by primary children?

What Generalizations Are Taught?

Four widely used sets of readers were selected to determine the phonic generalizations being taught in the primary grades. After a preliminary study of the manuals, workbooks, and readers, the manuals were selected as the source of the generalizations. The manuals presented the generalizations in three ways: (1) statements to be taught to the pupils, (2) statements to be derived by the pupils after inductive teaching, and (3) statements with no clear indications as to what was to be done. Generalizations presented by all three means were included in the analysis.

Five general types of generalizations emerged from the study of the teachers manuals. These types dealt with (1) vowels, (2) consonants, (3) endings, (4) syllabication, and (5) miscellaneous relationships. Arbitrary decisions were made in assigning some generalizations to one or another of the five types since certain statements might easily be classified under two or more headings.

If we eliminate from our consideration the miscellaneous type of generalization, a total of 121 different statements were located. There were fifty vowel generalizations, fifteen consonant generalizations, and twenty-eight generalizations in each of the ending and syllabication groups. In evaluating these figures it should be kept in mind that any statement was considered a separate generalization when its phrasing excluded or included different sets of words than another statement. For example, the generalization, "When there are two vowels side by side, the long sound of the first is heard and the second one is usually silent" and "When *ea* come together in a word, the first letter is long and the second is silent" were counted as two separate generalizations, although the second statement is a special application of the first.

While not directly related to our discussion here, note should be made of the wide variation of grade level of introduction, emphasis, and phrasing of the generalizations. Of the fifty different vowel generalizations, only eleven were common to all four series. None of these eleven was presented initially at the same half-year grade level in all four series. Some series gave a much greater emphasis to the generalizations than did other series. One publisher introduced only thirty-three of the one hundred twenty-one generalizations, while another presented sixty-eight. These comments are not meant to detract from the usefulness of basic materials, but simply to point out some of their differences. These differences do call for careful adjustments in the classroom when pupils are moved from one set of materials to another. The teacher who changes from series X to series Y may need to make some important revisions in his word recognition program. These findings may indicate also the need for further experimentation on emphasis and the developmental aspects of our word recognition program.

Which Generalizations Are Useful?

Forty-five of the generalizations given in the manuals were selected for further study. The selection of these was somewhat arbitrary. The main criterion was to ask, "Is the generalization stated specifically enough so that it can be said to aid or hinder in the pronunciation of a particular word?" An example or two will make our criterion clear. The generalization, "Long *o* makes a sound like its name," is undoubtedly a valuable generalization, but it was not specific enough to meet our criterion. On the other hand, the statement, "When a vowel is in the middle of a one syllable word, the vowel is short," was included because we could judge by reference to a word list how often one syllable words with a vowel in the middle do in fact have a short vowel sound.

Our next problem was to develop a word list on which we could test the generalizations. A reasonable approach seemed to be that of making up a composite list of all the words introduced in the four basic series from which the generalizations were drawn, plus the words from the Gates Reading Vocabulary for the Primary Grades. Once this list of some twenty-six hundred words was prepared, the following steps were taken:

1. The phonetic respelling and the syllabic division of all words were recorded. Webster's *New Collegiate Dictionary* was used as the authority for this information.

2. Each phonic generalization was checked against the words in the composite list to determine (*a*) the words which were pronounced as the generalization claimed and (*b*) the words which were exceptions to the generalization.

3. A "per cent of utility" was computed for each generalization by dividing the number of words pronounced as the generalization claimed by the total number of words to which the generalization could be expected to apply. For example, if the generalization claimed that "When the letters *oa* are together in a word, *o* always gives its long sound and the *a* is silent," all words containing *oa* were located in the list. The number of these words was the total number of words to which the generalization should apply. Then the phonetic spellings of these words were examined to see how many words containing *oa* actually did have the long *o* followed by the silent *a*. In this case thirty words were located which contained *oa*. Twenty-nine of these were pronounced as the generalization claimed; one was not. The per cent of utility became 29/30 or 97. This procedure was followed for all generalizations.

When the per cent of utility was computed for each generalization, we set two criteria as to what constituted a "reasonable" degree of application. We have no scientific evidence to demonstrate that these criteria are valid; it can only be said that they seem reasonable to us.

The first criterion was that the composite word list must contain a minimum of twenty words to which the generalization might apply. Generalizations with lower frequencies of application do not seem to merit instructional time.

The second criterion was a per cent of utility of at least 75. To state the matter another way, if the pupil applied the generalization to twenty words, it should aid him in getting the correct pronunciation in fifteen of the twenty words.

Table I gives the results of our analysis of the forty-five phonic generalizations. An inspection of the data leaves me somewhat confused as to the value of generalizations. Some time-honored customs in the teaching of reading may be in need of revision.

Certain generalizations apply to large numbers of words and are rather constant in providing the correct pronunciation of words. (See, for example, generalizations 19, 35, and 36.)

TABLE I. The Utility of Forty-Five Phonic Generalizations

*Generalization	No. of Words Conforming	No. of Exceptions	Per Cent of Utility
1. When there are two vowels side by side, the long sound of the first one is heard and the second is usually silent.	309 (bead)†	377 (chief)	45
2. When a vowel is in the middle of a one-syllable word, the vowel is short.	408	249	62
middle letter	191 (dress)	84 (scold)	69
one of the middle two letters in a word of four letters	191 (rest)	135 (told)	59
one vowel within a word of more than four letters	26 (splash)	30 (fight)	46
3. If the only vowel letter is at the end of a word, the letter usually stands for a long sound.	23 (he)	8 (to)	74
4. When there are two vowels, one of which is final e, the first vowel is long and the e is silent.	180 (bone)	108 (done)	63
*5. The r gives the preceding vowel a sound that is neither long nor short.	184 (horn)	134 (wire)	78
6. The first vowel is usually long and the second silent in the digraphs ai, ea, oa, and ui.	179	92	66
ai	43 (nail)	24 (said)	64
ea	101 (bead)	51 (head)	66
oa	34 (boat)	1 (cupboard)	97
ui	1 (suit)	16 (build)	6
7. In the phonogram ie, the i is silent and the e has a long sound.	8 (field)	39 (friend)	17
*8. Words having double e usually have the long e sound.	85 (seem)	2 (been)	98
9. When words end with silent e, the preceding a or i is long.	164 (cake)	108 (have)	60
*10. In ay the y is silent and gives a its long sound.	36 (play)	10 (always)	78
11. When the letter i is followed by the letters gh, the i usually stands for its long sound and the gh is silent.	22 (high)	9 (neighbor)	71
12. When a follows w in a word, it usually has the sound a as in was.	15 (watch)	32 (swam)	32
13. When e is followed by w, the vowel sound is the same as represented by oo.	9 (blew)	17 (sew)	35
14. The two letters ow make the long o sound.	50 (own)	35 (down)	59

* Generalizations marked with an asterisk were found "useful" according to the criteria.

† Words in parentheses are examples — either of words which conform or of exceptions, depending on the column.

TABLE I, Continued

*Generalization	No. of Words Conforming	No. of Exceptions	Per Cent of Utility
15. *W* is sometimes a vowel and follows the vowel digraph rule.	50 *(crow)*	75 *(threw)*	40
*16. When *y* is the final letter in a word, it usually has a vowel sound.	169 *(dry)*	32 *(tray)*	84
17. When *y* is used as a vowel in words, it sometimes has the sound of long *i*.	29 *(fly)*	170 *(funny)*	15
18. The letter *a* has the same sound (ò) when followed by *l*, *w*, and *u*.	61 *(all)*	65 *(canal)*	48
19. When *a* is followed by *r* and final *e*, we expect to hear the sound heard in *care*.	9 *(dare)*†	1 *(are)*	90
*20. When *c* and *h* are next to each other, they make only one sound.	103 *(peach)*	0	100
*21. *Ch* is usually pronounced as it is in *kitchen*, *catch*, and *chair*, not like *sh*.	99 *(catch)*	5 *(machine)*	95
*22. When *c* is followed by *e* or *i*, the sound of *s* is likely to be heard.	66 *(cent)*	3 *(ocean)*	96
*23. When the letter *c* is followed by *o* or *a* the sound of *k* is likely to be heard.	143 *(camp)*	0	100
24. The letter *g* often has a sound similar to that of *j* in *jump* when it precedes the letter *i* or *e*.	49 *(engine)*	28 *(give)*	64
*25. When *ght* is seen in a word, *gh* is silent.	30 *(fight)*	0	100
26. When a word begins with *kn*, the *k* is silent.	10 *(knife)*	0	100
27. When a word begins with *wr*, the *w* is silent.	8 *(write)*	0	100
*28. When two of the same consonants are side by side only one is heard.	334 *(carry)*	3 *(suggest)*	99
*29. When a word ends in *ck*, it has the same last sound as in *look*.	46 *(brick)*	0	100
*30. In most two-syllable words, the first syllable is accented.	828 *(famous)*	143 *(polite)*	85
*31. If *a*, *in*, *re*, *ex*, *de*, or *be* is the first syllable in a word, it is usually un-accented.	86 *(belong)*	13 *(insect)*	87
*32. In most two-syllable words that end in a consonant followed by *y*, the first syllable is accented and the last is unaccented.	101 *(baby)*	4 *(supply)*	96

* Generalizations marked with an asterisk were found "useful" according to the criteria.

† Words in parentheses are examples — either of words which conform or of exceptions, depending on the column.

TABLE I, Continued

*Generalization	No. of Words Conforming	No. of Exceptions	Per Cent of Utility
33. One vowel letter in an accented syllable has its short sound.	547 (city)	356 (lady)	61
34. When y or ey is seen in the last syllable that is not accented, the long sound of e is heard.	0	157 (baby)	0
35. When ture is the final syllable in a word, it is unaccented.	4 (picture)	0	100
36. When tion is the final syllable in a word, it is unaccented.	5 (station)	0	100
37. In many two- and three-syllable words, the final e lengthens the vowel in the last syllable.	52 (invite)	62 (gasoline)	46
38. If the first vowel sound in a word is followed by two consonants, the first syllable usually ends with the first of the two consonants.	404 (bullet)	159 (singer)	72
39. If the first vowel sound in a word is followed by a single consonant, that consonant usually begins the second syllable.	190 (over)	237 (oven)	44
*40. If the last syllable of a word ends in le, the consonant preceding the le usually begins the last syllable.	62 (tumble)†	2 (buckle)	97
*41. When the first vowel element in a word is followed by th, ch, or sh, these symbols are not broken when the word is divided into syllables and may go with either the first or second syllable.	30 (dishes)	0	100
42. In a word of more than one syllable, the letter v usually goes with the preceding vowel to form a syllable.	53 (cover)	20 (clover)	73
43. When a word has only one vowel letter, the vowel sound is likely to be short.	433 (hid)	322 (kind)	57
*44. When there is one e in a word that ends in a consonant, the e usually has a short sound.	85 (leg)	27 (blew)	76
*45. When the last syllable is the sound r, it is unaccented.	188 (butter)	9 (appear)	95

* Generalizations marked with an asterisk were found "useful" according to the criteria.

† Words in parentheses are examples — either of words which conform or of exceptions, depending on the column.

A group of generalizations seem to be useful only after the pupil can pronounce the word. Generalizations which specify vowel pronunciation in stressed syllables require that the pupil know the pronunciation of the word before he can apply the generalization. (See, for example, generalization 33.) This criticism assumes, of course, that the purpose of a generalization is to help the child unlock the pronunciation of *unknown* words.

The usefulness of certain generalizations depends upon regional pronunciations. While following Webster's markings, generalization 34 is rejected. Midwestern pronunciation makes this generalization rather useful, although we reject it because we used Webster as the authority. Such problems are natural, and we should not hold it against Mr. Webster that he came from New England.

If we adhere to the criteria set up at the beginning of the study, of the forty-five generalizations only eighteen, numbers 5, 8, 10, 16, 20, 21, 22, 23, 25, 28, 29, 30, 31, 32, 40, 41, 44, and 45 are useful. Some of the generalizations which failed to meet our criteria might be useful if stated in different terms or if restricted to certain types of words. We are studying these problems at the present time. We are also examining other generalizations which we did not test in this study.

Conclusion

In evaluating this initial venture in testing the utility of phonic generalizations, it seems quite clear that many generalizations which are commonly taught are of limited value. Certainly the study indicates that we should give careful attention to pointing out the many exceptions to most of the generalizations that we teach. Current "extrinsic" phonics programs which present large numbers of generalizations are open to question on the basis of this study.

This study does not, of course, answer the question of which generalizations primary children can apply in working out the pronunciation of unknown words. The answer to the question of the primary child's ability to apply these and other generalizations will come only through classroom experimentation. Also, this study does not establish the per cent of utility required for a generalization to be useful. The percentage suggested here (75) may be too high. Classroom research might reveal that generalizations with lower percentages of utility should be taught because they encourage children to examine words for sound and letter relationships.

The most disturbing fact to come from the study may be the rather dismal failure of generalization 1 to provide the correct pronunciation even 50 per cent of the time. As one teacher remarked when this study was presented to a reading methods class, "Mr. Clymer, for years I've been teaching 'When two vowels go walking, the first one does the talking.' You're ruining the romance in the teaching of reading!"

A Phonetic-Linguistic View of The
Reading Controversy

❖ ARTHUR J. BRONSTEIN AND ELSA M. BRONSTEIN

Reading commands so much attention among educators and concerned parents that the recent contributions of the speech scientist-linguist-phonetician to this study deserve careful reporting. The major purpose of the present paper is to summarize these contributions in the context of the long-continued and many-faceted controversy over methods of teaching reading. Indeed, a clear understanding of the contributions would be impossible without a rather detailed account of the pedagogical disputes and the dissatisfactions.

Approaches and Attitudes Toward the Teaching
of Reading Through the Midfifties

The more recent phases of the continued disputes are the more relevant to the present purpose, but neither the "whole-word method" nor "phonics" nor the "sentence-method" is a result of recent empirical studies. Part of the history of education in America, they can be found in the readers, the spellers, and the grammars published in the United States and used here from the early nineteenth century to the present. Nor is vigorous condemnation or defense new, for from at least the time of Noah Webster's *Dissertations on the English Language* in 1789 in this country and of John Hart's *A Methode or Comfortable Beginning for all Unlearned* in 1570 in England the arguments have been strong and unrelenting. During the two centuries or so prior to 1920[1] educators wrote about techniques involving the use of the alphabet, about the sounds of the letters in the alphabet, and mostly about their dissatisfactions with whatever method of teaching reading was being used at a particular time. Whenever these cries became loud enough, a "new" way of "doing the job" was introduced.

From *Speech Monographs,* 32: 25–35; March, 1965. Reprinted by permission. Arthur J. Bronstein is Professor of Speech, Queens College of the City University of New York, and Elsa M. Bronstein is affiliated with the New York City Public Schools. Portions of this paper were presented at the 1963 convention of the Speech Association of America in Denver, Colorado, at a sectional meeting jointly sponsored by the Secondary Schools and the Voice, Phonetics, and Linguistics interest groups.

[1] The four major historical periods were (1) the prerevolutionary period when the goal in teaching reading was predominantly religious; (2) the day of the *Blue-Back Speller,* during the early nineteenth century, when the standardization of the American language was of primary importance; (3) the late nineteenth century when graded readers, of which the McGuffey Readers were but one series, were introduced; and (4) the turn of the century when universal education began and disciplining the mind and "enhancing culture" became stressed. For details regarding these periods see Paul Witty, *Reading in Modern Education* (Boston: D. C. Heath & Co., 1949), ch. 1; and Nila Banton Smith, "Historical Turning Points in the Teaching of Reading," *National Educational Association Journal,* XLI (May, 1952), 280–283.

Shifting Approaches. The story is similar for the period from the 1920's to the beginning of 1950, during which time similar shifts in stress indicated that *a* satisfactory methodology had not yet been found. By 1920 the emphasis had become centered on rapid silent reading skills, with getting a central idea out of a paragraph, noting details, and following directions as the important elements,[2] and with a parallel neglect of oral reading. In 1925 the National Society for the Study of Education in its twenty-fourth Yearbook noted that a considerable proportion of the adults of that time had failed to master the basic reading skills. It suggested that the schools needed to develop a systematic program of instruction in reading that would be aimed toward developing a permanent interest in reading for leisure.

Fairly representative of the attitudes of educators in this period is the following quotation from the well-known and respected Paul Klapper: "The skeptic asks, 'Why all these pedagogical inventions: did not the old alphabetic method teach children to read?' The alphabetic method did teach us to read, but it cheated the child of the joy of the story for many years, and, in the end, often made of him a lip-reader."[3] This was the time of change-over from the *ABC*'s, and among the approaches phonics was the one of particular interest to the phonetician-linguist. The research worker finds in the literature of the 1920's innumerable references to both *phonics* and *phonetics.*[4]

Phonics from 1920 to 1955. These references indicate that the direct application of phonic drill to building reading skills was an accepted concept in the late 1920's[5] but that the method of application differed according to the practitioners. Klapper, for example, combined the teaching of the alphabet, phonics, and phonetics with the analysis of word, sentence, and story units,[6] whereas Anna D. Cordts eliminated isolated drill and used a method in which ". . . the pupil is never told a sound or any combination of sounds. He derives for himself the unknown parts of the word from key words which were learned as sight

[2] Witty, *loc. cit.*

[3] *Teaching Children to Read* (New York: Appleton-Century-Crofts, Inc., 1926), p. 109.

[4] These words often were used interchangeably, but the more careful writers made a distinction that followed closely the one made by Barrows and Cordts: "It is better to limit the word 'phonetics' to the science of speech sounds, and to use the word 'phonics' for the application of phonetics to the teaching of reading." Sarah T. Barrows and Anna D. Cordts, *A Teacher's Book of Phonetics* (Boston: Ginn & Co., 1926), p. 3. See also Arthur I. Gates, *New Methods in Primary Reading* (New York: Columbia University Press, 1928). Gates defined phonics as " 'ear training' and practice in the articulation of words and word elements" and phonetics as "the various forms of training in which pronunciations and sounds of word elements are associated with the equivalent printed word forms" (p. 33*n*).
Confusion concerning the terms still persists. They are used interchangeably in *A Critical Review of Research and Opinion on Phonics* (Albany: State Education Department, Division of Research, the University of the State of New York, 1963). For numerous examples of confusion in the use of these terms see C. C. Fries, *Linguistics and Reading* (New York: Holt, Rinehart & Winston, 1963), pp. 133–158.

[5] For a report of a study noting that all twenty-one of the most widely used reading systems included phonetic training in some way, see Arthur I. Gates, Esther Hemke, and Dorothy Van Alstyne, "Problems in Beginning Reading Suggested by an Analysis of Twenty-one Courses," *Teachers College Record,* XXVII (March, 1925), 572–591.

[6] In "analytic analysis" words are divided into letter combinations that are already familiar, and then these known combinations are used to sound out the new word.

words in the Primer or First Reader."[7] This may have been the point at which "Look-Say" began to replace systematic instruction in phonics in the classroom.

Opinions, of course, were as varied as the methods. Edward A. Dolch wrote that "The advantages of phonics in the first years may be and often are discounted by the teachers, but the question is, without phonics in the early years, how will the child acquire the sounding methods he ought to have later on?"[8] He called the sounding of letters "the most useful kind of phonic ability" (p. 90), and in addition decried the separate phonic drill and pleaded for systematic planning so that phonics could aid directly in reading. Dolch and Gates also favored systematic phonics instruction, not as the *only* training that the early reader should receive, but still as a form of training important in the total instructional picture.

A major turning point was the publication by Dolch and Bloomster of the results of a study that seemed to cast doubt upon the advisability of planned phonics instruction in the earliest years of reading — a view already strongly supported.[9] They concluded that, although there were individual differences, in general a child did not benefit from phonics instruction before reaching the mental age of seven. In the texts of the '40's this study was so often quoted that the inference is well founded that it contributed to the widespread delay of phonics instruction until at least second grade.[10]

Summary and Appraisal. The number of skills considered necessary for the proper preparation of the many future readers of America was rather large. Phonics, although always included in the lists in the texts, normally was placed towards the lower end.[11] Phonic readiness — not actual use — was the important consideration in first grade teaching,[12] and phonetic analysis was only one of the tools in reading classes in the second grade and beyond.

The earlier argument on the importance of phonetic training and analysis in the reading program had abated somewhat, but the convictions of those who preferred greater stress on phonetic skill remained strong and the scholars were not inactive. The prevailing approach, nevertheless, had become what has been

[7] *The Word Method of Teaching Phonics* (Boston: Ginn & Co., 1929), p. 5.

[8] *The Psychology of the Teaching of Reading* (Boston: Ginn & Co., 1931), p. 71.

[9] Edward A. Dolch and Maurine Bloomster, "Phonics Readiness," *Elementary School Journal,* XXXVIII (Nov., 1937), 201–205.

[10] In *A Critical Review of Research and Opinion on Phonics* a number of authors are cited on page 25 as agreeing that phonics should be delayed until the second grade.

[11] Nila Banton Smith used an order typical for the period: context, configuration, significant details, phonetic analysis, dictionary use, and word structure. "What Research Tells Us about Word Recognition," *Elementary School Journal,* LV (April, 1955), 440–446.

[12] See the works of Gates, Dolch, and Witty already cited. See also Albert J. Harris, *How to Increase Reading Ability* (New York: Longmans, Green & Company, 1940); Donald B. Durrell, Helen B. Sullivan, Helen A. Murphy, and Kathryn M. Junkins, *Building Word Power in Primary Reading* (New York: Harcourt, Brace & World, 1941).

Gray had the child wade through preprimers with a total vocabulary of about one hundred words, all to be recognized at sight, before receiving any instruction in attacking words independently. At the time that the child began doing wider reading Gray instructed the teacher to provide him with aids in the form of meaning clues, word-form clues, structural clues, and phonetic clues. William S. Gray and Lillian Gray, *Guidebook for Our New Friends* (Chicago: Scott, Foresman and Co., 1946), p. 19.

called "whole-word-look-and-say." On the surface at least, the controversy between phonics or phonetic training and Look-Say seemed quiescent.

Flesch as an Advocate of the Phonetic Approach

At this point Rudolph Flesch entered the controversy with the impact of an explosion. His trade book *Why Johnny Can't Read* quickly became a best seller. Perhaps because of the displeasure of some parents with the progress of their children in school or perhaps because of the mounting wave of talk against "permissiveness" that followed Sputnik and the growing demand for "basic education," Flesch's attack on current reading methods stirred a strong public reaction that educators and reading specialists, despite their distaste for Flesch and his methods,[13] could not ignore.

Summary and Critique of Flesch's Views. This potent skill as an advocate must be regarded as Flesch's chief contribution, for his system was not new in its essence[14] and was not always correct in its details. He defined phonics as "simplified phonetics for teaching reading"[15] — a definition that would have distressed Bloomfield greatly. Then he provided an introduction to phonics that was typical of the presentations in earlier reading texts, but that was noteworthy for such questionable phonetic statements as calling the *g*'s of *gem* and *go* "soft" and "hard" sounds, labeling the vowels in *mate, mete, mite, mote,* and *mute* "long vowels" rather than diphthongs (he confused letters with sounds), and classifying *au* as in *Paul* as a diphthong comparable with the *ou* of *spouse* and the *oi* of *noise* — again because of a confusion between sounds and spelling practices.

The instructional system itself, called "the natural sequence of *any* phonic method," consisted of five steps and was guaranteed to teach any child to read. The groups of phonemes and the order in which the pupil should master them were as follows:

1. The letters *a, e, i, o, u* and their short sounds followed by the seventeen consonants *b, d, f, g, h, j, l, m, n, p, r, s, t, v, w, y, z.* The "soft g" of *gem,* the *y* of *city* and the /s > z/ of *beds* should be avoided as yet.
2. Combinations of consonants (*lk* of *milk, sk* of *desk,* etc.) followed by the two inflectional endings of the plural morpheme /s ~ z/ as in *eats* and *crags;* then "the consonant combinations at the ends of words (*ng* of *ring, nk* of *pink, x* of *fox, sh* of *fish*). [These examples, even if regarded as elements in simplified instruction, are disturbing. The / ŋ / of *ring* is not a combination of con-

---

[13] Roger Brown in *Words and Things* (New York: Free Press of Glencoe, Inc., 1958), p. 68, notes that Flesch, whom he calls "a most vocal critic," was depreciated because of his rhetoric, his tendency to stack the cards, and his allegedly "cheap effort to scandalize the public." Brown's view is that Flesch's *methods* may have deserved attack but not necessarily his *conclusions.*

[14] Flesch admittedly based his approach on the ideas presented by Leonard Bloomfield, although the latter was an advocate of a linguistic, not a phonic, method. The works of Bloomfield from which Flesch developed his thesis are as follows: "Linguistics and Reading," *The Elementary English Review,* XIX (April, 1942), 125–130, and XIX (May, 1942), 183–186; *Language* (New York: Holt, Rinehart & Winston, 1933), esp. pp. 500–503 and Ch. 17, "Written Records."

[15] *Why Johnny Can't Read* (New York: Harper & Row, 1955), p. 22.

sonants, but a graphic combination of letters that represent a single consonant; similarly the *sh* of *fish* is a single sound and not a combination of two consonants, while the *x* of *fox* is correctly included in a group of consonant combinations.]

3. Vowel clusters (Flesch calls them "combinations") spelled with two letters: the *ee* of *sheep*, the *oo* of *book*, the *ah* sound of *pa* and *park;* the *or* of *lord*, the *er* sound of *bird*, the *ou* of *cow*, the *ai* sound of *say*, and the slightly different sound of *fair;* then the long *i, o,* and *u.*

4. Certain principles to be derived from a contrast of the long and the short vowels in such words as *fade* and *fad*, *Pete* and *pet*, *pine* and *pin*, *robe* and *rob*, *cute* and *cut*. The teacher should point out that *e* is the final letter of the first word of each pair and that adding *ing* to a word ending in a single consonant makes the vowel long: "Explain to him the important rule," Flesch stated on page 31, "that if you want to keep the vowel short in such *ing* words, you have to double the final consonant before adding the *ing*. For example: *bedding, shipping, trapping, humming, brimming, trimming*." [Actually Johnny should be taught these facts the other way around — that the long vowels remain long and the short vowels remain short when *ing* is added and that certain spelling conventions are ascertainable. In words with long vowels, such as *fade–fading*, the final letter is deleted before the *ing*, and in words with short vowels, such as *get–getting*, the final consonantal letter is doubled.]

5. The irregular spellings of *-sion* and *-tion* and the silent *k, w, t, l*, etc., in such words as *knife, write, whistle,* and *calm*.

Flesch's Influence. Some return from the position in which there was very little or no instruction in phonics was bound to occur, but Flesch certainly helped to speed the process.[16] Numerous journal articles and convention addresses on phonic, phonetic, and linguistic matters[17] followed the publication of *Why Johnny Can't Read;* and though the first reaction was that "Flesch's phonics" was a method that already had been tried, found lacking, and replaced with a "more complete approach," the outside pressure caused a re-evaluating that in time produced changes.[18]

One outstanding example of the consequences of Flesch's attack was a conference of reading experts called by James Bryant Conant on September 22 and 23, 1961, and supported by the Carnegie Corporation of New York. The meeting was "primarily aimed at preparing a public statement as to the place of phonics in a reading program and the constituent parts of such a program."[19] The outcome, despite the choice of conferees with divergent views, was almost unanimous. The majority report of sixteen pages was signed by twenty-seven of those attending, the minority report of eleven pages by only one member, and the supplementary statement dissenting from the minority report also by one.

[16] Other works, of course, followed his. Noteworthy among these is Sybil Terman and Charles C. Walcutt, *Reading: Chaos and Cure* (New York: McGraw-Hill Book Co., Inc., 1958).

[17] See, for example, the Conference Proceedings of the International Reading Association as published by *Scholastic Magazines*, VI (1961). Three especially perceptive articles in this issue on the contributions of linguistics to reading are those by Carl A. LeFevre, Priscilla Tyler, and Raven I. McDavid, Jr.

[18] See, for example, *A Critical Review of Research and Opinion on Phonics;* and *Learning to Read: A Report of a Conference of Reading Experts* (Princeton, N.J.: Educational Testing Service, 1962).

[19] *Learning to Read: A Report of a Conference of Reading Experts*, p. 1.

The majority report indicated that the skills of word recognition were grouped primarily under two types: "(1) Learning to respond to the phonic (sound) clues provided by the letters standing in the word. . . . This skill is usually spoken of as two separate skills: (a) phonics and (b) structural analysis. (2) Learning to recognize words by the meaning clues provided by the other words standing in the material being read."[20] The conclusion was that evidence supporting both extremes — the "no-phonics" and the "all-phonics" programs — was the exception. Editorializing, the authors added a note of caution: "We have recently witnessed some highly publicized attempts to force the favorable attention of the public on one or another reading book and its brand of teaching reading as though it were the single and indispensable answer to all our reading concerns. Often these attempts have been made by persons who know either little or nothing about the teaching of reading" (p. 16).

Both this use of anticipatory rebuttal and the slanting by the headline writer for the New York *Times* (not to mention the very holding of the conference) were evidence of the deep impression that Flesch had made upon both educators and laymen. The *Times* reported on the conference on June 4, 1962, under the headline "Phonics Stressed as an Aid in Reading" and the subsidiary headline "Conference says 'Look-Say' Method of Teaching Reading Is Not Adequate Alone." Not until the first paragraph of the article did the reader learn that the conference concluded that there was no single best way of teaching children to read. Thus, although the conference did not subscribe to Flesch's approach (i.e., only phonics as the guaranteed method), the newspaper through its headlines actually gave phonics strong public support.

Summary. Phonetic analysis in the forty years just past has been an important tool in the teaching of reading, but its relative role in the melange of methods has varied from period to period, from theorist to theorist, and no doubt from classroom to classroom. Most significantly, though, professionally trained phoneticians and linguists contributed almost nothing either to the attempts to improve teaching methods or to the succession of controversies. Ultimately the creation of a climate in which their knowledge will be welcome to the reading specialist may prove to be Flesch's most valuable contribution.

Potential Contributions of the Linguist

The delayed appearance of the linguist in the development of methods of teaching reading was not the fault of Leonard Bloomfield, who twenty years ago was ready to contribute. The reason that leading theorists derided his views was partly that they misunderstood his approach and suggestions[21] and partly that they were in the midst of what seemed to them to be a sensible and educationally sound revolution in reading methodology. Since this new method was consistent with the "whole child," "behavioristic," "progressive," "interest-centered" approach that was so strong in the 1930's, it was particularly attractive. Circumstances now are changed, though, and Bloomfield's system may

[20] *Ibid.,* pp. 8–9.

[21] For an account of some of the trials that Bloomfield faced see the introductory essay "The Story of the Bloomfield System," by Clarence L. Barnhart in Leonard Bloomfield and Clarence L. Barnhart, *Let's Read: A Linguistic Approach* (Detroit: Wayne State University Press, 1961), pp. 9–17.

at last be tried. His suggestions of a linguistic approach to reading, not to be confused with a phonics approach, are now being published in the Bloomfield-Barnhart series of readers *Let's Read*.

Such works perhaps will shift attention from phonics *vs.* nonphonics, a controversy that has not abated, to the more fruitful topic of the potential contributions of the linguist and the phonetician. The phonics approach, the "look-say" or whole word approach, and even both combined leave too much unsaid and unrecognized. The need is for a clear understanding of the linguistic principles involved in speaking, writing, and reading and of how they can contribute to an understanding of these activities. This information now is readily available, and the linguist believes strongly that some of the recent findings about linguistic phenomena should become a part of the knowledge of all teachers in our schools and especially of those teachers concerned with instruction in reading.

Some Major Resources. Important reference works already are available, and the literature that deals with linguistics and reading is growing very rapidly. The purpose of this section is not to review these resources generally but rather through the use of two examples to indicate something of the nature of the existing material.

Two especially fine books, both by psychologists from the Harvard University-M.I.T. complex, are John B. Carroll, *The Study of Language* (Cambridge: Harvard University Press, 1953), and Roger W. Brown, *Words and Things* (New York: The Free Press of Glencoe, Inc., 1958).

Carroll's book, an outcome of a report written originally at the request of the Carnegie Corporation of New York, surveys the field of linguistics, analyzes its status, and shows its connections with neighboring disciplines. It gives special attention to the possible implications of linguistic science to educational problems ranging from the kindergarten through the postgraduate level.

Within this extended discussion of linguistics and the teaching of the language arts, there are at least five points that are especially relevant to this present account: (1) One of the seven major perspectives of language study is "the recognition of the primacy of speech as contrasted with written communication — as a proper orientation for instruction in oral communication and in the teaching of reading" (p. 144). (2) A second major perspective is "an acquaintance with the phonemic structure of the language and its relation (or lack of relation) to orthography — as a preparation for the teaching of reading, writing and spelling" (p. 144). (3) The recognition that linguists[22] already had noted that the correct analysis of the relation between speech sounds and the orthography of the language could bring about improvement in reading instruction (p. 146). Sentences, Carroll said, should be taught with the recognition that given sounds may be graphically represented in a number of ways — a statement that again recognizes the primacy of the speech act.[23] (4) The

---

[22] He refers particularly to Bloomfield's work and to Robert Hall, *Leave Your Language Alone* (Ithaca, N.Y.: Linguistica, 1950).

[23] "The essential merits in the recommendations of Bloomfield are these: (a) Whatever the rationale a learning situation in early stages should be designed so that the perception of a printed word is conditioned to a previously established phonetic habit, instead of trying to condition an oral response to the printed word. (b) The child should be given an inkling of awareness about the nature of English orthog-

methods of teaching reading preferred at the time (1953) neglected a linguistic view of reading methodology, perhaps to their detriment. Dr. William S. Gray, perhaps the most eminent reading theorist of the 1930–1950's, Carroll states, viewed Bloomfield's suggestions with alarm in his *On Their Own in Reading* (Chicago: Scott, Foresman and Co., 1948). Gray wanted the child "to acquire phonetic word-analysis skills by generalizing from his experience in learning words as wholes, while Bloomfield [was] willing to present at least some of the bare facts about phonemic word analysis in the earliest reading lessons." Thus, "While Gray may scorn Bloomfield's approach as 'old-fashioned,' it is possible that a partially alphabetic approach, seasoned with refinements contributed by linguists and psychologists, may have considerable merit" (Carroll, p. 148). (5) Finally, Carroll corrects such misconceptions of Dr. Gray and other reading specialists as the belief that the linguists would denounce the learning of words as wholes in the early stages. Carroll is aware that ". . . the linguist would merely wish to give the child every kind of assistance in developing word-perception skills; he would regard instruction in the nature of sound-symbol relations as a highly effective kind of assistance" (p. 149).

These contributions, which clearly indicated a need for the "Look-Say" proponents to reconsider their approach, preceded Flesch's *Why Johnny Can't Read* by two years, but at the time Carroll hardly made a dent in the thinking of those primarily concerned with the teaching of reading. The long-range outlook is more hopeful.

Brown, too, has made contributions that promise to influence some of the future approaches to reading as a process. Some of the most important of these are the following: (1) A reinterpretation of Cattell's findings,[24] which had formed much of the "scientific" basis for the look-and-say method of teaching reading. Brown suggests that there is no proof that Cattell's subjects were not reading individual letters rather than "total word pictures" because the high level of redundancy in English makes it possible that they were generalizing from observed letters and not seeing words as units.[25] (2) The development of the positions that the use of whole words as teaching materials is as possible in phonetic training as in look-and-say recognition training and that phonetic generalizations are learned more rapidly and perhaps more certainly when explicitly stated than when developed inductively. "The educator who would claim that phonetic generalizations are better learned by incidental induction than by direct formulation with examples, assumes the burden of proof. His claim does not conform to popular belief nor has it been demonstrated in the laboratory. If you really want your pupil to learn a phonetic rule it seems

---

raphy even at the earliest stages. This is true even when a method emphasizing the learning of words as wholes is employed" (p. 147).

[24] J. M. Cattell, "Über die Zeit der Erkennung und Benennung von Schriftzeichen, Bildern, und Farbern," *Philosophische Studien,* II (1885), 635–650. Another source that advocates of the look-and-say method had relied upon for scientific support was L. E. Javal, "Essai sur la Physiologie de la Lecture," *Année d'Oculistique,* LXXXII (1878), 242–253.

[25] As partial support for this argument Brown points to R. S. Woodworth, *Experimental Psychology* (New York: Holt, Rinehart & Winston, 1948), p. 71: ". . . while the general shape of a word has some clue value, the clear view of the letters is a more important factor in word identification. . . . The adult reader is able to identify many words at a glance but it may be that this ability is best developed out of a letter-by-letter reading."

sensible to tell him the rule" (p. 74). (3) The presentation of the view that children *can* begin reading training by the phonic method about two years earlier than had been thought possible. After citing some empirical evidence in support of this position, Brown states, "It seems clear that children can gain from phonic training even before the first grade, and it would appear that a good way to build reading readiness is by instruction in reading" (p. 75).

Opportunities for Using Phonetic and Linguistic Resources.[26] Such scholarly contributions as those of Carroll and Brown, the effective agitating of Flesch, and shifting times in education generally now make it profitable for phoneticians and linguists to enter the field of reading. Educators have needed the help of those who could answer with linguistic accuracy the loud and strong "phonetics-only" advocates,[27] and linguists have recognized that leaving the field to the linguistically uninformed could result in errors reflecting upon their own discipline.[28] Furthermore, they have feared that silence would cause outsiders to place them in the "phonics-only" category in the reading controversy, and they have come to feel a responsibility for making it clear that any method of teaching reading that fails to recognize the grapheme-phoneme-morpheme relationship is deficient. And who but the linguistically trained can impart this information accurately?

Out of this atmosphere of deep interest certain major findings, viewpoints,

[26] Phonetics and linguistics, of course, are not interchangeable terms. The distinction between *phonics* (not a linguistic term, but the name of an educational method of teaching reading) and *phonetics* (a term dealing with the scientific analysis of the sounds of languages and the sound systems of languages) also should be maintained.

[27] One problem has been the failure of those advocating phonics to understand the difference between the phonic and the linguistic approaches to reading. See, for example, the review of Bloomfield and Barnhart, *Let's Read: A Linguistic Approach* in the *Council for Basic Education Bulletin,* VI (Feb., 1962), pp. 11–12, where the approach to reading by Flesch and Bloomfield are considered as identical. In the essay "Introduction to Teachers" in *Let's Read,* pp. 5–8, Prof. Robert C. Pooley says correctly that Flesch was on valid grounds in pointing out the significance of sound in deriving meaning from printed symbols (the phonics approach) but "what Flesch lacked, or at least did not utilize, was a command of the science of linguistics, which would have provided him with an understanding of the relationship between sound and written form. His protest against current methodology was supported by much specific evidence, *but his solution was inadequate* and did not strike at the heart of the problem" (*Let's Read,* p. 6). [Italics ours.]

Bloomfield, of course, despite Flesch's stated dependence on him, condemned the "phonic approach" or "phonic methods." See his essay "Teaching Children to Read," *Let's Read,* p. 28.

[28] Evidence concerning the current interest in linguistics and reading is burgeoning. See, for example, the Conference Proceedings of the International Reading Association, *Scholastic Magazines,* VI (1961); the Program of the National Council of Teachers of English Annual Convention, November, 1962; the report on the Conference on Learning to Read, May, 1962; *Let's Read: A Linguistic Approach;* Henry Lee Smith, Jr., review of *Let's Read* in *Language,* XXXIX (March, 1963), 67–78; B. Robert Tabachnick, "A Linguist Looks at Reading," *Elementary English,* XXXIX, (Oct., 1962), 545–548; C. C. Fries, *Linguistics and Reading.* Also indicative of the interest in linguistics and reading are the special session on Linguistics and Reading called by Priscilla Tyler of Harvard University at the Ninth International Congress of Linguistics held at Cambridge, August, 1962, and the six-day conference of linguists, psychologists, and reading specialists held at the University of Indiana, January 21–26, 1963, and reported in *The Linguistic Reporter,* V (April, 1963), 5–6.

and conclusions emerge as those the most likely to make major contributions to the evolving methodology of reading instructions.[29] The succeeding paragraphs identify and describe seven of these.

First, language is a system of spoken symbols represented by written symbols (or graphemes); it is not, as the reading teacher ordinarily sees it, a system of written symbols. The Indiana Conference, 1963, gave the first priority among its conclusions to the recognition that a fundamental part of the beginning stage of learning to read "is the acquisition of associations between the sounds of the language and the letters and spelling patterns used to represent them. Consequently, one component of any effective program of reading should be a body of material which is based on systematic analysis of the important correspondences [between the sounds and the symbols they represent]." This stress on the primacy of speech is essential to an understanding of the linguist's position: any improvement in the ability to read, he believes, will come from effective teaching of the correspondence of graphemes to sounds.

Second and following from the first, the unlocking of meaning in the process of reading occurs by going from the printed word through the spoken form that already is part of the reader's vocabulary. "Letters and the forms they compose," says James P. Soffietti, "will not become clues or triggers to meaning until they have been vocalized into the phonemes or morphemes or words they spell."[30] Thus, immediate association of letters and meaning does not occur; instead, as Pooley writes of the Bloomfield method, the child proceeds "from the translation of letters into sounds and sounds into meanings."[31]

Third, a reading methodology that has neglected to point out the way in which communication occurs has been only a partial system. Instruction should include the learning of the segmental and the suprasegmental sound features plus the grammatical signals that are an inherent part of spoken language. Ruth G. Strickland, after a three-year study, concludes, ". . . children [may] need help to recognize and understand the entire phonemic scheme of English, not only the basic phonemes that are built into morphemes, but also the suprasegmental phonemes of pitch, stress and juncture as they use them in oral speech."[32]

Word order, function words, grammatical inflection, and melody all play roles in the communication of meaning, and ignorance of their roles leads to word-by-word reading and to the false notion that language is a series of interrupted,

[29] Of all the sources for the ideas that follow, the only one published prior to 1960 was James P. Soffietti, "Why Children Fail to Read: A Linguistic Analysis," *Harvard Educational Review*, XXV (Spring, 1955), 63–84. Soffietti's attack on current reading methodology appeared in the same year as Flesch's diatribe and with almost the same title. His undramatic, lucid presentation has been hardly noticed, although his suggestions were at least as important as those advanced by Flesch and perhaps more so. Both writers based their presentations on Bloomfield with Soffietti the closer.

[30] *Ibid.,* p. 69.

[31] *Let's Read,* p. 7.

[32] *The Language of Elementary School Children,* Bulletin of the School of Education, Vol. XXXVIII, No. 4 (Bloomington: Indiana University, July, 1962), p. 106. In agreement with this view is an article by Priscilla Tyler, who reviews linguistic findings dealing with the supra-segmentals of stress, pitch, and juncture in "Sound, Pattern, and Sense," *Scholastic Magazines*, VI (1961), 249–253. Miss Tyler originally presented this material as a paper at the 1961 International Reading Association. She was one of the first to present these concepts in detail to reading specialists at one of their conventions.

isolated, fragmented forms. No one speaks the English language without using suprasegmental sound features, paralinguistic signaling devices such as vocal modifiers of volume and rate, both bodily and facial expressions, and the pertinent grammatical signals. No well-trained reader should remain unaware of these facets of communication.

Fourth, thinking of sentences as "expressions of complete thoughts" or as "sequences of words that normally end in periods," though traditional, is inaccurate. Words alone don't make sentences, but are merely one element in a complex series of signals that in combination can indicate that a sentence has been spoken. Syntactic forms, function words, inflectional forms, and patterns of intonation, pause, and stress are essential signaling devices. Graphemes thus are a secondary system of symbols, and the actual language is the system of spoken symbols.

A consequence of this revised and fuller view of the sentence is that the reading teacher is obligated to teach children that sentences (at least English) consist of phonemic, grammatical, and syntactic signals and patterns spoken in a certain order and with certain specific pitch levels and stresses culminating in certain terminal junctures or pauses. He also should make it clear that the graphic system indicates to the reader not only *what* the speaker says but, to quite an extent, *how* he says it. Failure to teach this relationship of the graphic signals to their oral counterparts is a failure to teach reading in its full dimensions.[33]

Fifth, the fact that reading is first and foremost a *language process* means that the training of teachers of reading must include the serious study of phonetics and linguistics. The study of such language activities as writing, reading, interpreting, discussing, and telling, though necessary, are not substitutes for basic knowledge of the language process. As the Indiana Conference stated:

Instruction in linguistics, emphasizing such relevant matters as the nature and functioning of language as well as the structure of English and its sound-symbol correspondences and dialects, should be a part of the education of elementary teachers and of the programs of inservice training for them. Support must be found for the preparation of textbooks for this, teaching grants for teachers, setting up of special institutes, and the training of specialists in linguistics and reading.[34]

Sixth, further knowledge of language as practiced by children may lead to the reexamination of some concepts now taken for granted and to improved instruction. Particularly needed are studies of the language of children in their different social environments and of their sound systems and grammatical, syntactic, and melodic patterns. Strickland observed rightly in her 1962 study on the language of children that their oral usage is far more advanced than the language used in their readers and that perhaps greater knowledge of their speech could lead to the construction of better textbooks.

Still other types of research, of course, also are needed. The evidence concerning the age at which the child can profitably begin to learn to read is incon-

[33] For a good discussion of graphics and the reading teacher see Carl A. LeFevre, "Language Patterns and their Graphic Counterparts," in the Conference Proceedings of the Reading Association, *Scholastic Magazines,* VI (1961), 245–249.
[34] *The Linguistic Reporter,* V (April, 1963), 5.

clusive, and the best time for terminating instruction in reading as a separate part of the elementary school curriculum is unknown.

Seventh, the realization that different languages present different problems to their respective native readers not only is a basis for profitable comparative studies but also is essential to the avoidance of naive transfers of experimental results from one language to another. Languages represented by a writing system in which the graphemes are highly consistent with the phonemic forms of the languages (such as Finnish, German, or Italian) create fewer reading hurdles than do those in which the writing and the phonemic systems are not so close (such as French or English). And, of course, languages that contain syllabaries (like Japanese) or ideographs (like Chinese) or that omit diacritics for vowel indication (like Modern Israel Hebrew) or that employ distinctive tones (like Thai) have special complexities. In all languages the written forms inevitably stand for the spoken ones, and the possibility that certain instructional techniques found useful in one may be applicable to others should not be overlooked; the point is that carry-over is uncertain, for the reading problems in one language cannot be completely equated with those in another.

Both experimenters and classroom teachers also must realize that the reading problems of native and of nonnative speakers are not alike and that even individuals within the same nationality may differ in language patterns.

Conclusion

The scholar of speech and language has become important, if not central, to the study of reading practices. Adding his knowledge to the contributions of the psychologist, the reading specialist, and the classroom teacher is essential to the further development of methods of teaching the most important skill in the process of education. The linguist, however, wishes to stress that if reading encompasses the skills of recognizing the associations between sound and letter-patterns and if (as seems clear to the writers) such sound-symbol associations are central to the acquisition of the skill we know as reading, then every elementary school teacher *must* be at least somewhat trained as a phonetician and grammarian. As a minimum he must acquire knowledge of the sound system of his own language, a clear understanding of the correspondences of sounds and symbols, and some degree of familiarity with the major spoken dialects and the essential grammatical forms and structures.

Interdisciplinary approaches to scholarly research and to pedagogical problems have become highly fashionable in American education, and careful thought leads to the conclusion that improvement in instruction in reading is among those endeavors in which cooperative effort is necessary. The traditional view that silent reading is outside the field of speech must be modified. Those within speech departments who specialize in phonetics and linguistics possess special knowledge that is essential to the development of a full, scientific, and thoroughly modern theory of (silent) reading.

Further Reading for Chapter 4

Artley, A. Sterl. "Phonic Skills in Beginning Reading," *Education*, 82: 529–532; May, 1962.

Bond, Guy L., and Eva Bond Wagner. *Teaching the Child to Read*. New York: The Macmillan Co., 1966. Chapter 8.

Burrows, Alvina Treut, and Zyra Lourie. "When 'Two Vowels Go Walking.'" *The Reading Teacher*, 17: 79–82; November, 1963.

Dawson, Mildred A., and Henry A. Bamman. *Fundamentals of Basic Reading Instruction*. New York: David McKay Co., Inc., 1963. Chapter 10.

DeBoer, John J., and Martha Dallmann. *The Teaching of Reading*. New York: Holt, Rinehart & Winston, Inc., 1964. Chapter 6.

Durkin, Dolores. *Phonics and the Teaching of Reading*. New York: Bureau of Publications, Teachers College, Columbia University, 1965.

———. "What Schoolmen Should Know About Phonics," *Nation's Schools*, 73: 72; April, 1964.

Gans, Roma. "How Shall We Teach Phonics?" *Grade Teacher*, 80: 540–544; November, 1962.

Gray, Lillian. *Teaching Children to Read*. New York: The Ronald Press Company, 1963. Chapter 11.

Groff, Patrick. "To Teach or Not to Teach Accents?" *Elementary School Journal*, 62: 218–221; January, 1962.

Harris, Albert J. *How to Increase Reading Ability*. New York: David McKay Co., Inc., 1961. Chapters 12 and 13.

Heffernan, Helen. "Are the Schools Teaching Phonics?" *Grade Teacher*, 81: 60; October, 1963.

Heilman, Arthur W. *Phonics in Proper Perspective*. Columbus, Ohio: Charles E. Merrill Books, Inc., 1964.

———. *Principles and Practices of Teaching Reading*. Columbus, Ohio: Charles E. Merrill Books, Inc., 1961. Chapter 7.

Hendrickson, W. A. "Fundamental Approach to Education: A Report on the Reading Program at Oakley," *California Education*, 1: 1–2; June, 1964.

Hester, Kathleen B. *Teaching Every Child to Read*. New York: Harper & Row, Publishers, 1964. Chapter 11.

Hunt, Lyman. "The Right Question About Phonics," *Education*, 82: 540–544; May, 1962.

Ibeling, F. W. "Supplementary Phonics Instruction and Reading and Spelling Ability," *Elementary School Journal*, 62: 152–156; December, 1961.

McKee, Paul. *Reading: A Program of Instruction for the Elementary School*. Boston: Houghton Mifflin Company, 1966. Chapter 4.

Ramsey, Z. Wallace. "Will Tomorrow's Teachers Know and Teach Phonics?" *The Reading Teacher*, 15: 241–245; January, 1962.

Robinson, H. A. "A Study of the Techniques of Word Identification," *The Reading Teacher*, 16: 238–242; January, 1963.

Sabaroff, Rose. "Comparative Investigation of Two Methods of Teaching Phonics in a Modern Reading Program: A Pilot Study," *Journal of Experimental Education*, 31: 249–256; March, 1963.

Smith, Henry P., and Emerald V. Dechant. *Psychology in Teaching Reading*. Englewood Cliffs, N.J.: Prentice-Hall, Inc., 1961. Chapter 7.

Smith, Nila Banton. *Reading Instruction for Today's Children.* Englewood Cliffs, N.J.: Prentice-Hall, Inc., 1963. Chapters 8 and 21.

Spache, George D. *Reading in the Elementary School.* Boston: Allyn and Bacon, Inc., 1964. Chapter 12.

————, and Mary E. Baggett. "What Do Teachers Know About Phonics and Syllabication?" *The Reading Teacher,* 19: 96–99; November, 1965.

Tinker, Miles A., and Constance M. McCullough. *Teaching Elementary Reading.* New York: Appleton-Century-Crofts, Inc., 1962. Chapter 7.

Witty, Paul A., Alma Moore Freeland, and Edith H. Grotberg. *The Teaching of Reading: A Developmental Process.* Boston: D. C. Heath & Company, 1966. Chapter 6.

✤ *5* ✤

Improving Comprehension

Reading is comprehending; unless the reader understands what he reads, he is not, in the truest sense of the word, reading. Although others may define reading as nothing more than pronouncing words on a printed page, the teacher cannot afford the luxury of such a loose definition. If our goal is to teach boys and girls to read, it must be clearly understood that we have not yet achieved that goal until we have taught them to understand the printed page.

A complete acceptance of this fact has certain implications for the reading teacher. It implies that teaching pupils the skills of translating a printed word symbol into the correct word sound is *not* reading unless the pupil can think the necessary meaning for that sound. Consequently, neither the correct application of phonic rules nor an artificial orthography with consistent symbol-sound relationships which are known to the pupil will make him a reader. They may lead him to word sounds, but it is his understanding, his comprehension, of the printed page that makes him a reader.

Reading comprehension is one facet of a general linguistic ability which includes listening, speaking, writing, thinking, and reading. The same linguistic symbols are used in these processes; only the forms of the symbols change. An acceptance of the place of reading comprehension in our general linguistic patterns, however, must not lead to the conclusion that it cannot or should not be taught in a series of specific reading-comprehension skills.

Far too often, a teacher's efforts to improve reading comprehension fail to take the form of direct instruction in specific comprehension skills. Sometimes there seems to be an almost mystical belief that these skills will emerge without direction if the child merely reads widely. Of course, every child should read widely, and there may be some who will develop some skills of comprehension unaided, but it is no more sensible to expect the child to do this without our direct help than to expect him to develop a full knowledge of our number system without our help.

In some cases our efforts to improve the child's reading comprehension may inappropriately take the form of exhortations to "try harder." Johnny is told to read a chapter in his social-studies text, subsequent questioning indicates that he has not comprehended the chapter, and, in our most severe tones, we tell him to read it again and, "This time, understand it."

As James B. Stroud points out in the first selection in this chapter, reading comprehension can be improved when we view it not as a general ability without subdivisions but as a series of abilities which can be directly taught.

126

These specific abilities include, among others, the abilities to use punctuation marks and typographical signals, to interpret metaphor, to see relationships between sentences, to discover the topic of a paragraph, and to select ideas for a given purpose.

In the second selection, Olive S. Niles divides reading comprehension into the three skills she considers most essential and then suggests specific techniques for developing these skills. In the following selection, Guy Wagner and Max Hosier suggest eight techniques the reading teacher may use to improve reading comprehension.

In the last selection, Paul Hollingsworth summarizes the results of a number of research studies which prove the value of certain kinds of listening exercises for improving reading comprehension. This area of teaching children to listen for certain specific purposes in order to improve their abilities to read for those specific purposes is an efficient, effective way to improve reading comprehension that is too often neglected.

Reading and Linguistic Behavior

✣ JAMES B. STROUD

Is there a special problem of reading comprehension? Reading comprehension appears to be simply a part of what we mean by comprehension of all forms of communicative behavior. The primary duty of the teacher of reading is to teach pupils to read, to develop what we call the basic skill of reading. Once a pupil has acquired this skill or to the extent that he has done so, he should be able to read any linguistic message that he is capable of understanding. He should comprehend it when he reads it as well as he does when he hears it. This, of course, does not deny that one may read, by one definition, things he does not understand.

Linguistic behavior is perhaps our best example of a generalized ability; better, or at least more remarkable, than counting. To be sure, one who has learned to count can count all things that are discernible to any of his senses, but he always uses the same names in the same order. In all of our discussion of transfer of training, we have largely overlooked the best example of it of all, the generalization of linguistic behavior. It is possible that the mature adult has never encountered precisely the same sentence twice in his life, except for quotations or in an occasional professor's lectures. In all the libraries of a great university, one probably could not find two sentences that are identical. Be this as it may, one's understanding of a linguistic message is in no wise dependent upon his having encountered it before.

There is another and remarkable sense in which linguistic behavior generalizes. Once a pupil has acquired command of the structure of a language and its symbols, he can utilize these in all the ways language can be used: in talking, listening, reading, writing, and thinking. In all cases, this is the same language, the same symbols, the same syntax. Only the mechanism varies. As Hockett has said, one can reproduce any linguistic message he undertands. It makes no difference whether he sees it, hears it, thinks it, writes it, or speaks it. The latter comes about from the fact of feed-back and internalization, as Hockett again suggests. Or, as Faris has said, when one is saying something to another, he is saying the same thing to himself.

It is not surprising that the correlations between reading comprehension scores and listening comprehension scores are about as high as those between two reading tests or those between two listening tests of comparable reliabilities. While there probably are some skills specific to each medium, the central problems of understanding are the same. Once a pupil has learned to read, he is in a position immediately to comprehend reading matter and to utilize reading in the development of his comprehension and of his mind. It is not necessary to teach him all over again to comprehend. At least this responsibility does not rest primarily with the teacher of reading. The development of reading comprehension takes place as the mind develops, once the art of reading has been mastered. The

From *Psychology in the Schools*, 1: 92–93; January, 1964. Reprinted by permission. James B. Stroud is Professor of Education and Psychology, University of Iowa, Iowa City.

educative process *in toto* takes care of this. Comprehension is a generalized ability. Probably no part of it is specific to or limited to reading. No one has succeeded in carrying reading comprehension, in a given pupil, beyond his general level of comprehension. All teachers contribute to the development of this general level, the reading teacher no less nor probably any more than the arithmetic teacher, the language teacher, the science teacher, and so on.

In reading, one must know what he is reading about, just as in talking, he should know what he is talking about. A fund of knowledge is required, not only in reading and talking, but in writing, thinking, and observing. This fund of knowledge is stored. It is a general fund that is drawn upon in all linguistic behavior. How it was acquired is of no consequence. One may have heard it, read it, observed it, or reasoned it out for himself. It generalizes to all linguistic behavior.

Happily, it is not the responsibility of the teacher of reading to supply this knowledge. The educational system and society supply it. He may have some part to play in it. This raises the question of the informational content of the basal reader series. The position taken here is that there are other overriding considerations in the preparation of such a series, or in choosing one. The primary function of the series is to teach the pupil to read, to develop the general skill of reading, to bring these skills into play and teach them. Perhaps interest value should be given a high place. Such matters as knowledge, citizenship, and moral values can be and are taught and learned elsewhere.

Obviously, a pupil brings to bear upon any reading situation his linguistic ability, including his powers of thought, and his knowledge wherever and however acquired. These he also brings to the problem of learning to read. If reading comprehension, apart from comprehension in general, can be taught so well, why is it so difficult to teach deaf-born children to understand what they read?

Of course, it is possible to learn to say the words on the page, and do so with considerable aplomb, without understanding much of anything. An occasional school child manages to do this as does almost any phonetician who "reads" a language unfamiliar to him. But this is not to deny that when one does read properly, he does so by linguistic generalization. A teacher could not prevent this, any more than he could prevent phonetic generalization.

Comprehension Skills

❖ OLIVE S. NILES

Middle-of-the-road reading teachers seem universally to agree that teaching students to read with comprehension is their major responsibility. Colleagues to the far right sometimes appear to leave the concept of comprehension out of their definition of reading. They talk as if they equated word pronunciation with reading. If this equation existed, phonics might indeed be the panacea for all ills. Colleagues on the far left, on the other hand, among them those who favor the more extreme forms of "individualized reading," often exhibit surprising faith that ability to comprehend will appear somehow with a minimum of specific teaching of comprehension skills.

Lists of comprehension skills which appear in professional books on the teaching of reading often seem formidable to teachers, who wonder how they can teach all the comprehension skills and also the word recognition and word meaning skills, the locational skills, the oral reading skills, and perhaps others. The question arises: Is it really necessary to teach all these skills separately? Are they truly basic or are they, perhaps, at least one step removed from those abilities, probably much fewer in number, which are truly fundamental to the process of comprehension?

The number of skills to be taught could probably be reduced if teachers got closer to an understanding of what is essential. Also, the time and effort expended in teaching skills would have a greater effect upon the student's power to read. In the writer's opinion, there are three abilities which clearly differentiate between the reader who comprehends well and the one who does not.

The first of these abilities is the power to find and understand thought relationships: in single sentences, in paragraphs, and in selections of varying lengths. Ideas are related to each other in many ways. Here is a simple example of the most common kind of thought relationship:

During our visit to the museum, we saw the first Stars and Stripes ever carried in battle; after that we enjoyed a collection of old silverware, later wandered into the room filled with Indian relics, and finally found ourselves absorbed in a display of old wedding gowns.

The parts of this sentence, obviously, are related to each other chronologically. We follow the trip through the museum in the time order in which the rooms were visited.

Now examine the same sentence parts arranged in a different way:

From *The Reading Teacher,* 17: 2–7; September, 1963. Also published as Improve-*ment of Basic Comprehension Skills: An Attainable Goal in Secondary Schools,* a Scott Foresman Monograph on Education (Chicago: Scott, Foresman & Company, 1964) and "Developing Basic Comprehension Skills," in *Speaking of Reading,* compiled and edited by John K. Sherk (Syracuse, N.Y.: Syracuse University Press, 1964). Reprinted with permission of Olive S. Niles, the International Reading Association, Scott, Foresman & Company, and John K. Sherk. Olive S. Niles is Director of Reading, Springfield Public Schools, Springfield, Massachusetts.

During our visit to the museum, we saw a collection of old silverware, an absorbing display of old-fashioned wedding gowns, a room filled with Indian relics, and the first Stars and Stripes ever carried in battle.

This sentence tells less than the preceding one. We know what the visitor saw, but we cannot follow him from room to room. The relationship present among the parts of this second sentence is a simple listing.

Here is another sentence:

During our visit to the museum, we enjoyed seeing the first Stars and Stripes ever carried in battle and the absorbing display of old-fashioned wedding gowns much more than we did the room filled with Indian relics and the collection of old silverware.

Now the ideas have a comparison-contrast relationship. The things the author saw have fallen into two groups: two displays which he enjoyed, two others he liked much less. An important *additional* meaning has been added because the relationship of the parts of the sentence is different.

Once more, observe the same facts but in a fourth relationship:

Because, on our visit to the museum, we had seen the first Stars and Stripes ever carried in battle, a room full of Indian relics, a display of old silverware, and a collection of old-fashioned wedding gowns, we were able to present a successful class program in which we compared relics of the past with their modern equivalents.

In this last sentence, we have a cause-effect relationship. The experiences of the museum visit have produced an effect: a successful class program.

These four kinds of thought relationship — time, simple listing, comparison-contrast, and cause-effect, plus others — occur in a great many combinations, some of them complex. The ability to observe and to use these relationships seems to be one of the basic comprehension skills.

The ability to set specific purposes in reading is a second important ability or skill. William G. Perry has reported a study done with fifteen hundred Harvard and Radcliffe freshmen to determine their habits of study when presented with a typical chapter in a history text.[1] In presenting his results, Perry has this to say:

We asked anyone who could do so to write a short statement about what the chapter was all about. The number who were able to tell us . . . was just one in a hundred-fifteen. As a demonstration of obedient purposelessness in the reading of 99 per cent of freshmen we found this impressive . . . after twelve years of reading homework assignments in school they had all settled into the habit of leaving the point of it all to someone else.

These same freshmen were able to do very well on a multiple-choice test based on the details of the material they had read.

If this purposelessness in study exists among students like those at Harvard, what must be the case with others less able? It might be argued that the moral

---

[1] William G. Perry, Jr., "Students' Use and Misuse of Reading Skills: A Report to the Faculty," *Harvard Educational Review,* Vol. 29, No. 3, Summer, 1959.

of the tale is that teachers should give better assignments in which they *tell* students what to look for. But it would seem more important to suggest that by the time young people are freshmen at Harvard, it is high time they know how to set their own purposes. It is obvious that Perry questions whether the students he tested had any real comprehension at all. They could answer multiple-choice questions, but they failed to get, as he says, the "point of it all."

Suppose, for example, that a student is studying a chapter about life on the Southern plantations. The inefficient reader plods straight through the material, often with wandering attention because his goal is only to "read the lesson." Contrast the careful attention to detail, the search for visual imagery of the student who studies the same chapter in order to make a drawing of the plantation grounds. Contrast again the procedures of the student who wants to compare the way of life of the Southern plantation with that in colonial New England. Or, again, the method used by a student whose responsibility is to report on one very specific topic: the duties of the mistress of the plantation. This last student, if he is reading efficiently, will skim rapidly through the chapter until he comes to a paragraph which seems to have a bearing on his special topic, then settle down to read carefully for detail. The student who thus reads with purpose, and its corollary, flexibility, has comprehension impossible to the student who merely "reads."

A third basic comprehension skill is the ability to make full use of previous learning in attacking new material. It is "reading readiness" in an extended form.

Jokes sometimes make an adult realize how a child must feel when he has to read something for which he does not have the requisite readiness. The following is supposed to be a story told by Helen Taft Manning about her father. When Taft was recuperating from a spell of illness, he wired a friend of his recovery and remarked that he had just taken a long horseback ride. The friend wired in reply, "How is the horse?"

Whether the reader sees anything funny at all in this story depends entirely upon whether he happens to remember from his previous reading or from pictures he may have seen that Taft was one of the heftiest of our presidents.

It is partly a matter of chance whether a reader happens to have a fact like this stored up in his head, but there is more to it than chance. Many students actually have the background information for full comprehension but fail to realize that they have it and to use it. Associational reading — the act of drawing upon all one has experienced and read to enrich what he is currently reading — is a skill which can be taught.

To summarize to this point: If an analysis is made of what lies at the foundation of comprehension, there seem to be at least three basic skills: (1) the ability to observe and use the varied relationships of ideas, (2) the ability to read with adjustment to conscious purpose, and (3) the ability to make full use of the backlog of real and vicarious experience which almost every reader possesses.

These basic skills are developed and strengthened in part by the kind of questioning which teachers use. Questions must be of the type which clarify thought relationships expressed in the material and which bring into focus meaningful associations with previous reading and experiences. "Thought" questions can turn a superficial test of comprehension into a learning experience.

Suppose, for example, that students have read an account of the Olympic Games. It is obvious that the first and last in the following set of four questions will make pupils use their comprehension skills, while the second and third will merely test their ability to skim or, if the exercise is unaided recall, to remember a couple of facts:

1. Why do the Olympic Games today feature a marathon race?
2. Who suggested that a marathon be added to the Olympics?
3. What is the official distance of the modern marathon?
4. Does anyone know of a famous American marathon race? Can you tell about it?

The kind of question is important. So, also, is the timing of the questions. Most questions should precede reading rather than follow it. If students knew *before* they read about the Olympics that they were to look for the cause-effect relationship required in Question 1 above and that they should be making the associations with previous knowledge called for in Question 4, they would read the account with better comprehension because the questions would guide their reading. Questions asked *before* help students set purposes; questions asked *after* may do little but test.

A second kind of guidance which helps students learn basic comprehension skills involves the application of the directed-reading-lesson pattern of teaching to lessons in the curricular areas such as social studies, science, and literature. Teachers in elementary schools are very familiar with the directed reading lesson, which appears so often in the manuals of basal readers. Applied to a lesson in one of the content areas, it starts with the development of background and purpose. The teacher builds readiness for the new lesson by introducing new vocabulary and concepts and by reviewing materials from previous lessons or from the students' experiences to show them how the new content connects with the old. He also helps them set purposes for study. After skimming through the pages of the lesson, looking at pictures, reading headings, reviewing what they already know about the subject, students are able to answer questions like these: "Is this a lesson we can read rapidly or must we study it carefully? Why? What are some of the things we should try to find out in this lesson? What questions can we anticipate *before* we read? How can we use this new information?"

It is during this first part of the directed lesson that students learn one of the basic skills: how to set purposes for reading.

The second step, silent reading and study, will be effective in proportion to the skill and thoroughness with which students are guided during the first step.

The third part of the lesson is the follow-up, usually some kind of questioning or testing. The type of questions and discussion the teacher uses determines how much students improve in their understanding of thought relationships and how much skill they acquire in making associations between what they are presently studying and the many other things they know — in fact, whether or not they get the "point of it all." Thus two more of the basic skills receive constant practice if the directed-reading-lesson pattern is used.

It is the writer's experience that some secondary teachers react negatively to this procedure. They may feel that it helps the student too much. He ought to be more on his own. The truth is that most students, even some very able ones, are not ready to study alone by the time they enter secondary school; we should be well content if they have acquired complete independence by the time they are ready for graduation. Skillful teachers know how to allow students to take more and more responsibility until one day, for most students not until some time late in senior high school, it is time to introduce SQ3R[2]. SQ3R is a grown-up directed reading lesson. The steps are virtually the same, but now the student is on his own. That Robinson's well-known technique is not more successful and popular stems from the fact that students have been expected to learn and use it before they are ready.

Teachers need to know what materials are available with which to help students learn comprehension skills. Many reading texts and workbooks have been written, some of them very useful, though, as has been implied earlier, the tendency has probably been to fragmentize the skills and perhaps to confuse both teachers and students by presenting too many *different* skills to teach and learn. Many of the exercises are tests of the application of the skills rather than devices for teaching them. Too often, they consist merely of passages to read followed by questions for students to answer. It is the unusual practice exercise which really shows the student how to see relationships, set purposes, and make associations.

Probably the very best materials for teaching comprehension skills are the regular textbooks in social studies, science, and literature. Because the student knows that the content of these books is important to him, he approaches them with a very different attitude from that with which he does a practice exercise in a workbook. He welcomes the teacher's help in seeing relationships and making associations which guide him in his task of understanding and remembering. Setting purposes for study makes sense to him. Every lesson in every textbook is a potential source for the best teaching of reading skills. Few secondary teachers seem to realize this. They are always searching for something different — something "special." Or, on the other hand, they make the assumption that the mere act of assigning reading in a textbook will insure growth in reading skill. Assigning is not synonymous with teaching. Only when the majority of teachers in secondary schools realize that purposeful teaching of reading skills is necessary in the everyday work of the content fields will the "reading problem" be solved.

What role does library or "individualized" reading have in this process of building comprehension skills? A very important one, but *not* the kind of role which most enthusiasts for "individualized reading" seem to visualize. Every bit of reading which a person ever does is a potential source of background understanding for all the reading he will do in the future. "Reading maketh a full man," said Francis Bacon, and he must have meant full of ideas, full of understandings, full of the background for rich comprehension. Any reader's experience can make this clear. He chooses a book or article on some subject with which he is familiar and reads easily with full and deep comprehension.

Contrast this experience with what happens when a reader undertakes to read a book in a field in which he has had no background of experience or previous reading. He can make no associations; he probably has no particular purpose except the very general one of getting some ideas about this new field; he misses many of the relationships which are obvious to the sophisticated reader in the field.

[2] Francis P. Robinson, *Effective Study*, Revised Edition (New York, Harper, 1961).

Here, then, is the reason why a broad program of individualized or library reading is essential to the development of comprehension skills, not that it is likely, as some authorities have claimed, that most teachers will be able to do a good job of teaching the skills as a part of the individualized program itself. Rather, through the reading of many books, children acquire the understanding and the background which make the teaching of full comprehension skills possible.

If the skills described here are accepted as fundamental to good reading, teachers must make sure that students themselves understand and accept them. The practice of a skill without the student's understanding of what and why he is practicing leads to success in only a hit-or-miss fashion. Strong motivation, so necessary in learning any skill, springs from two main sources: specific evidence of progress in learning the skill and proof of its practical application. The more teachers share their own purposes and understanding with their students, the more likelihood of success in their teaching.

Helping Them Hear and See What They Read ✤ Guy Wagner and Max Hosier

It might be useful as well as novel, if someone were to invent a device which showed a *red* light when a child was oblivious to meaning while "reading," and a *green* light when the words were registering on him. Of course, the device would be even more valuable if it had a rheostatic control to indicate *degree of comprehension (or misunderstanding)* by the relative intensity of the red or green light. Such a machine would be most helpful to the teacher of children who are just beginning to read, because that teacher has the important responsibility of helping children to see and hear as they read.

Communication involves both sender and receiver. We send by speaking or writing. We receive by listening or reading. When he reads, the child must hear the printed word with his ear instantaneously as he sees it with his eye. He must be made to realize that books and other reading material are only *printed talk*. The writer would be saying those words, if he were present.

Following are some practical suggestions which may help you teach your children to *hear, see,* and *understand* what their eyes report that the writer wanted to communicate.

I. Have pupils suggest ways in which they can better hear and see what they read:

You might explain that in a sense "you make your own private television show of what you read." When the children note that the teacher is interested

From *Grade Teacher*, 82: 96–100; March, 1965. Reprinted from *Grade Teacher* magazine by permission of the publishers. Copyright March, 1965, by Teachers Publishing Corporation. Guy Wagner is Director, Curriculum Laboratory, and Max Hosier is Supervisor of Student Teaching, Price Laboratory School, State College of Iowa, Cedar Falls.

in their learning to form "pictures complete with sound" as they read, they will be eager to share and listen to suggestions of classmates which will help them develop this reading skill. It is interesting to note the perceptive observations which pupils in one fourth-grade class offered in this connection . . . .

"You should draw your own picture in your brain as you read."

"The excitement of the book helps me see and hear it."

"Every time I read, I always have a picture in my mind, like if I am reading about the jungle and it says the drums started I can just feel and hear the drums pounding."

"When I read what people are saying I imagine what their voices sound like."

"Sometimes I stop reading and imagine that I'm seeing and hearing everything in the story."

Perhaps the best statement was made by a nine-year-old boy who said, "I compare what I'm reading with the same thing I normally hear and see. This way I can hear most anything in a book and can imagine pictures to go along with it."

II. Have pupils read orally what they have written:

Because the pupil *is* the writer he knows what he wants the reader to see and hear. Thus, you can encourage him to use the proper intonation and expression in conveying his meaning. The reader should explain to the listeners just what he is trying to help them "see and hear," and then show, by reading aloud, how he does this with proper expression.

Even letters to classmates who are ill, to relatives who have given them gifts, and to friends relating interesting events may be appropriate for this type of expressive oral reading.

The reading of original poetry is particularly effective. The following poem was shared with a fourth-grade class at Halloween. The nine-year-old girl who wrote it read with sparkling expression and with a face that radiated enthusiasm. The attentiveness of her pupil audience gave evidence that they were seeing and hearing the pictures painted by this budding poet.

> Hello, Mr. Pumpkin, round and yellow!
> You're such a funny, spooky fellow,
> With big eyes glaring like the sun,
> But I'm not afraid! I won't run!
>
> Hello, Miss Witch, black and scarey,
> You're nothing but a Halloween fairy,
> I hear you said "Boo!" — just in fun,
> But I'm not afraid! I won't run!
>
> How d' you do, Miss Ghost, dressed in white!
> I knew I'd meet you on Halloween night,
> Oh, but your face is a frightful one!
> But I'm not afraid! I won't run!
>
> Hi, Mr. Goblin with whiskers brown!
> Come on, chase me up and down!
> I know what mischievous tricks you've done,
> But I'm very brave! I won't run!

III. Have pupils illustrate paragraphs which they have read:

Parents of primary-grade children have long enjoyed the "artwork" their children do, illustrating stories or parts of stories. Intermediate grade teachers use this technique to a lesser extent but this type of pictorial activity does help bring meaning to the printed page and is one which could be worthwhile as voluntary homework.

Pupils can share their pictures with classmates, telling what it was that prompted them to illustrate as they did. This would be a good time to have pupils read orally the part from which a picture emerged. Other children, especially in a small group, might explain what kind of a picture they would use in interpreting the writing. *They should always read the paragraphs as they think the writer would have said them.*

Children should have practice in rethinking their pictures as they progress through the story or article so as to develop a clearer picture of what the writer had in mind. They also need to rehear the sounds of speech inherent in the reading matter, for example, as their understanding of the character of Grumpy evolves, they might note that he had a very complaining type of voice.

IV. Utilize instructional games which motivate expressive oral reading:

Games have intrinsic motivation as children want to see and hear through the game element. The more they do *see* and *hear* the clearer becomes the purpose and conduct of the game.

In our book, *Reading Games — Strengthening Reading Skills with Instructional Games* (Teachers Publishing Corporation, Darien, Connecticut), we describe a number of games which will help children to be better oral readers. One of them — "Wishing" — has for its purpose, to motivate interest in writing good paragraphs and, in turn, reading these expressively to the class. The teacher says, "If you could turn your chair into an airplane, what would you do?" The children then read their paragraphs to the class, using appropriate expression. In another — "Let's Act It Out" — the children practice interpreting what they hear or read. They write short stories which they read to the class, and then these stories are dramatized by a selected group. The rest of the children give their reactions to the actors' portrayal of the scene.

An example of one of these short stories is: "Mary and her mother are shopping in a department store for a new dress for Mary. A clerk comes up to help them. Mary looks at several dresses before choosing the one she wants. She would like to have a pair of shoes also, so she asks her mother if she may buy some." This and similar stories are quite short, but the readers or listeners are motivated to see and hear the scene portrayed by the writer, and thus reading is made meaningful.

V. Have pupils read silently or orally a short selection and then repeat it in their own words:

The teacher encourages the pupils to begin their interpretation by saying, "I think the writer is trying to say this." Direct this activity toward having the pupils *enjoy* reconstructing sounds and scenes as they, the listeners, interpret the writer. Discuss the reasons for various interpretations by different pupils, with each pupil reading orally the way he interpreted what the writer wished to convey.

You can help pupils realize the intended meaning of the writer. In order that more pupils may participate in this activity, several groups can function in various parts of the room, quietly, so as to not disturb the other groups.

VI. Have pupils tape their reading, and during the playback note inflections, intonations, and expressions used:

Tape recorders are becoming important classroom equipment, especially in the field of the language arts. This technique is both intriguing and practical.

Expect a certain amount of smiles when tapes are first played back and recognize that "It is rather funny at first to hear our voices played back, but it will help us to improve our oral reading. Let's listen especially to see if our voices really showed that we were reading like people talk. How can we show with our voices what the writer would say if he were right here with us?" If you keep tapes over a period of time, the children can listen back, to note improvement. Progress in this somewhat neglected skill of oral reading is perhaps the best motivator for a pupil; as he see that he is doing a better job at portraying what the writer has written, he tries harder.

Use of the tape recorder lends itself well to small group activities or even to individual work. When taping, constructive suggestions from classmates should be shared.

VII. Capitalize on the sociodrama:

Pupils present sociodramas which indicate a mere parroting of words without any evidence of understanding and then repeat them with a clear understanding of what was read. Children enjoy dramatics, as anyone can note by watching even preschool children play-act. Here we find the sociodrama with its role-playing technique to be a potent teaching method.

Choose two committees to portray the two situations. The entire class can offer appropriate suggestions, complete with oral reading to illustrate their points. However, the two groups need to work independently in their final preparations.

After each group presents its version, the class discusses the points illustrated by the actors.

This sociodrama should, of course, utilize actual reading, with the audience primed to note if they can *visualize* the scenes portrayed and *hear* the actual sounds inherent in the reading.

VIII. Make a judicious use of the coach-pupil system:

In this teaching technique, one child (the pupil) reads while the other (the coach) reports on what he has heard. Then the pupils reverse their roles.

In both instances, the coach tells *why* he heard what he did and reflects the expression used by the pupil. The pupil tries to read so that he truly says what the author would say if he were present. The coach offers only constructive criticism and is especially alert to note word pictures and sound effects.

This coach-pupil technique can be used in many types of school situations, but children need to be taught how to use the technique effectively. A demonstration worked out ahead of time by the teacher and a pupil would be helpful.

There are many other ways in which children can be guided to better see and hear what they read. For example, you show sound films, ask the children to put their heads on their desks for certain parts and just listen to form their own pictures of what is taking place. Then back the film up and show again with pupils matching *their* pictures with those seen on the screen. You can display pictures and have the children write short stories which relate to the pictures. Then they read the stories and explain how the story goes with the picture.

Can Training in Listening Improve Reading?

PAUL M. HOLLINGSWORTH

This question has been asked many times by teachers, administrators, and researchers. Will training in listening improve the pupil's reading abilities? Edna Lue Furness (6) in her study stated: "The modern academic term 'communication' acknowledges a basic relationship between reading and listening." Does this basic relationship between listening and reading mean, however, that improvement in the one skill will make an improvement in the other skill? To answer these questions, various studies in this area have been made.

Interrelationship Between Listening and Reading

Dow (5) reported approximately eighteen factors of reading comprehension that seem sufficiently similar to listening comprehension to consider these two receptive skills closely related. Just because they may be similar, however, does not indicate that they are identical. Wiksell (16) wrote that in reading one is able to adapt his own rate to the difficulty or nature of the reading material; however, listening demands a great deal more, inasmuch as the listener must follow the speaker no matter what the rate of speaking may be. Thus, in listening there is little time for reflection, which is so important in reading.

Hampleman (7) reported in his study of fourth- and sixth-grade pupils that skill in both listening and reading requires that active thinking be applied to symbols and that listening should be distinguished from mere hearing and reading from mere seeing.

Reading and listening do have things that they share in common and they are interrelated. Austin (1) reported that listening and learning to organize spoken language play an important role in understanding what is read. In her work with the primary grades she indicated that the listening program is an important aid to reading comprehension.

Cleland and Toussaint (4) determined the degree of relationship between selected tests of listening and reading. They found that the measure showing the closest relationship with reading was the Sequential Tests of Educational Progress Listening Test.

From *The Reading Teacher,* 18: 121–123, 127; November, 1964. Reprinted with permission of Paul M. Hollingsworth and the International Reading Association.
Paul M. Hollingsworth is Associate Professor of Education and Director, Reading Center, University of Nevada, Reno.

Vineyard and Bailey (15) did a study similar to that of Cleland and Toussaint, but this study was done with 114 second-semester freshmen students of Southwestern State College. Vineyard and Bailey found that reading ability, listening skill, and intelligence are highly related to one another.

Listening and Its Effects on Reading

Betts (2) reported a study in 1940 done at the fifth-grade level. He found a greater incidence of hearing impairment among the low achievers than among the high achievers. He felt that these findings may indicate a possible causal relationship, or that they reveal merely another difficulty for which the non-achiever must compensate. Hildreth (8) indicated that reading comprehension depends on comprehension of spoken language and that listening to correct English helps to improve recognition of the same expressions in print. Spache (13) suggested that measures of auding ability mark potential ceilings for reading ability.

Marsden (12) conducted a study to determine the effect of practice in listening (a) to decide upon the main idea of a selection, (b) to get the details on a given topic presented by a selection, and (c) to draw a conclusion from material presented. He tested the ability of 254 fifth- and sixth-grade pupils to read for these purposes. The lessons consisted of several short stories which were read by the teacher. Marsden concluded that the skills of reading a selection to note its main idea, to draw conclusions, and to note details were improved when opportunity to practice listening for these three purposes was given.

Lewis (10) conducted a study with intermediate grade pupils to determine the effect of training in listening (a) to get the general significance of a passage, (b) to note details presented on a topic by a passage, and (c) to predict the outcomes from a passage. Three hundred fifty-seven intermediate pupils in twelve classrooms were used. The program of training in listening consisted of thirty lessons of approximately fifteen minutes each. One lesson was given each day for six weeks. The teachers read the selections to the pupils. Each lesson included a listening exercise for each of the three purposes stated above. Lewis concluded that training in listening for the three purposes seemed to have a significant effect upon the ability of intermediate grade pupils to read for those same purposes.

Stromer (14) conducted a study to examine some of the relationships between reading, listening, and intelligence. He utilized three groups of students. These groups were: a listening group, a reading and listening group, and a reading group. The data collected seemed to indicate that the reading-listening method of training tends to increase the reading rate of the subjects.

Another research project, similar to those of Marsden and Lewis, was done by Kelty (9) in 1953 to determine the effect that training in listening for certain purposes had upon the ability of 188 fourth-grade pupils to read for those same purposes. The purposes referred to were: (a) deciding upon the main idea of a selection, (b) deciding upon the supporting details given in a selection, and (c) drawing a conclusion. The experimental group of ninety-four pupils was given thirty fifteen-minute lessons over a period of thirty days in listening. The control group received no instruction in listening. Kelty concluded that practice in listening for certain purposes favorably affects the ability of fourth-grade pupils to read for those same purposes.

Brown (3) pointed out that auditing ability supports reading ability during the first years in school, in which children learn to recognize the visual representation of words whose sound and sense already are familiar to a large extent.

Lubershane (11) conducted a study to determine if training in listening can improve reading ability. He had thirty-five pupils in the experimental group and thirty-seven in the control group, both groups from the fifth grade. The control group were given no listening exercises. The Metropolitan Reading Test for reading achievement was given before and after training. The experimental group was given auditory training exercises designed to improve written responses to oral commands. He concluded with a statement that auditory training may prove of value in reading programs, although no definite statistical proof of the value of these exercises in improving reading ability was found. The generally greater growth in reading ability in the experimental group suggested strongly that the auditory exercises had a positive effect on reading growth.

Conclusion

Can training in listening improve reading? Many of these research reports show that through the improvement of listening abilities reading can be improved. Listening does have a positive effect on reading achievement.

References

1. Austin, Martha Lou. "In Kindergarten Through Grades 3," *Methods and Materials for Teaching Comprehension,* Conference on Reading. Chicago: University of Chicago Press, 1960. Pp. 57–73.
2. Betts, Emmett A. "Reading Problems at the Intermediate-Grade Level," *Elementary School Journal,* 40: 737–746; June, 1940.
3. Brown, Don. "Auding as the Primary Language Ability," unpublished doctor's dissertation, Stanford University, 1954.
4. Cleland, Donald L., and Isabella H. Toussaint. "The Interrelationships of Reading, Listening, Arithmetic Computation and Intelligence," *Reading Teacher,* 15: 228–231; January, 1962.
5. Dow, Clyde W. "Integrating the Teaching of Reading and Listening Comprehension," *Journal of Communication,* 8: 118–126; Autumn, 1958.
6. Furness, E. L. "Improving Reading Through Listening," *Elementary English,* 34: 307; May, 1957.
7. Hampleman, R. S. "Comparison of Listening and Reading Comprehension Ability of Fourth- and Sixth-Grade Pupils," *Elementary English,* 35: 49–53; January, 1958.
8. Hildreth, Gertrude. "Interrelationship Among the Language Arts," *Elementary School Journal,* 48: 538–549; June, 1948.
9. Kelty, Annette P. "An Experimental Study to Determine the Effect of 'Listening for Certain Purposes' Upon Achievement in Reading for those Purposes," unpublished doctor's field study, Colorado State College of Education, 1953.
10. Lewis, Maurice S. "The Effect of Training in Listening for Certain Purposes upon Reading for Those Same Purposes," unpublished doctor's field study, Colorado State College of Education, 1951.
11. Lubershane, Melvin. "Can Training in Listening Improve Reading Ability?" *Chicago School Journal,* 43: 277–281; March, 1962.

12. Marsden, Ware. "A Study for the Value of Training in Listening to Achievement in Reading," unpublished doctor's field study, Colorado State College of Education, 1951.

13. Spache, George, D. "Construction and Validation of a Work-Type Auditory Comprehension Reading Test," *Educational and Psychological Measurement*, 10: 249–253; Summer, 1950.

14. Stromer, Walter Francis. "An Investigation into Some of the Relations Between Reading, Listening, and Intelligence," unpublished doctor's dissertation, University of Denver, 1952.

15. Vineyard, Edwin, and Robert Bailey. "Interrelationships of Reading Ability, Listening, Skill, Intelligence and Scholastic Achievement," *Journal of Developmental Reading*, 3: 174–178; Spring, 1960.

16. Wiksell, Wesley. "The Problem of Listening," *Quarterly Journal of Speech*, 32: 506; December, 1946.

Further Reading for Chapter 5

Bond, Guy L., and Eva Bond Wagner. *Teaching the Child to Read.* New York: The Macmillian Co., 1966. Chapters 9 and 10.

Dawson, Mildred A., and Henry A. Bamman. *Fundamentals of Basic Reading Instruction.* New York: David McKay Co., Inc., 1963. Chapters 11 and 13.

DeBoer, John J., and Martha Dallmann. *The Teaching of Reading.* New York: Holt, Rinehart & Winston, Inc., 1964. Chapter 7.

Gans, Roma. "They Read — But Do They Comprehend?" *The Education Digest,* 28: 48–50; April, 1963.

Gray, Lillian. *Teaching Children to Read.* New York: The Ronald Press Company, 1963. Chapter 12.

Harris, Albert J. *How to Increase Reading Ability.* New York: David McKay Co., Inc., 1961. Chapters 15 and 16.

Hester, Kathleen B. *Teaching Every Child to Read.* New York: Harper & Row, Publishers, 1964. Chapters 12 and 13.

McKee, Paul. *Reading: A Program of Instruction for the Elementary School.* Boston: Houghton Mifflin Company, 1966. Chapters 8, 9, 11, 12.

Newton, E. S. "Figurative Language: An Achilles Heel in Reading Comprehension," *Journal of Reading,* 8: 65–67; October, 1964.

Patterson, Charles W. "Pilot Project in Reading and Study Habits," *The Reading Teacher,* 17: 531–535; April, 1964.

Ruddell, Robert. "The Effect of Oral and Written Patterns of Language Structure on Reading Comprehension," *The Reading Teacher,* 18: 270–275; January, 1964.

Rushdoony, Haig. "Achievement in Map Reading: An Experimental Study," *Elementary School Journal,* 64: 70–75; November, 1963.

Schale, F. "Vertical Methods of Increasing Rate of Comprehension," *Journal of Reading,* 8: 296–300; April, 1965.

Shanker, Sidney. "Is Your Vocabulary Teaching Obsolete?" *The English Journal,* 53: 422–427; September, 1964.

Smith, Henry, P., and Emerald V. Dechant. *Psychology in Teaching Reading.* Englewood Cliffs, N. J.: Prentice-Hall, Inc., 1961. Chapters 8 and 13.

Smith, Nila Banton. *Reading Instruction for Today's Children.* Englewood Cliffs, N. J.: Prentice-Hall, Inc., 1963. Chapters 9, 10, and 22.

Tinker, Miles A., and Constance M. McCullough. *Teaching Elementary Reading,* New York: Appleton-Century-Crofts, Inc., 1962. Chapters 8, 9, 12.

6

Critical Reading

Modern reading programs are demonstrating an increasing awareness of the importance of critical reading. This growing emphasis may be coming from an appreciation of the increasing complexities of living today, or it may be simply a belated awakening to the fact that mere understanding of the printed page does not represent adequate reading maturity.

Critical reading is a special kind of critical thinking — it is critical thinking applied to the printed page. As such, it requires the reader to make various kinds of judgments about the author's ideas rather than to be satisfied with the simple understanding of those ideas.

Critical reading cannot be described adequately as a special kind of comprehension. It necessitates reading comprehension, of course, but it goes beyond this. To read critically, we must first understand what the author is saying, which requires us to use word-attack skills and to apply the various comprehension abilities which have been discussed previously. Beyond this, we must also be aware of the ideas the author does not state directly but which he implies. Once we understand what the author is saying to us, both directly and indirectly, we are able to apply critical-reading abilities to analyze his ideas.

Critical-reading abilities mature as the child progresses through school. There are some which we should begin fostering in the elementary grades but which do not reach full fruition until later years. There are others which, for many children, may be introduced most profitably when the child has attained an intellectual maturity normally occurring in later years.

Although we may not expect the pupil to attain complete mastery of critical reading in the elementary years, there are many reasons for beginning instruction at this level. First, the child develops certain habit patterns in reacting to what he reads, and a habit of blind acceptance should not become as firmly engrained as it may if left unchecked throughout the elementary grades. Second, the pupil will have many opportunities in the grade-school years to profit from this ability, for even at this level, there are reading materials which demand critical reading. Third, in a democratic society, it is essential that each individual attain the highest level of reading ability that he is capable of reaching. If our school programs are thoughtfully organized, an earlier start in critical reading may lead to more advanced ability in this area by the time the student leaves school.

As with many other learnings, pupils' abilities to read critically are greatly influenced by the general classroom environment that we engender. We cannot hope to help children develop a habit of questioning statements in print, which is necessary for effective critical reading, if, for example, we prevent pupils from questioning anything that we tell them.

But a free classroom environment only allows the seeds of critical reading to be planted; to nourish them, we must continually provide opportunities for growth and development through direct instruction and planned practice.

Some of the critical reading abilities which may be taught directly at the elementary-school level are (1) distinguishing fact from opinion, (2) recognizing assumptions and vague expressions, (3) recognizing propaganda techniques, and (4) judging the competence of a writer.

The three selections in this chapter present dimensions of critical thinking and reading and offer suggestions for developing them with students. The article by Robert H. Ennis deals with critical thinking of the type that could readily be applied to ideas expressed orally as well as to ideas expressed in print. It is, however, a brief, cogent explanation of various facets of critical thinking which can help the reading teacher understand some of the thought processes in which the good critical reader engages.

In the second selection, Helen W. Painter discusses the advisability of teaching critical reading and thinking in the primary grades. Although she does not favor specific lessons in critical reading, she offers fourteen different suggestions for ways in which this vital ability may be fostered in the early years.

In the last selection, Jeraldine Hill suggests several activities which may foster critical reading abilities in children in the middle grades.

A Definition of Critical Thinking

✤ ROBERT H. ENNIS

As a root notion, critical thinking is here taken to mean the correct assessing of statements. This basic notion was suggested by B. Othanel Smith (3): "Now if we set about to find out what . . . [a] statement means and to determine whether to accept or reject it, we would be engaged in thinking which, for lack of a better term, we shall call critical thinking." Since Smith's definition does not use any words like "correct," his notion is slightly different. Smith's concept of critical thinking, however, permits us to speak of "good critical thinking" and "poor critical thinking" without redundance or contradiction. Though this is an accepted manner of speaking, the predominant manner of speaking presumably builds the notion of correct thinking into the notion of critical thinking. Though the latter interpretation is used in this paper, it would be easy to restructure what follows and use Smith's concept. "Good critical thinking" in Smith's sense means the same as "critical thinking" as used in this paper.

Since there are various kinds of statements, various relations between statements and their grounds, and various stages in the process of assessment, we can expect that there will be various ways of going wrong when one attempts to think critically. In view of this fact, the aspects of critical thinking about to be presented, which may be looked upon as specific ways to avoid the pitfalls in assessment, are bound to make a rather heterogeneous list.

This list and the accompanying criteria for judging statements are based in a large part upon a study of the literature in education, philosophy, and psychology.[1] The list of critical thinking aspects is also based upon an analysis of a number of specimens of alleged justifications of statements, and a consequent realization of the places where these justifications can go wrong. One may look upon this list as a statement of a number of items that, if taught to students, will result in a greater likelihood that they will be critical thinkers. Further refinement of this list is a continuing task, and of course much remains to be done.

Major Aspects of Critical Thinking

A critical thinker is characterized by proficiency in judging whether:

1. A statement follows from the premises.
2. Something is an assumption.
3. An observation statement is reliable.

From *The Reading Teacher,* 17: 599–612; May, 1964. Reprinted with permission of Robert H. Ennis and the International Reading Association. Robert H. Ennis is Associate Professor of Education, Cornell University, Ithaca, New York.

[1] References that were of help can be found in Robert H. Ennis, "A Concept of Critical Thinking," *Harvard Educational Review,* 32: 81–111; Winter, 1962. The present article is a streamlined version of that article. The theoretical analysis of critical thinking and the proposals for needed research in that article also have been omitted here. The latter feature is expanded in an article entitled "Needed: Research in Critical Thinking," *Educational Leadership,* October, 1963.

4. A simple generalization is warranted.
5. A hypothesis is warranted.
6. A theory is warranted.
7. An argument depends on an ambiguity.
8. A statement is overvague or overspecific.
9. An alleged authority is reliable.

Although the root notion calls for its inclusion, the judging of value statements is deliberately excluded from the above list. This exclusion admittedly weakens the attractiveness of the list, but makes the job more manageable. So long as we remember that this exclusion has occurred, we should not be confused by the truncated concept. Perhaps this gap can at some future time be at least partially filled.

The exclusion of other important kinds of thinking (creative thinking, for example) from this basic concept of critical thinking does not imply that the others are unimportant, nor does it imply that they are separable from it in practice. This exclusion is simply the result of an attempt to focus attention on one important kind of thinking.

Another aspect which has deliberately been excluded from the list is proficiency in judging whether a problem has been identified. This is excluded not because it is unimportant, but because it resolves into one or another of the items on the list (or the judging of value statements) in each of the various meanings of "identifying a problem." This point will be developed later.

Each of the listed aspects of critical thinking will be examined and, if possible, criteria will be presented, clarified, and, when it seems necessary, at least partially justified.

1. Judging Whether a Statement Follows from the Premises

The concern of most logic books is with whether a statement follows *necessarily* from the premises. This is the judging of deduction. Reasoning in mathematics, "if-then" reasoning, and syllogistic reasoning all exemplify deduction.

The basic criterion is this: "A conclusion follows necessarily if its denial contradicts the assertion of the premises." Various rules have been developed for different types of deduction, but all see to it that this requirement is fulfilled. Well-developed sets of rules include:

1.1 The rules for handling equations and inequalities.
1.2 The rules of "if-then" reasoning:
    1.21 Denial of the "then-part" requires denial of the "if-part" but not necessarily vice versa.
    1.22 Acceptance of the "if-part" requires acceptance of the "then-part," but not necessarily vice versa.
    1.23 Instances of an "if-then" statement are implied by the "if-then" statement.
1.3 The rules for categorical reasoning.
    These rules may be summarized by the following: "Whatever is a member of a general class is also a member of whatever that general class is included in, and is not a member of whatever the general class is excluded from."

A number of cases of reasoning are parallel to strict deduction, but are different in that the generalizations in use as premises do not hold universally under any conceivable circumstance; they have exceptions and limits, not all of which can be specified. To extend Waisman's term (5), they are "open-textured." Reasoning from principles and hypotheses to the world of things, men, and events is inevitably of this sort. Sometimes the exceptions and limits are so far removed that we do not have to worry about them, and in such cases we can proceed as in deduction without fear of going wrong. Sometimes the limits and exceptions are close by, in which case, still approximating the deductive model, we use words like "probable," "likely," "barring unforeseen circumstances," etc., in the conclusion.

For an example of the latter case, consider the application of that standard law of economics, "If the supply is constant and the demand for a product decreases, the price will decrease." Two of the limits of the application of this law are within the knowledge of all of us. It is intended to apply to an economy free of government control and to a sector of it that is free of monopolistic control. Mention of these limits will suffice for present purposes, although there are others.

Now let us apply this law to a situation in which there is a decrease in demand for microscopes. Applying the law deductively, we are unalterably committed to a prediction of a price decrease. But it is not wise to be unalterably committed to such a prediction. For one thing, the well-known limits of the law might be breached: the government might decide to maintain the price of microscopes and pay for the destruction of the extras; or a monopoly might be formed to maintain the price.

But secondly, other things that are not yet explicitly built into the limits might go wrong. The makers of microscopes might form a trade association and decide incorrectly that with good advertising they *can* create a demand much greater than ever before, so that they can afford to raise prices. They therefore raise prices in anticipation of a nonexistent demand.

It is because of considerations like these that qualifiers like "probable" must be included in the application of many principles. The application of that law in that situation might be, "It is probable that there will be a lowering of price." But the application would not be this at all if it can be seen that a known limit is breached or that there is some other extenuating circumstance. The point is that the application of such principles should often not be stated any more strongly than this, even though the steps in reasoning parallel those of deduction.

Thus there are two kinds of following: strict necessity and loose following. The critical thinker can do both.

2. Judging Whether Something Is an Assumption

This topic is complicated because there are various logically different abilities that go under this title. These can be best approached through an examination of various uses of the word "assumption": the deprecatory use, the concluding use, the premise use, and the presupposition use.

2.1 *The Deprecatory Use and the Concluding Use.* The deprecatory use implies the charge that there is little or no evidence to support a given belief and that the belief is questionable. Here is an example: "You're just assuming that Frank didn't read the assignment." This deprecatory use is often found to be incorporated in the other uses, but sometimes it stands alone. As such its appearance is tantamount to a judgment that the view should perhaps be rejected, or at least be held in abeyance because of lack of support. No further discussion of the evaluation of this kind of assumption-claim is necessary here, since this is a general charge and is covered under discussion of the various other abilities.

In the concluding use, the term "assumption" is used to mark a conclusion, but the deprecatory use is involved too, since the conclusion is implied not to be fully established. Here is an example: "My assumption is that Hissarlik is at the site of Troy" (a statement made at the completion of a presentation of the evidence bearing on the location of Troy). We need not be concerned with discussing whether something is an assumption in the concluding sense; the important question is whether such an assumption is· justified and that question is covered elsewhere in this paper.

The first two uses of "assumption" were specified in order to keep them out of the discussion of the next two; the following discussion does not apply to them.

2.2 *The Premise Use.* This kind of assumption stands anterior to a conclusion in a line of reasoning, whether the conclusion be inductive or deductive. To call something an assumption is to say that the conclusion depends upon it, and that if the conclusion is to be accepted, the alleged assumption should also be accepted. Thus the location of assumptions (in this sense) is a useful step in the evaluation of conclusions.

Here are criteria for premise-type assumptions:

2.21 Of the various possible gap-fillers, the alleged assumption should come closest to making the completed argument, proof, or explanation a satisfactory one. (This criterion is necessary and sufficient.)
    2.211 The simplest gap-filler is ordinarily the one to choose.
    2.212 If there is a more plausible gap-filler among the more complex ones, it should be chosen. Plausibility, however, requires fitting in with existing knowledge — not being a special case.
2.22 Other conditions remaining the same, the state of affairs that is predicted could not occur (or probably would not occur) if the alleged assumption were false. (This criterion applies only to alleged empirically necessary assumptions, but for them it is necessary and sufficient.)
2.23 The community of experts in the field would not accept the position, conclusion, or argument without first believing the assumption to be true. (This criterion is neither necessary nor sufficient, but is a good ground.)

What is a gap-filler? Consider this piece of reasoning: "Since the demand for microscopes has decreased, the price may be expected to decrease." A gap-filler here would be:

1. When the demand for a commodity decreases the price will decrease. (It fills a gap in reasoning from the decrease in demand for microscopes to a decrease in price.)

It is not the only way to fill the gap, however. Consider these alternatives:

2. When the demand for goods and services decreases, the price decreases.
3. When the demand for optical instruments decreases, the price decreases.

4. When the demand for optical instruments (other than field glasses) decreases, the price decreases.

Since all four of these will fill a gap, it should be clear that being a gap-filler is not by itself a sufficient condition for being an assumption. The simplest gap-filler is ordinarily the one to attribute, thus ruling out No. 4. Simplicity might also be a ground for not accepting No. 2 as the assumption, since there is a conjunction of two things (goods and services) mentioned. But if the prevailing knowledge in economics admits no basis for distinguishing goods from services in the context of this principle, then simplicity is counter-balanced by the need to fit into existing knowledge. The first two gap-fillers would then be equally defensible (or indefensible) and either could be called the assumption.

Gap-filler No. 3 introduces a new twist, talking only about optical instruments. It is as simple as No. 1 but is not as general. Other things being equal, generality is to be preferred. A system of knowledge is better if it covers more cases. But if the more general gap-filler (1) should be false, and the less general one (3) true (or more likely to be true), the less general gap-filler is the one to choose.

Assumption-finding then is the locating of a gap-filler, the simpler the better, provided that it fits into and contributes to a system of knowledge. The assumption-finder should try to be generous to the person whose assumptions he is locating, generous in that he should try to find the best candidate for participation in a knowledge system. He should not accept a false gap-filler as the assumption until he has searched for one that fits into an acceptable body of knowledge. Put more simply in a way that covers most cases, he should search for one that is true.

While discussing gap-filling it would be well to note that there is one sometimes used criterion that is inapplicable: *logical* necessity. As exemplified by the four gap-fillers previously discussed, there is no single significant premise-type gap-filler which is logically necessary. It is always *logically* possible (though it may be extremely implausible) to compete an argument in more than one way, a point I have developed elsewhere (2).

Empirical necessity (2.22) is different. To the extent that empirical statements can be necessary, there can be empirically necessary assumptions. For example, a statement which predicts that the pressure in a fixed cylinder of confined air will increase is assuming that there will be a temperature increase. Since an increase in temperature in that situation *is* necessary for there to be an increase in pressure, the assumption is empirically necessary and can be pinned on the argument with confidence.

Criterion 2.23 mentions the experts. Although their considered opinions can be wrong, they do ordinarily know what fits into their body of knowledge. And they do know what is used successfully in the field to back up arguments and conclusions. So they can ordinarily be expected to know what an argument would need in order to be a good one.

2.3 *The Presupposition Use.* Presuppositions are sentences which must be true for a given statement even to make sense. This is the meaning of the term "presupposition" presented by P. F. Strawson (4). The claim, "The governor's mistakes have caused our present plight," presupposes that the governor has made mistakes. His not having done so would make nonsense out of either the affirmation or denial of the claim. If the governor has made no mistakes, it does not even make sense to say that his mistakes have caused our plight; nor does it make sense to say that his mistakes have not caused our plight.

Presupposition-finding is useful in avoiding being swayed by false presuppositions (if the governor has made no mistakes, we should be able to react to the presupposition that he has). And presupposition-finding is useful in grasping a verbal picture, and a part or the whole of a theory.

Judging whether something is presupposed by something else is simply a matter of stating the meaning of the "something else."

3. Judging Whether an Observation Statement Is Reliable

An observation statement is a specific description. Over the years, those fields most concerned with accuracy of observation have built up a set of rules for judging the reliability of observation statements. Here is a combined list of principles from the fields of law, history, and science:

3.1 Observation statements tend to be more reliable if the *observer:*
   3.11 Was unemotional, alert, and disinterested.
   3.12 Was skilled at observing the sort of thing observed.
   3.13 Had sensory equipment that was in good condition.
   3.14 Has a reputation for veracity.
   3.15 Used precise techniques.
   3.16 Had no preconception about the way the observation would turn out.
3.2 Observation statements tend to be more reliable if the *observation conditions:*
   3.21 Were such that the observer had good access.
   3.22 Provided a satisfactory medium of observation.
3.3 Observation statements tend to be more reliable to the extent that the *statement:*
   3.31 Is close to being a statement of direct observation.
   3.32 Is corroborated.
   3.33 Is corroboratable.
   3.34 Comes from a disinterested source with a reputation for veracity.
3.4 Observation statements, if based on a record, tend to be more reliable if the *record:*
   3.41 Was made at the time of observation.
   3.42 Was made by the person making the statement.
   3.43 Is believed by the person making the statement to be correct — either because he so believed at the time the record was made, or because he believes it was the record-maker's habit to make correct records.
3.5 Observation statements tend to be more reliable than inferences made from them.

4. Judging Whether a Simple Generalization Is Warranted

A simple generalization is a statement which covers a number of instances, and holds that they share some trait. For example, that red-headed people tend to have hot tempers is a generalization. It holds that red-headed people share the trait of tending to have hot tempers. A generalization is warranted:

4.1 To the extent that there is a bulk of reliable instances of it. The greater the variability of the population, the greater the bulk needed.

4.2 To the extent that it fits into the larger structure of knowledge.
4.3 To the extent that the selecting of instances is unbiased.
   4.31 A pure random sample is unbiased.
   4.32 A systematic sample is unbiased if a careful investigation suggests that there is not a relevant cycle or trend followed by the sampling procedure.
   4.33 Stratification of a population on relevant variables and unbiased sampling within the strata, is likely to be more efficient than 4.31 or 4.32 alone.
   4.34 An unbiased sampling of clusters of the population and unbiased sampling (or complete enumeration) within the clusters is likely to be an efficient way of sampling when access to separate individual units is difficult.
4.4 To the extent that there are no counter-instances.

The generalization that red-headed people tend to have hot tempers would be warranted to the extent that there is a large number of reliable instances of red-heads with hot tempers, to the extent that we are able to account for red-heads being hot-tempered, to the extent that our instances of red-heads are picked without bias, and to the extent that there is a lack of reliable instances of red-heads with even tempers.

5. Judging Whether a Hypothesis Is Warranted

Though the word "hypothesis" is often used to refer to a simple generalization, for purposes of marking off an important kind of statement which has a different relationship to its grounds than a simple generalization I will restrict the word "hypothesis" to the job of referring to this other kind of statement. Under this usage a hypothesis is a statement which is fairly directly related to its support by virtue of its power to *explain* this support, rather than being related by virtue of the support's being composed of instances of the hypothesis, as in the case for simple generalizations.

The hypothesis can be either specific (as is the case in law and usually in history) or it can be general (as is ordinarily the case in physical sciences and the social sciences of economics, sociology, and psychology).

Here is an example of a specific hypothesis: "Hissarlik is located at the site of Troy."

Here is an example of a general hypothesis: "The pressure in a liquid varies directly as the depth, assuming the pressure at the surface to be zero."

A hypothesis is warranted to the extent that:

5.1 It explains a bulk and variety of reliable data. If a datum is explained, it can be deduced or loosely derived (in the fashion of the application of principles) from the hypothesis together with established facts or generalizations.
5.2 It is itself explained by a satisfactory system of knowledge.
5.3 It is not inconsistent with any evidence.
5.4 Its competitors are inconsistent with the evidence. This principle is the basis of controlled experiments.
5.5 It is testable. It must be, or have been, possible to make predictions from it.

For purposes of illustration let us consider the bearing of each of the criteria on each hypothesis of the above two examples of hypotheses:

5.1 *Explaining a Bulk and Variety of Reliable Data.* Since Hissarlik is only an hour's walk from the sea, the Hissarlik hypothesis explains the reported (in the *Iliad*) ability of the Greeks to go back and forth from Troy several times a day. It explains why there are ruins at Hissarlik. These explained reports, it should be noted, can be derived from the Hissarlik hypothesis together with established facts or generalizations:

Hissarlik is at the site of Troy.
Hissarlik is one hour's walk from the sea.
People are able to walk back and forth several times a day between places that are one hour's walk apart.
Therefore it is probable that the Greeks were able to go back and forth from Troy to the sea several times daily (the explained fact).
Hissarlik is at the site of Troy.
A large city when abandoned tends to leave ruins.
Therefore it is probable that there are ruins at Hissarlik (the explained fact).

Of course explaining only those two pieces of evidence is not enough to establish the hypothesis. More evidence of different types must be provided.

The pressure hypothesis explains why water spurts farther from a hole near the bottom of a tank than from a hole in the middle of a tank. It also explains the proportional relationships between the following sets of readings of pressure gauges attached to the supply tank in a water system:

Distance from Top of Tank (in ft.)	Pressure Reading (in lbs./sq. in.)
0	0
5	2.1
10	4.2

These data can be derived from the hypothesis together with established facts or generalizations:

The pressure varies directly as the depth.
The greater the pressure at a hole, the farther the liquid will spurt.
The bottom hole is at a greater depth than the middle hole.
Therefore, the water spurts farther from the hole near the bottom (the explained fact).
The pressure varies directly as the depth.
The depth at 10 ft. is twice that at 5 ft.
Therefore, the pressure at 10 ft. (4.2 lbs./sq. in.) is twice that at 5 ft. (2.1 lbs./sq. in.), (the explained fact).

Again the explanation of these data alone does not establish the hypothesis. More explained data of various types are needed.

5.2 *Being Explained by a Satisfactory System of Knowledge.* If the Hissarlik hypothesis could itself be tentatively explained by established facts and generalizations, it would then be more acceptable. For example, suppose it were possible to show that the traits of the Trojans and the facts about the geography, climate, and nearby civilization at the time make it probable that the Trojan city would have developed at Hissarlik at the time that Troy was supposed to have existed. If it were possible to show that, the Hissarlik hypothesis would thereby receive support.

Similarly the pressure hypothesis is supported by showing that it can be explained, and thus derived, as follows:

> Pressure in a liquid is the numerical equivalent of the weight of a regular column of liquid extending to the top of the container.
> The weight of a column of liquid varies directly with its height.
> *Therefore,* the pressure in a liquid varies directly with the depth.

5.3 *Not Being Inconsistent with Any Evidence.* The Hissarlik hypothesis would be weakened if no springs could be found in the area of Hissarlik, since the *Iliad* mentions two springs in the area, one hot and one cold. The reasoning might go:

> Hissarlik is at the site of Troy.
> There were probably at least two springs at Troy, one hot and one cold.
> Springs tend to remain in existence over the years.
> *Therefore,* it is probable that there are at least two springs at Hissarlik, one hot and one cold.

Note that in using the absence of springs as evidence against the hypothesis, we are assuming that springs tend to remain and that the report of the *Iliad* is reliable. Either of these could be wrong. The less dependable these auxiliary assumptions are, the less dependable is our counterevidence.

The pressure hypothesis would be weakened by the discovery that water spurted out in the same amounts at the middle and the bottom, since the hypothesis implies otherwise. That is, it would be weakened if we did not previously have so much by way of other evidence built up in favor of the hypothesis — so much that, in this case, one would have a right to suspect such data.

5.4 *Its Competitors' Being Inconsistent with the Data.* A competitor of the Hissarlik hypothesis is the hypothesis that Bunarbashi is at the site of Troy. This competing hypothesis is not consistent with the data that Bunarbashi is a three-hours' walk from the sea and that the Greeks were able to go back and forth several times daily, if we assume that the Greeks walked.

A competitor of the earlier-stated pressure hypothesis might be one to the effect that the pressure increases directly as one gets closer to the surface of the earth. This hypothesis is inconsistent with pressure gauge readings on two independent tanks, one over the other, when the top tank has the pressure gauge at its bottom, and the bottom tank has its gauge at the top. The alternative hypothesis implies that the gauge in the upper tank would give the smaller reading. The data are just the opposite.

A controlled experiment is designed to rule out competing hypotheses by producing data inconsistent with them. When we test the hypothesis that a new fertilizer will increase the growth of corn, we put the fertilizer in a corn patch, develop a companion corn patch, the control, identical in every respect possible except for fertilizer, and watch the results. If there is a difference, the fertilizer hypothesis can explain it. But it would not be explained by heavy rainfall, warm weather, sunlight, etc., since both patches supposedly received the same amount. These alternative hypotheses would justify a prediction of no difference and would thus be inconsistent with the data.

It is, of course, impossible to develop a perfectly controlled experiment, since the perfect isolation and variation of a single variable is not possible. The important thing might be a *combination* of weather and fertilizer, or the important thing might have slipped by unnoticed. But we can still see in the controlled experiment an attempt to approximate the logical goal of eliminating hypotheses by turning up data that are inconsistent with them. The controlled experiment is an efficient way of eliminating hypotheses by this method.

It should be noted that there is an implicit assumption of standard or familiar conditions in the reasoning that leads to judgments of explanation and inconsistency. For example, the inconsistency resulting from Bunarbashi's being a three-hour walk from the sea is an inconsistency only if Bunarbashi was a three-hour walk from the sea at the time of the Trojan War. In declaring the data to be inconsistent with the competing hypothesis one is gambling that the sea was not at a significantly different level at that time.

This feature of reasoning from hypothesis fits in with the notion of loose reasoning presented under Aspect No. 1. There are always possible qualifications when we apply principles to the world of things, men, and events.

5.5 *Being Testable.* This is a logical criterion, not a criterion of practicality or even physical possibility. The criterion requires only that it must be possible to *conceive* of what would count as evidence for, and what would count as evidence against, the hypothesis. We have already seen that this is possible for each of our hypotheses. The fact that some conceivable tests are not practically possible is not important so far as this criterion is concerned. A conceivable, though presumably physically impossible, test of the pressure hypothesis would involve swimming to the bottom of the ocean with pressure and depth gauges, recording readings at various points along the way.

An hypothesis that appears untestable is this one: "Airplane crashes are caused by gremlins," since it does not appear possible to conceive of something that would count as evidence for and to conceive of something that would count as evidence against the hypothesis. The word "appear" is used deliberately, since the conceiving of evidence for and evidence against would immediately make the hypothesis testable — and would reveal to some extent the meaning of the hypothesis.

Most hypotheses that we consider are testable in this logical sense, so this criterion does not often discredit an hypothesis. But its fulfillment is absolutely essential for hypotheses about the world of things, men, and events.

6. Judging Whether a Theory Is Warranted

The difference between a theoretic system and an hypothesis of the type we have been considering is that the former is an involved network of relations between concepts, many of which are abstract and technical, while the latter is a simple relation between two or a small number of concepts, often less abstract and technical. Examples of theoretic systems are the kinetic theory of matter, the atomic theory, Gestalt psychology, the theory of evolution, Keynesian economics, Turner's frontier theory, and classical English grammar. Obviously the evaluation of theories is a demanding task. It demands more than we can ordinarily expect of elementary and secondary students. Undergraduates are sometimes better equipped, and graduate students are expected to become equipped to perform this task.

Evaluating theories is comparable to evaluating hypotheses, but much more complex. In general the same criteria apply but on a broader scale. Two modifications should be noted: the addition of the criterion of simplicity and the weakening of the effect of contrary evidence.

The criterion of simplicity calls for choosing the simpler of two competing systems, other things being equal. The classic example of the application of this criterion is the preference of the Copernican system, which considered the sun the center of the universe, to the Ptolemaic system, which looked upon the earth as the center. The Copernican system was simpler since it needed fewer cycles and epicycles to explain the movements of the planets.

Since theories have so many parts, contrary evidence does not usually result in outright rejection, but rather in adjustment to fit the contrary evidence — until the whole system becomes more complex than a competitor. The criterion of simplicity then functions.

Following are the criteria for theoretic systems. There will be brief comments, but no attempt to exemplify the operation of each will be made, because to do so would be a monumental task and would make rather laborious reading for those not versed in the fields chosen. You are invited to provide examples from a theoretic system in a field you know.

A theoretic system is warranted to the extent that:

6.1 It explains a bulk and variety of reliable data. Within the system, furthermore, the less abstract statements should be explained by the more abstract ones.

6.2 It is explained by broader theories. Some theories are so broad already that, with our present state of knowledge, to demand fulfillment of this criterion is often to demand speculation.

6.3 It is not inconsistent with any evidence. As indicated earlier, occasional inconsistency can be handled by adjusting the theory. Sometimes the inconsistency must just be accepted for lack of a better theory, and we say, "The theory does not hold for this kind of case."

6.4 Its competitors are inconsistent with the data. Again a single inconsistency does not destroy a competitor, for it too can be adjusted, but a larger number of inconsistencies damage it.

6.5 It is testable. When adjusting a theory to fit the data, people are sometimes tempted to make the theory impregnable by making it untestable. Freudian psychology is sometimes accused of being untestable.

6.6 It is simpler than its rivals. As theories are adjusted to fit new data, they may become extremely complicated, as had happened to the entire Ptolemaic system at the time of Copernicus.

7. Judging Whether an Argument Depends on an Ambiguity

The ambiguity can appear anywhere in an argument, but most frequently it appears in a shift of meaning from the sense in which the conclusion is proved to a sense in which it is applied. There is such a shift in the following line of reasoning:

There are people who sincerely believe on religious grounds that medication is wrong. They believe this because they believe that any treatment of human beings with medicine is a violation of their religious principles. "Medication" means anything intended for the prevention, cure, or alleviation of disease.

Since the chlorination of water is intended for the prevention of disease, it is medication. To chlorinate water is thus to violate their religious principles.

The statement, "Chlorination is medication," is proven when the statement has one meaning: "Chlorination is something intended for the prevention, cure, or alleviation of disease." And it is applied with a different meaning: "Chlorination is treatment of human beings with medicine."

Obviously arguments that depend on ambiguities are to be rejected. No criteria can be given that will serve as guides to students in detecting ambiguities, although you can exhort them to be alert with such statements as, "Make sure that the key words are used in the same sense throughout," or "Check the argument using the key word in its ordinary sense, and if it fails, check it using the word in any technical senses that might be employed."

8. Judging Whether a Statement Is Overvague or Overspecific

For the purposes of a given situation, a particular statement might be too vague to provide guidance. In such situations the statement should be rejected or inquired into, since in its condition its truth or falsity is irrelevant.

The statement, "Education has disappeared from the schools" (or "There is more education in the schools than ever before") is useless in decision-making about curriculum and school finance until the terms, "education," "disappeared," and "the schools" are clarified. The statements are not specific enough to be tested and applied. They are too vague.

On the other hand, in a war-ravaged country it might be quite meaningful to say that education has disappeared from the schools (since they are now used for hospitals or housing). In this situation, "education," even loosely defined, has disappeared from the schools.

This aspect requires consideration of the purpose of the discourse and requires the judgment, "This is (or is not) specific enough for our purpose." If the purpose is to come up with curriculum and budgetary recommendations for a school system long in existence, the statement is not specific enough. If the purpose is to make a report to the leader of a war-ravaged country, it is specific enough.

It might be thought that this aspect of critical thinking is one in which people do not make mistakes. In concrete situations this tends to be true, but in abstract situations it is easy to go wrong by forgetting to put questions and answers in the context of situations with purposes. Crawshay-Williams develops this point well (1).

9. Judging Whether an Alleged Authority Is Reliable

In order to assess the statements made by an alleged authority, one must appraise his credentials. Certainly other aspects of critical thinking should also be applied, if one is able to do so. But there are times when one must make a judgment about a statement solely on the basis of the credentials of the person making the statement. An alleged authority should be accepted to the extent that:

9.1 He has a good reputation.
9.2 The statement is in his field.

9.3 He was disinterested — that is, he did not knowingly stand to profit by the results of his statements (except that he may have stood to have his reputation affected).

9.4 His reputation could be affected by his statement and he was aware of this fact when he made his statement.

9.5 He studied the matter.

9.6 He followed the accepted procedures in coming to his conclusion (although there are legitimate exceptions to this requirement).

9.7 He was in full possession of his faculties when he made the statement.

The Reduction of Problem Identification to the Other Aspects

Different kinds of judgments go under the label, "problem identification":

1. Judging that a want has been identified, as when someone says, "My problem is to learn to appreciate poetry." In this sense the judgment that the speaker has identified his problems is tantamount to the judgment that this is something the speaker, who might also be the judge, really wants to do. Problem identification here is identification of wants, either one's own, or someone else's. If they are one's own introspect wants, then critical thinking is not involved. For a person to know his wants (felt needs) is something that he cannot fail to do.

If they are someone else's wants, then identifying problems is the same as establishing explanatory hypotheses, as is the case for all subconscious wants, one's own or someone else's, for example, "Mark's problem is to get attention." Judging the identification of someone else's problem and of subconscious wants are then critical thinking of a type already discussed — judging hypotheses.

2. Judging that a valuable goal has been selected. Here is such a problem identification: "Our problem in Culver City is to increase respect for law and order." Insofar as that is a statement of an end rather than a means, the judgment that it is an adequate identification of a problem is a value judgment. For reasons indicated earlier, this type of judging, though important, is excluded from this analysis of critical thinking.

3. Judging that a means decision is adequate. For example, if the broader objective were respect for law and order, the following might be a statement of a means decision: "Our problem in Culver City is to establish a youth bureau." The judgment here that the problem has been identified does at least these two things: (1) implies endorsement of the goal of respect for law and order (this part of the judgment then is a value judgment); (2) says that the means selected will facilitate achievement of the goal and that they will be at least more likely to facilitate it than any other course of action, within the limits of existing resources and goals. These limiting goals, by the way, are another instance in which values are impressed on problem identification. To judge that the problem has been identified is to judge that no unjustified goal violation would take place if the problem were solved.

To apply the means interpretation to our example: it is there implied that the establishment of a youth bureau would increase the likelihood of winning respect for law and order, and would be more likely to do so than any other course.

Judging a means decision is judging the application of a principle and judging the acceptability of the principle. To judge whether a youth bureau in Culver City would result in increased respect for law and order is to judge whether a principle about the effectiveness of youth bureaus, applied to this situation, gives us this statement with sufficient probability; and to judge whether the principle is acceptable. Judging principles comes under judging generalizations, hypotheses, or theories, depending on the principle in question.

In summary, problem identification is many different things and often a combination of them. Elements capable of being treated under the proposed notion of critical thinking are (1) judging the alleged identification of the wants of others and of subconscious wants (explanatory hypotheses), and (2) judging the assertion of a means of reaching a goal (judging the application of principles and judging the principles themselves). Each of these types of judging is treated elsewhere.

Summary

There has been presented a root notion of critical thinking: the correct assessing of statements, and the presentation and clarification of a list of nine major aspects of critical thinking, which are based upon the root notion. These aspects get at the most important ways people can go wrong in assessing statements and can serve as a statement of elementary and intermediate goals in the teaching of critical thinking.

It has not been the purpose of this paper to suggest how to teach critical thinking, since that would vary so much from one level to another and one subject to another. Perhaps the examples will suggest teaching ideas.

References

1. Crawshay-Williams, Rupert. *Methods and Criteria of Reasoning.* London: Routledge and Kegan Paul, 1957.
2. Ennis, Robert H. "Assumption-Finding." In B. Othanel Smith and Robert H. Ennis (eds.), *Language and Concepts in Education.* Chicago: Rand McNally, 1961. Pp. 161–178.
3. Smith, B. Othanel. "The Improvement of Critical Thinking," *Progressive Education,* 30: 129–134; March, 1953.
4. Strawson, P. F. *Introduction to Logical Theory.* London: Methuen, 1952.
5. Waisman, F. "Verifiability." In Antony Flew (ed.), *Logic and Language.* Oxford: Basil Blackwell & Mott, 1952.

Critical Reading in the Primary

Grades ❧ HELEN W. PAINTER

In her book *I Will Adventure,* Elizabeth Janet Gray (4) has her main character, Andrew, scorning study and school. He expresses his feelings to his new friend, an actor and playwright named William Shakespeare. Shakespeare says to him: "Ignorance is a curse, Andrew, knowledge the wing by which we fly to heaven. If you get a chance to pluck a feather from that wing, make the most of it."

Surely in our world today the informed individuals who can read and think are of vital importance. Kathleen Hester (6) writes about a boy in second grade in Puerto Rico. He read: "We wish to read good books, in order not to be ignorant, in order not to be slaves." What better reasons do we need for critical reading?

What is critical reading and how early can we teach it? Dr. Nila B. Smith (8) has pointed out the popularity of the term *critical reading* today and the fact that many people are using the term to refer to many skills in reading. She sees three types of thought-getting processes: (a) literal comprehension, getting the primary meaning from words; (b) interpretation, getting a deeper meaning from words in addition to simple, literal comprehension; and (c) critical reading, including the first two but going further in involving personal judgment on and evaluation of the "quality, the value, the accuracy, and the truthfulness of what is read." Critical reading involves critical thinking.

How early can we start teaching critical reading? Is it possible in elementary school, particularly in the primary grades? Research findings reveal that critical thinking can be taught from kindergarten through college. Dr. Leo Fay (3) points out: "Actually children at ages well before those at which they enter school are able to make valid judgments in relation to their experiences and their maturity levels."

Critical reading *in its highest form* is complex, and a young child usually would be unable to do such involved reading. Second graders may be critical readers, Heilman (5) says, but "no one would suggest that their interpretation of the Constitution is adequate for our society." But they can evaluate in terms of their maturity, their backgrounds and experiences. Stauffer (10) tells of a six-year-old questioning how three ducks in a story could be a "long parade of ducks." The child knew ducks, had seen them walk in single file, had reached a reaction to *long* and *short,* and could figure out what a parade was. He obviously was doing critical thinking.

Are teachers teaching the skills of critical reading? In the Harvard report of reading in elementary schools, *The First R* (1), the staff reported that not until Grades 5 and 6 did school systems estimate "considerable" attention was given to critical reading, a situation "very much in keeping with the prevailing opinion among administrators and teachers that only older children are able

From *The Reading Teacher,* 19: 35–39; October, 1965. Reprinted with permission of Helen W. Painter and the International Reading Association. Helen W. Painter is Professor of Education, University of Akron, Akron, Ohio.

to think and read critically." More than half of the school systems devoted "little" or "no" time to such skills in Grades 1 and 2. In observations in the classroom, the field staff rarely found teachers trying to help children in those activities that contributed to critical reading. Therefore, among their recommendations the authors proposed that "a definite program be initiated in which all children are taught critical and creative reading skills appropriate for their development, and that teachers find ways to stimulate thinking beyond the literal meaning of passages read."

It is apparent that critical reading skills do not appear automatically but must be taught. All authorities agree that a teacher must so direct the reading of children that they can think critically. A teacher herself must be a critical reader and thinker. She must give practice in the skills. She must remember that "critical thinking abilities are difficult and they are slow agrowing" (7). She must help children gain background and experiences. She must encourage critical thinking and be pleased by the questioning of children, not annoyed by it. She must create the setting for critical reading. Too often a teacher asks merely for simple recall.

A teacher must be skillful in teaching critical thinking: we want to develop questioning attitudes in children, but we do not want teachers or classes always to be unduly suspicious, to question everything and thus deny themselves opportunities to lead lives full of satisfaction (2). A teacher must use logic in promoting sound and proper attitudes.

Exactly how, then, can critical reading and thinking be taught? Probably the best way is to guide classroom discussion as it occurs. Dr. Smith writes (8):

Rarely should a teacher plan to "give a lesson" in critical reading, particularly in the primary grades. More direct work can be done at times in the upper grades. Leads into critical reading activities usually arise from discussion of reading content.

Children themselves often offer leads to critical reading. The wise teacher keeps herself ever on the alert for such leads, encouraging them with commendation for good thinking and stimulating further research for facts with tactful questions or remarks.

Surely, the primary school curriculum provides a fertile field for critical thinking. Basal reading selections and individual books, as well as materials in content fields, offer many opportunities to a teacher. Critical reading may be taught to a large or small group or to an individual pupil.

It is obvious, therefore, that critical reading is possible with young children, but that the amount and kind of such activity rest upon the teacher. To assist teachers, here are some examples and applications of critical reading at the primary school level.

Primary school children can question whether a situation is truth or fantasy. Russell (7) mentions first graders making such distinctions after hearing "The Day It Rained Cats and Dogs." Primary grades include the age for the start of interest in fairy tales, and children can be led to distinguish between fantasy and truth. Could someone sleep for a hundred years? Could a pumpkin become a coach? Could such events take place? Why or why not? We can help children to look for clues that signal a fairy story, such as the once-upon-a-time beginning and the fairy prince and princess.

A child may decide if action is plausible in stories not labeled fairy stories. Look at Phyllis McGinley's "The Horse Who Lived Upstairs." Have you ever heard of a horse living upstairs? It is possible? How does the author make the situation seem plausible? Are animals, insects, and birds able to talk, as Wilbur, Charlotte, and Templeton do in *Charlotte's Web?* Why or why not? Is there a land where the wild things are?

Young children can be led to judge the competence of an author. Chibi could distinguish the cry of crows under different circumstances. Can this be? Laura Ingalls Wilder in *The Little House in the Big Woods* tells of Ma and Laura going out to milk the cow after dark and finding a bear in the barnlot. Did bears come to farms then? What would your clothes, your house, or your parents' work have been a hundred years ago? Why did not Laura's father take an automobile or jet plane?

Such materials call for checking on an author. Is the author writing about what he or she actually knows? How can we find out? It is unfortunate that notes about authors and how they happen to write their stories do not appear somewhere within the covers of books to offer quick proof of competency.

Children can judge how fair and just another is. Should Peter Rabbit have been punished, or should Ping have gotten a smack for being last? Is an author right to make such things happen? Why do you think so?

Characters can be judged as lifelike or real. Does Fern do things that you would if you owned Wilbur? Is Templeton just what a greedy, selfish rat ought to be? Why does the little old man set out to find a cat? Why did he want to please the little old woman?

Perhaps discussion can lead to some understanding of the motives of characters, why a giant was bad and why a hero's deeds are good, for example.

Sometimes a title can be appraised. Children can judge such a title as *The Courage of Sarah Noble.* Does it seem a good one? Why? How do you think Sarah will show her courage? Was she brave? Would *you* have been? Children might judge a title by deciding whether it gives the idea of the story and sounds interesting.

Children can judge pictures. Children can do some critical thinking about the pictures in a book, though they are too immature yet to evaluate the technical quality of the art. They can see if a picture is true to the story. Most children are very much aware of details and catch discrepancies before adults do. One first grader was much disturbed at a picture of a little girl in a clean dress, because on the previous page the girl had fallen into a mud puddle. How, then, could her clothes be clean? As Lynd Ward once said, illustrations should be part and parcel of a book.

By being exposed to good illustrations, even young children can begin to build standards of art appreciation. They can offer some good reasons for their preferences.

Children can judge likenesses and differences in books dealing with children of other lands. Why did the boys and girls make fun of Chibi? Why did Ping live on a houseboat? Why did Pelle take a boat to the store and pay for the dye for the wool with a shilling? Family stories of people of other countries or races may lead to animated discussions and serious thought.

Various types of comparisons can lead to critical thinking. A child may compare biographies about the same person for details and authenticity, for example, the d'Aulaires' *Abraham Lincoln* with another book or TV program about Lincoln. A book, *Little Toot,* may be checked against a film or filmstrip in deciding how much the two are alike. Different versions of a story (or song) may be compared, as *Frog Went A'Courtin'* and "The Frog He Would A'Wooing Go." Some very capable children may check the original copy of a book against a simplified copy and try figuring out why the story has been made easier to read. The popularity of book clubs, even for young children, also leads to critical evaluation.

A child should be ready to evaluate his own oral or written reports. Even a young child, under guidance, can be taught to look up material for a report and judge what material is pertinent and what sources are best. Second and third graders are reading more widely than ever for information, and they must be led to dictionaries and encyclopedias. They must learn to check on accuracy. Even small children must be led to examine copyright dates in order to determine if material is up-to-date, an aspect of critical evaluation particularly important in content areas. With dictionary work a teacher must lead her class to develop awareness of multiple word meanings, that the right meaning may be chosen for the material being read.

A teacher may teach children to detect propaganda. One of the most common means of propaganda is television. According to David Russell (7), many children before starting school have developed critical thinking abilities with regard to this medium. He cites the five-year-old saying with a smile, *"All the TV ads say they have the best breakfast cereal."* While more chances are offered in the upper grades, probably we can teach children to detect propaganda as early as Grade 3 and help them recognize some of the techniques (8).

The child must be alert to figurative language. Figurative language is common. Many such expressions as "It's off the record" constantly confront the child. The young reader who has been taught to think critically will ask what the material really means.

A child can become alert to words that arouse emotions. A child may find a poem about rain personally pleasant. If he wants to play in the yard he may be dismayed by rain, however, just as may his mother who wants to hang the washing outside. He can be led to realize that a man whose fields are drying up may be delighted with rain. Words arouse emotions. Some understanding comes when meaning can be brought into the critical thinking of the child.

Finally, a child will select books according to his preferences. How does a child choose reading materials outside school? Spache (9) says that children begin as early as the primary grades to offer comments about their enjoyment of books. They can compare events and experiences in a book with their own. They can be led to think critically about the author, what he wants them to see as his purpose, what words he uses, and what his characters are like. Evaluative skills and appreciation call for the personal involvement of each individual.

In summary, children of primary grades will be able to think critically about those situations which are a part of their own experiences or can be related to them. Many children will not do critical reading or thinking unless the teacher directs or challenges them. Surely critical reading by children calls for teachers who are critical thinkers themselves.

References

1. Austin, Mary, and Morrison, Coleman. *The First R.* New York: Macmillan, 1963.
2. Dallmann, Martha. "Critical Evaluation," *Grade Teacher,* 75: 46–47; September, 1957.
3. Fay, Leo. *Developing the Ability to Read Critically.* Reading Promotion Bulletin No. 28. Chicago: Lyons and Carnahan, n.d.
4. Gary, Elizabeth Janet. *I Will Adventure.* New York: Viking, 1962.
5. Heilman, Arthur W. *Principles and Practices of Teaching Reading.* Columbus, Ohio: Charles E. Merrill, 1961.
6. Hester, Kathleen B. "Puerto Rico — Leader in a Spanish-American Reading Program," *Reading Teacher,* 17: 316–321; April, 1964.
7. Russell, David H. "The Prerequisite: Knowing How to Read Critically," *Elementary English,* 40: 579–582, 597; October, 1963.
8. Smith, Nila B. *Reading Instruction for Today's Children.* New York: Prentice-Hall, 1963.
9. Spache, George D. *Reading in the Elementary School.* Boston: Allyn and Bacon, 1964.
10. Stauffer, Russell G. "Children Can Read and Think Critically," *Education,* 80: 522–525; May, 1960.

Teaching Critical Reading in the Middle Grades

❖ JERALDINE HILL

One of the purposes in teaching children to read is that they may ultimately be able to think for themselves. A good reader is not only one who can read, but one who does read, enjoys reading, and knows how to use what he has read. A search through literature on teaching reading reveals much written on teaching children to read and to enjoy reading. However, there is very little practical material available on teaching a child how to use what he has read, or, put another way, to do critical reading. Most of the material found

From *Elementary English,* 39: 239–243; March, 1962. Reprinted with the permission of the National Council of Teachers of English and Jeraldine Hill, Instructor, P. K. Yonge Laboratory School, University of Florida, Gainesville.

has been written on teaching critical reading through the content areas above the elementary school level.

Spache[1] lists six skills necessary for critical reading: (1) investigating sources; (2) recognizing authors' purposes; (3) distinguishing opinion and fact; (4) making inferences; (5) forming judgments; and (6) detecting propaganda devices. These are separate from comprehension skills that require a lower level of inferences and interpretations. These are skills that go beyond the comprehension skills needed. Although you would not expect younger children to think as maturely as those in high school, this does not prove that middle-graders cannot be taught to think critically. In fact, middle-grade children are at the point in their development when they are questioning. They ask, "Can you prove it?" of their peers, their teachers, and their parents. They are skeptical when proof is not available. Content areas can be used to teach critical reading to these children. Beyond this, the very books read for recreation or as part of an individualized reading program can also be used to teach the skills necessary to do critical reading.

One of the types of books that is of interest to children is biography and biographical fiction. A way to help children grow in their ability to do critical thinking is to compare various biographies and fictionalized stories about one famous person. For example, the life of Benjamin Franklin might be used. The child could read *Ben and Me*[2] and the one the D'Aulaire's wrote on Benjamin Franklin[3] and use some reference book's account of the life of Benjamin Franklin. The three accounts could be compared as to what phases of the person's life are covered, any bias shown by the author, what is historically true, what is perhaps legend and what perhaps is pure fiction. For the more able readers, adult versions and the children's versions of the biography of a famous person written by the same author can be used. The four-volume biography of Abraham Lincoln by Sandburg[4] and the book he wrote for children, *Abe Lincoln*,[5] or Ester Forbes' factual account of *Paul Revere*[6] and *Johnny Tremain*,[7] the fictionalized account of Paul Revere, can be studied for the author's different purposes in each book, variations in style between adult and children's versions, as well as distinguishing fact, legend, and fiction.

Books about families are another kind of book of interest to the middle-grade child. These include books such as *The Moffats*,[8] *The All-of-a-Kind Family*,[9] the *Little House*[10] books. Children can discuss the different types of families, their homes, their standards of living, their ideas of discipline, etc. This helps

[1] George Spache, *Toward Better Reading* (Champaign, Illinois: Garrard Press, 1961), Chapter 5.

[2] Robert Lawson, *Ben and Me* (Boston: Little Brown & Co., 1939).

[3] Ingri and Edgar P. D'Aulaire, *Benjamin Franklin* (Garden City, New York: Nelson, Doubleday, Inc., 1950).

[4] Carl Sandburg, *Abraham Lincoln* (4 Vols., New York: Harcourt, Brace and Co., 1928).

[5] Carl Sandburg, *Abe Lincoln, The Prairie Years* (New York: Harcourt, Brace & Co., 1928).

[6] Ester Forbes, *Paul Revere* (Boston: Houghton Mifflin Co., 1942).

[7] Ester Forbes, *Johnny Tremain* (Boston: Houghton Mifflin Co., 1943).

[8] Eleanor Estes, *The Moffats* (New York: Harcourt, Brace & Co., 1941).

[9] Sidney Taylor, *The All-of-a-Kind Family* (Chicago: Wilson & Follett Co., 1951).

[10] Laura Ingalls Wilder, *Little House* books (New Uniform Edition; New York: Harper & Bros., 1953).

to build the understandings of how families differ and yet are basically alike. Books such as *Elder Brother*,[11] *Thirty One Brothers and Sisters*,[12] *Henner's Lydia*[13] and other De Angeli books give a picture of other cultures, ethnic and social groups and their type of family life. Books such as these also aid in developing more understanding of human interrelations.

Similar to the books about families are books about particular boys or girls. Such books as *Shen of the Sea*,[14] *The Courage of Sarah Noble*,[15] *Caddie Woodlawn*,[16] *Adam of the Road*,[17] *Isle of the Blue Dolphins*[18] can be used to discuss the problems of the main character, his fears, his dreams, and how he shows courage beyond his fears. The personality of the main character can be studied as to his strengths and weaknesses shown in the story, his values and judgments, and whether he is shown to have strong biases or prejudices. Children can consider what they would do under similar circumstances and project what would have happened if the children's suggestions were followed.

Puzzles are a challenge to middle-grade children that they find hard to resist. A way to use books to stimulate puzzles is to have children write their version of how a book came to be written, or write how they would have ended a particular book if they had written it. Then the children can go even further and write to publishers and authors and ask about the story behind the books. This would also give children an opportunity to learn more about the publication of books and give them more knowledge of authors as real people. There is, of course, already published, *The Story Behind Modern Books*,[19] but it is quite old. It might serve as a starting point to write about more current books.

Writing to publishers and authors can serve yet another purpose in teaching critical reading. A complete study can develop from writing to various publishers of books that are familiar and favorites of the children. This can take the form of a study of all of the books of a particular author or illustrator. This can lead to a discussion of a particular style of one author, expressions he uses in more than one of his books, similarity of characters or locales. It can be a study of the new books for the year that will be published by one company, their variety, the subject most popular for that year. Sometimes publishers will lend a school original manuscripts, galley sheets, or original illustrations. This can lead to an appraisal of the field of publishing, the cost, the way books are advertised, the format, and so forth. The impact that publishers have on what is available for children to read can be discovered from such a study. The people who write books are of much interest to young readers. They enjoy trying to find out as much as they can about the authors'

---

[11] Evelyn S. Lampman, *Elder Brother* (Garden City, N. Y.: Doubleday, Inc., 1950).

[12] Reba P. Mirsky, *Thirty One Brothers and Sisters* (Chicago: Wilson & Follett, 1952).

[13] Marguerite De Angeli, *Henner's Lydia* (Garden City, N. Y.: Doubleday, Inc., 1936).

[14] Arthur Chrisman, *Shen of the Sea* (Garden City, N. Y.: E. P. Dutton, 1925).

[15] Alice Dalgliesh, *The Courage of Sarah Noble* (New York: Charles Scribner's Sons, 1954).

[16] Carol Brink, *Caddie Woodlawn* (New York: Macmillan Co., 1937).

[17] Elizabeth Janet Gray, *Adam of the Road* (New York: Viking Press, 1942).

[18] Scott O'Dell, *The Island of the Blue Dolphins* (Boston: Houghton Mifflin Co., 1960).

[19] Elizabeth Montgomery, *The Story Behind Modern Books* (New York: Dodd, Mead & Co., 1949).

lives and families. *The Junior Book of Authors*[20] and magazines such as *Horn Book* and *Elementary English* can be of much help to them in seeking information about authors. Of course, writing to the author is always a way to learn how he lives, how he chooses his plots, his philosophy of writing, his family, and his interests.

The pictures in books fascinate young children. As they grow older they still enjoy pictures, but their books have fewer and fewer illustrations. Children's picture books can be used by older readers for a different purpose. The different styles of various illustrators can be compared. The study of the style and media of one illustrator can be made by collecting as many books as possible and comparing the earlier books of an illustrator with his more recent books. One can never forget the change of style of Robert McCloskey from *Make Way for Ducklings*[21] to *Time of Wonder*.[22] It is very hard to believe that they were done by the same person. Another use of illustration is the comparison of media, color depth, and the aesthetic aspects of illustrations. Older readers can appraise the part that the illustrations play in the stories in picture books. A more mature appraisal can be made by a consideration of how illustrators have affected the entire development of children's books.

Many of the basal reader series have a watered down version of famous children's books. Children can read the original books and compare the stories in the readers. They can evaluate the similarities and the differences of the two versions as to simplicity or difficulty, degrees of descriptive language, style, and interest. Readers also have simplified versions of folk and fairy tales which can also be compared. Another comparison can be made between the original versions of classics, such as, *Little Women*,[23] *Tom Sawyer*,[24] *Treasure Island*,[25] and series of these that are published in simpler and more attractive form by some book publishers. Don't be surprised if some children do not prefer the original! Studies such as these may include possible reasons for making more than one version, the job of editing, the place of illustrations, differences in cost, and so on.

Children can examine the advantages of various kinds of book clubs in learning how to build up their own personal libraries. Such clubs as the Junior Literary Guild, the Arrow Book Club, the Weekly Reader Book Club, will be good for this. Some readers may move into the adult Book-of-the-Month Club, the Literary Guild Book Club, *American Heritage*. Then there are the scientific types of monthly books, such as *Around the World Program, Know Your America, Nature Program, National Aviation*. The good periodicals for children should be introduced to them, also, for lighter and shorter reading periods. We build discriminating adult readers by helping children to be discriminating in their reading tastes.

One of the many of the mass media that can be used in the classroom to help children develop the ability to read critically is the newspaper. The ac-

[20] *Junior Book of Authors* ed. S. J. Kunitz & Howard Haycraft (2nd Revised Edition; New York: Wilson & Co., 1951).

[21] Robert McCloskey, *Make Way for Ducklings* (New York: Viking Press, 1941).

[22] Robert McCloskey, *A Time of Wonder* (New York: Viking Press, 1957).

[23] Louisa M. Alcott, *Little Women* (Boston: Little Brown & Co., 1934). (1868)

[24] Mark Twain (Samuel Clemens), *Tom Sawyer* (New York: Harper & Bros., 1917). (1876)

[25] Robert L. Stevenson, *Treasure Island* (New York: Charles Scribner's Sons, 1924). (1882)

counts of important events can be compared in several newspapers. The newspaper can also be used as a springboard into the study of how news is gathered and reported, the effect that the printed words has on the children's lives. More advanced readers may be interested in the *New York Times,* the *Commercial Appeal.*

Poetry is one of the best ways to help children to read critically. For poetry is an abbreviated thought. The poet must leave so much to the reader's imagination. A keen interest in poetry is not developed in a short time. Poetry takes much tasting, much thinking, much time to assimilate the thoughts presented. But for these reasons it must not be neglected. Poetry, as all other reading, should be partly for enjoyment. It should never be presented to young children for analysis of structure, meter, or rhyme. It should be presented for the beauty of the thought it brings, the release of emotion through verse. It can be used, without hindering any of these, to discuss and appraise the thought presented and its effect on the reader. Children should be encouraged to see that they, too, can write poetry. However, if we use poetry with children as we should, they will soon discover this for themselves.

There are many sources that a teacher can have in her classroom to help children develop an ability to use and learn more about books, authors, and illustrators. Besides many and varied trade books, there are bibliographies put out by the American Library Association, listing books of various age levels and subjects. There are bibliographies of adult books that young people will enjoy. This association also publishes *Libraries Bulletin.* The University of Chicago Children's Book Center publishes an excellent book list about books, their authors, and illustrators. The *New York Times* Book Review Section and Supplement has valuable articles, also. The *Saturday Review* and the *Atlantic Monthly* magazines will be of interest to more mature readers. There are many more, but one of the best is a teacher or librarian who tells children of new books, shows them or reads from them to children. This personal appraisal means more to most children than a printed account, no matter how well done the printed account may be. Children, too, can be instrumental in encouraging others to read favorites by preparing bibliographies that they feel other children may enjoy.

The role of a school librarian in helping children grow in interest and ability with books is very important. The public librarian is also important. One who reads and tells stories to children and discusses their reading with them is invaluable. She is the spirit of the library to children. How she helps and guides children with books is one indication of how they will continue their use of libraries in the future. A good librarian will encourage children to feel at home in the library, to enjoy it. She will help children learn the aids the library can give. It is possible for even young children to became acquainted with the card catalog. As they grow older, the librarian can introduce the indexes that are available, and help them to discover aids to their own book needs. If teacher and librarian work together, the ways they can help children keep growing and stretching their abilities to use books are unlimited.

Any one of these suggestions may be used as a starting point to get children to thinking for themselves and interacting with the material that they are reading. There are, of course, many other ways in which this can be done. However, the first step is to begin. The questioning middle-grade mind will take up from there. Children will begin to develop better ways to think about what they read if they have the training to do so. Then we have started them on the path toward becoming readers and thinkers who will not be fooled by the language of emotional persuasion. They will be able to recognize propaganda that, unless understood, can result in the enslavement of the minds and enslavement of the people themselves.

Further Reading for Chapter 6

Criscuolo, N. P. "A Plea for Critical Reading in the Primary Grades," *Peabody Journal of Education,* 43: 107–112; September, 1965.

Groff, Patrick J. "Children's Attitudes Toward Reading and Their Critical Reading Abilities in Four Content-Type Materials," *Journal of Educational Research,* 55: 313–318; April, 1962.

Heilman, Arthur W. *Principles and Practices of Teaching Reading.* Columbus, Ohio: Charles E. Merrill Books, Inc., 1961. Chapter 9.

Hester, Kathleen B. *Teaching Every Child to Read.* New York: Harper & Row, Publishers, 1964. Chapter 16.

Krebs, Stephen O. "Teaching Critical Thinking," *Education,* 81: 153–157; November, 1960.

Livingston, H. "Investigation of the Effect of Instruction in General Semantics on Critical Reading Ability," *California Journal of Educational Research,* 16: 93–96; March, 1965.

McKee, Paul. *Reading: A Program of Instruction for the Elementary School.* Boston: Houghton Mifflin Company, 1966. Chapter 10.

Oppenheim, June. "Teaching Reading As A Thinking Process," *The Reading Teacher,* 13: 188–193; February, 1960.

Russell, David H. "The Prerequisite: Knowing How to Read Critically," *Elementary English,* 40: 578–582, 597; October, 1963.

Smith, Nila Banton. "What Is Critical Reading?" *Elementary English,* 40: 409–410; April, 1963.

Stauffer, Russell G. "Children Can Read and Think Critically," *Education,* 80: 522–525; May, 1960.

Stauffer, Russell G. "'Critical Reading at Upper Levels," *The Instructor,* 74: 75, 101–103; March, 1965.

Wolfe, Evelyn. "Advertising and the Elementary Language Arts," *Elementary English,* 42: 42–44; January, 1965.

7

The Disadvantaged Child

During very recent years there has been a growing awareness of the needs of disadvantaged children. This awareness has received its greatest impetus from the various federal programs which concentrate on helping such children.

As in many areas, the terminology used has often been inexact and has seemingly contributed as much to misunderstandings as to understandings. Terms such as *economically deprived, culturally deprived, disadvantaged,* and others have been used interchangeably by some authors, while other authors have used the same terms to denote differing classifications of students. In this chapter there will be no quarrel with either group. Here the term *disadvantaged* refers to any children who have not shared in the kinds of preschool and out-of-school opportunities which most teachers have come to expect for most children. Certainly there is no sharp division between children who are disadvantaged and those who are not. There is, instead, a continuum from children who have been most markedly deprived to those whose rich backgrounds of experience serve as fertile bases for school learning. The children at the lower end of this continuum are the disadvantaged.

These children, then, find their in-school learnings hindered in at least two major ways. First, the values and goals which have been built and are continuing to receive reinforcement in their homes and communities are not in line with the values of the school or the goals of the teacher for his students. A disadvantaged child may admire and want to emulate an older teenager in his community who has mastered the art of stealing hubcaps. Such a child may not be strongly motivated by the promise of a gold star after his name on a wall chart for every book he reads. Instead, he runs a great risk of being classified as lazy and indolent by his teacher when, in reality, he is basically neither; he merely sees absolutely no value in pursuing the particular kinds of endeavors his teacher thinks he should want to pursue.

In addition to the motivational differences which may lead the disadvantaged into school disfavor, a second major hinderance is his differing experiential background, which simply has not prepared him to profit from the kinds of school learnings offered — particularly in the area of reading. The child who lives where no reading matter is to be found may also live in a home where language patterns differ so markedly from those in school that, for all practical purposes, the in-school communication is a foreign language to him.

It is essential, however, that we do not assume that all disadvantaged children lack facility in oral communication. The total quantity of words in their listening and speaking vocabularies when they enter school may approximate that of their more favored peers; it is just that a large number of these words may not be the kind that a teacher would use or even permit in the classroom. Similarly, their language patterns may be completely adequate for their purposes out of school. But the child who shows possession by saying "me dog," may have difficulty when called upon to read the simple sentence, *It is my dog.*

The reading skills such children should acquire do not differ significantly from those all children should acquire. These pupils, too, should learn to unlock words, to comprehend printed materials, and to read with some degree of critical ability. The basic differences must come from our modifications of approaches, and these modifications grow from an understanding of the particular characteristics of each disadvantaged child with whom we work.

The three selections in this chapter put major emphasis on the characteristics of these children and suggest procedures which have proved successful for working with them. Charles A. Glatt explores the question of who the disadvantaged are and reaches a valuable conclusion, though it may be more complex than some would wish to believe. Mildred Beatty Smith suggests some procedures for working with the disadvantaged child and with his parents. The last selection, by Rupert A. Klaus and Susan W. Gray, describes programs in Tennessee and Washington, D.C., which have been used successfully in coping with some of the problems of the disadvantaged.

Who Are the Deprived Children?

✤ CHARLES A. GLATT

Educators are given to attaching labels to special concerns and interests that affect their profession. *Life adjustment education* is one such label. *Education of the whole child* is another. And *dropouts* is a third.

Life adjustment education had its heyday, as did education of the whole child. And enough has been written about dropouts to set the stage for a proper study of those who remain in school.

During the past two years a new concern has taken its place beside the others. I am thinking of the problem — rather difficult to label and more difficult to define — of "culturally deprived children."

Since President Johnson's antipoverty proposals were made to Congress, suggestions have been rampant that educators ought to be involved in the crusade to bring relief to depressed areas. In discussions of the war on poverty that is being waged in this country the expressions *culturally deprived* and *depressed areas* are often used. The expressions remind us that all Americans do not share equally in the fruits of the American dream. But how many thoughtful writers are satisfied with these labels?

A child does not have to be deprived culturally to receive only a small share of the benefits that ought to be the birthright of every American. A child may be deprived in other ways. Or he may be only *disadvantaged*. The word *disadvantaged* signifies perhaps a lesser evil than *deprived*. The terms, of course, are subject to interpretation, and writers and speakers differ in their interpretations. Riessman, for example, employs the expressions *culturally deprived, educationally deprived, deprived, lower class, underprivileged, disadvantaged,* and *lower socioeconomic group* interchangeably in his writings.[1]

As a child, I was perhaps one of the culturally deprived. But then many children who grew up during the depression years were culturally deprived. As a teacher in the public schools, I have taught students who fit current definitions of the deprived. And I have had workshop experience in dealing with cultural deprivation at the university level. Drawing on this background, I suggest that at least four propositions underlie the over-all concern with deprivation.

First, identification of deprived children may be difficult, but it is clear that some children are much more restricted in their experiential backgrounds, in their store of enriching memories, than other children are. Within the same neighborhood, the same school, the same classroom, some students are affluent

From *The Elementary School Journal*, 65: 407–413; May, 1965. Reprinted from "Who Are the Deprived Children?" in *The Elementary School Journal* by Charles A. Glatt by permission of The University of Chicago Press. Copyright © 1965 by The University of Chicago. Charles A. Glatt is Associate Professor of Education, The Ohio State University, Columbus.

[1] Frank Riessman, *The Culturally Deprived Child* (New York: Harper & Row, 1963), p. 1.

in qualities and characteristics that bespeak unstinted advantages: other students are almost bankrupt in these qualities.

Second, in America we have not quite decided which is more desirable, a monocultural or a multicultural existence. Certainly, at times the expectations of a particular culture are overriding. (For example, if one wants to climb the social ladder, one is guided by the expectations of a particular culture.) At other times a diversity of heritage may be an asset. To label someone as *culturally deprived* is to attach importance to one way of life as compared with another. Actually, in one environment a child may be wealthy in "subcultural" attributes. In another environment, the same child may be impoverished.

Third, educators who write and talk about the deprived child are dealing with a sensitive domain, as the proposition just stated suggests. Deprivation may be quite obviously related to certain ethnic and religious groups, to certain social classes and residential districts. But to say so is to invite a whirlwind of unfavorable reaction. Therefore, much of the literature on cultural deprivation is not so lucid as one might desire.

Fourth, deprivation is relative — relative to the culture, to the social system, to one's in-group and to the out-groups, to the time, the place, the particular situation. One of the most difficult tasks involved in studying this problem is to arrive at norms. Can levels or standards be defined? Can the definitions then be used to categorize individuals? I contend that to derive such norms is not only difficult, perhaps even impossible, but also undesirable. I suggest rather that the first task is to identify the social and cultural influences that affect individual development. After this task has been accomplished, the behaviors that result from these influences can be identified. Once the influences and the behaviors have been identified, it will be easier to determine the kind of growth that is needed to overcome personal deprivation.

From my experiences with students, I do not believe that such terms as *culturally deprived* and *culturally disadvantaged* are needed in the educator's professional vocabulary. The need is to recognize that each of us is deprived or underdeveloped in some ways. What one person needs to grow and develop may not be what another needs. I have found several guidelines useful in assessing the growth needs of individuals.

The first guideline: the causes of deprivation in children are manifold. Some of the causes are common and often they can be easily identified. These include economic status, housing, previous formal education, physical and mental health, and access to religious instruction. Other reasons for differences among individuals are just as significant but less readily specified. These include family attitudes and values, use of free time, maturation, interests, appreciations, and accessibility of learning materials that supplement and enrich those available in the classroom — books, art, music, movies, television, lectures.

The students who come into our schools bring with them diverse backgrounds that reflect differences based on these and other causes. Growth and development that occur in the classroom often tend to accentuate rather than to ameliorate such differences.

The second guideline: each child's background is unique, and each child's personal behavior is an expression of his unique background. The evidence we use to identify individual deprivation can usually be classified under the following categories of attitudes and behaviors: use of acceptable language;

relations with others; and social amenities (dress, manners, gestures, toilet habits). Other categories include respect for property, personal beliefs, values, attitudes, preconceptions, appreciation for aesthetic experiences, and the ability to relate ideas with events and entities.

These are clues that can lead a perceptive teacher to the causes of deprivation. The lists are not complete, but they suggest evidence that can be helpful in identifying areas of needed growth. The traits do not usually occur in isolation. Certain speech patterns, mannerisms, attitudes, and beliefs are commonly clustered and are associated with specific social classes, ethnic groups, economic levels, and family structures.

When Values Clash

Certainly conflict between opposing value systems is a basic factor in differential development. A child from a French home in southern Louisiana may be deprived in his use of the English language if only a French dialect is spoken at home. Navajo students from an Arizona reservation may hold values regarding property rights that are different from the values held by most Americans. A Catholic child may feel extremely uncomfortable if he is forced to sing hymns that express Protestant religious beliefs. Middle-class attitudes toward home life may be meaningless to children of migrant workers. Attitudes toward thrift and economic self-sufficiency may mean nothing to a boy whose major ambition is to grow up and get his name on the welfare rolls, as his father did. Cafeteria courtesies may be alien in a home where food is never plentiful and second servings are unknown. Open-mindedness may be next to impossible for the daughter of a family whose religious or political commitments are so strong that they preclude objectivity on any issue.

Truthfulness may be no virtue to a child who has never considered lying a vice. Honesty may not be seen as the best policy by the lad who has been taught at home to steal. Purity may be a meaningless notion to the girl whose mother prostitutes herself. Love may hold no attraction for a child who has only been tolerated. The teacher who has insight into these differences is wise indeed.

Four Children

In my work with young people in the South, the West, and the Northeast, I have come to know the culture of many families. From my experience I would like to present portraits of four children. Other teachers across the nation, I am sure, have known boys and girls like these. From Frank, John, Lulu Mae, and Margaret Smith we can learn to look behind the label *culturally deprived* to the unique needs of a single child.

Frank is a Spanish-American boy in a southwestern city. His father is on public relief. The family is Catholic and lives in a less desirable neighborhood in a house that is long past the stage of just needing repairs. The four-room home has a radio, a television set, and many pulp magazines, but few books. Frank has three sisters and four brothers, all of whom live at home. Except for one week when the family visited relatives in rural Colorado, none of the children has ever been more than thirty miles from his neighborhood. The only English spoken in the home is profane: everyone knows and uses the four-letter words. Liquor, when available, is consumed freely by the parents and the older children, and the sex act requires no privacy. Pocket money for the children comes from odd jobs and petty thievery.

Is Frank's way of life at home the culture to be examined? If so, Frank is not deprived. His life is enriched by the experiences that have been forced upon him. Is the way of life taught and encouraged at Frank's school to be examined? If so, Frank is quite deprived. He has a strong in-group allegiance; his language is foul and coarse; his personality is acutely twisted and antagonistic; art and music as aesthetic interests leave him cold and unresponsive; his dress, his appearance, his haircut, and his toilet habits are not at all in accord with campus expectations; his attitudes toward property and other persons are unacceptable; he cannot relate ideas and events that he has not experienced. Frank's growth needs are quite evident to his middle-class, Anglo, Protestant teacher. To him, Frank is one of the culturally deprived.

More important, however, Frank is a marginal person; that is, he is not a fully participating member of any one social group. As he adopts the ways of the school, he becomes less at ease at home. As the family pressures him (through formal and informal means), he finds school life less and less acceptable. Like many others he may gradually reject either the one way of life or the other, but he will continue to be influenced by both.

John is typically American. Like Frank, he is in seventh grade. His father is an assistant manager of a manufacturing firm and a member of several civic organizations. His mother attends the "right" meetings and belongs to the acceptable clubs. They are Protestant. John is the second of three children. The family has travelled extensively; they attend "cultural" activities; and plans for higher education for each child have already been made. The family is successful, well fed, and lives in spacious surroundings. Basically no conflicts characterize the home and the school environments. Can John possibly be one of the deprived?

At first glance one should probably answer in the negative. As his teacher came to know John, however, certain traits that are not immediately obvious were revealed. John's language at home and in the classroom is not the same as his language on the playground. Most of the four-letter words Frank uses John also uses, but only when he is with his peer group. His exemplary behavior in the presence of adults changes when adults are absent. The pictures he draws and the verses he pens on walls of the lavatories are a far cry from the art and the poetry to which he is exposed at home and in class. Frank could not care less about his school marks: John could not care less about how he makes his high marks. Cheating is acceptable: the only sin is being caught. John can relate ideas and events, but the relationships he draws in private are not in accord with the values and the beliefs he ostensibly holds.

Is John deprived? Does he need enrichment? Does he need new and different growth experiences? The reader can supply the answers. Frank is being forced to learn a new way of life. John is choosing a new (and hopefully not a permanent) way of life which fits needs that are probably not comprehended by his parents or his teachers.

Each of these boys is deprived in his own way. Each needs supplemental experiences. Each is caught in a world of conflicting values and expectations from which escape is difficult.

Lulu Mae is Negro and, by legal standards, illegitimate. In the Louisiana parish where she was born, Negroes know better than to apply for a marriage license. At best they would merely be ridiculed for making such a request; at worst they might be "taught a lesson" physically. Lulu Mae lives in a two-room shotgun shack in one of the several "Nigger Quarters" of the town where she, her mother, and several other children reside. The man who lives with her mother now is the third "daddy" that Lulu Mae recalls.

Food is never plentiful in the shack, which has only tar paper to keep the damp winter cold from coming through wide cracks in the walls. Only two beds can be seen: most of the children sleep on hard pallets on the floor. The stove, which also serves as a heater, burns wood, which is brought home each day from the lumber mill where "Daddy" works. No books, magazines, or newspapers can be found, except those that are laid under the cheap linoleum or that have been used as wallpaper in the front room. The family is regular in church attendance (Baptist), the only planned social activity in which they engage. Each of the older children has been "converted" and baptized in a nearby river.

Lulu Mae is the same chronological age as Frank and John, but in the two-room segregated school she attends she is barely doing fourth-grade work. No audio-visual aids can be seen there, and books of any kind are at a premium. Those that are available were sent over after they were no longer useful at the "white" elementary school.

By all measuring devices, Lulu Mae is deprived. Unlike Frank, however, she is not becoming a marginal person. Her teacher, also a Negro, is sensitive enough not to tease her students with unrealistic goals. Much of her teaching is oriented toward how black people can best get along in a white man's world.

Yet, Lulu Mae is wealthy in some respects. She knows about sex; she knows how babies are born and how to care for them; how to stay warm under thin blankets on a cold night; how to dig bait and catch catfish; how to say "Yes, suh" and "No, ma'am" with a toothy smile; how to wash clothes without a machine; how to cook collard greens, fatback, and cornbread. She knows something about sewing and planting a garden. She knows how to go barefoot without getting stickers in her feet and how to make an ice-cream cone last a full ten minutes on a hot summer day.

She cannot do most of the things that John or even Frank can do in school, but they could not do many of the things she can do at home. She needs an enriched curriculum — but only if her future is more promising than her mother's was. This year a pair of eyeglasses would help her work in school more than a new dress or a different book would, but no one in her family has ever owned glasses. The educator who wants a "specimen" for enrichment might well think seriously of the thousands of Lulu Maes throughout the land.

Margaret Smith (born Margarita Salmini) is — or was — Italian. Two years ago her parents moved from the Italian neighborhood, legally changed their names, and began making a new circle of friends. Margaret and her mother bleached their hair to an orange shade, while the males in the family got crewcuts to replace the longer hair styles they had worn for years. Visits back to see relatives are becoming very rare.

The Smiths bought an encyclopedia and subscribed to several upper-middle-class magazines. Their new house is neat, the lawn is well trimmed, and the usual back-yard outdoor cooking equipment stands beneath a shade tree. Clothes, shoes, accessories — all are in good taste, bought with the help and advice of friends who have also made the cultural switch the Smith family is making.

Margaret does well in school. She is an *A* student who is well liked by peers and teachers. No one at school thinks of her as Italian, but she lives with the fear that some day they might. She has learned to hate her old neighborhood and her former friends and is careful to associate only with children of the dominant social group. Margaret and her family have deliberately chosen to deprive themselves of a cultural background in order to cope better with what to them is a more desirable way of life. In making this change, they have sacrificed lifetimes of informal learnings. Mr. and Mrs. Smith are under no delusions about their own escape from the ethnic stigma — the break will not be complete for them. Their hope, however, is that their children will successfully make the great transition across subcultural lines without recurring problems.

Margarita's heritage was very rich: Margaret's heritage must begin anew. She has had many enriching experiences, but these must now be woven into the fabric of her new life. Fortunately, she will not be caught in school-home conflicts because her family depends in part on what she and her sisters learn at school for their new guideposts at home.

Deprivation and the School

Examples such as these are too numerous and too well known to merit further portrayal here. Certainly not all American children fit these descriptions. Each portrait is unique although each is, in many ways, similar to the others.

Some children are deprived of self-confidence, of a definite and well-defined role that is compatible with roles developed by their peers. Other children, including many upper-class boys and girls, are deprived of playmates, of friends, of understanding and appreciation. Still others lack skills, knowledge, pets, toys, and childhood myths.

The school cannot and should not try to assume responsibility for making up all the deficiencies in each child's life, but each educator is accountable for being aware of these differences. Moreover, it is incumbent upon members of the teaching profession to supplement previous experiences with new ones that properly fit the role of the school.

Enrichment, experiences, good education for all children — these are legitimate and necessary concerns of the school. But before we, as educators, make our definitions complete, many and diverse factors must be considered. Lest we do more harm than good, we must carefully select the criteria by which deprived children are to be identified.

Reading for the Culturally

Disadvantaged ✤ MILDRED BEATTY SMITH

> *Every teacher and probably every parent knows that it is imperative for boys and girls to learn to read adequately.*
>
> PAUL McKEE

Educators have been talking about a high quality of education for all children for many years. Most would quickly agree that every boy and girl should benefit from quality education tailored to his or her particular needs; yet the door to opportunity is not easily made available to every child.

One of the problems currently receiving considerable attention, particularly in urban centers, is how to cope with the deficiencies that burden too many children when they begin school. This paper suggests that a different approach is needed to teach culturally disadvantaged boys and girls to read.[1]

Reading, as we all know, opens the door to learning. Reading unlocks the portals to world splendors, to adventure, to all the fascinating knowledge about people, animals, places, things. Yet, reading does not do this for the disadvantaged youngster. For him, the first experiences of reading can present fear and ego-shattering barriers to all future learning. Such a child requires what we know to be good instruction — *and something more.*

It is the content of this "something more" that puzzles and all too often baffles educators. Before proceeding on this topic, let us examine the social-psychological setting of the disadvantaged, which creates the need for attention.

The Socialization Process

The good teacher knows that a child's behavior is learned through the socialization process, one of the inevitable functions of our society.[2] Chief among the socialization agencies in our society are the home and the school, each of which shares an essential role. The family, however, exerts the first and perhaps the predominant social influence upon the child. As a primary group, the family

From *Educational Leadership,* 22: 398–403; March, 1965. Reprinted with permission of the Association for Supervision and Curriculum Development and Mildred Beatty Smith. Copyright © 1965 by the Association for Supervision and Curriculum Development. Mildred Beatty Smith is General Elementary Consultant, Flint Public Schools, Flint, Michigan.

[1] In this context, the term "culturally disadvantaged" refers to the many children who lack the necessary environmental motivation to achieve. Reading, for example, has not been made to seem important for them and they, therefore, do not "want" to read.

[2] *Socialization* is referred to as the process of inducting the individual into the ways of the group. For further discussion of this concept, see W. B. Brookover, *A Sociology of Education,* New York: American Book Company, 1955; Bernard Barber, *Social Stratification: A Comparative Analysis of Structure and Process,* New York: Harcourt, Brace and Co., 1957; and Mildred B. Smith, "Interpersonal Influence on the Occupational Expectations of Sixth Grade Students," unpublished Ph.D. dissertation, Michigan State University, 1961.

defines the basic ideas, values, and emotions that are to influence the child throughout his life span.

If a child's family members read extensively in his presence, the child soon realizes that learning to read is important. No other communication is necessary for this value to be transmitted to the child. Similarly, an uneducated father can indicate to his son the importance of a college education by admiring in his presence a friend who attends college. Working-class parents who demonstrate interest in books or formal education transmit their values to their children. Other parents can limit their children's values to areas of entertainment-satisfaction or possessing a car. As the child interacts with members of his family group, he internalizes the expectations of these "important" people, and their values become his.

Although it is the first socializing agent, the family is not the only one for the child. When the child enters school, the teacher becomes for him an additional important person. It is at this stage that the expectations of both parents and teachers influence the attitudes, values, and aspirations of children.

Culturally disadvantaged children who are underachievers possess characteristics that are usually identifiable. This underachieving child invariably exhibits a poor attitude toward classroom work as well as unsatisfactory work habits.

This child is frequently without pencil or paper, but is likely to have an assortment of gum or candy wrappers in his desk. His notebook (if he has one) is untidy. He can be described as "working with one eye on the teacher and the other on his paper." He may talk to and poke other students the moment the teacher turns his back to write on the chalkboard. He plays with gadgets kept in his pockets or desk, and spends considerable time eating candy, pretzels and the like. The disadvantaged child (a) is not interested in his school work; (b) sees little value in it; and (c) finds himself forced into a strange and often a hostile environment.

On the other hand, the child who comes to school from a home in which he is required to complete a job on time, is rewarded for doing it well, sees his parents reading books and magazines, and is encouraged by his parents, has a good chance for success in reading. This student is motivated from within to achieve. He acquires the determination, desire, and ambition to learn. These qualities seem to contribute as much as native ability to success in reading.

The importance of the home environment as a factor in reading achievement should be understood by the educator. The sympathetic teacher understands that the culturally disadvantaged child is severely handicapped by an environment which he did not request and over which he has no control. Such a child may read and perform in other subjects at a level far below that he is capable of achieving.

The Reading Program. All children require good basic instruction in reading. However, additional motivation techniques and material must be employed in such instruction to compensate for the deficiencies that are inherent in the disadvantaged child's environment. Ideally, motivation should come not only from the teacher, but from the parent as well. Since many parents of disadvantaged children are unaware of the importance of stimulation, it becomes the task of the teacher and the administrator to bring this to their attention so that together, educators and parents can provide the child with the kinds of experiences that will encourage him to want to read.

Prereading Experiences. The disadvantaged child often enters school with a subnormal vocabulary which severely retards his reading progress. An effective, well-designed preschool program can enhance intellectual stimulation and greatly improve verbal language ability.

What causes the experience void of these children? In most cases, parents do not challenge their boys and girls to explore their environment — by asking questions, answering questions, and calling attention to details. Such parents overlook obvious points: (a) differences in colors of objects (*red chair, blue ball, blue and green boxes*); (b) differences in sizes of things (*large chair, small box*); (c) differences in shapes of things (*square table, round ball*); (d) words that express how objects feel (*damp cloth, soft sponge, heavy iron, fuzzy chicken*).

Educators will agree that disadvantaged children need a variety of experiences but it should be noted that these children, however, do not *intellectually experience* their present environment because they are not challenged to "see," to "distinguish," to "know about" it. Many of these children frequently relocate both within the city and from city-to-city — frequently moving to other sections of the country. Yet, all they can say about such traveling is an expression such as, "we went south." They are unable to identify cities, buildings, animals, highways, rivers, and historical landmarks along the route. This situation occurs because parents, brothers, or sisters have not encouraged the children to examine their surroundings for detail. They are not asked, "Did you see . . . ?", and "Did you notice . . . ?"

This "pattern of thinking" or behaving is learned at an early age through interaction with adults and older siblings. A good preschool program should not only help the child develop this "pattern of thinking," but should help to unlock the child's door to intellectual experience about his total environment.

Experience and Vocabulary. Closely allied with intellectual stimulation about things, places, and ideas is vocabulary. If the child observes detail and "tests his experiences" by talking about them, he then learns specific vocabulary.[3] In this manner, the child enlarges his speaking and listening vocabularies. Both types must be developed. It is not enough for the teacher to say the appropriate words. The child must say them also; and he will be reluctant to do so when such words are never spoken in his home. The teacher must realize that the child is experiencing a language that is "foreign" to him.[4] At this point, he must teach it as a foreign language (for example, using the word in a sentence and having the child repeat it).

In summary, disadvantaged preschool children need (a) to build ideas and concepts through intellectual stimulation and (b) to develop oral language facility. An effective program must include both direct and vicarious experiences. Direct experiences would include trips to such places as the grocery store, drug store, hardware store, zoo, library, fire station, farms (fruit, vegetable, animal), and horticultural gardens. Vicarious experiences would include

---

[3] It is believed that this kind of learning and behaving causes children to earn a higher score on standard intelligence tests. If this assumption is correct, intelligence tests do not adequately reflect the potential of culturally disadvantaged children.

[4] Since so much of the language spoken by the teacher is foreign to the disadvantaged child, English should be approached in this setting for what it is — a foreign language to the child.

the use of filmstrips, recordings, storybooks, and imitation realia, as toy fruits, vegetables, flowers, and animals, all of which can help build concepts and vocabulary.[5]

Involving Parents in Preschool Program

A parent educational program is an indispensable part of any preschool program for disadvantaged children. Parents not only can assist the teacher on field trips, but should be encouraged to learn along with the children. Parents can be taught the finger plays, songs, and games their children are learning, allowing for carryover experiences in the home.

All parents need to be encouraged to read daily to their children, and many need to be taught how to do this.[6] A take-home library that is managed by volunteer parents can provide read-aloud materials for the entire family.

School and Home Reading Experiences. The prereading program described earlier, emphasizing ideas, concepts and vocabulary development, should be continued in the kindergarten and primary years.

It is important that children not be forced into formal reading instruction before they are ready. However, undue emphasis must not be placed upon "waiting" until they are "ready to read." Instead, action is best directed toward getting children ready to read and providing materials that are meaningful in relation to their life experiences. Real-life stories which utilize the culturally disadvantaged child's own experiences and vocabulary make excellent beginning-to-read material.

Typewriters are ideal for creating interest in reading. The teacher types stories of children's experiences as told by them. These then are distributed as "reading stories." Children not only enjoy reading about their own happenings, but get an extra incentive from seeing their thoughts in print. Classrooms equipped with typewriters facilitate this teaching method. Children should also be encouraged to use the typewriter.

The regular reading program can be augmented by many good trade books. Children should be motivated to read trade books both at school and at home. Since many disadvantaged children are poor readers, additional techniques are very helpful. One technique is to begin a Bookworm Club, offering every child an incentive to read trade books. Another idea that usually works is to take the time following a library period to allow each child to get started reading the story. Otherwise, boys and girls are likely to forget the book soon after taking it home. With the reading of the story started at school, they are already interested in it and more apt to continue reading once they are at home.

The teacher should frequently read to the class and see that there always are

[5] It is not uncommon for these children to be unable to identify common fruits and vegetables, even though they may frequent the grocery with parents (an indication that parents are not calling their children's attention to details in their immediate environment).

[6] A booklet, "How to Help Your Child with Reading," has been used at parent meetings to explain techniques of reading aloud to parents in Flint, Michigan. (It should be noted that an illiterate parent can encourage his child to enjoy books by looking at storybooks and discussing the pictures with him. The very fact that this parent takes time with a book "shows" that he values reading and wants the child to learn to read.)

many interesting books in the classroom. The teacher who reads books for her own enjoyment lets the students know that their teacher likes to read.[7] It is important that the teacher set a time for sharing reading experiences with the students. In this way, the teacher becomes a member of the learning group, sharing in the excitement and interest.

Children who already have experienced failure with a standard reading program find the basal reader most formidable. Such materials may be eliminated in lieu of some type of multilevel self-help reading materials. These consist of short stories which can be completed during a single reading period. This approach gives the child immediate reinforcement and a feeling of accomplishment. A typical result is that children like the self-help reading material because it "puts us on our own more and the teacher does not have to tell us what to do all of the time."[8]

Parents and Reading Achievement. Parents may be invited to the school to help in many ways. A successful involvement can be achieved by invited parents during the library period. In addition to assisting the teacher with clerical chores, mothers show their children that they not only want but *expect* them to learn to read.

Fathers, too, can provide this encouragement by taking turns with library duties as well as reading to the class during the library period. They thus demonstrate to their children, particularly boys, that men value reading. Culturally disadvantaged boys especially need this type of masculine approval, since most prodding to achieve is normally associated with mothers or female teachers. All too often boys look upon their chums who take school work seriously as "sissies."

Mothers can help, also, by making single-story reading booklets. The child who finds thick hard-covered books difficult to "read for fun" will be delighted to discover he can finish a thin booklet and he gets the added satisfaction of reading several books. One mother simply cut up outdated reading books into individual stories under the teacher's direction. They then added covers.

Underachieving students require special help with vocabulary development. A file box of word cards enables the child to keep his own record of words that cause him difficulty. He can study these words at school, and also take them home for study. Again, teachers should instruct parents so they can help by flashing the word cards.

The following are suggested study steps that can be explained to parents as a guide for helping their child study reading words. The child should:

1. Look at only one word at a time. Think about how it begins and ends.
2. Say it softly. Think about how it sounds.
3. The meaning should be in *your own words*.
4. Your sentence should be a good sentence — it should make sense.
5. Check to see that you have given the correct meaning and have used it in a sentence.

---

[7] It is a paradox that the person who teaches reading and who is constantly encouraging children to "enjoy books" is seldom if ever seen doing the same by the students.

[8] A quotation from a Flint, Michigan, elementary class.

Another suggestion is to encourage parents to provide dictionaries and other reference books for home study. This produces an academic atmosphere in the home, facilitating the desire to learn. A quiet period in the home every evening can be managed by parents. Such a reading and study period helps all the children in the home to complete their homework, to read, write, or play games quietly. Parental support of this kind strengthens the school program, instilling an interest in reading beyond the regular school day.

Summer Reading Activities. Summer carryover of reading experience is very important in maintaining interest, fluency, and vocabulary. For this reason, summer reading activities that parents can manage are suggested. Suggestions[9] for parents may include: (a) continuing the daily "quiet time" in the home for individual reading, reading aloud to children, and playing quiet games; (b) having educational materials available — trade books, educational records, encyclopedias, dictionaries, and newspapers; (c) taking children to the library regularly; (d) encouraging children to make out grocery lists from newspaper advertisements; and (e) while riding in the car, encouraging children to read road signals and posters and see how many states they can identify by recognizing license plates.

A New Role for the School. As this article has emphasized, culturally disadvantaged children require special programs, teaching techniques, and materials to compensate for the areas of lack in their life experiences. This cultural lack, attributable in part to their homes and in part to their community environment, calls for stepped-up educational efforts if achievement is to match individual potential.

It is important to point out that such a realization does *not* mean that the school should simply take over and do everything for the child, thereby assuring his educational development to a satisfactory level. In the first place, the school, as structured in our society, cannot assume such control over the child. Secondly, no outside agency, school or otherwise, should assume the proper role of the parent.

Rather, the rightful role for educators is seen to be that of teaching and of assisting parents to assume their responsibilities, and of assuming their obligations to the public for the educational development of all children. The ideal and productive relationship, then, is the cooperative sharing of mutual responsibilities by the parents and the schools, working together to bridge the cultural gap with purposeful planning and educational programing.

---

[9] A more comprehensive list of suggestions could be printed for distribution or could be explained to parents at meetings during the last month at school.

Murfreesboro Preschool Program for Culturally Deprived Children

❦ RUPERT A. KLAUS AND SUSAN W. GRAY

The major purpose of the Early Training Project, initiated in the spring of 1961, is to study the feasibility and effectiveness of conducting a preschool intervention program designed to offset the progressive retardation in cognitive development and school achievement that characterizes the culturally deprived child as he passes through school.

The theoretical position from which the investigators chose to work follows:

1. There are identifiable and definable group differences between the privileged and the deprived that have a major bearing on a child's later adjustment to school and his academic performance.

2. The differences which handicap the deprived child's academic performance are subject to change, which may be effected by providing appropriate preschool activities through the application of sound educational and psychological principles and practices.

3. The remedial efforts will be most effective if the program is initiated at the preschool level so that the program will be developmental rather than remedial.

4. The proposed changes will enhance the child's emotional health rather than affect it adversely.

Major differences selected for final consideration fell into four categories:

First, the groups differ in their attitude toward achievement. While middle-class children generally are motivated to achieve, and particularly to achieve in school work, culturally deprived children often show little motivation to excel academically, an achievement which is probably little valued in the home. The deprived are less inclined to forego immediate gratification for potential future gain; and they do not demonstrate much persistence in the process of completing a task or achieving a goal, particularly with respect to academic tasks or goals. Many of the attitudes listed above may be related to the fact that the deprived seemingly have not internalized a standard of excellence to the same degree as the middle class and that for this reason they fail to have a standard against which to evaluate their performance.

A *second* major consideration was that of aptitude for achievement. There is adequate evidence that deprived children differ from the more privileged in language development, both quantitatively and qualitatively. Qualitatively,

From "Murfreesboro Preschool Program for Culturally Deprived Children," by Rupert A. Klaus and Susan W. Gray, *Childhood Education*, 42: 92–95; October, 1965. Reprinted by permission of the Association for Childhood Education International, 3615 Wisconsin Avenue, N.W., Washington, D.C. 20016. Rupert A. Klaus is School Psychologist, City Schools, Murfreesboro, Tennessee, and Susan W. Gray is Professor of Psychology, George Peabody College, Nashville, Tennessee. The research project reported in this article was supported by the National Institute of Mental Health, under Mental Health Project Grant 5-R11-MH-765-2.

deprived children use language with more concrete and functional connotations, while privileged children are inclined to utilize abstract language categories with greater frequency. The authors have observed that deprived children have greater difficulty in making, or at least reporting, perceptual discriminations with respect to pictures, printed forms, and words. Privileged children show a higher level of conceptualization. Language development, concept formation, and perceptual discrimination may be closely interrelated and interdependent; which one is of primary importance may be a matter for further investigation and research.

Third, the patterns of social interactions demonstrated by deprived children were considered. Deprived adults as well as children frequently show a distrust of strangers. Also, one finds that deprived children seem more aggressive in relationships with their peers but appear more passive in their interactions with authority figures. This suggests that deprived children interact less with strange adults and also less with their environment in the presence of strange adults which should have an inhibiting effect on school performance.

A *fourth* factor of concern was the general state of physical health, which probably needs no further elaboration or documentation.

In an attempt to give a theoretical explanation for the above differences the authors selected two major contributing variables — stimulation and reinforcement. With respect to stimulus variables, it is suggested that a difference in variety and richness of environmental stimulation is far more important to the deprived child than the amount. Perhaps more important than either of these is the order in which stimuli are either presented by adults or selected from the environment by adults for more intensive interaction on the part of children. The middle-class parent who is more knowledgeable about child development will provide children with materials and activities, many of them school related, which are more appropriate for their interests and abilities.

Concerning reinforcement variables, it was felt that most deprived children would receive less reinforcement from adults and, as a result, more from peers and self through general motor activity, resulting in a lower level of reinforcement. Also, middle-class children frequently would be reinforced for the kinds of behavior exploratory in nature and suggesting development of an internalized standard of excellence, while the reinforcement for the deprived child might be more inhibitory in nature. Response to behavior in the middle class is specific in that behavior is evaluated in terms of right and wrong, while among the deprived the response is directed more toward an individual's being good or bad because of his performance or behavior. Finally, reinforcement might also vary as to whether it is verbal; social nonverbal (such as pats, gestures and facial expressions); or by means of concrete objects. It is suggested that privileged children are more frequently exposed to verbal reinforcement.

It should be emphasized that the authors are well aware that there is great variability within socioeconomic groups with respect to any and all the above variables and that there is a great deal of overlap between groups. Differences enumerated above should suggest activities and methods to be used with groups of children that would be appropriate to effect constructive change. Individuals, however, have to be considered on the basis of their demonstrated orientation and response.

Sixty children were selected for the demonstration project in Murfreesboro, Tennessee, a town of approximately twenty-five thousand; and twenty-seven children were selected in a similar neighboring community. All the children were born in 1958 and expected to enter school in the fall of 1964. The children in Murfreesboro were randomly assigned to three groups. One training group participated in ten-week summer school sessions during 1962, 1963, and 1964. A second training group participated in the ten-week summer school sessions in 1963 and 1964. The third Murfreesboro group served as the local control group, and the one in the neighborhood community served as the distal control group.

One feature of the project was the home-visitor program. A well-qualified primary teacher with extensive training in sociology made weekly visits to homes of children in the training groups. These home contacts were initiated the first summer the children were in school, 1962 for the first group and 1963 for the second group, and continued through the academic year 1964–1965, the first year the children were in elementary school. The home visitor supplied parents with books, magazines, and materials and instructed the parents as to how they might use these with their children. Emphasis was placed upon getting parent and child to interact, particularly at the verbal and conceptual level. The home visitor also suggested numerous activities parents and children might engage in jointly so as to broaden the child's experiential background. Examples are gathering of leaves and seeds in the fall, experiments with freezing and thawing of water in winter, study of plant growth and flowering in the spring, visits to places of interest in the local community, and increased and effective use of the local public library. The home visitor also suggested how the mothers might more appropriately respond to the child in terms of activities reported and materials brought home from school. The program of activities and the proposed attitude changes we were hoping to effect in the children were explained to parents. It was hoped this would elicit parents' interest and approval and would aid them in responding more appropriately to any indication on the part of the child that the proposed changes were being effected.

The ten-week summer sessions were staffed to permit a low pupil-teacher ratio. For each group of twenty children a well-qualified primary teacher served as the coordinating teacher. In addition, four teacher-helpers, well-motivated college students who had shown interest in working with young children, served as small-group teachers (five children per group). The coordinating teacher was responsible for the instructional program and selected the over-all topics for consideration and study. She also was responsible for instruction when the children met in the large group of twenty. The small-group teachers were supervised by the coordinating teacher and were responsible for instruction in the smaller groups.

The children arrived in school at 9:00 A.M. and for the first thirty or forty-five minutes met in the large group under supervision of the coordinating teacher. Activities at this time set the general theme for the remainder of the day. Following this, the children met with their small-group teachers, who had planned various activities, Numerous activity centers — books, perceptual materials, arts and crafts, housekeeping, music, blocks, and toys — were set up throughout the building. The small-group teachers moved from one activity to another, each activity lasting, approximately thirty minutes. The children were given a snack of juice and crackers in mid-morning and nourishing lunch at noon. Shortly before leaving at 1:00 P.M., they reconvened in the large group to review and discuss the day's activities under the direction of the coordinating teacher.

The small-group teachers planned their activities so that the children were given maximum individual attention. Planned activities were always related to major areas of emphasis in the project: achievement motivation, delay of gratification, persistence, language development, perceptual discrimination, concept formation, improvement of personal social relations, and evidence of concern for general physical health. It was hoped that the entire school day would be an intensified specialized instructional activity geared toward effecting some of the changes that we hoped would take place with the children. The performance of each child was carefully evaluated and recorded, and suggestions were made for needed additional activities. These recommendations were discussed with the coordinating teachers, and appropriate plans were made to provide the necessary experiences within both the large and the small groups.

Numerous field trips were made to local points of interest. The children were prepared for the trips by discussions and audiovisual materials, and the teachers carefully planned the activities so that they might make a maximum contribution to the topic and variables emphasized at that time. During the trip significant aspects were selected from the environment for major focus of attention, and the teacher attempted to engage the children in conversation concerning these. Following the field trip, the activities were reviewed and the children were encouraged to discuss and relate their experiences.

Personal hygiene and good health habits were stressed throughout the project. The children were all given an annual physical examination, either by their private physician or through the local Public Health Clinic. The initiative for this was assumed by the project.

One of the concerns of the project was that the adults involved quickly would be seen as major reinforcing individuals. A carefully planned program was instituted so this might be achieved. The teachers were instructed to be particularly alert to any signs of behavior that would suggest that the children were responding in terms of the major variables under consideration. The reinforcement that followed was immediate and specific. Early in the program, teachers were encouraged to utilize concrete, social and verbal reinforcement together so as to be sure to reach the child through one of these means. As the program progressed emphasis shifted more toward verbal reinforcement. Also, it was hoped that by having the child compare his performance with an internalized standard of performance he would be able to utilize self-reinforcement.

The data collected thus far seem very encouraging. To date, measures of general intellectual performance on tests such as the Binet indicate that the progressive retardation of intellectual functioning has begun for the control groups but has been arrested for the training groups, with a possibility of improvement.

Language development, as measured by the Peabody Picture Vocabulary Test and the Illinois Test of Psycholinguistic Abilities, consistently favors the training groups over the control groups. Measures of reading readiness administered in the fall of 1964 showed the children in the training groups performing better than the control groups.

Analysis of the results of achievement tests administered in the spring of 1965 are not complete. The data available suggest that there has been a diffusion effect in Murfreesboro where one of the control groups has been in constant contact with the treatment groups and that the performance of the former has been enhanced.

Our somewhat guarded conclusion, thus far, is that a carefully planned developmental program can offset significantly some of the cumulative effects of cultural deprivation on a child's later school performance.

Further Reading for Chapter 7

Black, Millard. "Characteristics of the Culturally Disadvantaged Child," *The Reading Teacher*, 19: 465–470; March, 1965.

Byers, June. "Using Poetry to Help Educationally Deprived Children Learn Inductively," *Elementary English*, 42: 275–279; March, 1965.

Brazziel, W. F., and Mary Terrell. "For First Graders! A Good Start in School," *Elementary School Journal*, 62: 352–355; April, 1962.

Crosby, Muriel. "Primary Reading Needs," *Education*, 84: 462–465; April, 1964.

Dale, Edgar. "Vocabulary Development of the Underprivileged Child," *Elementary English*, 42: 778–786; November, 1965.

Deutsch, Martin. "The Role of Social Class in Language Development and Cognition," *American Journal of Orthopsychiatry*, 35: 78–88; January, 1965.

Duggins, James, H. "Reading and Social Difference," *English Journal*, 54: 284–288; April, 1965.

Edwards, Thomas. "The Language-Experience Attack on Cultural Deprivation," *The Reading Teacher*, 18: 546–551; April, 1964.

Gomberg, Adeline W. "The Lighthouse Day Camp Reading Experiment with Disadvantaged Children," *The Reading Teacher*, 19: 243–246; January, 1966.

Krueger, M. G. "Choosing Books for the Disadvantaged: Children's Materials," *Chicago School Journal*, 46: 254–255; March, 1965.

Lloyd, Helene. "What's Ahead in Reading for the Disadvantaged?" *The Reading Teacher*, 18: 471–476; March, 1965.

Meiselman, Max S. "The 1964 Summer Elementary School Program in New York City," *The Reading Teacher*, 19: 485–487; March, 1965.

Mingoia, Edwin M. "A Program for Immature Readers," *Elementary English*, 51: 616–621; October, 1964.

Olsen, James. "The Verbal Ability of the Culturally Different," *The Reading Teacher*, 18: 552–556; April, 1965.

Riessman, Frank. "Are the Deprived Non-Verbal?" in *Mental Health of the Poor*, Frank Riessman, Jerome Cohen, and Arthur Pearl (eds.). New York: The Free Press of Glencoe, 1964. Pp. 188–193.

Schwab, Rose L. "After-School Study Centers in New York City," *The Reading Teacher*, 18: 482–484; March, 1965.

Wachner, Clarence W. "Detroit's Great Cities School Improvement Program in Language Arts," *Elementary English*, 41: 734–742; November, 1964.

Wittick, Mildred Letton. "Language Arts for the Disadvantaged," in *Teaching the Culturally Disadvantaged Pupil*, John M. Beck and Richard W. Saxe (eds.). Springfield, Ill.: Charles C Thomas, 1965. Pp. 109–149.

8

Reading and the Gifted Student

The term *gifted students* is defined in many ways by those who have written about the education of the gifted. Although there is no single, generally accepted meaning for it, most often it refers to (1) those students who have already attained high academic achievement or (2) those students whose potential for learning is very high. In the latter case, the student's actual achievement may not be unusual but he may demonstrate potential for learning through some measure of academic aptitude such as an intelligence test.

These students, who, by definition, deviate markedly from their age-mates, suffer all of the problems engendered by these differences, plus some special ones. They require the attention of each good teacher as he provides for individual differences. Since these students deviate toward greater abilities, however, the teacher must offer opportunities which are more challenging than those that he normally provides for his students.

Although few disagree that a child will learn most effectively when he is taught to read at his learning level, and although most teachers at least make an effort to provide instruction at appropriate levels for slower-learning students, the "teach-them-when-they're-ready" principle often is not used in teaching the gifted. If appropriately applied, it must mean that some gifted pupils would be taught skills which average students would normally learn at higher grade levels. It must mean, for example, that some gifted third-graders would be receiving instruction in fourth- or fifth-grade reading skills, which their non-gifted classmates would not receive until one or two years later.

This form of vertical enrichment is a completely logical extension of our generally accepted belief in providing for individual differences, but it is an extension many are unwilling to accept. The main stumbling block to its acceptance seems to be "grade-level thinking" rather than "child-oriented thinking." If we can concentrate on the child rather than on grade levels, we may break the grade-level lockstep which too often stands in the way of the most adequate instruction for our gifted students.

An alternative to vertical enrichment is horizontal enrichment, which provides opportunities for the child to broaden his learnings at any grade level but does not cut upward across grade-level lines. For the gifted student, there can and should be many opportunities for wide reading in a variety of fields. Such reading can broaden his background of information and provide many opportunities for him to apply the reading skills that he has learned. It should not, however, be the entirety of his reading program when he shows readiness to profit from instruction in higher-level skills.

The most effective kind of enrichment will be a judicious mixture of horizontal and vertical enrichment that allows gifted students to participate in many broadening reading experiences *and* master the higher-level skills for which they are ready.

We must not assume, however, that the greater potential for learning that these students possess will automatically lead them to uncover, without our assistance, the most effective techniques of reading. In fact, sometimes, the gifted develop ways of reading that hide their deficiencies in essential skills. For example, a very young student may memorize words with great facility and use this memory in place of the word-attack skills he has not mastered. An alert teacher must note this weakness and provide instruction in the needed skills so that the void will not be detrimental in later reading activities.

One method of occupying the time of gifted students which warrants careful analysis is that of making them helpers for slow-learning students. This method is often justified as teaching social responsibility, but sometimes it benefits only the slow-learning student. Although we have very real responsibilities to the slow-learning students in our classrooms, we also have responsibilities to the gifted. Both should be helped to grow in reading abilities at their own levels of development. It may sometimes be a good practice to have our gifted students help the less gifted, but this procedure should not be carried on at the expense of the gifted students' growth.

The three articles in this section give additional information about the gifted and offer suggestions for stimulating their reading growth. In the first article, Ruth Strang suggests various procedures for the classroom.

In the second article, John J. DeBoer discusses "creative reading" in relation to the gifted student. The term *creative reading* demands a moment of our time. It is used to imply going beyond the understanding of what an author says and, as used by DeBoer, even going beyond critical reading (see Chapter 6). A clear definition of creative reading which differentiates it from other kinds of reading and post-reading, however, has not been forthcoming. For example, DeBoer includes throughout his selection a number of examples of creative reading which could just as adequately be classified as critical reading. He also classifies the understanding of metaphor as creative reading, but some others see it more logically as a kind of comprehension ability. There is no intent here to discount the many valuable activities Dr. DeBoer recommends for gifted readers; I merely wish to point out that the classification of these activities as creative reading is one with which not all reading specialists agree.

In the last article, Dan Cappa and Delwyn G. Schubert describe the results of a questionnaire study which elicited information about reading stimulation in the homes of the gifted.

The Able Reader

✢ RUTH STRANG

It sometimes seems that able readers are born, not made. Asked how they learned to read, they say, "I don't know. I just began to read." Without consciously following any particular process, they associated printed words with their meanings and developed their own system of phonics. Many able readers could read when they entered school.

Other able readers recall having had some reading instruction during their preschool years. They were taught the alphabet, given word-picture games to play, or were helped to sound out words that they wanted to learn. Experiments by Dr. O. K. Moore and others have shown that preschool children with a wide range of ability can learn to "read" — as each experimenter defines it.

Children who are reading before they come to school tend to have certain environmental conditions in common. Their parents or other adults have read aloud to them, encouraged their verbal curiosity and interest, answered their questions, and told them the words they wanted to know. These children have been to interesting places, seen and done interesting things, and talked about their experiences. Other things being equal, children whose parents take time to talk with them tend to be superior in language development.

In kindergarten, the child has further opportunities to explore, to listen, to talk, and to discover "the delight that lies between the covers of books." Activities, such as painting, cutting out pictures, and building things help to develop eye-hand coordination. The child also obtains practice in visual and auditory discrimination. These prereading experiences are especially important for children from economically disadvantaged homes, or homes where English is not spoken.

For children who have already begun to read, these activities may seem like a waste of time. However, able readers need activities in which they can learn to work cooperatively with other children. The skillful kindergarten teacher, like the wise parent, encourages these children to take the initiative in their learning, and provides an environment conducive to it.

Some first-grade teachers regard the child who already knows how to read as a problem. He definitely isn't. He should be given basic instruction in reading, along with other able learners. Even though he may be able to read the first-grade books, he may not have acquired the reading skills he will soon need for reading on his own. He should be expected to learn the same skills as the other pupils, but it is natural that he will learn them faster.

However, he should not be bored with explanations that he already understands, or with drills that he does not need. The danger of requiring a child to persist in activities that are below his level of readiness is obvious. He may lose his eagerness to read, become disillusioned with school, lose interest in

From *The Instructor,* 74: 83, 108–109; March, 1965. Reprinted by permission. Ruth Strang is Professor of Education, The University of Arizona, Tucson.

purposeful reading, or seek attention and excitement in obstreperous or disobedient behavior.

Able readers who did not learn to read before they came to school will "catch on" quickly; they should soon be separated from the group that needs more instruction. They can be on their own part of the time. Most of them can soon be grouped with the youngsters who learned to read before they came to school.

Able readers may get the social experience and the sense of service that they often need by occasionally helping other children with their reading difficulties. In such a team learning situation, an able reader may prevent the other from continuing to practice errors which the busy teacher might not detect.

The teacher can easily identify the able reader. When given a choice of activities, he often goes to the book corner. When the class is reading an experience story, he knows all or most of the words instantly. He reads for the teacher out of the primer or first-grade books.

It is more difficult to identify the potentially able reader — the child who has high mental ability but has not acquired commensurate reading ability. His failure to read up to capacity may be due to visual or auditory defects, low energy level, deficiency in oral language, retarded ego development, lack of experiences that give meaning to words, conflicts and worries that interfere with his ability to concentrate, or poor physical coordination. He may be afraid of the teacher or the other children in the room, or unable to relate himself to other people.

Some children develop a resistance to reading as a consequence of being nagged to read at home, or being given premature formal instruction by anxious or impatient parents. Any of these conditions may prevent a bright child from learning to read. If the teacher can get some indication of the possible cause from daily classroom observation, from test results, and by talking with his parents, she may be able to correct the conditions that are preventing the child from profiting by his instruction.

Throughout the primary grades and the intermediate grades, the same principles and procedures are applicable:

1. Ascertain the child's readiness for reading, his present proficiency, and his learning ability.
2. Don't bore him with instruction and practice that he does not need.
3. Provide him with a progression of meaningful and enjoyable reading experiences, including free choice of suitable books, creative writing, dramatizations of stories and poems, and discussions of stories that he has read.

It is preferable to broaden the child's reading interests by giving him supplementary materials on his present reading level, rather than giving him books that he will read in the next higher grade. Let him prepare simple reports on a topic; set up bulletin-board displays; keep a scrapbook of his experiences; and prepare practice material on visual discrimination and categorization, basic sight vocabulary, or sentence building, for children who need drill.

Able readers will often suggest other activities. They like to take initiative, and work hard on their own projects. As they look back over their elementary-school experience, children often recall with great satisfaction their special reading projects. One sixth-grade boy became absorbed in the subject of conservation and taught the unit on conservation to the whole class.

The able "bilingual" child benefits by frequent participation in informal group discussion and conversation, dramatization, and choral speaking. He needs expert help in learning to pronounce the English sounds that are different from those used in his native tongue.

Although he usually likes to read aloud to others, the able reader must be prepared to read a selection fluently and with expression. The importance of oral reading decreases as the student goes through the grades.

It often happens that bright children in primary grades are diagnosed as reading problems. In many cases their difficulty does not become apparent until after the first grade, perhaps because they have depended upon their superior memory and have not acquired the basic word-attack, comprehension, and vocabulary-building skills which all pupils should be taught at each grade level. This factor should be taken into careful consideration in accelerating a child; he may be physically, socially, and emotionally mature, but the teacher should be sure that he does not lose out on the basic reading skills.

If the able learner has difficulty with certain words and letters, he should be helped to note their similarities and differences, and to observe how they are used in sentences. One way of making him look more closely at words causing difficulty is to give him a number of sentences with the choice of three words, only one of which makes sense in the sentence:

was

The boy sat the dog.

saw

Exercises of this kind also give him practice in the use of context clues and several other word-recognition skills.

The teacher should ask the able reader questions that require him to think. To answer questions that ask "Why?" he needs to use the facts in reaching his own conclusion.

The able reader should also learn to ask and to answer his own questions. He should have access first to picture dictionaries, then to junior dictionaries, and finally to adult dictionaries. Junior encyclopedias and the World Almanac are also essential reference materials.

The reading interests of able readers widen rapidly. Beginners Books (Random House), biographies such as those in Row-Peterson's American Adventure Series, The Childhood of Famous Americans Series (Bobbs-Merrill), and the new social studies and science books published by the Garrard Press are only a few of the many fascinating series for children and young people that are being published in a continuous stream. Able readers follow the same general interest sequence but are usually about two years ahead. If they have access to a well-stocked library, they individualize their own curricula — provided they have acquired the skills that are necessary for effective reading.

Creative Reading and the Gifted

Student ✤ JOHN J. DEBOER

The term "creative reading" has had much currency in recent years. Is it a euphemism, intended to reinforce the impression of a modern classroom as a dynamic environment in which all emphasis is placed on stimulation as opposed to lesson-learning? Or is it merely a faddish expression for plain "good reading"?

Traditionally, we have thought of the writer as the one who "creates," while the good reader enters the author's world and passively permits that world to act upon him. Thus the skills involved in increasing one's perception span, vocabulary, word recognition, speed, and recall have been taught in order to facilitate the process of efficient reception in reading. The purpose has been to provide the child with a new language, an indispensable, vast means of symbolic communication.

Certainly the factor of receptivity is essential to good reading. When the reader goes to the printed page with mind fixed, with views and emotions previously established dominating the reading, the author is powerless to communicate with him. The reader must let the author take the lead. He must give himself, at least temporarily, over to a "willing suspension of disbelief" as the author spins a tale, or he must follow obediently as the philosopher expounds his doctrines — not necessarily to accept, but to understand. Thus only can the child enter new worlds and let enchantment or excitement or surprise delight him.

But there is another side to the coin. For every action there is a reaction. All the skills enumerated in a previous paragraph call for selective effort on the part of the reader. In Emerson's phrase, one must be an inventor to read well. There can be no efficient receptivity in reading without active response. The good reader keeps supplying from his own experience. And in the discriminating evocation of personal experiences lies the source of true creativity in reading.

Thus effective reading shares with other types of creative effort one purpose: to combine and recombine the materials of language to achieve a meaningful result. This means that (a) the creative reader is an active agent, not merely a passive recipient; (b) he is a seeker and an experimenter; and (c) he is both a builder and a leveler.

Reading, of course, is inseparable from thinking. Creative thinking involves all the higher-order mental processes: perception, concept formation, seeing relationships, drawing conclusions, making comparisons, making applications. Teaching creative reading must therefore be accompanied by instruction in creative thinking, insofar as creativity is a thing that can be taught.

From *The Reading Teacher,* 16: 435–441; May, 1963. Reprinted with permission of John J. DeBoer and the International Reading Association. John J. DeBoer is Professor of Secondary Education, University of Illinois, Urbana. This article was adapted from a chapter by the author, "The Concept of Creativity in Reading," in *Perspectives on English: Essays to Honor W. Wilbur Hatfield,* ed. Robert C. Pooley (New York: Appleton-Century-Crofts, Inc., 1960), pp. 199–211.

Creativity in the Gifted

In the sense in which we are employing the term, creativity is essential to reading growth from the earliest stages. The appeal to creativity must be made to learners of all levels of ability. But it is the cultivation of genuine creativity in the gifted pupil that provides probably the most difficult of all challenges to the teacher of reading. The creative act is aways a unique response, personal to the individual.

Although the differences *among* gifted children are as great as those between the gifted and the average, we may reasonably expect that most gifted children have greater capacity for perceiving or educing relationships, greater original-ity in utilizing the fruits of past experiences, greater daring in drawing con-clusions from data, greater hospitality to the new or unexpected, greater will-ingness to challenge authority. As in creative writing, the gifted student flourishes in an atmosphere of freedom, acceptance, and stimulation.

We may not assume, of course, that pupils of high potentiality necessarily display their talents in reading. It appears that the correlation between mental ability and reading comprehension is high, and it is reasonable to expect that the academically gifted boy or girl will do well in reading. We know, however, that many bright students are under-achievers in reading. They are in just as great a need of systematic instruction and encouragement as are the re-tarded readers.

And what of those young people who score normal in reading tests (and sometimes below normal) who exhibit extraordinary talent in music, art, the dance, the mastery of quantitative concepts, or practical and mechanical opera-tions? Since interests and creative abilities are usually associated, the teacher will make every effort to draw on the child's existing resources of creative interests to foster his growth in creative reading. A person's aptitudes may vary from one area of interest and competence to another, but human abilities are not generally highly compartmentalized. General intelligence, combined with such factors as experience, motivation, interest, and parental pressures, is com-monly the basis for exceptional achievement in specific fields. Kirk illustrates the many categories of special aptitudes as the socially talented, the mechan-ically talented, the artistically talented, the musically talented, the physically talented, the linguistically talented, and the academically talented (1). The concepts and mental constructs developed in various categories of experience should be drawn upon in the reading process, which will in turn enrich and amplify the world of creative discovery and achievement outside of reading.

To avoid nebulous objectives in the cultivation of creative reading abilities, the teacher should learn to view creativity in its more specific manifestations. While creativity cannot be "taught," in any direct sense, it is possible for the teacher to help free the child from the roadblocks, emotional and technical, which impede his path to the unique expression of which he is capable. By seeing clearly some of the major tasks involved in creative reading, the young learner can assume attitudes toward the printed page which will effectively promote the kind of independence and active response that we seek in reading. Suggestive of these tasks are the following: (a) creative inquiry, (b) creative interpretation, (c) creative integration, (d) creative application, and (e) creative criticism. The list is by no means exhaustive, and the resourceful teacher will find additional specifics as she works with groups or individual children.

Creative Inquiry

Modern schools have shifted their emphasis from mere subject-matter mastery and the rentention of ready-made "learning products," in the Morrisonian sense, to the growth of a lively curiosity, a reaching-out for meaning, a re-examination of alternative "solutions" to old problems, and the discovery and definition of new problems. Under this new emphasis, the idea of communicating established principles, sometimes even by the lecture method, is not eliminated. But in all learning, the reader or listener is an active participant, and he learns only as he re-creates within himself the thing to be learned. The first step in such re-creation is the adventure of asking questions. In each problematic situation the versatility and individuality required of the learner take on the quality of creative thinking, or "creative" reading. Such creativity is called into play in reading at various levels.

The first task, then, is to learn how to ask the *right* questions.

At a simple level, the satisfaction of curiosity, the questions may be fairly obvious ones, such as, "What will happen next?" or "Why was Linda so quiet at Christmas dinner?" Questions may reveal a more mature kind of critical curiosity, as illustrated in a letter by a third grade boy written to an author in care of her publishers: "I've been reading your book at school called *Let's Take a Trip to the Firehouse*. Now what I'd like to know is why you call the aerial truck and the hook-and-ladder truck the same thing." He politely discusses the differences between the trucks and concludes by asking again why the author wrote as if they were same (3).

Basic to this boy's capacity to make intelligent inquiry was the fact that he had had enriched experiences with toy fire equipment, had probably visited the fire station several times, and, perhaps most important, the fact that he was called upon to make comparisons among many books on the subject.

For older students, the questioning aroused by a very dramatic account of the detonation of the first atomic bomb presents a greater challenge. "It was the nearest thing to doomsday that one could possibly imagine. . . . But Laurence thought it might be the dawn of a new day for mankind, not doomsday at all. He shared the exuberance of the scientists, who leaped to their feet . . . shouting with joy."

In one class, such questions as these were raised after reading about the bomb: "What other inventions were motivated by defense and armament?" "How have such inventions affected the nation's economy?" "What peaceful uses could atomic energy serve?" "Was the discovery of atomic fission and fusion fortunate or unfortunate?" "Was Laurence right in thinking that atomic energy did not spell out doomsday but a great new hope for mankind?" "What steps could we as a nation take to reduce the danger of nuclear war?"

These questions were stimulated, but not demanded, by the story. They arose out of experience with previous reading and discussion, and out of the relationship between the passage and the day's news. It is in this perception of relationships and their formulation in words that the element of creativity is to be found.

Such an approach to creative inquiry, especially by talented children, has fundamental implications for the organization of the curriculum. Few questions that young people ask are limited to a single discipline. The answers must be drawn from a variety of subject fields. If the questions are worthwhile, they will concern situations and problems rather than neatly categorized items of information. The domain of reading is as broad as the world itself.

Creative Interpretation

Creative inquiry is a search for answers to questions which the reader asks to meet a need or satisfy curiosity; creative *interpretation* involves an intensive effort at reconstructing the author's precise meaning. Such reconstruction is not "free" creation, because it is sternly limited by the clues and symbols found in the reading matter. Nevertheless, interpretation at its best is a creative process because the ideas on the page must be built anew in the mind of each reader. Since minds of readers differ, and since some minds are both better informed and more creative than others, interpretations of literary materials may vary widely. Witness the conflicting interpretations of passages in the Bible or Shakespeare.

A familiar example of the need for creative interpretation is the expression found in newspapers almost daily, "the free world." In ascertaining the writers' intent when they use the word "free" in this context, a reader might examine the various classical definitions of "freedom," such as "absence of external restraint," or "power to choose and pursue a line of action," or "exemption from arbitrary domination." Some acquaintance, however, with the common use of the expression, "the free world," in America and Western Europe soon leads the perceptive reader to recognize that it refers to all the countries outside of the Communist orbit, except perhaps the uncommitted nations. The fact that these "free" countries include Franco's Spain, the dictatorships of Latin America, and the white supremacist Republic of South Africa, and that nations ground down by poverty and starvation cannot be considered really free, does not alter the true intent of the writer. "Freedom" in this sense may be a politically motivated euphemism, but to the sophisticated reader the writer's meaning is clear.

The understanding of metaphorical language, too, calls for a kind of creative interpretation. When Margaret Sidney writes, in *Five Little Peppers and How They Grew*, "It was just on the edge of twilight," she calls on the child to interpret the figure which borrows from space to describe time. Creative effort is involved in this simple translation, which the fluent reader almost unconsciously makes as he follows the sweep of the story. When an author calls his book, *Out of the Jaws of Victory*, the student must quickly supply the original metaphor and relate the inversion to the political analysis with which the books deals — Truman's election in 1948. This kind of interpretation, which calls for the formation and utilization of mental constructs on the part of the reader, is a creative activity, although on a relatively simple level.

Creative Integration

We have seen that creativity in reading means putting things together — words, concepts, images — to create something new in the reader's mind. But this "putting together" extends also to the constituent factors in a remark, a situation, a plot, or the sayings and deeds of a character. The essential moments of insight in reading occur when the reader has perceived what the various factors "add up to." The "adding up to," however, is not a mere process of addition, but a perception, sometimes unexpected, of a central impact, a mood, a value, an attitude toward life.

To the creative reader, the "moment of insight" has value insofar as he is able to relate it to the body of his previous experience, his previous attitudes, his perception of reality, his outlook on life. *Integrating* what one reads (or hears on the radio, or sees on the stage or the television screen) with one's beliefs about self or others or the world or values is a process that must be unique to each individual, and is, therefore, in a true sense creative.

Let us take as an example the Biblical story of David and Goliath. The reader is moved by the story — the spectacle of a young man exhibiting great faith and courage, of the mighty defeated by the weak, of the arrogant brought low by the humble. But from this point on, each reader makes his own connections with past knowledge and experience — connections which heighten the emotional impact of the narrative, but which also give new meaning to a much broader cluster of events, issues, problems, goals, beliefs. Thus, one reader, following David as he ran forward to meet the giant, remembered that David was a pastoral poet, the "sweet singer of Israel," who was not merely a military hero but also one of the towering figures in the ancient and cultural tradition of the Jewish people. The reminder made him see in clearer perspective the nature of the barbaric mind which harbors anti-Semitism. The reaction was not one of free association; it was a creative transference from a single dramatic episode to a generalized insight or emotion. The task of the student is to build a structure fit for the cultivated mind to dwell in.

Creative Application

One of the skills of reading frequently mentioned is the ability to apply what one reads. It is reasonable to question whether application is a proper part of reading itself. A closer examination of the mental processes involved in reading, however, will reveal that application is integral to creative reading. To construe what one reads, one must know what the reading matter *implies* for a variety of related situations.

The process of application may be illustrated by the simple examples of a housewife following a recipe and of a chess addict trying to solve a chess puzzle. In these instances, the reading is accompanied by other activities, but the reading itself is focused upon the ways in which the printed words are to be applied. Considering the relative simplicity of these examples, one might hesitate to use the term "creative" in this connection. No one, however, would dispute the creative quality of applications made when the reading material is abstract or when it calls for subtle distinctions of meaning.

To the extent that reading may affect one's thinking in general, or that an idea encountered on the printed page may reshape one's beliefs about related matters, whether they concern social organization or public health or penology, reading has brought about a kind of "application" that is truly creative.

Creative Criticism

Discussions of critical reading have usually been concerned with the negative aspects of the process. They have stressed analysis rather than creation. If critical reading is essentially a process of acceptance and rejection, attention has been focused chiefly upon rejection. Thus, the reader has often been encouraged to look for pitfalls and errors, to beware of logical fallacies, of various propaganda devices, of stereotypes and emotionalized language. Critical reading has too often engendered mere skepticism and a purely defensive attitude.

While defense against the wiles of Madison Avnue experts and clever propagandists is important, it is not enough. Our youth must learn to seek a strategy of conquest, to develop philosophies of their own. Reading is a search for answers. The creative reader accepts, rejects, puts together, raises questions, draws inferences, and comes to (at least) tentative conclusions. He makes a declaration of independence of the author. He knows when he can draw independent conclusions, when he must suspend judgment, when he must trust the author.

The question of trust is crucial in creative criticism. The reader trusts the acknowledged expert with respect to facts. Without a degree of trust in the writer, very little learning could take place through reading. But always it must be guarded trust, a willingness to examine accompanied by a readiness to challenge.

Critical thinking and critical reading must lead to conclusions upon which one can act. Creative criticism does not result in a vacuum or intellectual stalemate. It is goal-oriented.

The creative reader comes to the printed page with a body of values and information against which he tests what he is reading. He revises his values and corrects his information if the material appears valid to him. For such a task, wide knowledge and experience and clear purposes are needed.

The elements of creative reading described in the foregoing paragraphs provide manageable targets for instruction, but in the reading process itself they often operate simultaneously and interactively. The key is wide reading rather than single-textbook instruction, and frequent challenges by the teacher as to the reader's purposes and standards of judgment.

References

1. Kirk, Samuel A. *Educating Exceptional Children*. Boston: Houghton Mifflin, 1962. P. 39.
2. Pooley, Robert C., and others. *All Around America*. Chicago: Scott, Foresman. P. 167.
3. Schatz, Esther E., Roberta Utterback, Mary E. Wilsberg, and Alexander Frazier. *Exploring Independent Reading in the Primary Grades.* Columbus, Ohio: The Ohio State University. Pp. 66–67.

Do Parents Help Gifted Children

Read? ❧ DAN CAPPA AND DELWYN G. SCHUBERT

There has always been considerable discussion of what teachers should and shouldn't do to help children read. But it is a serious mistake to assume that reading is solely the responsibility of teachers and the school. A child spends more time at home than he does in school and a great deal depends on what happens there. What is the parents' attitude toward their children's reading? Do they feel the school is doing a good job of teaching reading to their children? Do they provide physical conditions and special reading materials for their children? Books? Magazines? Questions such as these are particularly important when considering the reading development of gifted children. Research shows that gifted children are mentally hungry and that their cerebral appetites often are met through wide reading. Since the school frequently is unable to provide enough free periods for gifted children to satisfy their insatiable desire to read, most of their free reading, if it is going to take place at all, must occur in the home.

With the cooperation of a number of experienced elementary teachers enrolled in the writers' classes, the authors were able to gather information about the home reading environment of eighty-three gifted intermediate grade children. The study grew out of questionnaires filled out by twenty-nine fourth-, thirty-three fifth-, and nineteen sixth-grade children. Two additional children were included, although no grade designation for them was available. Intelligence quotients ranged from 130 to 185 with an average of 137.8. Approximately one-third of the total number of children began to read before entering school.

Among other things, the children were asked how many books at home belonged to them, if magazines came to their home just for them, and the names of such magazines. They also were asked how much time they spent daily, out of school, reading for fun.

When questioned as to how many books at home belonged to them, two of the eighty-three children answered with an ambiguous "many." One child failed to respond. The remaining eighty, as evidenced in Table I, indicated having personal libraries ranging in size from two to five hundred books. The average size was forty-one books. Perhaps the most impressive aspect of these data is variability. Although no child reported owning no books, almost 20 per cent of the children reported having small libraries (two to ten books); and a minority group indicated tremendously large libraries for this age level. In general, however, it is reassuring to find that forty per cent of the children owned substantially large libraries of twenty to one hundred books.

Forty-seven children in this study answered affirmatively the query, "Do any magazines come to your home just for you?" Table II shows that twenty-one different magazines were subscribed to by parents, with four — *Children's*

From *The Journal of Educational Research*, 56: 33–36; September, 1962. Reprinted by permission. Dan Cappa and Delwyn G. Schubert are Professors of Education, California State College at Los Angeles.

TABLE I. "How Many Books at Home Belong to You?"

Number of Books	2–10	12–20	21–40	50–101	105–500
Children Responding	20	21	16	18	5
Average per Child	41 books				

Digest, Boys' Life, Jack and Jill, and *Calling All Girls* — enjoying a popularity accounting for 65 per cent of the total number. As a sidelight, it is interesting to note that most of the magazines are juvenile in their appeal. A few adult magazines, such as *Saturday Evening Post* and *Look,* also are represented. In several instances, the magazine titles reported by the children are in error.

Table III shows the varying amounts of time the gifted children in this study devote to reading for fun outside of school. Seven children failed to commit themselves in this regard. But of the seventy-six who did respond, it is reassuring to find that well over half of them are devoting more than one hour daily to free reading outside of school.

"In the home, where do you do most of your reading?" To this question, the authors received multiple responses. Fifty-five children (56 per cent of the total responses), answered: "my room." Another twenty-seven children (28 per cent of the total responses) said that they did their reading in the "living room." The remaining answers varied and included: "den," "kitchen," "spare room," "study," "in a corner," and "tree house." Three children failed to answer the question. The responses given, however, indicate that well over half of the gifted children in this study are provided with a suitable reading

TABLE II. "What Magazines Come to Your Home Just for You?"

Name of Magazine	Frequency
Children's Digest	17
Boys' Life	8
Jack and Jill	5
Calling All Girls	5
Movie Magazine	2
Children's Friend	2
Child's Life	1
Around the World	1
Reader's Digest	1
Linn's Weekly Stamp News	1
Look	1
Girls' Life	1
Comic Books	1
American	1
Children's Activities	1
Photoplay	1
Sport	1
Saturday Evening Post	1
Wee Wisdom	1
Junior Natural History	1
American Girl	1

TABLE III. "About How Much Time Do You Spend Daily, Out of School, Reading for Fun?"

Length of Time in Hours	¼–1	1–2	2–3	3–5
Number of Children	30	29	15	2
Average per Child	1.16 hours (70 minutes)			

environment. Certainly it can be assumed that when a child reads "in his room," an optimal reading environment probably is to be found.

The last section of the study was devoted to studying parents' attitudes toward the reading habits of their children. Table IV shows that of a total of 217 responses, 176 involved criticisms of the children. On the other hand, statement *j* evoked forty-one commendatory responses and statement *i* rated none at all. If we can put credence in the judgment of the children who filled out the questionnaires used in this investigation, the parents represented are happy with the school. None of them feels that the school is doing a poor job of teaching reading.

Statements *a* through *d* show that the parents are more interested in encouraging slow reading than fast reading. Of the two kinds of reading, oral and silent, the former is more subject to criticism. This is understandable, since shortcomings are more obvious when children read out loud.

Statement *e* shows that a substantial number of the parents (34 per cent) want their children to do more reading. In a few instances, according to *f*, parents have juvenile bookworms who constitute a problem by doing too much reading.

Not only are these parents interested in having their children read more, but, according to statement *g*, 22 per cent of them would like to see more difficult books read. Only one parent in the entire sample felt that his child should read

TABLE IV. "Check One or More of the Following Statements That Best Describe Attitudes of Your Parents Toward Your Reading Habits"

a.	6	you should read faster orally
b.	17	you should read slower orally
c.	7	you should read faster silently
d.	9	you should read slower silently
e.	28	you should read more
f.	5	you should read less
g.	18	you should read harder books
h.	1	you should read easier books
i.	0	you are not being well taught to read at school
j.	41	you are being well taught to read at school
k.	6	you should know more words when you read
l.	15	you should do a better job of sounding out words
m.	2	you should understand better what you read
n.	23	you should remember more of what you read
o.	13	you shouldn't read in bed
p.	17	you should read a greater variety of books
q.	9	others:_____

easier books. Apropos, too, is the parents' desire to have children include in their reading a greater variety of books (statement *p*).

Statements *k* and *m* don't prove to be of concern to parents, but *l*, on the other hand, reflects the current interest in phonics. Eighteen per cent of the parents feel that their children "should do a better job of sounding out words." This tends to corroborate an earlier study by one of the authors, showing that gifted children do not make much use of structural or phonetic analysis in attacking unknown words.

About 28 per cent of the parents are concerned with the inability of their children to remember what they read. Their preoccupation with statement *n* may be a reflection of the layman's conception that an educated mind is encyclopedic in nature. This insistence on retention has been given impetus by the numerous "Champagne for Caesar" types of television shows which glorify the ability to retain information.

The last item, *q*, involves nine miscellaneous criticisms of children's reading such as: "you shouldn't read at the dinner table," "you should appreciate poetry more," "you should get more interested in books," etc.

In summary, it seems evident that the parents of the gifted children in this study are assuming responsibility in extending the reading skills of their children. The majority of them are buying books and subscribing to magazines for their children to read. They are providing time and a place in their homes where free reading can take place. As a group, parents are critical of their children's reading and are interested in raising the quantity and quality of the reading done by them. Parents do not, however, level any criticisms against the school.

Further Reading for Chapter 8

Barbe, Walter R. "Reading Aspects," in *Curriculum Planning for the Gifted*, Louis A. Fliegler (ed.). Englewood Cliffs, N.J.: Prentice Hall, Inc., 1961. Pp. 213–243.

————, and Dorothy E. Norris. "Reading Instruction in Special Classes for Gifted Elementary Children," *The Reading Teacher*, 16: 425–428; May, 1963.

Dawson, Mildred A., and Henry A. Bamman. *Fundamentals of Basic Reading Instruction*. New York: David McKay Co., Inc., 1963. Chapter 8.

Durr, William K. *The Gifted Student*. New York: Oxford University Press, 1964. Chapters 4 and 9.

————, and Robert R. Schmatz. "Personality Differences Between High-Achieving and Low-Achieving Gifted Children," *The Reading Teacher*, 17: 251–254; January, 1964.

Gross, Calvin E. "Language Arts Experiences for the Mentally Superior: Kindergarten through Grade 8, Pittsburgh," in *Educating the Academically Able*, Lester D. Crow and Alice Crow (eds.). New York: David McKay Co., Inc., 1963. Pp. 320–326.

Isaacs, Ann F. "Should the Gifted Preschool Child be Taught to Read?" *The Gifted Child Quarterly*, 7: 72–77; Summer, 1963.

Jacobs, Leland B. "Books for the Gifted," *The Reading Teacher*, 16: 429–434; May, 1963.

McCracken, Robert A. "Accelerating the Reading Speed of Sixth-Grade Gifted Children," *Exceptional Children*, 27: 27–29; September, 1960.

Sabaroff, Rose E. "Challenges in Reading for the Gifted," *Elementary English*, 42: 393–400; April, 1965.

Sister Josephina. "Actual and Expected Reading Scores of Gifted and Average Pupils," *Peabody Journal of Education*, 42: 28–31; July, 1964.

Torrance, E. Paul. "Helping Gifted Children Read Creatively," *The Gifted Child Quarterly*, 7: 3–8; Spring, 1963.

Witty, Paul A. "A Balanced Reading Program for the Gifted," *The Reading Teacher*, 16: 418–424; May, 1963.

——, Alma Moore Freeland, and Edith H. Grotberg. *The Teaching of Reading: A Developmental Process*. Boston: D. C. Heath & Company, 1966. Chapter 15.

9

Organizing for Instruction

In addition to trying out a variety of teaching methods and techniques, school personnel have also experimented with different types of grouping arrangements in an effort to improve reading achievement. These organizational efforts have included intraclass as well as interclass arrangements.

At the present time, in the vast majority of schools in which these arrangements are being tried out, teachers are providing for individual differences within a classroom through the use of reading groups. Although there is no standard number of groups, most teachers use three, with some additional individualization for the very few pupils who are exceptionally strong or exceptionally weak in reading skills in relation to the rest of the class. A single basal-reading series may be used, with children reading at different levels within the series, or a multi-basal approach may be used, with a different series for each group.

In contrast to this, some teachers are experimenting with an individualized reading program. The essential characteristics of this approach are pupil selection of reading matter and individual reading — i.e., each child chooses what he wishes to read from a wide variety of reading materials and reads alone, without regard to what the other children in the room are reading. Generally, in this program, a basic-reading series is not used.

Proponents of intraclass grouping also support the value of a large amount of independent reading for all children and recommend that pupils should have many opportunities to read widely from materials of their own choosing. They believe, however, that complete individualization of instruction is likely to lead to a detrimental deemphasis of reading skills and that children should not be expected to learn to read without more direct instruction in skills than they are likely to receive when a purely individualized approach is used.

Proponents of individualized reading usually reject a merger of the two approaches. They believe that the grouping approach is ineffectual and should not be used. Although they generally contend that the teacher will continue to teach reading skills to individual pupils, they do not concentrate on skills and provide no clear-cut understanding of how a sequential skill-development program can or should be maintained.

The first two selections in this chapter deal with this issue of groups versus individualized reading. The article by Russell G. Stauffer presents well-reasoned descriptions of the two approaches. With objectivity and sound reasons for his decisions, Dr. Stauffer concludes that the approaches are not mutually exclusive and that the wise teacher of reading will find his pupils benefiting from a combination of the two.

The following report by Alton L. Safford describes an evaluation of one year's growth in reading for a group of students who were engaged in an individualized reading program. As Dr. Safford points out, his study was designed to measure what *had* happened when individualized reading was introduced into a regular, on-going program — not what would happen if it was tried in a classical experimental-control study. The results are striking.

The second kind of organizational arrangement which has been tried is one in which children are placed into classrooms on bases other than years in school. One of these, the non-graded approach, is designed to completely eliminate grade-level designations and to permit children to progress through the non-graded portion of the school at paces which are most appropriate for them. For example, if a school replaces Grades 1, 2, and 3 with a non-graded primary, some children might complete this portion of their educational program in two, three, or four years, but there would be no "passing" or "failing" from year to year. Teachers in schools in which this approach has been used generally favor it.

Another organizational change by which children are grouped into rooms is the Joplin Plan. In this arrangement, children are heterogeneously assigned to grade levels for the major portion of the school day, but they are homogeneously grouped according to reading achievement for reading instruction. This program of semi-departmentalization is designed to narrow the range of individual differences within a classroom.

The last three studies in this chapter deal with the effects of grouping children into classrooms in different ways. The studies by Maurie Hillson *et al.* and Mary King Skapski report the effects of non-graded programs on reading. Although the methods of comparing results in these two studies are quite different, the conclusions are the same and should provide definite direction to those who wonder about the value of this kind of grouping arrangement.

In the final selection, William F. Moorhouse examines the results of a five-semester Joplin-Plan study. The changing results from semester to semester show the effects of a new approach on the initial reading achievement of pupils.

Individualized and Group-Type Directed Reading Instruction

❧ RUSSELL G. STAUFFER

As long ago as 1888 educators were vehemently denouncing the lockstep method of instruction. Lockstep meant that all pupils in a class, as one, were required to move forward at the same rate, in the same book, mastering the same amount of material to the same degree of thoroughness. Preston Search, who was strongly opposed to the lockstep practices, was hailed as the first voice in America to be raised in protest (10).

Today, in most instances the whole-class lockstep pattern has been broken. Now the common practice is to organize a class into three groups. Stewart, in a study of 120 school systems, reported that the consistent practice at the primary level was to have three groups, and that many of the schools had two or more groups at the intermediate level (8).

What has happened, though, in all too many instances where children are grouped for reading instruction is to commit the same lockstep errors on a group basis as were previously committed on a whole-class basis. Frequently children are put in groups, and regardless of the label used, are known as "poor," "average," and "good" readers. A pupil is usually so classified at the first-grade level and is so passed on from year to year and is seldom, if ever, reclassified.

To a degree, the shortcomings of any form of lockstep procedures were recognized and criticized in the Twenty-Fourth Yearbook of the National Society for the Study of Education, Part II, *Adapting the Schools to Individual Differences*. The basic intent for the breaking of the lockstep was stated there as "the individualization of instruction." It was pointed out that individuals must be given an opportunity to follow their own tastes. Then, being social-minded, they will want to discuss what they read and profit by the discussion. It was also pointed out that small groups, spontaneously formed, were best to stimulate the turning over of ideas in the mind, of seeing their significance and relationships, and otherwise digesting and assimilating them. To accomplish this kind of classroom organization and directing of learning, teaching would need to be vigorous, inspiring, and highminded.

In Part I of the Twenty-Fourth Yearbook, the Committee on Reading explains that, if reading instruction is to develop desirable attitudes, habits, and skills, then each teacher must study the needs of her pupils so as to provide appropriate group and individual instruction. What the Committee sought was to have each pupil attain maximum growth with the least amount of wasted effort and the most satisfaction. It recognized two extreme positions: mass instruction,

From *Elementary English*, 37: 375–382; October, 1960. Reprinted with the permission of the National Council of Teachers of English and Russell G. Stauffer, Professor of Education, University of Delaware, Newark.

and individual instruction; and it advocated a classroom organization that allowed for both group and individual instruction.

Between the twenties and the fifties teachers broke away from the whole-class pattern for reading instruction. Arranging children in a class into three groups became the common practice. In three decades it became evident, though, that what was happening was merely the replacement of a whole-class lockstep with a three-group lockstep. The common question asked by teachers was: "What do the pupils in Groups I and II do while I teach Group III?"

Publishers of basic readers tried to provide the answers by providing more workbooks. Next, they added two basic books at a level, and today they have reached the "parallel reader" stage. None of this has solved the dilemma! Teachers have discovered that, regardless of the added materials, they still cannot be in three different places at one time.

It seems almost a paradox that, in answer to this challenging three-group, one-teacher circumstance, the movement during the fifties should be toward complete individualization of instruction. Is it any wonder that teachers with questions about how to handle three groups should revolt? If they are concerned — and they have a right to be — about the handling of three groups, just to think about teaching thirty children individually can be distressing.

A brief review of the circumstances that may have led to the grouping dilemma seems in order. Much of the effort toward grouping resulted from the advent of standardized tests, increased knowledge of individual differences, and the expanding supply of materials. Accordingly, practices were modified so that the good readers could move ahead in a book while the slow ones were allowed to drop behind and move slowly in the same book.

Grouping within the bounds of a basic reader was soon found to be inadequate. So publishers of basic readers provided two books for each grade level beyond first grade, and five books for first grade. This in turn led to the practice of bringing into a classroom a supplementary basic reader to be used by the third, or slow group. Now the three groups were provided with materials; but the teachers, rigorously following plans outlined in Teachers' Manuals, found themselves trapped even more completely than before. They just could not do the things recommended and meet each group once a day.

For a while teachers tried to get around this time-material barrier by having Groups II and III do workbook activities. The end result was that workbooks were used as "busy-work," since the teacher did not have time to guide or check this work. This misuse was so common that many school administrators forbade the purchase of workbooks.

Next, independent reading of other basic readers was tried, but pupils soon discovered that basic readers were not tradebooks. Bringing other basic readers into a classroom immediately raised questions about the use of basic books that did not have the same grade-level designation as the grade in which they were being used. The supplementary readers had to be at or below the grade level of a class. Again, administrators protested as they found their book closets filled with six or seven different sets of basic readers.

To pick up the "no-workbook" slack, the market next became flooded with special phonetic skillbooks. And strangely enough, many administrators approved the purchase of these materials, even though they refused to buy study-books planned to parallel a basic reading program.

Is it any wonder that out of all this came two movements — on the one hand, homogeneous grouping on an interclass basis and the use of one book was practiced (2), and on the other hand, individualized reading instruction. The shortcomings of the whole-class lockstep method with its meager diet and insufficient daily portion does not need to be reviewed again, but the dimensions of group instruction and individualized instruction warrant defining.

Since the early 1920's many studies have been made to determine the quality of performance by individuals and by groups (4). These studies have dealt with groups formed in different ways, from the *ad hoc* group (or just-assembled group) at one end of the continuum to the well-established, traditional group at the other end. The traditional group is here thought of as an organized group with some mutuality of purpose.

Since each pupil is in a class he is always a part of a group. He may be a member of an interacting face-to-face group using the same basic reader. Or, he may be in the non-interacting face-to-face group — the climatized group — as in a class using individualized reading procedures.

As members of a class the pupils are influenced by the membership according to the degree of interaction. In other words, pupils assigned to the same classroom are influenced constantly by one another. Even though each one may be reading a different book, even though the difficulty level of the books used may vary by as much as eight levels of readability, even though the purposes for reading vary from vague, undefined reading for pleasure to specific, clearly-stated question-seeking information, these pupils are not isolated; they are not in solitary. Each child has a fairly good idea of what the other is doing, how well he can read and think, and how responsible he is.

Certainly these children are cooperative. They work together, helping each other clarify purposes, locate materials, handle word-attack needs, deal with comprehension problems, and discuss findings. Certainly there is a spirit of competition. The spirit is different from that in a traditional group situation, and this is to be expected. It is vastly different from the unfortunate circumstance that exists in those classrooms where pupils are grouped unwisely and inappropriately. In those situations the negative aspects are a pernicious influence and can corrupt and undermine the spirit.

All this is mentioned here to focus attention on the degree of cooperation and of competition that influences a circumstance best defined as "individualized reading instruction" and one best defined as a "group-type directed reading activity." In both situations motivation for reading and purposes accomplished by reading reflect the dynamics of a group as well as the interests and needs of the individual pupil. There is a practical need for specifying these conditions in order to understand how both types of reading activities are interrelated and how both procedures have their legitimate place in a sound reading program and are complementary rather than contradictory, as was pointed out in the Twenty-Fourth Yearbook. This is why the definition of individualized reading that is perhaps most widely quoted has specific significance. May Lazar (3) says:

Individualized reading is a way of thinking about reading — an attitude toward the place of reading in the total curriculum, toward the materials and methods used, and toward the child's developmental needs. It is not a single method or technique but a broader way of thinking about reading which involves newer concepts concerned with class organization, materials, and the approach to the individual child. The term Individualized Reading is by no means fully descriptive, but for want of a better term most proponents of this approach continue to use it.

This definition does not present a panacea or a skewed emphasis. It does not offer a quick and simple solution to a complex problem. Rather, it reflects the insights and creative efforts of qualified, dedicated teachers. The teaching of reading requires a dynamic approach — one that breaks sharply with the piece-meal, memoriter, story-parrotting, non-thinking approach so roundly condemned by each National Committee on Reading since 1924.

An attitude toward the function of reading predicated on pertinent findings in the basic human sciences is difficult to quarrel with. As Laura Zirbes (11, pp. 166–167) says:

If we are sensitive to developmental needs we look at reading differently and go at it differently. We go at it as creative guidance. The materials are not subject matter. They are resources we use.

What are the boundaries of the two approaches? It seems best to define the group-type activity boundaries first because teachers are more familiar with grouping. Boundaries of a group-type directed reading activity are:

1. Pupils are grouped for instruction on the basis of reading appraisals that have placed them at about the same instructional level.

2. All pupils in a group read the same basic-reader story at the same time under teacher direction.

3. Purposes for reading are declared by the pupils. At times all may read to accomplish the same purpose. At times each may have individual purposes. At times two or three in the group may have the same purposes. In the group rests the authority to discipline each pupil's conjectures by reference to the facts at hand in the story. Each pupil is encouraged to have the strength of his convictions until proved right or wrong.

4. The purposes declared reflect the pupil's ability to use information provided by the total-story context to conjecture, to reason, and to evaluate. The purposes also reflect each pupil's ability to make discriminate use of his experiences, interests, and language abilities.

5. Answers found are reported to and discussed with the group. Again, with the *group* rests the authority to accept or reject. Lines in the story may be read orally to the group to prove points.

6. The teacher directs the reading-thinking process by use of provocative queries such as "Why do you think so?" "What do you think will happen next?" She stands by during the silent reading to give help as requested with word-attack needs and in clarifying meanings. She does not teach so-called new words or concepts in isolation before a story is read. Since she is using material that is structured according to controls of vocabulary, new concepts, and interests, she allows her pupils to put to work the word-attack skills and the comprehension skills that they know. One of the chief reasons why basic readers are carefully structured is to permit pupils to use skills learned in a situation where the demands of the material will not frustrate them.

7. Fundamental skill training in word attack and in comprehension is provided as prepared in a systematized studybook program. Some pupils do all of the activities; some do most of them; some do only a few.

8. Additional skill activities are suggested in an accompanying manual. In addition, the manual defines a variety of methods for directing the reading-thinking process for each story.

9. Recommendations are given in the manual for related follow-up activities subsequent to the reading of the story.

10. Other stories are recommended to be read either in school or at home.

Items 3 to 6 differ sharply from those commonly practiced where basic readers are used. During the past three decades teachers have had foisted upon them such malpractices as motivating the reading of a story by telling part of the story; explaining to pupils that the story to be read is a surprise story; asking pupils to read to see what Tom or Dick or Harry said; saying that the first sentence on the next page will tell what happened and when it happened; telling children that "today's story is about a merry-go-round," showing pictures of a merry-go-round and telling how people get off and on and ride horses that go up and down. This is the kind of pablum which results in teaching and reading that becomes "uncreative by responding to requirements, following directions, and waiting to be told what to do" (11, p. xxii). This kind of intellectual stripping down in the erroneous belief that children cannot think has foisted on teachers, and, in turn, on children, a "waiting-to-be-told" and a "rote-parroting" attitude and performance. Whereas, quite to the contrary, creative teaching of reading is intended to direct children to think about implications, to consider their ideas and test them as they read and think, and to realize that reading is a continuous and creative process.

Children bring with them to school many concepts and opinions that can be used while reading. What is required is that the teacher direct reading as a thinking process in order that the children may put to work their experiences and make comparisons and judgments. This means that children must be taught to reflect over relevant antecedent events from their own experiences so that they may set their own purposes for reading, reason while reading, and subsequently accept or reject what they find as proof for their conjectures. This way of directing reading teaches children to take full advantage of past learning while reading to accomplish the new purposes before them now (7).

In a group situation the children benefit from shared experiences, estimates, and predictions — as each one reads the same selection or story. This permits each member of a group to compare his predictions with those of others to see how different members manipulated story information in order to predict, to compare his conclusions with those reached by others, to evaluate the skills he has used and note whether or not others used the same skills and why, and to scrutinize the way others extended and refined concepts and generalizations gained through the reading. Furthermore, in a group where all deal with the same material, authority for the acceptance of proof rests with the group as well as with the teacher. Each member serves as an auditor, examining and weighing proofs and conclusions presented — frequently by oral rereading (10).

The boundaries of an individualized-type directed reading activity are as follows:

1. Primarily, pupils are not placed in traditional groups. Each pupil is free to work without interruption in order to pursue an interest. Two, three, or more may work together to pursue the same interest.

2. The materials read are in a large measure self-selected. Included for selection are textbooks in other curriculum areas which give sufficient facts and skills, tradebooks, basic readers, newspapers, and magazines at different degrees of complexity.

3. Purposes for reading are largely self-declared and reflect each pupil's interests, abilities, and needs. Purposes may vary from vague, undefined desires for reading fiction, to specifically declared goals requiring versatility in rate adjustment such as when reading to skim, to scan, or to study.

4. In dealing with answers, self-responsibility and reliance are as essential as they were in declaring purposes. However, a completely self-reliant pupil would certainly be a rare person. Individuals are social minded. They want to discuss what they read and to profit by the discussion; they want to share with others.

So the group or class may often serve as judge or critic while the reader defends and supports his answers. Lines may be read orally to prove points. Papers and talks may be prepared to substantiate claims.

5. The teacher is constantly available to give help as requested in attacking words not recognized at sight, and in clearing comprehension needs.

6. Skill training is provided as needed by using either teacher-prepared materials, studybooks designed to accompany basic readers, and other skill books. Pupils with similar needs may be grouped for instruction. They may meet as a group for two or three periods or for three or four weeks.

7. Pupil as well as teacher records are kept of reading done, purposes accomplished, and needs declared and resolved. Pupil schedules are maintained.

8. Teacher pacing is done to direct each child to locate materials in keeping with his interests and skills, to develop purposes that are clearly defined, to organize knowledge gained, to appraise understandings gained, to adequately share with others, to provide needed skill training, to foster new interests in wide reading. All this must be done at a tempo that will assure a maximum amount of success and a minimum amount of frustration.

Even this specific defining of boundaries shows that there is a great deal of overlap between the two approaches. Group-directed activities stimulate a great deal of individual thinking and reading and reasoning. Individualized activities include a lot of group work. Each has elements of strength and weakness (5).

It is also readily recognizable that when reading instruction is individualized, teaching does not need to deteriorate to the point at which it deals only with the whims and fancies of ordinary life, so that learning becomes undirected and unmethodic. Quite to the contrary, teaching reflects knowledge of the results of research and investigation into child growth and development, knowledge about how in many ways reading is synonymous with thinking, and knowledge of what is available for children to read.

For a child to behave as an individual and yet respect the rights and comforts of the other members of the class, he must view his reading performance as having a place among the reading patterns of the other children. There must be some controls over each pupil's reading performance and that of the entire class which result in a system sound enough to maintain an orderliness and stability of expectation.

Rules must be developed that encourage some behavior patterns and inhibit others. Controls must be developed so that each pupil learns to exercise some authority over himself and also feels responsible for the making of the rules.

The spirit motivating the room must be such that the success of one pupil in the class is gratifying to all and that the failure of one pupil results in a letdown feeling in the others. The spirit of class unity must be strong. Each pupil must show respect for the purposes, values, and actions of every other pupil.

At first some pupils may find it difficult to assume responsibility and to participate in group action. They may be passive and acquiescing; they may be aimless, or they may display anger or frustration. For these pupils both the teacher and the class must feel a responsibility. Above all, though, controls must be exercised in so humane a way that a pupil's willingness to express himself and to participate in group actions will not be inhibited. He must not necessarily be joined with others in pursuing an area of interest or need but, rather, he must be led to recognize and pursue his own interests and needs.

Certainly skills are taught and maintained during self-selection time. This is not an undirected, unmethodic time. Some of the skills accomplished are:

1. Locating materials. Pupils need to learn not only where different materials are located but also how to use them. They must learn where such materials are kept as textbooks, tradebooks, magazines, encyclopedias, dictionaries, newspapers.
2. Identifying and declaring likes and dislikes and purposes.
3. Searching persistently for answers and being resourceful.
4. Distinguishing between reading just for fun and reading to learn.
5. Reading extensively and intensively.
6. Acquiring concepts through the use of context clues, a glossary, and a dictionary.
7. Extending and refining concepts by means of encyclopedias, textbooks, periodicals, pictures, films, and consulting specialists.
8. Assembling and organizing information for oral and written reports.
9. Keeping records.
10. Using word-attack skills when dealing with material in which the vocabulary and concept burden are not controlled as they are in a basic reader.
11. Knowing how and when to share ideas learned.
12. Learning how to listen attentively and to ask questions.
13. Using wisely leisure to think and reflect.

It is recommended, then, that a modified basic-reader approach be used. To do this effectively one must, first, drop the notion that a basic-reader program in and of itself is final and sacred. It is not. Second, one must drop the notion that time can be equated with equality. Not every group must be met every day for the same length of time. Third, the idea that a basic book recommended for a grade level must be "finished" by all pupils in a grade before they can be promoted must be discarded. Fourth, teaching reading as a *memoriter* process by presenting new words in advance of the reading and then having pupils tell back the story must be stopped. If reading is taught as a thinking process, even short basic-reader stories will be read with enthusiasm.

Fifth, one of the major comments made by pupils taught in classes where instruction has been individualized is: "At last reading is interesting. Now we enjoy reading" (3). Such comments are severe indictments of what has been happening as a result of the misuse of basic readers. So teachers must be sure to provide many books and to allow children to make their own selections.

Sixth, effective skills of word attack must be taught. Basic reading books do not provide for such skill training; neither do tradebooks. Such skills are presented in detail only when studybooks or workbooks are well organized. The studybooks designed to parallel the basic-reader programs should be used and the skills should be taught systematically. Teachers' manuals do not provide all the needed activities for skill training. Teachers' manuals are not studybooks.

Seventh, the reading program should be divided so as to allow about half of the time for each approach — a basic reader program and an individualized program. This might be done by using the group approach with basic readers for a week or two, and then the individualized or self-selection approach for a similar period of time. Where a pupil is free to select day after day for two or three weeks, he is almost forced to examine his interests and decide more carefully what he wants to do.

The reasons for these recommendations might be summarized as follows:

1. A modified basic-reader approach allows for the use of basic readers designed to develop reading-thinking skills in a group situation. The individualized reading program allows for seeking, self-selection, and pacing — with a library as the source of materials.

2. Both group and individualized reading activities provide different classroom organization. Self-selection time requires resourceful teacher-pupil planning. Structured basic-reader programs provide compact, organized, systematized plans.

3. Pupil motives for reading can be activated and honored differently in both situations. Both set the stage differently so that pupils encounter reading experiences promoted by varied ideas, by varied organization of ideas, and by different materials.

4. Different skills are taught in each. The basic-reader material provides the vehicle for training in purpose-setting, hypothesizing, examining the facts, reaching relevant conclusions; in versatility in reading, in systematically checking comprehension and work-attack skills. Self-selection time provides training in the resourceful use of skills acquired in group-directed activities as well as in the refinement and extensions of skills acquired when performing individually.

In conclusion, the philosophy of the modified basic-reader approach might be referred to as Sir Russell Brain (1) speaks about his philosophy when he says:

Philosophies illustrate the fairy story of the Emperor's clothes in reverse. The philosophy claims to be naked — the naked truth — but the eye of a child sees it to be wearing the oddest collection of old clothes, some inherited from the past, and some painstakingly made by the philosopher, like a caddis-worm, from such materials as he happened to have at hand. Indeed, we may come to the conclusion that the important thing about truth is not that it should be naked, but what clothes suit it best, and whether it should not sometimes dress up for special occasions.

References

1. Brain, Sir Russell. *The Nature of Experience.* London: Oxford University Press, 1959.

2. Goodlad, John I., and Robert H. Anderson. *The Nongraded Elementary School.* New York: Harcourt, Brace and Co., 1959. Pp. 15–20.
3. Lazar, May. "Individualized Reading: A Dynamic Approach," *The Reading Teacher*, 11: 75–83; December, 1957.
4. Lorge, Irving, David Fox, Joel Ravitz, and Harlin Brenner. "A Survey of Studies Contrasting the Quality of Group Performance and Individual Performance, 1920–1957," *The Psychological Bulletin*, 55: 337–372; 1958.
5. Sartain, Harry W. "A Bibliography on Individualized Reading," *The Reading Teacher*, Vol. 13; April, 1960.
6. Stauffer, Russell G. "A Directed Reading-Thinking Plan," *Education*, 79: 527–532; May, 1959.
7. ———. *Teaching Reading as a Thinking Process.* Philadelphia: The John C. Winston Co. (In preparation [at the time this article was published]).
8. Stewart, David K. "How Do Schools Organize for Reading Instruction Today?" *School Briefs.* Chicago, Ill.: Scott, Foresman & Co., January-February, 1958. P. 2.
9. Stock, Dorothy, and Herbert A. Thelen. "Emotional Dynamics and Group Culture," in *The National Training Laboratories.* New York: New York University Press, 1958.
10. *Twenty-Fourth Yearbook of the National Society for the Study of Education.* Chicago: University Press, 1923.
11. Zirbes, Laura. *Spurs to Creative Teaching.* New York: G. P. Putnam's Sons, 1959.

Evaluation of an Individualized Reading Program

❖ ALTON L. SAFFORD

Hardly an educational journal appears today without at least one article extolling the merits of self-selective reading. As a result of this general enthusiasm, local elementary school districts throughout the nation are showing an increased interest in this method of teaching reading. Specifically, with the support of the California Department of Education, and with the enthusiastic endorsement of the Los Angeles County Superintendent's Office of Education, many workshops and institutes have been held in Los Angeles County to demonstrate these new techniques and to discuss the advantages of this method for teaching reading. As a consequence many local assistant superintendents in charge of instruction have encouraged the teachers in their districts to adopt, or at least to experiment with, self-selective reading in their classrooms.

From *The Reading Teacher,* 12: 266–270; April, 1960. Reprinted with permission of Alton L. Safford and the International Reading Association. Alton L. Safford is Psychologist and Coordinator, Special Educational Services, Santa Barbara County Schools, Goleta, California.

Despite the whole-hearted, enthusiastic endorsement of self-selective reading by so many authorities in this field, it was thought prudent to substantiate these claims within our own district. As Dr. Constance M. McCullough said in one of the few opinions in the literature expressing any reservations about these new methods for teaching this critically important skill: "In the meantime, have we, as citizens of a country struggling for survival in a highly competitive world, the right to jeopardize the quality of education by the widespread use of an unproven method?" (1)

Hence, in June, 1958, as partial requirement for an M.S. in Education, an evaluation was made of the effectiveness of the self-selective reading program in one of the local elementary school districts.

Procedures

The school district lies in an unincorporated, upper-middle-class residential community in Los Angeles County, bordering the southern edge of the San Gabriel Mountains, and it is made up of 72 classroom teachers in four elementary schools serving some 2,485 pupils from kindergarten through the sixth grade. A survey was made to locate all classes which had been taught during the past three years with individualized reading techniques.

The criteria for including a class in the study were: (a) whether or not all of the children in that class had the opportunity to select by and for themselves the books that they wanted to read during the regular reading period; (b) whether they read those books (silently or aloud, to themselves or to another child, or to and with the teacher — it did not matter) individually and mainly by themselves, as opposed to group situations where everyone reads either silently or aloud out of the same book at the same time; and (c) whether or not the children of the class did read consistently in this individual fashion, periodically every day, all of the school year, as *the* regular reading program.

Such criteria did not mean that the teacher could not give help in reading, either individually or by temporarily forming groups to give instruction as needed in phonics, syllabication, consonant blends, accents, word attack, use of the dictionary, etc. The main criterion was not whether groups were formed or were not formed, but rather whether the groups were formed temporarily and for the purpose of specific instruction, and were not used to structure permanent group reading situations.

Seven such classes were identified: they included Grades 3, 4, 5, and 6. The total number of children in the sample was 183. Growth in reading was measured by the reading section of the California Achievement Test Battery, Primary and Elementary, Form DD, which is administered in October of each year to all of the children in this district, Grades 2 through 6. The individual growth of each child in the above-defined sample was computed by subtracting his score made in October of the year of the study from his corresponding score of the following October, as he entered the succeeding grade.

Next, average, or mean growth, increments were computed for each of the seven classes in the sample. These mean class increments were compared with the national norms of 1.0 years and with the district norms[1] of approximately 1.25 years of gain in reading.

---

[1] From published data of the school district, "Report to the Board of Trustees," February, 1958.

Then comparisons were made between the reading gains of a group of forty-eight "superior" students, with I.Q.'s of 120 and above, and the gains of seventy-six "average" students with I.Q.'s of 90 to 110. (All I.Q. scores were derived from the California Short-Form Test of Mental Maturity, Elementary and Primary Batteries. These tests are administered generally every October to all children in this district in Grades 1, 3, and 5.) These two groups were taken from the total sample of 183 children and comprised all with I.Q. scores within those ranges.

Following that, a breakdown was made of the total reading scores of fifty students from two of the fourth-grade classes, and a comparison was noted between their mean reading vocabulary gain and their mean reading comprehension gain.

Students who transferred into these classes during the school year, or who left, or who were not in the district the following year in October when the reading test was again administered, were dropped from the statistics of the study.

There were no retentions among the pupils in the sample classes.

Rationale

No effort was made to balance or to equate these seven classes with model or "normal" classes within the district. This study was not conceived as a "classical" experiment — like the Walker (3), McChristy (1), and other studies, where efforts were made to determine what *might* happen under a given set of circumstances — but as a survey of what *had* occurred with a given set of methods. The matched-sets-of-classes design was considered, but was rejected for the following reasons. It was thought that the very act of identifying, isolating, labeling, observing, and teaching and testing such matched classes would, of and in itself alone, sufficiently change the attitudes of the children about themselves and toward their work to such a degree as to significantly disturb and change their individual rates of learning. (To say nothing of effecting gross changes in the intensity, time, effort, and preparation spent by the teachers of such classes.)

In short, an observed class is not a normal class. The observer distinctly and often critically influences his field of observation. Briefly, it was thought that, in this case, the very effort to isolate and control the independent variables would introduce other and more complex and intangible variables than it would control and eliminate.

The seven classes of this study were all identified, labeled, and "observed" after the teaching was done and after the measurements of instruction were completed, not during or before. Also, all testing of the children in the sample classes was done in the normal course of testing all of the pupils in the district. Furthermore, not even the teachers of the seven classes constituting the sample were themselves aware that at some time in the future their classes would be used as the basis for this study.

The author of this study and the members of the faculty committee who originally proposed this design deem the aforementioned delineation to be of some importance.

However, mean I.Q. scores for each of the seven classes were compared with the district mean of 117, and since the differences of those means, divided by the standard error of the differences of the same means were below the critical ratio of 2.58, the hypothesis that these seven classes were samples from the same total population of school children within the district — as regards their basic ability to learn, or to receive instruction, and, specifically, reading instruction — was considered tenable.

Results

From but a brief inspection of Table I, two main observations may be made.

First, none of these seven classes, as a group, came even close to the national norm of a gain of 1.0 year, let alone to the district's higher norm of a gain of 1.25 years in total reading achievement.

Second, the statistics indicate that the children in each of these classes entered the grade in which they were taught reading by these new methods considerably above the national level of expectancy in that skill. It is the fact that these children, as a group, as a class, did not make more growth during that period of specialized reading instruction that is so pertinent. This fact becomes the substance of the conclusion of this study.

On the other hand, considered individually, of the total number of 183 children, 49, or 26.7 per cent did achieve a model gain of 1.0 or greater in total reading achievement. This left, however, some 73.3 per cent of the total sample who fell below what might be considered a national mean, or "average" gain in reading.

By separating the total sample into groups of children on the basis of their mental maturity scores, the following data were noted: The total mean reading gain for one year of the forty-eight "superior" students was .46, while the corresponding gain of the seventy-six "average" students was .366. This difference is statistically insignificant.

Not enough "below-average" students could be found to justify any conclusions about this method based upon an analysis of their gains.

In a comparison of the reading vocabulary gains with the reading comprehension gains of the fifty children in two of the fourth-grade classes, it was noted that their mean reading vocabulary gain was .61 and their mean reading comprehension gain was .52 of a year's growth. This difference is statistically insignificant and could be due to chance.

TABLE I. Growth in Reading Achievement

Class	No.	Grade	Calif. Read. Score I*	Calif. Read. Score II	Mean Gain in Read.
1	21	3	4.20	4.63	.43
2	23	4	4.70	5.33	.63
3	27	4	5.16	5.67	.51
4	27	4	5.33	5.49	.16
5	31	5	7.10	7.38	.28
6	26	6	7.46	8.14	.68
7	28	6	7.04	7.83	.79

* Score I is the score received in October of the year entering the grade shown; Score II is the score made the following October upon entering the next grade.

Conclusions

It may tentatively be suggested that: (a) For the majority of the individual pupils in the seven classes, the use of individualized reading techniques resulted in lower gains in reading achievement over a period of one calendar year, when contrasted with the results of other methods of reading instruction that are currently being used in this district and throughout the nation. (b) The use of self-selective reading methods achieved no significantly different results with the superior students than with average students. (c) The use of individualized reading techniques resulted in no significant difference in growth between reading vocabulary and reading comprehension.

Speculative Considerations

Two questions immediately arise: Why has self-selective reading given such unsatisfactory measured results in this district? Are the self-selective reading plans, methods, and techniques that are now being used in the other, adjacent, elementary school districts actually working with the degree of success claimed?

It must be admitted that the conclusions of this study are in contradiction to conclusions based upon the results of several other studies in this field. However, all of the other studies, whose results imply the superiority of self-selective reading methods over the older, group methods of instruction were so designed that both the children and the teachers of the classes involved were keenly aware of the nature and implications of what they were doing.

It might now be profitable to carry on further studies of a similar design. It would be interesting to survey in other districts the results of individualized reading programs as used with other "unobserved" classes, where all of the teaching is finished and all of the testing is done, where the children are now in junior high and high school, and the teachers themselves are shifted about in grade level or transferred out of the district. Certainly, the data are available.

References

1. McChristy, Antoinette. "A Comparative Study to Determine Whether Self-Selective Reading Can Be Successfully Used at the Second Grade Level," unpublished Master's Thesis, The University of Southern California, Los Angeles, June, 1957.
2. McCullough, Constance M. "Opinions Differ on Individualized Reading," *NEA Journal*, 47: 163; March, 1958.
3. Walker, Clare. "An Evaluation of Two Programs of Reading in Grades Four, Five, and Six of the Elementary School," unpublished Doctoral Dissertation, New York University School of Education, New York, 1957.

A Controlled Experiment Evaluating the Effects of a Non-Graded Organization on Pupil Achievement

✼ MAURIE HILLSON, J. CHARLES JONES,
J. WILLIAM MOORE, AND FRANK VAN DEVENDER

A recurrent criticism of the educational system of this country has been that many programs and procedures have been put into large-scale operation in the schools on the basis of the subjective impressions or the evangelistic zeal of their proponents, and once instituted, have been continued, in some cases for many years, with little or no effort being made at systematic evaluation. Hilgard (4) and others (1) have pointed out the tendency of educators to force psychological principles, without regard to their relevancy, into educational theory, using psychological labels as justification or support for existing educational practices.

In recent years the public elementary schools have shown increasing interest in non-grading as a possible solution to many of the academic problems encountered in the primary grades. In addition to an interest in improving achievement, there has been an understandable concern over the effects of academic failure on young children, estimates of the failure rate under the present grades system running as high as 18 per cent on a national basis. The non-graded system has been promoted, not as a change in instructional method, but as a *reorganization* of the primary levels of instruction whereby children may progress at a rate appropriate to their abilities and without the disorganizing effects of the threat of failure. Other specific advantages claimed for the non-graded system in addition to improved achievement and reduction of tensions and anxieties for both pupils and teachers have been: instruction can be adjusted to individual spurts and lags in development; children will compete with their own records rather than with each other; teachers need not fear encroaching on "materials for the next grade" or be required to bring all children up to the same levels of achievement without regard to the ability of some children to achieve these norms; and children, after absence from school, may resume at the point where they left off. Moreover, those who attest to the worth of non-grading, state that a unique outcome of this procedure is that achievement is increased at all levels of pupil ability.

From *The Journal of Educational Research,* 57: 548–550; July-August, 1964. Reprinted by permission. Maurie Hillson is Professor of Education, Rutgers, The State University, New Brunswick, New Jersey; J. Charles Jones and J. William Moore are Professor of Education and Chairman, Department of Education, respectively, at Bucknell University, Lewisburg, Pennsylvania; and Frank Van Devender is Principal, Shamokin Public Schools, Shamokin, Pennsylvania. The research reported in this article was supported in part by the Susquehanna Valley Program, Bucknell University, through a grant from the Ford Foundation.

A procedure which promises so many benefits, with few if any drawbacks, is worth careful evaluation. To date, such evaluation as exists is largely subjective, anecdotal, and at the level of demonstration rather than experimentation.

Typical are results reported for a non-graded program in the Elmira Heights, New York, elementary schools which indicate that it is not uncommon for 90 per cent to 95 per cent of the non-graded pupils to be reading at a fourth-grade level at the end of three years, this in contrast with the 60 per cent typical of the pupils in a conventional graded program (5). Similar results are reported for the Linda School District, Marysville, California, by R. A. Anderson (6). Other non-graded programs make comparative claims. However, some critics question the reliability of such evidence. The third edition of the *Encyclopedia of Educational Research* notes that "non-grading is supported by some plausible sounding claims and theories rather than by research" (2). It could be suggested that the apparent success of non-graded programs might be attributable to a number of uncontrolled variables, e.g., selection of the most able teachers for the non-graded groups, establishing in-service training programs for teachers and administrators prior to and during the program, development of special materials for use in the program and improved parent orientation and interest. The possibility is thus raised that demonstrated gains may result from the operation of one or more of these variables rather than from the change from a graded to a non-graded organization. The purpose of this investigation was to assess in a controlled experimental situation, the effects of a non-graded program on the reading achievement of a group of elementary-school pupils. This is a preliminary report covering the first one and one-half years of the experimental period; the complete experiment will extend over three years.

Method

Subjects. All first-grade students entering the Washington Elementary School (2) for the academic year 1960–61 were randomly assigned to either experimental ($N = 26$) or control groups ($N = 26$). Subjects remained in their respective groups for the academic years 1960–61 and 1961–62 and continued into 1962–63. Subjects identified as a part of the experimental program included only those initially assigned to these groups. Transfers or new entries were randomly assigned to experimental or control groups but were not included in the evaluation. Reading-readiness levels for all children in both experimental and control groups were determined during the first two weeks of the school year and three levels of reading ability were established for each group.

Teachers

All teachers, whether assigned to experimental or control groups, were selected for participation on the basis of their excellence in teaching. Selection was made by the administration and an attempt was made to match the teachers on the basis of their past effectiveness. They were then randomly assigned to experimental or control groups. All teachers, whether experimental or control, participated in workshops in preparation for the non-graded program; all received the assistance of a reading consultant in selecting materials, carrying on their programs, and the observation and assessment of pupils for placement in reading groups.

Procedure

Non-grading for the experimental group proceeded on a year-by-year basis; children were permitted to move from reading level to reading level as their level of performance dictated, there being a total of nine possible reading levels through which a pupil might progress during a three-year period. By the third year non-grading for Grades 1 through 3 will be completed and the designations of first, second, or third grade eliminated.

Pupils in the control group were placed in one of three reading-level groups within a conventional graded program and instruction was adapted to the ability levels of the groups. At the end of each school year the entire class, with the exception of those classified as failures, was promoted to the next grade and again subdivided into three reading-level groups. No child was assigned to a reading group except those contained within his own grade level, e.g., no child was assigned to a second-grade reading group who was not in his second year of school and only those second-year children who had failed first grade were assigned to reading groups below the three contained within the second grade.

Results

The effects of the non-graded organization on pupil achievement were evaluated at the end of the third semester of the experimental period by the use of three achievement tests. The first was the Lee Clark Reading Test, the second and third were the Paragraph Meaning and Word Meaning tests of the Primary Battery of the Stanford Achievement Test.

The results of the comparisons of the mean grade placement using the t-test analysis (two-tailed test), for the experimental and control groups for the Lee Clark Reading Test, Word Meaning, and Paragraph Meaning tests are presented in Table I.

TABLE I. A Comparison of Mean Grade Placement on Reading, Word Meaning and Paragraph Meaning Achievement Tests

Test	Experimental Group $N = 26$	Control Group $N = 26$	t	p
Lee Clark Reading	3.19	2.81	2.71	.01
Word Meaning	3.33	2.86	3.13	.01
Paragraph Meaning	3.27	2.90	1.95	.06

It can be observed in Table I that the E group for grade placement was significantly higher than the control group on all three measures of achievement.

Discussion

Since it was the primary purpose of this investigation to provide more reliable data covering the effects of the non-graded primary organization on reading achievement, any conclusions which are drawn must be evaluated in terms of the soundness of the design of the experiment as well as the statistical analysis of the data. From this point of view, an evaluation of the design indicates that in general the variables were sufficiently controlled so that data resulting from the experimental situation were reliable. The only portion of the design in which greater control seemed desirable and was not possible within the limits of this investigation was teacher variability. Although care was exercised in the matching and the random assignment of teachers, because of the small number (N = 6), it is possible that some systematic differences still existed.

Turning to the statistical analysis of the scores obtained by the students on the related measures of reading achievement, it was found that the non-graded pupils performed at a higher academic level on all three measures. Specifically, a comparison of mean grade levels for reading as measured by the Lee Clark Reading Test was significantly (.01 level) in favor of the non-graded primary organization. Comparison results were obtained when mean grade levels for related measures of reading (word meaning and paragraph meaning tests) were compared statistically. As observed in Table I, the mean grade level on the word meaning test was significantly greater for the non-graded group at the .01 level of significance, and the paragraph meaning was greater in the same direction at the .06 level. These results are in keeping with a number of previous research findings supporting the use of the non-graded primary organization (6).

Since confidence can be placed in the design of the study and the resulting empirical evidence is strongly in favor of the non-graded group, it can be inferred that the superior achievement in reading of pupils in the non-graded group in this experiment was attributable to the organizational structure rather than to either superior pupil ability and/or teaching methods.

Conclusions

Generally it can be concluded that pupils participating in a non-graded primary organization (all other things being equal) will achieve at a significantly higher level on measures of reading ability and related measures of reading than will pupils participating in a graded organization. Specifically, it may be stated that pupils of all levels of ability achieved at a higher level than pupils in a graded situation. Further, it is concluded that the increased achievement of the participants in the non-graded primary program is primarily related to organizational structure when methods of teaching are held constant.

Summary

Ss (N=52) were taught reading in one of two public school organizational structures (graded versus non-graded). At the end of one and one-half years of the three-year experimental period, analyses of grade level achievement for three measures related to reading achievement favored the non-graded organization at a level which was statistically significant.

References

1. Davis, Robert A. "Applicability of Applications of Psychology with Particular Reference to Schoolroom Learning," *Journal of Educational Research,* 37: 19–30; 1943.

2. *Encyclopedia of Educational Research,* 3rd ed. (The American Educational Research Association). New York: The Macmillan Co., 1960. P. 22.
3. Goodlad, John I., and Robert H. Anderson. *The Nongraded Elementary School.* New York: Harcourt, Brace and Co., 1959.
4. Hilgard, Ernest R. "The Relation of Schools of Psychology to Educational Practices," *The California Journal of Elementary Education,* 8: 17–26; 1939.
5. "Non-Graded Primary Unit Plan," unpublished report, The Elmira Heights Control Schools, Elmira Heights, New York, December, 1959.
6. Personal communication to Dr. Anderson as reported in a speech to the American Association of School Administrators, Atlantic City, New Jersey, February, 1960.

Ungraded Primary Reading Program:
An Objective Evaluation   ❖ MARY KING SKAPSKI

More and more elementary schools are replacing their first three grades with so-called ungraded primaries. In these units, groups of children who show about equal readiness for learning are allowed to progress through the primary work at rates appropriate to their ability.

In the ungraded primaries, learning is so paced that the child may experience success at every step of the way. Slow learners are not pushed into learning to read before they are ready, a practice sometimes followed in the hope that the children will be able to "pass" into second grade at the end of one year.

Gifted children spend as little time as possible on the extremely simple reading matter at the preprimer and primer levels and can be given a good deal of enrichment material. In short, the aim of the ungraded primary is to insure that provisions are made to meet individual differences.

Many descriptions of ungraded primaries can be found in educational literature (1). Although teachers and administrators who are working in ungraded primaries feel that the children benefit greatly from the programs (2), there have been few objective evaluations of the results of instruction in ungraded primaries. This study arose from an unusual opportunity to evaluate such a program.

For several years one public elementary school in Burlington, Vermont, has had an ungraded primary program in reading, while instruction in other subjects has been carried on under the traditional, graded system.

At the beginning of the study the writer administered the Stanford Achieve-

Reprinted from "Ungraded Primary Reading Program: An Objective Evaluation," in *The Elementary School Journal,* 61: 41–45; October, 1960, by Mary King Skapski by permission of The University of Chicago Press. Copyright © 1960 by the University of Chicago. Mary King Skapski is at present serving as Senior Chemistry Mistress, Holy Child College, Lagos, Nigeria, under the auspices of the Ford Foundation.

ment Test, Primary Battery, to all the second- and third-graders in this school; that is, to all children who were doing second- or third-grade work in subjects other than reading. The children's achievement in reading was then compared with their achievement in arithmetic.

There was some question as to which children should be chosen for the comparison. There were three possibilities: The achievement of all children of the same grade placement could be compared. Or the achievement of all children who had spent the same length of time in the primary unit could be compared. Or the achievement of only the modal-age children (those children who entered first grade in September of a particular calendar year and spent one year in each grade) could be included.

As Table I shows, all three comparisons led to similar results. For reasons given in the detailed description of the study (3), the grade-equivalent scores on the Primary Paragraph Meaning Test were used as the measure of reading achievement, and the grade-equivalent scores on the Primary Arithmetic Computation Test were used as the measure of arithmetic achievement. The grade placement of the children at the time of testing was 2.5 (that is, fifth month of the second grade) for second-graders and 3.5 for third graders.

The study emphasized the difference in achievement in two situations: first, when ample provisions were made for individual differences and, second, when virtually no such provisions were made. For this reason, it was decided to limit the comparison to the modal-age children, thus eliminating the children for whom provisions for individual differences were made in arithmetic through repeating or skipping a grade.

The Detroit Group Intelligence Test was administered to the children by the writer. The average intelligence quotient of the second- and third-graders in this school was 116. If the children were achieving in accordance with their ability, the average achievement should have been well above their grade placement. It can be seen from Table I that such was the case in reading, in which children of every ability level were presumably receiving instruction of an appropriate level of difficulty. In arithmetic, however, all children, regardless of ability, were being given instruction at the level of their grade placement. This procedure is reflected in the lower average arithmetic achievement

TABLE I. A Comparison of the Reading and Arithmetic Achievement of Children in a School with an Ungraded Primary Reading Program

Group	Number	Average Reading Achievement	Average Arithmetic Achievement	Difference
All second-grade children	38	3.2	2.4	0.8
All third-grade children	47	4.7	3.3	1.4
All children in their second year in the primary	36	3.4	2.5	.9
All children in their third year in the primary	39	4.7	3.2	1.5
Modal-age second-graders	34	3.2*	2.5†	.7
Modal-age third-graders	36	4.8‡	3.3§	1.5

*Standard deviation = 0.8.   ‡Standard deviation = 1.2.
†Standard deviation = 0.1.   §Standard deviation = 0.4.

of the children and also in the fact that the spread of the arithmetic scores (as indicated by the standard deviations) was much narrower than the spread of the reading scores.

Table I also shows that, in reading, the third-graders were achieving at a point further above their grade placement than the second-graders, who had spent one year less in the ungraded situation. This result is understandable, since (with one or two exceptions) all the children started at the same point at the beginning of the first year in the primary unit.

Guilford's formula for the standard error of a difference in correlated data was used to find whether the differences between reading and arithmetic achievement at each grade level were statistically significant (4). Both differences were found to be very significant, the t ratio being 5.4 for the second-graders and 7.5 for the third-graders.

The difference between achievement in the two subjects might have been due at least in part to the fact that the learning of reading is very different from the learning of arithmetic. For this reason, a second comparison was made.

The writer administered the same tests to all the second- and third-graders in two other elementary schools in the same city. The average intelligence quotients, as measured by the Detroit Group Intelligence Test, of the children in these two schools were found to be 116 and 115, as compared to the average of 116 in the school first studied.

The socioeconomic backgrounds of the children, the training and experience of their teachers, and the amount of time devoted to reading instruction in the three schools also proved comparable.

The reading achievement of the children in these two schools was compared with the reading achievement of the children in the first school. Since there was grouping (on an ability basis) within each grade for instruction in reading in the two schools with traditional primaries, this second comparison did not contrast the results of giving individualized instruction with the results of giving identical learning experiences to all children regardless of ability, as the first comparison had done. Rather, the second comparison was a comparison of the results of two methods of providing for individual differences. That the children in the ungraded primary reading program were achieving at a higher level than the children in the traditional primaries can be seen from Table II. Since the different schools had different promotion policies, the achievement of all the children who were in their third year in school, regardless of their formal grade placement, was used in this comparison.

There was no statistically significant difference between the reading achievement of the children in School 2 and the reading achievement of the children in School 3. The reading achievement of the children in School 1 (the school with the ungraded reading program) was significantly higher than that of the children in the other two schools combined, at the 1 per cent level of confidence ($t = 2.8$).

That the ungraded reading program did not result in lowered achievement in areas other than reading can also be seen from Table II.

On the average, the children were benefiting from the ungraded reading program. The question remained whether children of all ability levels were benefiting. To answer this question, the children were arbitrarily divided into three groups on the basis of intelligence quotients according to the Detroit

TABLE II. Average Reading, Spelling, and Arithmetic Achievement of All Children in Their Third Year in Each of the Three Schools

Children in Their Third Year	Number	Average Achievements in		
		Reading	Spelling*	Arithmetic
School 1	38	4.7†	4.0	3.2
School 2	33	4.2†	3.8	3.1
School 3	39	3.9‡	3.6	2.9

*Some children in each school attained perfect scores on the spelling test; therefore their actual achievement was higher than the total average scores would indicate.
†Standard deviation = 1.2.
‡Standard deviation = 1.1.

Group Intelligence Test: average, with intelligence quotients ranging from 88 to 112; superior, with intelligence quotients ranging from 113 to 124; and very superior, with intelligence quotients of 125 or higher. Since the standard deviation of the distribution of Detroit intelligence quotients in the general population is 12.5, the "average" classification included all the children who were within one standard deviation of the mean; the "superior" classification included the children whose intelligence quotients fell between one and two standard deviations above the mean, and the "very superior" classification included the children whose intelligence quotients were more than two standard deviations above the mean. There were no children in the sample with intelligence quotients lower than 87.

Table III shows a comparison of the reading and arithmetic achievement of the children of each ability level in their third year in the ungraded primary reading program. It can be seen that children of each ability level were doing considerably better in reading than in arithmetic. The difference was greatest for the very superior children. In arithmetic, these children were achieving exactly at the point of their grade placement: that is, at the point at which instruction was being given. The average and superior children were not achieving up to this level. In reading, in which appropriate instruction was being given to children of each level of ability, there were great differences between the average achievements of the children of different ability levels.

Table IV shows the reading achievement of the children of each ability level in each of the three schools. Again it is evident that children of each level of ability were benefiting from the individualized instruction they were receiving in the ungraded primary reading program, and again the difference was greatest for the children of very superior intelligence.

TABLE III. Average Reading and Arithmetic Achievement of Children of Different Ability Levels in the School with the Ungraded Primary Reading Program

Ability Level	Number	Average Reading Achievement	Average Arithmetic Achievement	Difference
Average	17	4.1	2.9	1.2
Superior	12	4.8	3.4	1.4
Very superior	9	5.8	3.5	2.3

**TABLE IV. Average Reading Achievement of Children
of Different Ability Levels in Each School**

Ability Level	School 1	Average Reading Achievement of Children in School 2	School 3
Average	4.1	3.7	3.3
Superior	4.8	4.4	4.1
Very superior	5.8	4.6	4.9

It should be mentioned that at the other end of the intelligence scale, under the ungraded plan, less than half as many children spend four years in the primary as would if the question of promotion came up at the end of their first year of school.

The ungraded primary, then, benefits all the children. Gifted children are not allowed to underachieve, nor are slow learners frustrated by repeated failure. All children progress steadily from level to level, each child at his own rate.

Notes

1. See, for example, Florence C. Kelly, "Doing Away with Grade Levels," *NEA Journal*, 37: 222–23; April, 1948. Some standard textbooks of educational psychology (for example, J. B. Stroud, *Psychology in Education*, p. 269; and L. J. Cronbach, *Educational Psychology*, p. 225) also describe this method of organization of primary instruction.
2. See, for example, Florence C. Kelly, "Ungraded Primary Schools Make the Grade in Milwaukee," *NEA Journal*, 40: 645–646; December, 1951.
3. Mary K. Skapski, "Individualized Instruction in the Ungraded Primary School and Its Effect upon the Achievement of Second and Third Grade Children of Different Ability Levels." Unpublished Master's thesis, University of Vermont, October, 1956.
4. J. P. Guilford, *Fundamental Statistics in Psychology and Education.* New York: McGraw-Hill Book Co., 1950.

Interclass Grouping for Reading

Instruction ❧ WILLIAM F. MOORHOUSE

During the first three years of elementary school, the range in reading level among pupils becomes wider and wider. It is common to find five to seven reading levels represented by the pupils in a fourth-grade class. Beyond fourth grade, reading differences become even greater. Teachers of average-sized classes have the problem of providing effective instruction in reading for several reading levels.

Fourth-, fifth-, and sixth-grade teachers have found it difficult to challenge the best readers and to give special help to poor readers when all are in the same class. To meet such problems, some school systems provide reading specialists who work with individual pupils and small groups. This solution usually requires additional staff and additional classroom facilities.

In 1954, Floyd reported that the Joplin, Missouri, public schools had developed a highly successful grouping plan.[1] The plan for teaching reading in the intermediate grades did not require additional staff or facilities. Nationwide interest and discussion of this plan seem to have been stimulated by publicity received through the article, "Johnny Can Read in Joplin," by Roul Tunley, which appeared in the *Saturday Evening Post* for October 26, 1957.

In February, 1958, an experiment was begun in two public elementary schools of Laramie, Wyoming, to determine whether interclass grouping for reading in Grades 4, 5, and 6 would produce readers superior to those grouped conventionally by grade levels for reading. The experiment was evaluated at the end of one semester, at the end of three semesters, and again after five semesters.

Standardized reading tests were used to measure the reading level in grade equivalent of all pupils in the experiment. The pupils' intelligence quotients were also obtained. The two elementary schools are referred to as School A and School B. The growth in reading achievement by pupils in School A was compared with that of the pupils in School B. The pupils in School A are referred to as the experimental group. At the beginning of the experiment there were 189 pupils in each group. As a test for significant differences, the statistical method of analysis of covariance was used to treat the grade equivalents obtained periodically during the five semesters.

Each school had two fourth-grade classes, three fifth-grade classes, and two sixth-grade classes. Seven teachers were assigned to each school for these classes.

For this experiment the fourth, fifth, and sixth grades of School A were ranked on the basis of their reading level as measured by the first reading test. Some adjustments were made on the basis of previous test scores, intelligence

From *The Elementary School Journal,* 64: 280–286; February, 1964. Reprinted from "Interclass Grouping for Reading Instruction," in *The Elementary School Journal* by William F. Moorhouse by permission of The University of Chicago Press. Copyright © by The University of Chicago. William F. Moorhouse is Coordinator for the Regional Educational Data Processing Center, Santa Clara County, California.

[1] Cecil Floyd, "Meeting Children's Reading Needs in the Middle Grades; A Preliminary Report," *Elementary School Journal,* 55: 99–103; October, 1954.

quotients, and teacher judgments of school performance. The ranked list was divided into seven groups. Starting with the second semester of the school year, pupils who had similar levels of reading achievement were placed together for reading instruction for fifty minutes each day.

The pupils in the three grades were intermingled during the reading period. Each of the seven regular teachers in School A taught a reading class. Pupils spent the other portions of the school day in their regular fourth-, fifth-, or sixth-grade classrooms.

Table I shows how the ranked list of pupils in School A was divided into seven groups. The number of each group is listed in the first column. Group 1 had the highest reading level, and other groups follow in order. The number of pupils who were provided with each level of textbook is indicated in the second and third columns. For example, in Group 1 eleven pupils used eighth-grade reading textbooks and eighteen used seventh-grade reading textbooks. The three columns on the right side of the table show the number of pupils who came from each graded classroom to comprise the number listed in the second column. The reading textbook of about one-fourth of all the pupils was at the same level as their regular grade placement. The books these pupils used were at the same level of books they would have used had they not been regrouped for reading. But three-fourths of the pupils were reading material either above or below the level they would usually be asked to attempt in the graded system.

**TABLE I. Organization of Seven Reading-Level Groups in
School A at the Beginning of the First Semester**

| | | | Number of Pupils from Graded Classes | | |
Group*	Number of Pupils	Grade Level of Material	Fourth Grade	Fifth Grade	Sixth Grade
1	11	8	2	4	5
	18	7	1	9	8
2	12	7	2	5	5
	13	6	1	9	3†
3	30	6	8	11	11†
4	30	5	6	19†	5
5	30	4	11†	9	10
6	17	3‡	10	4	3
	9	3§	4	5	0
7	10	3§	7	3	0
	3	2‡	2	1	0
	4	2§	3	1	0
	1	1‡	0	1	0
	1	1§	0	0	1
Total	189		57	81	51

* Numbers indicate level of reading proficiency, in descending order. Group 1 has the highest reading achievement; Group 7, the lowest.
† Pupils were supplied with reading materials intended specifically for the grade they were in.
‡ Pupils were supplied with reading materials intended for second semester of given grade.
§ Pupils were supplied with reading materials intended for first semester of given grade.

Pupils in the same grades of School B, who served as a control group, were not assigned to interclass groups but remained in their graded classes for their reading instruction fifty minutes a day. The organization of their classes and their instruction in subjects other than reading were the same throughout the school day as the organization and the instruction of the experimental group. The teachers were free to form intraclass groups at their discretion. Teachers of the classes in the control group had access to the same test data that teachers of the experimental group used to rank their pupils to form interclass groups.

Teachers in School B were encouraged to make use of the test scores and personal observation to identify the individual reading needs of their pupils and to meet these needs as best they could in their graded classes. Supplementary reading materials for all reading levels were available for use with either individual pupils or small groups of pupils, as the teacher saw fit. Primarily, pupils used a basic reading textbook written for the grade they were in.

It was necessary to purchase a different series of basic readers for School A so that pupils reading below their grade level would not be repeating material they had attempted in former grades. Funds were not available to purchase the same series for School B.

The pupils in School A were told that they were assigned to reading groups where they would make the most progress. They were also told that no grades would be given for this particular reading period but that, at the end of the semester, a written report on their work in reading would be sent to their parents.

The pupils in School B were encouraged to work very hard on their reading and were told that they were being tested to see whether they could make more progress than pupils in School A. They were told that pupils in School A would be taught to read in a "different way" as an experiment.

In all instances, no significant differences in mean intelligence quotient were found between the various project and control groups that were compared throughout the experiment.

The mean gain in reading level of the experimental group was double that of the control group during the first semester. At the end of the first semester 169 pupils remained in each group. Table II shows mean gains of the experimental and the control groups, the mean differences, and standard errors of the differences of the various groups. Table II also shows the levels of significant difference in mean gain in reading level between various experimental and control groups during the first semester. The levels of significance were at the .05 level or better. The results indicate that the reading gain made by the experimental group over the control group during the first semester was greater than can be attributed to chance.

When the experimental and the control groups were compared on the basis of grade level, reading level, and intelligence quotient, pupils in School A showed strikingly greater gains than the pupils in School B, with the exception of those who ranked in the lower fourth nationally in intelligence quotient. Interclass grouping did not appear to influence the reading growth of pupils whose intelligence quotients were below 90.

During the first semester, results of this experiment were very much the same as those reported in other sources. The teachers and pupils were very much pleased with the interclass grouping plan.

TABLE II. Mean Gain in Reading Level in Control and Experimental Groups During the First Semester and Analysis of Covariance*

Group	Number of Pupils in Experimental or Control Groups	Mean Gain in Years Control Group	Experimental Group	Mean Difference	Standard Error of Difference	Analysis of Co-Variance $F y \cdot x$†	Level of Significance of Difference‡
Grade							
Four	54	.54	1.09	.55	.21	10.40	.001
Five	67	.55	1.14	.59	.21	7.62	.01
Six	48	.75	1.49	.74	.26	6.42	.05
	169						
Intelligence Quotient							
110 and above ..	74	.94	1.55	.61	.21	13.34	.001
91 to 109	70	.40	1.14	.74	.30	12.81	.001
90 and below	25	.18	.52	.34	.25	.01	not sig.
	169						
Reading Level							
1 and 2	49	.53	1.33	.80	.28	5.23	.05
3, 4, 5	80	.68	1.29	.61	.21	6.61	.05
6, 7	40	.57	1.07	.50	.17	8.95	.01
	169						

* Mean gains were made during a period of time which covered half a school year. The mean gains in reading level of experimental and control groups, their mean difference, and the standard error of the mean difference are stated in terms of years of reading level as measured by standardized reading tests.
† The $F y \cdot x$ values were used to determine the levels of significance of differences shown in the right-hand column.
‡ With the exception of pupils whose intelligence quotients were 90 or below, all experimental groups made gains over control groups which are not likely due to chance.

After three semesters, differences in reading level between the experimental and the control groups from the beginning of the first semester to the end of the third semester were still significant at the .05 level; however, the levels of significance had dropped below the level obtained after the first semester. The reading growth that had taken place during the second and third semesters was not significant at the .05 level.

As time passed, differences diminished. Pupils in School A who were tested five semesters after the experiment began did not show significant gains in reading level over pupils in School B. This was true, not only of the pupils who were tested in junior high school two semesters after interclass grouping had been terminated, but also of the pupils who spent five semesters in the interclass grouping plan.

The means in reading level for pupils in attendance at various times when tests were administered are plotted in Figure 1. Data were available for 126 pupils who remained in each group after two and a half years. The solid line represents the growth of the control group and the broken line represents the growth of the experimental group.

Figure 1: Comparison of Rate of Mean Gain in Reading Level of Experimental and Control Groups, by Grade-Level Group

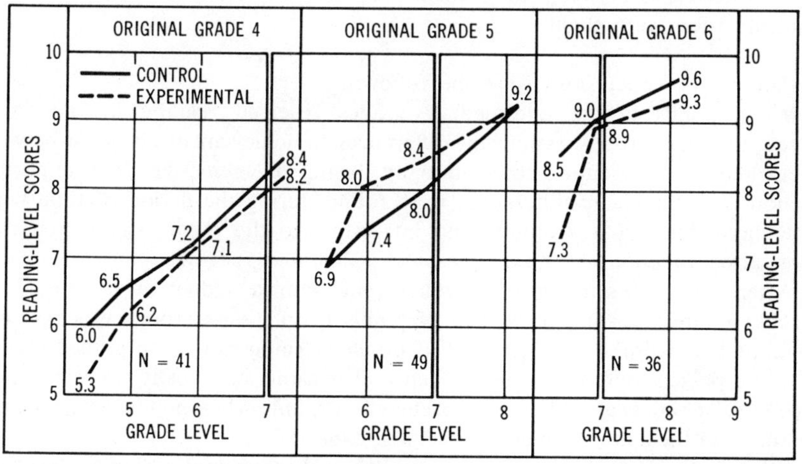

Note: The mean gain in reading level is shown for a period of two and a half years for the original fourth- and fifth-grade groups and for a period of one and a half years for the original sixth-grade groups. The means are based on the scores of pupils who still remained at the end of the experiment.

The units on the vertical scale represent reading-level scores as measured by tests. The horizontal scale is divided into three sections, one for each grade group, to indicate the grade level of pupils at the time of testing. The double line at Grade 7 indicates the time when groups left the experiment and entered junior high school.

The original Grade 4 and Grade 6 groups were not alike in mean reading level. The standard deviations of the distributions ranged from 1.2 in the fourth grade to 1.8 in the eighth grade.

The following observations are based on the results shown in Figure 1:

1. The rate of growth in mean reading level of each of the control groups is steady and about the same as the rate of the national group. This is evidenced by the upward, diagonal direction of the lines which form approximately a 45-degree angle with the coordinates.

2. The rate of mean growth of each of the control groups was slightly greater during the first semester than it was later.

3. The greatest rate of mean growth of each experimental group took place during the first semester and in each instance was higher than the rate of the corresponding control group.

4. The greatest rate of mean growth during the first semester was made by the sixth-grade experimental group. Next was the fifth-grade experimental group, and last was the fourth-grade experimental group.

5. The rate of mean growth of each experimental group was lower during the second and third semesters than it was during the first semester.

6. During the second and third semesters the fourth-grade experimental group was the only experimental group to show a rate of mean growth greater

than that of its control group. The sixth-grade experimental group was no longer in the experiment and showed the least mean growth during the second and third semesters.

7. Differences between final means of the experimental group and the control group were slight.

Among the conclusions were the following:

When pupils in the intermediate grades received reading instruction in seven interclass groups, significant differences in achievement occurred between them and pupils grouped conventionally during one semester. It is important to note that significant differences were found during the period of time when interclass grouping was unique and interesting to the pupils and served as a motivating function.

After the first semester and concurrent with a reduction of pupil and teacher interest, reading-level gain of pupils in interclass groups was no more than, and sometimes less than, that of pupils learning to read in graded classes. As time passed, differences diminished and became statistically not significant. The lack of significant differences occurred at a time when pupils were reaching maturity in their development of reading skills.

When a group of pupils was reading below its measured potential, interclass grouping served to bring the group up to its measured potential in reading level.

When a group of pupils was reading at its measured potential, initial accelerated gains were offset by later decelerated gains, and, as time passed, little if any influence of interclass grouping was apparent.

The evaluation of each pupil, which was necessary to determine his placement in an interclass group, was very useful. The task of forming interclass groups required a more thorough analysis of pupils' individual differences than might otherwise have been made. Teachers, elementary-school counselors, and principals found time to pool their knowledge of pupils' needs. The result was a better working relationship among staff members and a better understanding of pupils' reading achievement and potential than had existed in the school before the use of the grouping plan.

The growth toward reading maturity of pupils in interclass groups was accelerated. It is possible that the pupils received certain personal benefits because they developed certain reading skills at an earlier time. Through the development of greater reading efficiency at an earlier age, the demands of routine work in other subjects where reading skill is used may be reduced.

Interclass grouping had other advantages. It increased pupil interest and motivation and added variety to the school day for pupils and teachers. Pupils whose reading level was below their grade level seemed to participate more freely in reading-level groups than in grade-level groups. Teachers reported that they had more time to assist individual pupils because the problem of selecting reading materials on the basis of reading level was reduced.

No disadvantages in interclass grouping for reading instruction were found as far as pupil progress in reading was concerned. However, when the extra time involved in organizing interclass groups, the time involved in changing rooms, and the need for additional textbooks are considered, the advantages may not be sufficient to warrant use of the plan.

Possibly this study has merely shown again that when teachers and pupils become enthusiastic and put in extra effort, instruction and learning are favorable.

Further Reading for Chapter 9

Artley, A. Sterl. "An Eclectic Approach to Reading," *Elementary English,* 38: 320–327; May, 1961.

Balow, I. H., and A. K. Ruddell. "The Effects of Three Types of Grouping on Achievement," *California Journal of Educational Research,* 14: 108–117; May, 1963.

Carson, Roy M., and Jack M. Thompson. "The Joplin Plan and Traditional Reading Groups," *Elementary School Journal,* 65: 38–43; October, 1964.

Clymer, Theodore. "Working with Groups," *The Instructor,* 74: 79, 108; March, 1965.

Crosby, Muriel. "Organization for Reading Instruction," *Elementary English,* 37: 169–173; March, 1960.

Dawson, Mildred, A., and Henry A. Bamman. *Fundamentals of Basic Reading Instruction.* New York: David McKay Co., Inc., 1963. Chapter 9.

DeBoer, John J., and Martha Dallmann. *The Teaching of Reading.* New York: Holt, Rinehart & Winston, Inc., 1964. Chapter 12.

Duker, Sam. "Needed Research on Individualized Reading," *Elementary English,* 43: 220–225, 246; March, 1966.

Emans, Robert. "Teacher Evaluations of Reading Skills and Individualized Reading," *Elementary English,* 42: 258–260; March, 1965.

Frymier, Jack R. "The Effect of Class Size Upon Reading Achievement in First Grade," *The Reading Teacher,* 18: 90–93; November, 1964.

Groff, Patrick. "Comparisons of Individualized and Ability-Grouping Approaches as to Reading Achievement," *Elementary English,* 40: 258–264; March, 1963.

———. "Comparisons of Individualized and Ability-Grouping Approaches to Teaching Reading: A Supplement," *Elementary English,* 41: 238–241; March, 1964.

Harris, Albert J. *How to Increase Reading Ability.* New York: David McKay Co., Inc., 1961. Chapter 5 and 6.

Hester, Kathleen B. *Teaching Every Child to Read.* New York: Harper & Row, Publishers, 1964. Chapter 21.

Kierstead, Reginald. "A Comparison and Evaluation of Two Methods of Organization for the Teaching of Reading," *Journal of Educational Research,* 56: 317–321; February, 1963.

Lofthouse, Yvonne. "Individualized Reading: Significant Research," *The Reading Teacher,* 16: 35–37, 47; September, 1962.

Powell, William. "The Joplin Plan: An Evaluation," *Elementary School Journal,* 64: 387–392; April, 1964.

Rittenhouse, Gloria. "An Experiment in Reading by Invitation in Grades One Through Four," *The Reading Teacher,* 13: 258–261; April, 1961.

Rothrock, Dayton G. "Heterogeneous, Homogeneous and Individualized Approaches to Reading," *Elementary English,* 38: 233–235; April, 1961.

Sartain, Harry W. "The Roseville Experiment with Individualized Reading," *The Reading Teacher,* 13: 277–281; April, 1960.

Smith, Nila Banton. *Reading Instruction for Today's Children.* Englewood Cliffs, N. J.: Prentice-Hall, Inc., 1963. Chapters 6 and 7.

Spache, George D. *Reading in the Elementary School.* Boston: Allyn and Bacon, Inc., 1964. Chapters 4 and 11.

Tinker, Miles A., and Constance M. McCullough. *Teaching Elementary Reading.* New York: Appleton-Century-Crofts, Inc., 1962. Chapter 13.

Veatch, Jeanette. "Evaluating Differentiation of Learning in Reading Instruction," *Educational Leadership,* 22: 408–411; March, 1965.

————. "In Defense of Individualized Reading," *Elementary English,* 37: 227–234; April, 1960.

Vite, Irene W. "Grouping Practices in Individualized Reading," *Elementary English,* 38: 91–98; February, 1961.

❖ *10* *❖*

Materials for Reading Instruction

Probably no single factor influences the reading instruction that our children receive more than the materials we use to provide that instruction. Certainly basic readers have had a great effect on the reading instruction that we provide. The use of an artificial orthography for introducing reading to children requires the use of reading materials in which that orthography is used. An individualized reading program cannot operate without a wide variety of appropriate reading materials from which children may choose. Although materials do not blindly dictate method, the method we select depends upon the availability of appropriate instructional materials.

Although there are no sharp divisions between categories, classroom reading materials may be classified into three major categories. First are those materials which are primarily designed to assist in teaching reading skills and improve reading achievement. As stated previously, the most widely used of these materials are the various basic-reading series, consisting of children's readers, teacher's guides, workbooks or skillbooks, and a number of kinds of supplementary materials for each reading level. The educator, in selecting a basic series, should carefully evaluate each of these parts of the series, before deciding which one he wishes to use. The quality of selections in the child's reader, the suggestions for developing needed skills as given in the teacher's guide, and the types of practice exercises in the workbook all require a careful, critical analysis before a selection is made.

In addition to the basic series, there are various other kinds of materials which are primarily designed to teach pupils how to read more effectively. These include supplementary workbooks, which often aim at some specific skill such as phonics; a wide variety of reading games designed to teach skills such as structural analysis or to build sight vocabulary; various types of machines which aim to increase reading rate; and programmed reading materials.

Although the emphasis in this section is on materials to improve reading ability, the other two major categories of reading materials merit mention. The second classification comprises materials that are primarily designed to provide information through reading, including many kinds of texts, such as history or geography, and a wide variety of supplementary reference books dealing with study topics. The third category includes tradebooks and children's magazines, which are basically intended to be read for enjoyment. Although the books in these last two classifications serve useful functions in their own right, the effective reading teacher will also find opportunities to use them to teach or provide practice in many reading skills and abilities.

As noted previously, the selections in this chapter deal with materials designed to improve reading abilities. In the first selection, Arthur I. Gates explores the value of vocabulary control at the third- and fourth-grade levels in a basic-reading series. Although his findings support such control for at least some pupils through the third-grade level, they cast doubt on the necessity of vocabulary control in such materials above this level.

The author of the second selection, Eunice Shaed Newton, is also concerned with vocabulary control, but she approaches the problem at a different grade level and with a different emphasis. Forcefully demonstrating the broad range of meanings which may be associated with many of the most common words introduced at the first-grade level, Dr. Newton contends that this variety allows for much richer linguistic experiences within the confines of a controlled vocabulary than is normally supposed.

In the final selection, Jane Bissell Levine presents an evaluation of the advantages and disadvantages of programmed reading instruction and explores a number of issues which will determine the direction that such programming might take.

Vocabulary Control in Basal Reading Material ❖ Arthur I. Gates

This article deals with two related problems, the course of the development of the ability to work out the recognition and meaning of "new" words and the control of "new" words in basal reading material.

Beginning several decades ago, efforts were made to control the introduction of new words in the primary grades in order to foster the development of word-recognition and word-meaning skills and to enable the pupils to read the "study" or basal material with reasonable fluency and comprehension. Control was also made more comprehensive by selecting "new" words more carefully, by introducing them at more uniform intervals, and reviewing them more frequently and systematically, by providing more careful analysis of their visual and auditory features, and in other ways. Control was gradually extended upward until within recent years most basal series provide, and many teachers now demand, some degree of vocabulary control, at least a list of "new" words through the fourth grade, and occasionally later.

Vocabulary control is one of a number of refinements of basal reading materials which have increased the costs of the books appreciably. Some of the controls may have been carried so far, moreover, as to be useless, if not disadvantageous.

The present study consists in comparing the ability of pupils to work out the recognition and meaning of words previously introduced (and presumably studied) in a basal series with their ability to handle the "new" words introduced in later books in the same series. The first study, conducted in 1958, employed as subjects 310 pupils then near the end of the third grade. The pupils were members of twelve classes in New York City Public Schools 28 and 109 in the Bronx, 102 in Manhattan, and 127 in Brooklyn, which had used the Macmillan Readers as basal books from the beginning of Grade 1 to the time of the tests. The test, called a "Reading Puzzle," consisted of forty exercises, half of which were based on words introduced in the third-grade books, called the "old" words, and half of which were "new" for these children in the sense that they appear for the first time in the fourth-grade readers. The words selected were those which appeared at approximately regular intervals in the published lists of words in order of appearance in the third- (or earlier) and the fourth-grade manuals, respectively. Sample exercises follow.

In these illustrations, but not in the tests, the key word is italicized:

THIRD GRADE

A *buffalo* is

    an animal   a tree   a house   a curtain

FOURTH GRADE

A *tortoise* is

    an animal   a tree   a house   a curtain

From *The Reading Teacher*, 15: 81–85; November, 1961. Reprinted with permission of Arthur I. Gates and the International Reading Association. Arthur I. Gates is Professor Emeritus, Teachers College, Columbia University, New York City.

THIRD GRADE

An *umbrella* is something you take when it is

raining   singing   late   friendly

FOURTH GRADE

Medicine is something you take when you are

sick   proud   happy   asleep

THIRD GRADE

A *sailor* is a person who goes to

the mountains   a doctor   the jungle   sea

FOURTH GRADE

A *student* is a person who goes to

war   China   a doctor   school

THIRD GRADE

A *candle* will give you

food   light   rain   music

FOURTH GRADE

A *cramp* may give you a

reward   pain   lift   friend

In constructing the test the writer undertook to match each third-grade word with a fourth-grade word of the same general type (noun, verb, etc.) as shown in the illustrations above, and to have the context and the incorrect choices similar in character and difficulty, and composed of words of lower frequency in the Thorndike word list than the key word.

The results are shown in Table I. The most significant fact shown by this table is that these third-grade pupils recognized the form and meaning of almost as many of the words first introduced in the fourth grade as they did of the words previously studied in the third grade. More than half of these third graders got substantially all of both the "old" third-grade words and the "new" fourth-grade words correct.[1] The average third-grade child scores only a half-word less on the fourth-grade than on the third-grade words. The ablest children handle correctly about 97 per cent as many "new" fourth-grade words as the "old" previously studied third-grade words. Even the children who got the lowest scores succeeded in recognizing 90 per cent as many "new" fourth-grade words as the "old" third-grade words.

A second study was conducted in 1959 to see how second-grade pupils would compare with third-grade youngsters on both third- and fourth-grade words. For this test we secured the records of fifty-five pupils in the third grade and forty-seven pupils in the second grade of P. S. 108, New York City. The four classes

---

[1] In such tests any child, however able, is likely to slip on one or two items. Hence a score of 19 is likely to be substantially as good as a perfect score of 20.

TABLE I. Scores of 310 Third-Grade Pupils on
Third- and Fourth-Grade Words

Number of Third-Grade Words Right	Number of Fourth-Grade Words Right	Difference in Favor of Third-Grade Words	Difference per 100	Number of Pupils	Cumulative Percentage of Pupils
20	19.5	0.5	2.5	125	40
19	18.4	0.6	3.1	43	54
18	17.4	0.6	3.3	26	63
17	16.2	0.8	4.6	17	68
16	15.0	1.0	5.5	12	72
15	14.2	0.8	5.3	12	76
14	13.1	0.9	6.4	10	79
13	12.1	0.9	6.9	9	82
12	10.8	1.2	10.0	7	84
11	9.8	1.2	10.9	8	87
10	8.7	1.3	13.0	12	91
9	7.8	1.2	13.3	8	93
8	7.2	0.8	10.0	10	96
7	6.3	0.7	10.0	6	98
6	5.3	0.6	10.0	5	100

in this school had all used the Macmillan Readers from the first grade.[2] The results are shown in Tables II and III.

Although the third-grade pupils had not finished the third-grade readers, more than half of them got substantially perfect scores on both the third- and fourth-grade words. Here, as in the schools used in the first study, there were no zero scores, and the pupils with the smallest number correct handled the fourth-grade "new" words almost as well as the third-grade words.

The second-grade children were, on the average, only two-thirds of the way through Grade 2, and none of the third- or fourth-grade words had as yet been encountered in their basal books. Six of these pupils got perfect scores on both lists, and three more, included in the group of seven who averaged 17.3 and 17.1, got 19 of one or both lists. Thus a fifth got substantially perfect scores on both third- and fourth-grade words. None of the forty-seven pupils got a zero score. The average (median) child in the second grade recognized and understood correctly about 60 per cent of the "new" third-grade, and about 57 per cent of the "new" fourth-grade, words, even when they were presented in multiple choice exercises, which are typically difficult for children of their age. The context clues in the tests (see samples above) are not only meager, consisting only of a synonym or an example of the word's use or effect, but if the child does not recognize the key word, he is confronted by three misleading clues along with the one correct one. The typical second- and third-grade books give far more helpful clues than do these tests. Had the children encountered these words in a fuller and less artificial context, such as in the basal readers, they would have shown a higher percentage of successes.

[2] No doubt more or less similar results would have been obtained had any one of several other basal series been used.

**TABLE II. Scores of Fifty-Five Third-Grade Pupils on
Third- and Fourth-Grade Words***

Mean Number Right on Third-Grade Words	Mean Number Right on Fourth-Grade Words	Difference	Number of Pupils	Cumulative Percentage of Pupils
20.0	20.0	0	20	36
19.5	19.4	0.1	7	49
19.0	18.8	0.2	7	62
17.0	16.5	0.5	7	75
12.1	12.0	0.1	7	87
7.2	6.8	0.4	7	100

* Entries represent the number of children getting perfect scores followed by the mean scores of the remaining pupils in groups of seven.

A pupil's ability to recognize words not as yet encountered in his basal reading is due to two major factors. The average child by the end of Grade 3 in a good school — such as the schools used in this study — has done extensive reading outside of his basal books. Work in the basal books should be regarded as similar to the formal "lesson" in dancing or golf — it should comprise but a fraction of the total activity. Thus the average child reads extensively a wide variety of other material with uncontrolled vocabulary during which he encounters and learns far more words than those presented in the basal book lessons. Some careless critics of education seem to have assumed that the child's reading is limited to the material in the basal readers, and that his reading vocabulary is consequently restricted to that of the basal books. This view is grotesque; it embodies a complete misunderstanding of the nature of the total reading program.

The child's success in learning words during his reading of any material depends upon his techniques of working out, by himself, the recognition, pronunciation, and meaning of the unfamiliar words in context. A number of different skills and insights — not merely one such as some particular type of phonetic procedure — are needed to handle most efficiently all the varieties of words and verbal contexts and patterns encountered in a child's reading. That the New York City pupils have learned to use such a variety of techniques efficiently is shown by the fact that they can handle words not previously encountered in their basal program. Children halfway through the second grade do this very well, and of course they will be much better after they have had another year in school. As one of the teachers stated, "I think my pupils are adept at independent word recognition. They can usually figure out the word for themselves from structural, phonetic, context or other clues, some words by one approach and others by others. We, in fact, make it a practice to have each child figure each word out himself. None of the others is allowed to tell, at least not until the pupil has tried all the methods he knows." When these teachers discover a pupil who lacks an important technique, they teach it to him.

In Summary. Third-grade children of average ability in the thirteen classes from four different New York City public schools, as a result of the abilities

**TABLE III. Scores of Forty-Seven Second-Grade Pupils on
Third- and Fourth Grade Words***

Mean Number Right on Third-Grade Words	Mean Number Right on Fourth-Grade Words	Difference	Number of Pupils	Cumulative Percentage of Pupils
20.0	20.0	0	6	13
17.3	17.1	0.2	7	28
13.7	13.2	0.5	7	43
10.6	10.0	0.6	7	57
9.2	8.5	0.7	7	72
6.8	6.1	0.8	7	87
5.3	4.4	0.9	6	100

* Entries represent the number of children getting perfect scores followed by the mean scores of the remaining pupils in groups of seven.

they have acquired to work out the recognition and meaning of unfamiliar words and the experience they have had in reading by themselves, appear to have little more difficulty with the "new" words in the fourth-grade basal books which had not as yet been used in school than with words already encountered in earlier basal books in the series. For such children the listing and conventional controls of such "new" words in Grade 4 seem to be a waste of time in teaching and a needless expense in book production. Third-grade pupils have encountered most of the "new" fourth-grade words in reading other material, and if not, they can handle most or all of them when they encounter them in normal context. The fact that a word is "new" in the basal materials is an unreliable indication of its difficulty at fourth-grade level. This is true for the poorer students also, who during the second half of Grade 3 have only slightly more difficulty with the "new" fourth-grade words, on the average, than they have with the "old" third-grade words. Indeed the top quarter of youngsters two-thirds through the second grade have so little trouble with both "new" fourth- and third-grade words as to make conventional vocabulary control of doubtful value to them. Too few data were available in this study, however, to test the value of conventional "new" word control in basal third-grade readers for pupils of relatively low abilities.

The Basal Primer May Be Deceptively
Easy ❋ EUNICE SHAED NEWTON

Even though the battle over Dick and Jane, Bob and Judy, Jack and Janet continues without abatement, educators perhaps should approach vocabulary revisions of basal primers with thoughtful hesitancy. It could very well be that the field of linguistic science offers ammunition for the fray which can adequately state the case for controlled vocabulary in initial developmental reading texts. Could it be that the frequently derided, repetitious vocabulary of the basal primer is serving a developmental function? Lincoln Barnett, in a provocative article in *Life* (1), presented a veritable windfall to the educator who is interested in this problem.

Barnett's discussion of ". . . our frustrating, wonderful, irrational, logical, simple and now universal tongue — the English language . . ." suggests a need for those Anglo-Saxon tool words which occur so frequently in American basal primers. One of Barnett's major points is that since modern English is not highly inflectional, its morphological simplicity may be misleading. In this regard, he illustrates the semantic variations of several of our monosyllabic words of high frequency of use. Their proliferation of meanings challenges credibility.

When words such as *get, give,* and *make* are combined with certain versatile prepositions, numerous idiomatic phrases result. These phrases demand non-literal interpretation and can pose prodigious comprehension problems for the unwary reader. Barnett astutely demonstrates this point by presenting possible meanings of the phrase *give up.* It can mean *cease, cede, desert, discontinue, forego, forsake, relinquish, renounce, resign, sacrifice, stop, succumb, surrender, vacate, withdraw, yield,* and perhaps other things.

Of particular interest to the teacher of reading, too, is Barnett's reference to Basic English. The linguistic studies by I. A. Richards and G. K. Ogden (3, 8) have deep implications for any discussion on the essential words for the beginning reader. In the 850 words of Basic English compiled by them, there are included only sixteen verbs and two auxiliary verbs which are deemed necessary to indicate basic human action. Twelve of the verbs (*give, get, take, put, come, go, keep, let, make, say, see,* and *send*) are fundamentally simple body or manual action. These vital verbs totally permeate all forms of English expression. Richards and Ogden both argue that no acceptable form of English is possible without frequent recourse to them.

When the twelve verbs mentioned above along with the verbs *do, have, be, seem,* and the auxiliaries *may* and *will* are combined with certain flexible prepositions and other words, they can take the place of many other verbs. The extent to which other verbs can be replaced, without loss or change of essential meaning, by phrases containing Basic English verbs is possibly the most significant contribution of Richards and Ogden's research.

From *Elementary English,* 40: 273–274, 334; March, 1963. Reprinted with the permission of the National Council of Teachers of English and Eunice Shaed Newton, Associate Professor of Education, Howard University, Washington, D.C.

It may be wise to recall at this point, too, that Irving Lorge (4) had noted the problem of the prepositional phrase in American English syntax. It was his belief that the prepositional phrase (frequently composed of little-verb-plus-preposition) was central in comprehending the English sentence. It was for this reason that he stressed its importance in estimating readability, for he perceived that the prepositional phrase is the key to substantive relations.

The most cursory examination of a basal preprimer or primer in wide adoption in the United States will reveal the extent to which the textbook writers utilize the vital verbs of Basic English. (The monumental vocabulary studies of Dale, Dolch, Gates, and Thorndike show the frequency of use of the same words which Richards and Ogden discovered in their linguistic analyses.) The deriders of the controlled introduction of words in the American primer have termed the resulting context nonsensical jargon. Could it be that what appears to the adult as gibberish is not gibberish to the child at all? Could it be that there are subtle semantic variations in the simple content due to the flexibility of these vital verbs? Is it not possible that the young pupil needs to be inducted gradually into this peculiarity of English?

In a primer of wide adoption (6), one may encounter within few pages of each other the variations in the meaning of *make, be,* and *go* which follow:

> Did you *make* a ball for me? (contrive, construct, compose)
> *Make* her put it down. (force her to, compel her to, induce her to)
> Help me *make* your bed. (arrange, straighten properly)
>
> Where can mother *be?* (physical position or whereabouts)
> Make her *be* good. (become good, conform to accepted conduct)
> I will let her *be* a rabbit. (assume the characteristics of)
>
> Tip can *go* "bow-wow." (can utter, can say, can articulate)
> *Go* and let mother see you. (move physically: run, walk, etc.)
> Let me *go.* (release me, cease annoying me, give me permission)

It must be remembered that the illustrations just given are not unusual; one does not have to search assiduously to find them. Hall (2), Marckwardt (5), Sturtevant (9), Whitehall (10), and other distinguished linguists have attested to this vagary of English. Its pervasiveness should strongly suggest to us that controlled induction into our flexible syntax is necessary.

In his classic essay on "Basic English and Its Application," I. A. Richards has a message concerning the difficulties of learning a language which all who desire improved developmental reading instruction would do well to consider:

. . . All success and security in language learning depends upon the undisturbed growth of patterns. The worst disturbers are rival unconnected patterns which thrust in and confuse them. You can only protect, foster, and confirm a growing pattern if you know what you are doing as a teacher. And you can only know what you are doing if the words you are dealing with are few. . . . In brief, you cannot really help a learner if you allow him to attack the language on too wide a front. If you teach him too many words at once, you cannot give him the exercise in using them that he needs. (7)

References

1. Barnett, Lincoln. "The English Language," *Life:* 76–83; March 2, 1962.
2. Hall, Robert A. *Linguistics and Your Language.* Garden City, N. Y.: Doubleday and Company, 1960.
3. Johnsen, Julia E. (ed.). *Basic English.* New York: H. W. Wilson Company, 1944.
4. Lorge, Irving. "Predicting Readability," *Teachers College Record,* 45: 404–419; March, 1944.
5. Marckwardt, Albert H. *American English.* New York: Oxford University Press, 1958.
6. McKee, Paul, M. Lucile Harrison, Annie McCowen, and Elizabeth Lehr. *Jack and Janet,* Reading for Meaning [Series]. Boston: Houghton Mifflin Company, 1957.
7. Richards, Ivor A. "Basic English and Its Applications," in *Basic English.* New York: H. W. Wilson Company, 1944.
8. Richards, I. A., and G. K. Ogden. *The Meaning of Meaning.* New York: Harcourt, Brace and Company, 1949.
9. Sturtevant, Edgar H. *An Introduction to Linguistic Science.* New Haven, Conn.: Yale University Press, 1960.
10. Whitehall, Harold. "The English Language," *Webster's New World Dictionary of the American English Language.* New York: The World Publishing Company, 1957.

Let's Debate Programmed Reading Instruction ❖ JANE BISSELL LEVINE

Intensive programming of the reading curriculum is currently getting under way. A few unrelated segments of an elementary-school reading program are now available commercially, and small sections of a comprehensive developmental reading program are being tested this year in some New York City public schools, prior to commercial release. Some university teachers are beginning to program reading instruction, or are considering whether it is worthwhile.

What is programming? It means analyzing a subject into its component strands; arranging them in proper sequence; dividing them into the smallest possible bits of instruction; planning to test a student's understanding at each step, to minimize error, and to reinforce correct responses.

While reading specialists, other than those involved in active programming efforts, may look upon programmed reading instruction with interest, most of them view it as entirely a future development. On the contrary, there is no

From *The Reading Teacher,* 16: 337–341; March, 1963. Reprinted by permission. Jane Bissell Levine is affiliated with the Reading Clinic, Graduate School of Education, University of Pennsylvania, Philadelphia.

better time than the present to raise and discuss many questions about its suitability for teaching reading.

Potential Advantages

Programming sounds like a lot of trouble, and indeed the almost complete lack of programs in the field of reading attests to the particular difficulties of programming reading instruction. Is automated instruction worth the trouble? That question could be answered finally only by writing and putting into use a complete reading program — a process which would take years. Before that process is undertaken, one would naturally try to decide whether the potential advantages make the effort worthwhile. Some of the assets would be as follows:

1. The techniques of master teachers would be available to everyone, anywhere, at any time. If auto-instruction is successful, the caliber of reading instruction ought to improve generally and be more uniform nationwide.
2. The classroom teacher would be released from drill work and its correction and free to exert a humane influence.
3. Each student could proceed at his own pace.
4. Reinforcement (correction or reward) would be given to every student at every step of learning.
5. The automatic teacher would be inhumanly patient with every pupil.
6. A student's errors would be recorded, giving the teacher a clue as to where the student was having trouble, or as to areas where the program was weak.
7. Programs completed could serve as a record of progress.

Aside from the above potential classroom advantages, there are two advantages of programming reading which pertain to the education of reading teachers. First, widespread attempts to program could hardly fail to result in a clearer general understanding of the components of reading skills and the sequences of teaching them. Second, all the many theories about teaching reading could be tested under more control than has ever been possible, because the teacher's personality and skill, and the classroom social setting for learning, would be removed as factors. The teachers' enthusiasm for their own methods has often accounted for favorable results which were not duplicated when the methods were tried by others. The removal of the teacher variable and greater control of the classroom social factor seemingly would make programmed reading instruction an ideal research instrument. Furthermore, each step of the program can be tested for effectiveness and varied as necessary. Even if it proved not suitable for general classroom use, programmed instruction might survive for research uses.

Possible Difficulties

Against the potential advantages of programmed instruction, one ought to consider the possible difficulties of programming reading. Mature reading skills are more complex than any others that have been programmed, and the learning situations are more diverse. The student must not only read, but listen to stories, and tell them, sing songs, play word games, study pictures, write, do library research, and many other things to acquire the full repertoire of reading behavior.

Furthermore, learning to read starts with very immature children and unfolds as they mature physically, mentally, and socially. The sequence of child development and readiness to learn has received no attention in the literature on teaching machines. In fact, one of the implicit goals of such literature is to have more children learn more than ever at earlier ages. Will this run up against limits fixed by the child's level of maturation, or will our present theories of child development be revised?

Not least of the complications is that learning to read from a written program calls for the very ability which is being taught — reading. This is not an insoluble puzzle, if lower reading skills are used to teach higher ones, but the crucial question is whether reading can be programmed in tiny bits without teaching bad reading habits. Would reading the short, independent frames of programmed instruction contribute to or detract from the growth of perception by phrases, the ability to read long passages, or the ability to skim for some specific fact?

Aside from these general objections, there are specific areas where instructional devices cannot function. Pronunciation cannot be given or checked by a teaching machine, except on tapes with a teacher auditing, as in foreign language laboratories. Neither can oral reading be checked nor aural discrimination training and tests given. In time, electronic devices which respond satisfactorily to the human voice will probably be perfected, but they will be very expensive, and they will never be "good listeners."

Also, spontaneous questions cannot be addressed to a teaching machine if the child has difficulty in reading instructions. This objection applies to any subject programmed, for a program must be readable at the level of use. A reading teacher ought to be part of each team writing elementary-school programs, to adjust the readability level.

How could programmed instruction build up skills of reading long passages? What could it do to shepherd the development of independent reading activities and interests? What substitute could it offer for class discussions, story-telling and dramatizations?

How Programs Might Be Used

Turning from what programming cannot accomplish in teaching reading, let us consider its possible uses. Could it be used to teach entire units, as in basal readers? Certain oral parts of the experience couldn't be included, like pronunciation and class discussions, although a film or recording could introduce the unit. The work of introducing vocabulary and word analysis skills before the lesson and comprehension checks and workbook exercises after the lesson could be programmed. Perhaps the reading itself ought not to be cut up into short programmed frames, because the pupils need to practice reading unit-length materials.

The other approach to programming is to use it for isolated skills, such as the development of visual discrimination in the pre-reading program. And in beginning reading, by combining pictures of well-known objects and their printed names, plus tape-recorded instructions, one could condition a basic sight vocabulary. Several other parts of the reading program could be programmed: vocabulary development, word recognition from context clues, structural analysis, phonetic analysis, and comprehension development. They might be programmed en masse by using bits of each in connection with a basal reading unit. Or they could be done as separate strands, but in short segments closely coordinated with the student's reading level. Many workbook exercises could be adapted for programs. Certain study skills could be programmed — learning how to use indexes and tables of contents, to alphabetize, use diacritical marks, learning to use atlases, encyclopedias, the dictionary, and the card catalog, to read graphs and tables, and learning how to summarize and outline.

How could programmed materials be dovetailed with standard instruction? Would entire reading units be used as the main form of instruction? This is possible, especially experimentally. Its widespread adoption would depend on experimental results.

Or, programmed instruction could supplement the repertoire of independent activities the reading teacher makes available. Teachers often provide word games, workbook exercises, picture matching, etc., for independent practice in reading skills. Is there much difference other than hardware and step-by-step correction between the two?

If teaching machines were used as a supplement to regular instruction, which children might benefit? Advanced skills could be learned by avid readers; this would give a more solid foundation to their independent reading. Pre-grade reading, review, and remedial work could be given to slower readers. Special programs always involving written responses could be made for those students who profit from kinesthetic reinforcement. Braille could even be provided. Home study could proceed during prolonged absences, or skills that were missed during absences could be learned after return to school.

Another use of programs might be teaching adult illiterates to read.

Who Should Program?

Despite the many difficulties forseeable in programming reading, the advantages which have been glimpsed seem to make the attempt worthwhile. The next questions are, how should it be done, and who should do it?

There is certainly no one correct way to program reading, both because there are several theories of how best to teach reading and because there are no set rules of programming. One can search the literature without finding any but the most general guideposts on how to program — nothing that would show exactly how to do it. It is an art acquired through practice. Fortunately, one is not expected to write a perfect program on the first try. Programs are developed empirically from the first draft by being tested on students and revised until their flaws are removed, on the assumption that if the student does not learn, the program is at fault.

Ideally, a programmer must know something about three things: programming, the teaching problems of the particular subject, and the content of that subject. Some people have developed a talent for programming and subsequently taken the time to master the content of various subjects, and there also has been some programming by cooperation between subject-matter experts and skilled programmers.

If programming seems desirable, should reading teachers fold their hands and wait until it is available commercially? Hopefully not. It would be highly beneficial for many teachers to try their hands at writing programs, because this would increase the variety of ideas from which programs could be developed. The field is in its infancy, and there is great freedom to experiment. Experienced reading teachers, with their knowledge of subject matter and skill in presentation, have a good start and need only the practice of writing programs. Cooperative workshops would be an excellent way to do it.

Programs should be written as the subject matter requires. Later a mechanical device may or may not be used to present the material to the students, but no particular auto-instructional device should be allowed to dictate the shaping of the program. Purchase of any device or general adoption of a program should not occur before thorough testing of the program compared with standard classroom instruction.

Suggested Reading List

Cook, Desmond L. "Teaching Machine Terms: A Glossary," *Audiovisual Instruction,* 6: 152–153; April, 1961.

Fry, Edward B. "Teaching Machines and Reading Instruction," *Reading Teacher,* 15: 43–45; September, 1961.

Gates, Arthur I. "Teaching Machines in Perspective," *Elementary School Journal,* 62: 1–13; October, 1961.

Hively, Wells. "An Exploratory Investigation of an Apparatus for Studying and Teaching Visual Discrimination, Using Pre-School Children," in *Teaching Machines and Programmed Learning, A Source Book,* A. A. Lumsdaine and Robert Glaser, eds. Washington: Department of Audio-Visual Instruction, National Education Association, 1960. Pp. 247–256.

Komoski, P. Kenneth. "Teaching Machines and Programmed Reading Instruction," in *Controversial Issues in Reading and Promising Solutions,* Helen M. Robinson, comp. and ed., Proceedings of the Annual Conference on Reading, Vol. 23, Supplementary Educational Monographs, No. 91. Chicago: University of Chicago Press, December 1961. Pp. 109–120.

Noall, Mabel S. "Automatic Teaching of Reading Skills in High School," *Journal of Education,* 143: 1–71; February, 1961.

Popp, Helen M., and Douglas Porter. "Programming Verbal Skills for Primary Grades," *Audio Visual Communication Review,* 8: 165–175; Fall, 1960.

Pressey, S. L. "Certain Major Psycho-Educational Issues Appearing in the Conference on Teaching Machines," in *Automatic Teaching: The State of the Art,* Eugene Galanter, ed. New York: John Wiley & Sons, 1959. Pp. 187–198.

Pressey, S. L. "Some Perspectives and Major Problems Regarding 'Teaching Machines,' " in Lumsdaine and Glaser, cited above. Pp. 497–505.

Rowan, Helen, ed. " 'Tis Time He Should Begin to Read," *Carnegie Corporation of New York Quarterly,* April, 1961.

Smith, Nila Banton. "An Experiment to Determine the Effectiveness of Practice Tests in Teaching Beginning Reading," *Journal of Educational Research,* 7: 213–228; March, 1923.

Further Reading for Chapter 10

Bear, David, E. "Two Methods of Teaching Phonics: A Longitudinal Study," *Elementary School Journal,* 64: 273–279; February, 1964.

Bond, Guy L., and Eva Bond Wagner. *Teaching the Child to Read.* New York: The Macmillan Company, 1966. Chapter 6.

Burns, Paul C. "Instruction in Literature in Elementary School," *The Reading Teacher,* 15: 38–42; September, 1961.

Byers, Lorella. "Pupil Interests and the Content of Primary Reading Texts," *The Reading Teacher,* 17: 227–233; January, 1964.

Corliss, William. "Elementary School Libraries," *Elementary English,* 38: 494–496, 505; November, 1961.

Cruiscuolo, Nicholas. "Exploring the Value of Basal Readers," *Peabody Journal of Education,* 42: 98–104; September, 1964.

Dane, Chase. "The Role of Reading Guidance in the Total Guidance Program of the Elementary School," *The Reading Teacher,* 15: 102–109; November, 1961.

Gates, Arthur I. "Teaching Machines in Perspective," *Elementary School Journal,* 62: 1–13; October, 1961.

————. "The Word Recognition Ability and the Reading Vocabulary of Second- and Third-Grade Children," *The Reading Teacher,* 15: 443–448; May, 1962.

Hester, Kathleen B. *Teaching Every Child to Read.* New York: Harper & Row, Publishers, 1964. Chapters 19 and 20.

Hollingsworth, Paul M. "The Effect of Two Listening Programs on Reading and Listening," *Journal of Communication,* 14: 19–21; March, 1964.

Huck, Charlotte S. "Changing Character of Basic Reading Materials," *Educational Leadership,* 22: 377–381; March, 1965.

Martin, John Henry. "Report on Automated Reading Instruction," *Teaching Aids News,* 5: 6–10; February, 1965.

McCollum, John A. "An Evaluation of the Carden Reading Program," *Elementary English,* 41: 600–612; October, 1964.

Rogers, Helen, and H. A. Robinson. "Reading Interests of First Graders," *Elementary English,* 40: 707–711; November, 1963.

Smith, Nila Banton. *Reading Instruction for Today's Children.* Englewood Cliffs, N. J.: Prentice-Hall, Inc., 1963. Chapter 5.

Spache, George D. *Reading in the Elementary School.* Boston: Allyn and Bacon, Inc., 1964. Chapter 3.

Stiles, Lindley J. "What Shall We Do About Poetry in the Schools?" *The Elementary School Journal,* 65: 175–178; January, 1965.

Talbert, Dorothy, and C. B. Merritt. "The Relative Effectiveness of Two Approaches to the Teaching of Reading in Grade V," *The Reading Teacher,* 19: 183–186; December, 1965.

Tinker, Miles A., and Constance M. McCullough. *Teaching Elementary Reading,* New York: Appleton-Century-Crofts, Inc., 1962. Chapter 15.

Way, Olivia, R. "How Elementary School Teachers and Librarians Work Together," *The Reading Teacher,* 17: 159–163, 169; December, 1963.

West, M. "Criteria in the Selection of Simplified Reading Books," *English Language Teacher,* 18: 146–153; July, 1964.

Williams, J. P. "Reading Research and Instruction: Programmed Teaching Systems," *Review of Educational Research,* 35: 151–152; April, 1965.

❖ *11* ❖

Perception

Much of the research now being carried on which relates perception to reading concentrates on the perceptual problems of children who have reading difficulties. An increased understanding of the general perceptual patterns of children, however, may provide some important guidelines for ways in which all children can be taught to read more effectively.

For example, research studies show that beginning readers may recognize words by noticing certain striking characteristics, such as tall letters at the beginnings and ends of words, but that they sometimes find it very hard to move from these outlines or silhouettes of words to letters within the words — especially when their reading vocabularies have developed to the point where they include many words that are similar in appearance. Thus it would seem that emphasizing general word configuration may further delay the child's ability to read.

But the implications of research should be analyzed very carefully before they are applied in the classroom. For example, it has been reported that eight-year-old children pay particular attention to the initial letter of a word and then substitute words of the same general structure. Rather than being a characteristic of eight-year-olds, however, it is very likely that this is a characteristic of children of any age *when they are taught to read by a certain method*. Studies done during the 1930's which purported to show *the* age at which a child should begin reading and *the* age at which he should receive phonics instruction have long since proved untenable because the researchers did not consider the different reading methods which could be used successfully with children at other age levels. As educators, we should be aware of such pitfalls so that we will not act upon the same kinds of generalizations again.

In the first selection in this chapter, Agnes D. Fitzgerald explores perception from two basic directions. First, she looks at the total perceptual development of the child from birth to first grade; then, she moves from the perceptual aspects of the child's development through listening to speaking to reading to writing. In the second selection, M. D. Vernon summarizes a number of research reports on perception which may have a direct bearing on methods of teaching reading. In the third selection, Newell C. Kephart explains the various perceptual growth patterns of the child and describes how these emerging perceptual patterns are interrelated.

Perception Skills and Beginning

Reading ❖ AGNES D. FITZGERALD

The babbling and flailing of a baby on the floor may seem to the noncritical observer to be simply babbling and flailing on the floor. However, these overt personal expressions are not purposeless actions. They represent progress in the dynamic process of growth. To the baby, they are probings in a world of unexplored, undefined pleasure-pain complexes; they are his desperate efforts to relate himself to his environment; they are his only means of continuing to perceive, to experience and thus to learn and develop. To us, they are recognizable landmarks of progress in normal developments; to us they are significant devices by which we can appraise his personal ability to control himself in his environment.

The discussion of this paper is focused on the basic learned skills of perception as they develop in the young child and the relation of these skills to a successful start in reading. The perception process begins with gross motor awareness. The random movements of a child in the early stages of development are not consciously controlled. As the child grows, control develops. At an early age, perception takes the form of comparing and relating the objects of which a child is made aware through the excitation of his sensory organs. Coordinating the eye and the hand, sensing the right side from the left side, extending this knowledge of laterality to determine a set direction, distinguishing figure and ground in objects viewed, and placing observations in appropriate space are the primary demonstrations of a child's capacity to control himself with basic perceptual skill. This control is a direct product of continuous comparing, relating and integrating in light of one's immediate "set" and one's past experience. It is a control that is vitally necessary in beginning reading. Adjusting to the terms of our mechanized world of today, it is helpful to examine the human machinery of the child. We may be unable to adjust the machinery which is involved in basic perception but at least we may know what parts are not working.

Seeing what we recognize as a clock, hearing what we recognize as its chimes, and reaching out to touch the cool smoothness of the glass face of the clock — the sensual recognition of any form — is vague and undefined in the young child. The Gestalt psychologists have given to us our present understanding that we tend to perceive in wholes. In the global form of perception skill, a child responds to a group of sounds rather than to actual sounds that make up the pattern. Research cites a case of a child responding in the same way to *"Ou est la fenêtre?"* and *"Wo ist das Fenster?"* It is accepted that we speak in phrases and stresses rather than in individual elements. In the global stage of perception, the toddler calls all men "daddy" and all four-legged animals "dog."

At a later stage, children differentiate details in visual and auditory percep-

From *Elementary English*, 40: 415–419, 427; April, 1963. Reprinted with the permission of the National Council of Teachers of English and Agnes D. FitzGerald, Reading Specialist, North Colonie Central Schools, Newtonville, New York.

tion. In doing so, however, sometimes they lose the form as a whole and are left with nothing but a mass of details. Conversely, normal adults see the pattern, not the separate elements. For example, how often do we miss an extra *the* in re-reading a manuscript? The same concept is treated in completion tests, such as the Street (12) Gestalt test, in which one first perceives a broken outline or the details of a figure and later mentally fills them in to make the whole pattern, thus demonstrating the principle of closure. Similarly, in reading, the phonic sounds of *c-a-t* are just separate sounds of *c-a-t* to certain children who do not perceive the auditory pattern. The acuity is clear but not the pattern. Early identification of such a lack saves both teacher and pupil many futile hours. The time is better spent approaching the reading task from another direction while working to supply experience to develop the missing skill if possible. A classroom teacher may use a simple test in auditory discrimination when she suspects that a child is having difficulty in this area. Joseph Wepman (14) of Chicago University has developed a simple test for this purpose.

In visual perception, difficulty occurs when certain details alone are used as a clue to a word. For example, Kephart (7) describes the word *toot* which has elements that stick up at the front and back of the word. It is not necessary for the child to see the word as a whole, but he recognizes these characteristics and gets the desired result. Kephart further states that this type of child deceives the teacher at first by not showing any difficulty in learning sight words. Later trouble develops. With the word analysis method, the child is taught to break the word down into its parts and to sound out the phonic elements. "How can this be done by the child that still only sees the global mass? He cannot break it up into parts if he sees no parts to begin with." Some children see a word as we first may see an incomplete figure. He attends to one part. As he does this, he loses the other parts. He fails to see the *form*. Vernon (13, p. 15) summarizes the results of some studies pertaining to visual perception by saying "children . . . are less likely to see words as wholes than as meaningless jumbles of details with no apparent relationship between these." Most teachers who have worked with inept readers have remarked that those readers are the ones who notice the tiny flaws of the printer or the speck in the paper. The better reader scarcely sees them.

Space as well as *form* is a necessary part of perception. Without form and space, we cannot reproduce and, sometimes, we cannot even identify objects such as a square or a written word. Form and space are important for the same reason. They establish relationship. Form establishes the relation within the figure and space establishes the relation between the figures.

By the age of five a normal child can make a square. It is hard for us to realize what this simple task involves. To copy a square, a child must locate a beginning point. This he does with reference to his own body. He must get his hand to the exact starting point and distinguish one direction from another. According to Kephart, the idea of laterality leads to the idea of direction. If a child has not established which is right and which is left, certain relationships in space will be meaningless. Some lines and circles that make up printed letters are the same except for position. Since it is the perception of letters, words, and phrases that concern us in reading rather than the perception of squares and other forms, let us consider this further.

As Kephart states, without laterality, there is no difference between the letters *b* and *d*. (7, p. 32) "It is not that the child is confused. It is not that he has not learned the difference. It is not that he reverses the letters. The fact is that, for this child, no difference exists. . . . No direction exists, so no difference based on direction can exist." The perceptive teacher is aware that this skill must be present in order to teach the complicated activities involved in reading left to right across the line and returning to the next line at the left. One may cite further findings such as Vernon states. "There is general agreement that a child does not observe (or only with difficulty) orientation of shapes and their order or direction in sequence." In light of this paper, shapes may be called *form* and "order and direction" may be called *space*. The idea of space location for objects and letters gives the child a way to compare them. In order to get a relationship between elements, a child must establish a system of fixed direction. If one is to distinguish any difference between *left* and *felt,* one must have a consistent way of seeing letters in a fixed direction.

The experiments of Senden (7, p. 16) throw very interesting light on this space-form relationship. A blind person given sight by surgery was taught to distinguish a square and a triangle. After thirteen days, he could not report which form was which without counting the corners. Thus, the details were perceived first as elements in themselves. After he counted the corners, the total pattern or grouping of the elements emerged. It is not hard to relate this type of process to Anderson's (1, p. 272) description of the developmental process in reading. "The rank beginner is prone to identify words with certain compelling and dominant letters. The pattern materializes only through practice. . . . Gradually more and more details are enlisted until the word is organized as a unit and perception is complete." Thus Anderson states that reading by syllables or "dominating complexes" represents an intermediate stage in this process. The ultimate goal, of course, is to perceive quickly the constructual form of the word or word group or sentence. We often expect this involved process to appear full-blown in the young child and we minimize the amount and type of practice needed for such flexibility of perception.

Another example that Senden cited concerned a person with restored sight who could name a cube of sugar on the table but would not recognize the sugar when it was suspended by a thread. A teacher observes this same phenomenon with a child who is able to recognize a word at the blackboard but who is unable to recognize the same word in print in his book. This is sometimes referred to as a "category shift." The child has not learned flexibility of the pattern or "set." He may have learned to do it successfully in talking and he may readily respond to the spoken word such as "ball" in various categories — "bounce the ball," "throw the ball," "kick the ball." He must gain the same flexibility in reading.

The reading teacher's problem is to build up an integrated perceptual pattern that brings meaning to relationships within a figure and between figures. A child must learn to do with his eyes alone what formerly he did with his hands, arms, and total body. The teacher must realize that perhaps he has not yet done enough with these motor controls and may need the support of head nodding, finger, or marker in reading.

At the 1958 IRA Conference, Robinson (10) concluded that the most significant visual conditions for reading are "eye coordination difficulties involving depth perception, visual fusion and lateral and vertical eye-muscle balance." Harris (6) comments on these problems in eye coordination, stating that they "raise suspicions of inadequacy in the neurological controls of the eye rather than in the eye itself." Thus we return to the importance of perception in the child who does not have any sensory defect. Perhaps the ocular machinery is in order, but the child has not learned to use it efficiently. Optimistically, we can attempt to help him as much as possible.

A sense of space is necessary in order for a child to have an awareness of objects behind him. A young child backs into his little chair with great caution for the space behind him is not structured. So the older slow-learning child may feel that the ball on a string which he has tried to hit has gone out of existence when it swings behind him. For the child who is lacking in these basic perceptive motor skills, Kephart suggests that classroom teaching involve attention to perception and motor ability combined. He stresses the important feedback or matching between them. He considers emphasis in this area to be equal in importance with the attention usually given to integrating the child's ideas with his experience and understanding. Because of his belief in the cyclical nature of the learning process — input, integration, output and feedback — he advocates physical education as a necessary part of reading readiness. He considers muscular activities and intellectual activities as inseparable components of the total activity.

To change our emphasis on the development of basic perceptive skills themselves to emphasis on the beginning reader, let us consider the perception development from the point of view of the total Language Arts Program. Speech is the first link in this chain. It is closely related to auditory perception. The baby first listens to sounds. Then he imitates them. People talk in phrases which the baby hears. He gets meaning from the phrase as a whole, a global perception. Later he learns to break the phrase down into words. He may have some difficulty with the next step — that of breaking down the word itself. As Harris (6) puts it, "if the child could actually perceive the difference between *brother* and *bwuvvuh,* he would make the correction himself." Listening must be developed. The perceptive ability to distinguish the part within the whole (which we have previously described) is undeveloped in the child who recognizes that "fish" and "dish" are not the same but who cannot tell why. The ability to recognize the Gestalt as well as the separate elements in the slowly blended syllables of a word requires more than vague global perception. It is a constructive, integrated process. It is apparent that training in the skill of attentive listening is a very important factor in speech development and thus in beginning reading. Contrast in sound is the easiest to recognize. This suggests an order for the introduction of beginning sounds. It further suggests beginning with "dependable" sounds such as *s, l,* and *m.*

Continuing along the language-arts chain from listening to speech and then to reading, we note that words that ring true to the ear are the easiest to read. Hildreth uses this reasoning to suggest that the experience chart made up of the child's own words is a natural starting point for formal teaching. This upholds the theory of global perception preceding constructual perception. Anderson suggests for children who are not yet ready to read that one cover the print and have the child tell the story to the teacher. He suggests going along in the picture material as far as the child's perceptive skills will take him. He suggests another intermediary step as memory reading. Memory, that is, past experience, influences and changes perception. The research done by Goins (4) stresses the place of memory in holding the idea of the word as a whole, the Gestalt, while the child analyzes its parts. The ease with which this is done affects the ease of reading. Durkin notes that memory is a quality that all very young readers have in common. The lack of this, combined with underdeveloped auditory perception, presents many problems for the beginning reader.

The ability to write is the last link in the chain of language arts and is therefore dependent upon the preceding links. Attempt to avoid confusions should be made by integrating writing into instruction even at the sight-word stage. Careful attention to the sequence and pattern of the letters is necessary. The kinesthetic activity of writing or tracing strengthens the image. The teacher stresses the similarities and differences of letters and sounds that exist in the child's stockpile of sight words. Thus the total approach is emphasized.

The classroom teacher should be aware of the re-enforcement to perception that activities such as typing may give. The child looks at the word, says it, then types it. The child is helped to gain an impression of letters organized in space. As he sees the word in the book, it may be just a *form* to him. To type it, he must translate that form into *space* and thus develop his perceptive learning. As Gesell suggests, more emphasis should be placed on perception instead of looking. Filmstrip viewing of words or sentences may aid perception by controlling the images viewed.

Since reading involves the nervous system, it involves a total response of the child — eye, ear, hand, body, and, most important of all, that mysterious realm, the mind. As Vernon (13, p. 205) states, "We do not really know what he (the child) sees or hears." It is a delicate relationship between the inner ideas in his mind, his "set," and the outer stimuli. The teacher must constantly explore and check the results to approximate the child's degree of perception. In the same way that the beginning reader uses all learned clues to develop his idea of the word, so the teacher uses all clues observed in the child's responses to develop the instruction and to take the child as far as he can go on his way to successful reading. As we learn the significance of the basic perception skills, our own adult perception of the process of reading continues to grow and deepen.

Summary

The perception process begins with gross motor controls through the stages of eye-hand coordination, laterality, directionality, and form and space relations. It involves comparing, relating, and integrating, which is a continuous process that changes with one's immediate set and one's past experiences. These basic skills are assumed to be developed at first-grade age. At any stage, however, maturation may be delayed. Cases have been given to illustrate vague global perception; to illustrate perception which responds to separate unrelated units rather than whole-part relationship; to illustrate the importance of form and space relationship. The presence or absence of these basic skills has significance for the teacher and the awareness of this should control method, materials, and procedures.

Bibliography

1. Anderson, I., and W. C. Dearborn. *The Psychology of Teaching Reading.* New York: Ronald Press Co., 1960.

2. Boomsliter, Paul. *Lectures on Speech Development.* Albany, New York: New York State College for Teachers, 1958.
3. Durkin, Dolores. "Children Who Learn to Read before First Grade," *Elementary School Journal;* October, 1961.
4. Goins, Jean T. *Visual Perceptual Abilities and Early Reading Progress.* Supplementary Educational Monographs, No. 87. Chicago: University of Chicago Press, 1958.
5. Hildreth, Gertrude. *Teaching Reading.* New York: Henry Holt and Company, 1958.
6. Harris, Albert J. "Perceptual Difficulties in Reading Disability," in *Changing Concepts of Reading Instruction.* International Reading Association Conference Proceedings, Vol. 6. New York: Scholastic Magazines, 1961. Pp. 282–289.
7. Kephart, Newell C. *The Slow Learner in the Classroom.* Columbus, Ohio: Charles E. Merrill Books, 1960.
8. Koffa, K. *The Growth of the Mind.* New York: Humanities Press, 1951.
9. Piaget, J., and B. Inhelder. *The Child's Conception of Space.* London: Routledge and Kegan Paul, 1956.
10. Robinson, Helen M. *Clinical Studies in Reading,* No. 77. Chicago: University of Chicago Press, 1957.
11. ————. "The Findings of Research on Visual Difficulties and Reading," in *Reading for Effective Living,* International Reading Association Conference Proceedings, Vol. 3. New York: Scholastic Magazines, 1958. Pp. 107–111.
12. Street, R. F. *A Gestalt Completion Test.* New York: Teachers College, Columbia University, 1931.
13. Vernon, M. D. *Backwardness in Reading.* Cambridge: Cambridge University Press, 1957.
14. Wepman, Joseph M. *Manual for the Wepman Auditory Discrimination Test.* The author: Universiy of Chicago, 1958.

Major Approaches to Word

Perception ❋ M. D. VERNON

Clearly the ability to read must depend in the first place on reasonably accurate perception of printed words and the letters from which they are formed. Yet, as was noted in a previous paper by the author published in *Education* (1), children only slowly develop the capacity to perceive accurately the details of relatively complex shapes and the exact relationships of their parts.

That young children have little natural tendency to analyze shapes into their constituent details was shown by Ames *et al.* (2) with the Rorschach ink-blots. The shapes of the blots were responded to as wholes, but vaguely and inaccu-

Reprinted from the April, 1966, issue of *Education*. Copyright, 1966, by The Bobbs-Merrill Company, Inc., Indianapolis, Indiana. M. D. Vernon is Professor of Psychology, University of Reading, Reading, England.

rately, by children under three years; though some organization of parts began at three to four years. But in a later investigation Ames and Walker (3) found that kindergarten children of under six years who showed greater clarity and accuracy of response to detail subsequently became better readers than did those who, at the kindergarten stage, still continued to give gross global responses.

Recognizing Words as Wholes

If children, when they start learning to read, are only just beginning to be able to perceive complex shapes, it would seem particularly difficult for them to recognize words, which are shapes of great complexity, [since] their characteristics [are] dependent upon the relationships of their constituent parts, the letters. Many psychologists and educationists, aware of this difficulty, have supposed that children learn to read in the first place by perceiving words as "wholes" — rather vague outline shapes which they learn to recognize as the names of objects shown in pictures. This notion then suggested that the "look-and-say" or "whole-word" method was the most suitable for teaching beginners reading. It was claimed that the Gestalt theory supported the notion, since it emphasized that we normally perceive "wholes" or total patterns, often overlooking their constituent details.

But the "wholes" of the Gestalt psychologists in general possessed some striking and obvious pattern or form which . . . was easy to perceive as a whole, and had nothing like the irregularity and complexity of word shapes. Psychologists such as Meili (4) showed that patterns were perceived as wholes only when their outlines were fairly simple and obvious. If they were complicated, or if the details were relatively salient, the child tended to perceive these rather than the outline of the whole.

This suggests that in some circumstances a child may perceive dominant letters, such as the ascending and descending letters, and that the only characteristic of the outline of the whole word perceived may be its length. The latter might then enable children to differentiate between words of very different length. However, Davidson (5) found that only 16 per cent of the errors made by children of a mental age of four years who were learning to read were substitutes of words of the same length. Many other errors were due to confusion of individual letters.

Recognizing Words by Salient Letters

It would thus appear that words may often be recognized not so much from their general outline shape as from certain salient letters. Of these, probably the initial letters are the most important. Thus Wilson and Flemming (6) showed a strong tendency among children of six to seven years to substitute for the correct word another word with the same initial letter. Diack (7) found that a child of three years could pick out the word *caravan* from several other meaningful and nonsense variants such as *carve, caramel, varacan, racavan,* and *naracan.* Diack concluded that the correct choice was based partly on length (since *carve* was seldom selected); partly because it had no bit sticking up at one side, like *caramel*; and partly because at one end there was a convex curve, found in the letter *c*.

Different children may identify by means of different letters, but the ascending letters seem to catch the eye. Children of eight years, only just beginning to read (8), appeared partly to see the words, attending principally to the initial letter, and then to substitute possibly more familiar words of the same general structure, such as *chickens* for *clucked*. However, some substitutions were nonsense, such as *chimly and clickle*. Again, Ilg and Ames (9) found substitutions of words of similar form, such as "scratchily" for "scarcely," to be frequent in normal readers up to the age of seven years.

What we may conclude is that there is in the early stages no *systematic* analysis of word structure and of the letters composing the word, though Daniels and Diack (8) found analysis more apparent with children taught by the phonic method than partly by whole-word methods. Piaget (10) showed that there was little capacity for systematic direction of attention to the significant features of complex forms below the age of six to seven years.

Recognizing Letters

It would appear at first sight that letters themselves would be difficult to perceive and remember accurately, since many differ from each other by small details only. Moreover, children have to learn to distinguish between significant differences between letters, and minor variations such as those of different type faces. Yet many children seem to learn at least the commoner letters surprisingly easily.

Gibson *et al.* (11) carried out experiments in which they presented, to children of four to eight years, twelve forms shaped like letters, each with a number of "transformations," that is to say, slight variations of shape. The children were required to match each of the twelve forms against its counterpart grouped with the variations. The total number of confusions decreased from 58 per cent at four years to 20 per cent at eight years. Few children confused the standards with variants in which the lines of the originals were broken or closed up. Confusions between curved and straight lines were numerous at first but decreased to zero by eight years; and the same was true of rotations and reversals.

Similar results were obtained with real letters among the younger children who had not learned to read, though the total errors were fewer. Confusions between reversed letters such as *b* and *d* have been observed by many experimenters. Their experiments have shown that young children do not discriminate at all clearly between the same shapes in different orientations. These errors disappear among normal readers at seven to eight years, but they persist among backward readers for considerably longer.

At some point before words can be recognized correctly individual letters must be analyzed out and correctly perceived, or at least, individual "graphemes" — letter groups. This is necessary before the child can associate these with the corresponding "phonemes" or sound groups. The essential feature of the phonic method is to teach children to recognize easily the most common and regular graphemes and phonemes. It is impossible to say whether at this stage the child perceives *every* letter in the word individually. But probably certain individual letters, for instance those which are responsible for differentiating words of similar general appearance, must be separately perceived and learned.

However, it is quite possible that young children are relatively slow to extract what are the most important letters. Thus Ghent (12) found that even at eight years children had some difficulty in picking out simple figures "embedded" in more complex wholes. This inability might be matched by difficulties in picking out important letters in whole words.

Perceiving Correct Letter Order

But no sooner have letters been isolated than they must be recombined or "blended" in the correct order to form the whole word again. There is ample evidence to show that even after the letter shapes have become thoroughly familiar, their order in the word still produces difficulties. This is partly inherent in the English language; who can remember, without a mnemonic, when *i* comes before or after *e*?

But Piaget and Inhelder (13) found that children under five to six years could reproduce correctly the order of beads on a string only by copying, bead by bead, from a model. At about six years they began to understand order as such, and to be able deliberately to reverse it. This is a much easier task, however, than remembering the correct order of letters in words in which the order may vary only slightly.

It is not surprising that up to seven to eight years there are frequent confusions in reading between words consisting of the same letters in a different order (9). What are more surprising are the complete reversals of words, such as *was* for *saw*, since it would appear here that the whole structure of the word is altered. Although these reversals are commoner in backward readers, they are also found among normal readers.

Perception Through Context

Finally, to achieve fluent reading, the child must cease to perceive every letter in the word, and even every word in the sentence. An average adult reader makes five to six fixation pauses of about one-fifth of a second each in every line of print; and rapid readers make considerably fewer. The scope and duration of a fixation pause are such that only certain words in the line are seen clearly; the remainder are inferred from the context. And indeed it appears from studies of tachistoscopic reading that, if they know what to expect, adult readers can reconstitute whole words when only a few letters have actually been perceived (7).

Even parts of letters may be sufficient. Thus Huey (14) showed that if the lower parts in a continuous text were obscured, this could be read quite easily, though not when the upper parts of the letters were omitted.

Now it is known from an experiment by Draguns and Multari (15) that even pictures of real objects, when blurred and partly obscured, are recognized with more difficulty by children aged under nine to ten years than by older children. Thus it seems possible that up to a certain age children may be precluded from perceiving and reading rapidly because they are slower than adults to infer whole structures on the basis of partial cues.

Backwardness and Poor Perception

To what extent may backwardness in reading be caused by inaccurate or defective perception of words? There is evidence that some backward readers are less competent than are normal readers in perceiving and reproducing the complex forms of the Bender Gestalt Test (16, 17). Kinsbourne and Warrington (18) found some backward readers to be retarded in the WISC Block Design and Object Assembly Tests. And Tjossem *et al.* (19) demonstrated a poorer performance by backward readers on an "embedded" figures test.

These findings suggest that it is not so much the immediate perception of form which is deficient as the capacity to analyze shapes and extract certain significant characteristics from them. It is improbable that this capacity is deficient in all backward readers. But it may often be so in those cases in which there are EEG abnormalities and minimal brain damage is suspected (20, 21). Defects of this kind may occur in other dyslexic children, but not in all (22). Again, it is probable that they are only seldom the main cause of dyslexia. When associated, as they often are, with language disorders, dyslexia may be particularly severe (23).

We may conclude, therefore, that the types of perception involved in reading words, including the accurate analysis of complex shapes and their reconstitution from partial cues, may indeed cause children some difficulty until they have reached the appropriate stage of maturation. Most children, however, do develop naturally the ability for these types of perception. Some backward readers may show a maturational lag in perceptual development, though probably the effects of this are commonly aggravated by other deficiencies.

References

1. Vernon, M. D. "The Development of Visual Perception in Children," *Education*, 78: 547; 1958.
2. Ames, L. B., *et al.* "Development of Perception in the Young Child as Observed in Responses to the Rorschach Test Blots," *Journal of Genetic Psychology*, 82: 183; 1953.
3. ————, and R. N. Walker. "Prediction of Later Reading Ability from Kindergarten Rorschach and I.Q. Scores," *Journal of Educational Psychology*, 55: 309; 1964.
4. Meili, R. "Les Perceptions des Enfants." *Archives de Psychologie*, 23: 25; 1931.
5. Davidson, H. P. "An Experimental Study of Bright, Average, and Dull Children at the Four-Year Mental Level," *Genetic Psychology Monographs*, 9: 119; 1931.
6. Wilson, F. T., and C. W. Flemming. "Reversals in Reading and Writing Made by Children in the Kindergarten and Primary Grades," *Journal of Genetic Psychology*, 53: 3; 1938.
7. Diack, H. *Reading and the Psychology of Perception.* Nottingham, England: Skinner, 1960.
8. Daniels, J. C., and H. Diack. *Progress in Reading.* Nottingham: University of Nottingham Institute of Education, 1956.
9. Ilg, F. L., and L. B. Ames. "Development Trends: Reading Behavior," *Journal of Genetic Psychology*, 76: 291; 1950.
10. Piaget, J. *Les Mecanismes Perceptifs.* Paris: Presses Universitaires de France, 1961.
11. Gibson, E. J., *et al.* "A Developmental Study of the Discrimination of Letter-like Forms," *Journal of Comparative and Physiological Psychology.* 55: 897; 1962.
12. Ghent, L. "Perception of Overlapping and Embedded Figures by Children of Different Ages," *American Journal of Psychology*, 69: 575; 1956.

13. Piaget, J., and Inhelder, B. *The Child's Conception of Space.* London: Routledge and Kegan Paul, 1956.
14. Huey, E. B. *The Psychology and Pedagogy of Reading.* New York: Macmillan, 1910.
15. Draguns, J. G., and G. Multari. "Recognition of Perceptually Ambiguous Stimuli in Grade School Children," *Child Development,* 32: 541; 1961.
16. De Hirsch, K. "Gestalt Psychology as Applied to Language Disturbances," *Journal of Nervous and Mental Disease,* 120: 257; 1954.
17. Lachmann, F. M. "Perceptual-Motor Development in Children Retarded in Reading Ability," *Journal of Consulting Psychology,* 24: 427; 1960.
18. Kinsbourne, M., and E. K. Warrington. "Development Factors in Reading and Writing Backwardness," *British Journal of Psychology,* 54: 145; 1963.
19. Tjossem, T. D., *et al.* "An Investigation of Reading Difficulty in Children," *American Journal of Psychiatry,* 118: 1104; 1962.
20. Cohn, R. "Delayed Acquisition of Reading and Writing Abilities in Children," *Archives of Neurology,* 4: 163; 1961.
21. De Hirsch, K. "Studies in Tachyphemia: IV: Diagnosis of Developmental Language Disorders," *Logos,* 4: 3; 1961.
22. Ingram, T. T. S. "Delayed Development of Speech with Special Reference to Dyslexia," *Proceedings of the Royal Society of Medicine,* 56: 199; 1962.
23. Borel-Maisonny, S. "Les Troubles du Language dans les Dyslexcs et les Dysorthographiques," in *L'Apprentissage de la Lecture et ses Troubles.* Paris: Presses Universitaires de France, 1952.

Perceptual-Motor Aspects of Learning Disabilities

✤ Newell C. Kephart

The following discussion outlines a portion of the rationale for dealing with the child with learning disabilities developed by the author over the past twenty-five years. It is based largely upon clinical observation of the behavior of many such children and forms the basis of the therapy program of the Achievement Center for Children, Purdue University.

Most of the learning experiences which the public school presents to the child are oriented toward symbolic materials. Visually, we present words, diagrams, and similar representations on a printed page. Verbally, we manipulate conceptual items and deal in intricate, logical sequences. Underlying such presentations is a fundamental assumption: that the child has established an adequate orientation to the basic realities of the universe — space and time. It is well known that the ability to deal with symbolic and conceptual materials is based upon consistent and veridical perceptions of the environment. Numer-

From *Exceptional Children,* 31: 201–206; December, 1965. Reprinted by permission.
Newell C. Kephart is Professor of Education, Purdue University, Lafayette, Indiana.

ous, normative studies have indicated that the child, under normal conditions, has established a stable world by the age of six years when he comes to us in the public schools. Therefore, our fundamental assumption is legitimate.

However, in a significant percentage of children, accidents occur during the developmental period. The accident may be any one of a large number of events. Its effect is to interfere with the establishment of a stable perceptual-motor world. As a result, many children come into our school system lacking the fundamental assumptions which underlie so much of the material which we present.

For the child who has been unable to establish the three dimensions of Euclidean space in his visual world, the words on a page of print may become an unintelligible mass of meaningless marks. They may not hold together into the compact groups, words and phrases, with which we deal. They may not hold still, but float about on the page. Worst of all, they may look different to him at different times and under different circumstances.

For the child who has been unable to establish a firm temporal dimension in his environment, the verbal discussions which we present may be no more than a meaningless jargon of sounds. Our intricate, step by step logical procedures may be difficult to organize without a temporal dimension along which to arrange them. Consider the difficulty which many children have in organizing the sequence of steps in long division.

For this significant percentage of children, the materials which we present in the classroom may cause difficulty, not because of the content or inability to deal with the content, but because of inability to deal with the mechanics of the presentation. Where the mechanics of the task break down, the content of necessity suffers. It may be that the child has not so much difficulty in learning to read as he has in seeing the words on the page. It may be that he has not so much trouble in understanding arithmetical reasoning as he does in organizing the steps of this reasoning in time.

Environmental Interactions

The child's first interactions with his environment are motor. His first learnings are motor learnings. His first attempts to organize the environment are based upon these motor interactions. For a very large number of children, the learning difficulty begins at this early motor stage. He learned to use his motor responses to accomplish certain ends, but he failed to expand or generalize these motor responses so that they formed the basis of information gathering. He has learned a motor response for a specific end, but has not developed a motor interaction with his environment.

The difference here is that between a motor skill and a motor pattern. A motor skill is a motor act which may be performed with high degrees of precision. However, it is limited in extent; it is designed for a specific result, and only limited variation is possible. The motor pattern on the other hand involves lesser degrees of precision, but greater degrees of variability. Its purpose is much broader, and extensive variation is possible.

Consider the difference between walking as a motor skill and walking as a part of a locomotor pattern. The young child first develops a walking skill. He learns how to maintain an upright position while he puts one foot in front of the other. This process allows him to move from point A to point B. However, most of his attention must be devoted to the motor process itself — what part must move and how must it move. Very little attention can be devoted to the purpose of the movement. The skill is very limited and little variation is possible. Thus, if he encounters an obstacle in moving from point A to point B, he may well have to stop and give up the entire task. He cannot veer around the obstacle or step over it because these adjustments involve greater variation than his limited skill will permit.

Consider on the other hand the locomotor pattern of the older child. He can get from point A to point B by any one of a number of specific skills. He can walk; he can run; he can skip; he can jump, and so on. If an obstacle looms in his way, he can veer around or go over or under it as the problem demands. In all of these extensive variations, he does not need to expend attention on the motor act itself. This act has been generalized; it is no longer specific. As a result, he can shift directions or shift movement sequences without undue attention to the process itself.

With the walking skill the child is limited to rather specific purposes and ends. The process does not involve a continuous, changing, viable relationship with the environment. Only through a locomotor pattern can the child maintain a consistent, uninterrupted interaction with the environment surrounding him. The development of a stable body of information about this environment demands such a continuous, reliable interaction. Thus motor patterns become essential for information-gathering at this basic early stage in the development of the world of the child.

There are four of these motor patterns which appear to be of particular significance to us in the field of education.

Balance and Maintenance of Posture. All spatial relationships in the world about us are relative. Right and left, up and down, behind and before are relationships which are not given directly by perceptual data. They develop out of the observation and organization of relationships between objects. A well organized system of such relationships will include the three Euclidean dimensions of space. All of these relationships, however, are relative. Each object is related to each other object, and there is no objective direction. The child must systematize this set of relationships through the learning resulting from his interaction with the objects in his environment.

The point of origin for all such relationships is the force of gravity. It therefore becomes important for the child to establish a relationship to the force of gravity and to be able to maintain this relationship and the awareness of the center of gravity throughout all of his activities. It is only through a constant and stable relationship to gravity that a point of origin for spatial relationships can be established. This stable relationship to gravity is achieved through the motor pattern of balance and posture. By maintaining the relationship of his body to the force of gravity, the child identifies the direction of the line of gravity and maintains this constant throughout his interactions with the environment.

The child should be able to maintain his balance and relationship to gravity under many conditions and with his body in a large number of different positions. He should not lose balance or lose his awareness of gravity when the position of his body changes or when its motion alters. On the other hand, his relationship to gravity should be variable so that he can maintain this relationship under a large number of conditions. His balance and posture should be dynamic and fluid rather than rigid. It is only through such a dynamic relationship to gravity that a continuous awareness of its direction can be maintained.

Locomotion. The locomotor skills are those motor activities which move the body through space: walking, running, jumping, skipping, hopping, rolling, etc. It is with the pattern of locomotion that the child investigates the relationships within the space around him. By moving his body from one point to another, he learns to appreciate the properties of this surrounding space and the relationships between the objects in it. Out of such knowledge a space world with stable coordinates will develop. Locomotor skills should be variable. They should permit the child to divert his attention from the movement itself to the purpose of the movement. They should permit the child to adjust to changes in the environment and to obstacles which may lie in the path of his movement.

Contact. The contact skills are those motor activities with which the child manipulates objects. Involved are the skills of reach, grasp, and release. It is with the contact skills that the child investigates through manipulation the relationships within objects. In order to obtain this information, he must be able to reach out and make contact with the object; he must be able to maintain this contact through grasp until he has obtained the necessary information, and he must be able to terminate this contact through release and move on to the next object. From the knowledge so gained, form perception and figure-ground relationships will develop.

The skills of reach, grasp, and release should be established well enough so that the child can divert his attention from the motor acts to the manipulation. They should also be sufficiently variable to permit him to make complex manipulations in search of information.

Receipt and Propulsion. With the skills of locomotion, the child has investigated the relationships in the space around him. With the skills of contact, he has investigated the relationships within an object. However, many of the problem situations with which he must deal involve the movement of objects in space. It is with the skills of receipt and propulsion that he investigates movements in space.

Receipt skills involve those activities by which the child makes contact with a moving object. Such skills include, not only the pursuit of the moving object, but also the interposition of the body or parts of the body in the path of the moving object, as in catching. The skills of propulsion involve those activities by which the child imparts movement to an object. Included are throwing and batting, and the like. Also included are the more continuous skills of pushing, pulling, and the like.

Through the use of these four motor patterns, the child investigates the vast array of relationships in the environment around him. Out of this investigation he puts together a system of these relationships. The initial information is motor. It comes from the interaction through movement of the child with his environment. To develop a system, however, these interactions must be extensive, and they must be consistent. If the interactions are not sufficiently extensive, the system will not be sufficiently inclusive. If the interactions are inconsistent so that the observed relationships are not stable, the development of a system is impossible. To develop such extensive and consistent investigations, motor patterns as opposed to motor skills are required. Therefore, we are not interested in whether or not the child can walk; we are interested in whether or not he can locomote in order to obtain information about objects in space. We are interested in a sort of motor generalization by which the repertory of movements, whatever they may be, available to the child are used for the purpose of gathering information about the environment around him.

Many children find the motor learning required for a learning pattern difficult. As a result, they stop with a motor skill. They require additional help and additional learning experiences to continue this motor learning until a level is reached which will permit the use of movement, not only for specific purposes, but for the more generalized purpose of information gathering. It becomes the responsibility of the public schools to offer this aid and to help the child expand his motor learning.

Directional Relationships

Out of these motor investigations of the environment comes a system of relationships. At this point the system is primarily a motor system. It exists within the child's own body. The directions of space are beginning to develop, but they are limited to the movement relationships which occur in his body. The vertical direction has developed and stabilized out of his use of balance and posture. Out of his more extensive motor activities he has developed a laterality among his own movements. He now knows when a movement is on the right side of the body, and when it is on the left; and he knows how far to the right, or how far to the left it may be. He has developed a sort of a right-left gradient within his own movement system.

For further progress, however, this system of directional relationships must be transferred to outside objects. Since he cannot investigate in a motor fashion all of the objects in his environment, he must learn to investigate them perceptually. These perceptual data, however, do not at this point possess the spatial relationships which his motor data possess. Perceptual data come to have such relationships by projecting motor information onto perceptual information.

It is through the perceptual-motor match that the child makes this projection. As he manipulates an object or relationship motorwise, he observes the perceptual data which he is receiving concurrently and particularly he observes changes in these perceptual data. Through a matching of the motor data and the perceptual data, these two areas come to give him the same information. Now perceived objects have a right and a left, just as manipulated objects have a right and left. Now he can *see* up and down, just as previously he learned to feel up and down. Through such a projection process, the perceptual world comes to be systematized and organized in the same fashion that the motor world was organized. It is only through such a projection that a veridical organization of the perceptual world is possible.

Important here is the control of the external sense organs. The sensory avenue which gives us the greatest amount of information, and which is most subject to control, is that of vision. The visual information is controlled by the direction in which the eye is pointed. The pointing of the eye in turn is controlled by the extraocular muscles. The child must learn to explore an object with his eye in the same way in which he previously explored it with his hand. It is important, however, that the exploration with the eyes duplicate the exploration with the hand, and that the resulting information match the earlier information.

Two problems arise at this point. First of all, the child must learn to manipulate his eye through the development of patterns of movement in the extraocular muscles. The second, and perhaps a more important problem, is that of learning to manipulate the eye in terms of the incoming information. The only way in which the child can know that his eye is under control is to evaluate its information. The criterion of ocular control is the visual information which results. However, the child is only now developing a stable visual world with which to evaluate the present perception. Therefore, the body of information which should provide the criterion for ocular control is not yet present. On the other hand, without ocular control the incoming contributions to the body of visual information are inconsistent and spotty. Thus the control of his eye is hampered by his lack of a stable visual world while at the same time the stability of his visual world is impaired by his lack of ocular control.

The solution to this dilemma is in motor manipulation. The child investigates motorwise. He then experiments with the movement of his eye until it gives him information which matches his motor information. Since the body of motor information is reasonably stable, he stabilizes the visual information when a match occurs. Through many such experiments, he develops a visual world which duplicates his motor world. He has established a perceptual-motor match. When this match is adequate, he can drop out the intervening motor manipulation and use his now stable visual information to control the eye and thus control new visual input. Now all information — motor or perceptual, sensory input or motor response — is a part of a stable over-all system which gives consistent information wherever it is tapped. Control of perceptual information and of motor response are both possible and are both a part of one consistent system.

It is obvious that such learning will be difficult and will require extensive experimentation. Here again the learning process frequently breaks down with the result that an adequate match between perceptual information and motor information is not accomplished. For such children there is limited stability in the perceptual world. They cannot *see* the relationships of right-left, up-down, and so on. For them, the letters on our page do not present a stable directional relationship. If you cannot *see* a difference between right and left, it is very difficult to distinguish between a *b* and a *d*. If you do not *see* a difference between up and down, it is easy to confuse a *b* and a *p*. Thus, for such children the mechanics of the reading task become extremely difficult. To deal with our symbolic material, the child requires a stable spatial world. Such a stable spatial world can be established only through the development of a system of spatial relationships learned first in the motor activities of the child and later projected onto perceptual data. Such a system must be both generalized and extensive.

Other Relationships

The behavior of the child occurs not only in space but also in time. For this reason there is another dimension of behavior which must be generalized and systematized. This is the temporal dimension. There are three aspects of time which are important to us in education: synchrony, rhythm, and sequence.

The basis of temporal judgments arises through synchrony. The child must first be able to appreciate simultaneity in time before he can appreciate serial events in time. Synchrony is the point of origin of the temporal dimension.

Having developed a point of origin through synchrony, the child requires a temporal scale. This scale must be characterized by stable, equal intervals. Rhythm provides such a temporal scale. It is through rhythm that he can estimate and evaluate temporal intervals.

Sequencing is the ordering of events in time. It is obvious that such ordering is difficult or impossible unless there is a temporal scale upon which to superimpose this order. Unless the child can appreciate temporal intervals it is difficult to organize events in terms of their temporal relationships.

As with the relationships in space, relationships in time also developed first in the motor activities of the child. Synchrony is observed when muscles move in concert. Rhythm is developed when muscles move alternately or recurrently. Sequence is observed when movements occur in coordinated patterns. From the generalization of many such observations, a temporal system evolves, and a temporal dimension develops.

This motor-temporal system must then be projected onto outside events just as the motor-spatial system was projected onto the perception of outside objects. Now auditory rhythm develops and speech begins to be rhythmical. Now the eyes move rhythmically across a page of print preserving the temporal relationships of the material as well as the spatial relationships. Now the step by step procedures of logical reasoning can be organized in time.

When these two systems are adequate, the child can translate activities from one to another. Consider the task of drawing. The child first looks at the copy. His visual perception gives him a simultaneous spatial presentation of the material. As he begins to draw, however, he must translate this simultaneous spatial impression into a series of events in time which will preserve the continuity and relationships of the whole. If the copy is a square for example, he must translate the four simultaneously presented lines into a series of directional movements performed one at a time, but resulting in a square form.

As in the development of spatial relationships, so in the development of a temporal relationship, many children experience difficulty. As a result, they have difficulty organizing events in time, and they have particular difficulty with our educational materials in which temporal sequence is vital. We must be prepared to aid these children in the development of a temporal dimension of behavior.

Conclusion

Since the materials and activities which we present in the public schools are so frequently highly symbolically oriented, we have a tendency to look primarily at the child's symbolic response and at the symbolic aspects of his performance. Perhaps our preoccupation with symbolic variables has blinded us to the more fundamental problems of many children. It is possible that their orientation to the physical universe which surrounds them is disturbed. It is possible that, as a result of this disturbance, their difficulties are not so much with the content of our activities as with the mechanics involved. Greater attention to the child's methods of handling the mechanics of our tasks might result in less frustration for us and more learning for the child.

References

Bartley, S. A. *Principles of Perception.* New York: Harper and Brothers, 1958.

Gesell, A., Florence A. Ilg, and G. E. Bullis. *Vision — Its Development in Infant and Child.* New York: Hoeber Medical Division, Harper and Row, Inc., 1941.

Jersild, A. T. *Child Psychology.* Englewood Cliffs, N. J.: Prentice-Hall, Inc., 1954.

Kephart, N. C. *The Slow Learner in the Classroom.* Columbus, Ohio: Charles E. Merrill, 1960.

————. *The Brain Injured Child in the Classroom.* Chicago: National Society for Crippled Children and Adults, 1963.

————. "Perceptual-Motor Correlates of Education," in S. A. Kirk and W. Becker (editors), *Conference on Children with Minimal Brain Impairments.* Urbana, Ill.: University of Illinois, 1963. Pp. 13–25.

Piaget, J., and B. Inhelder. *The Child's Conception of Space.* London: Routledge and Kegan Paul, 1956.

Small, V. H. "Ocular Pursuit Abilities and Readiness for Reading," unpublished masters thesis, Purdue University, Lafayette, Ind., 1958.

Strauss, A. A., and Laura E. Lehtinen. *Psychopathology and Education of the Brain Injured Child,* Vol. I. New York: Grune and Stratton, Inc., 1947.

————, and N. C. Kephart. *Psychopathology and Education of the Brain Injured Child,* Vol. II. New York: Grune and Stratton, Inc., 1955.

Further Reading for Chapter 11

Almond, Eugenia B. "You've Got to Crawl Before You Can Read," *Scholastic Teacher,* 5: 21; November, 1964.

Balow, Irving H., and Bruce Balow. "Lateral Dominance and Reading Achievement in the Second Grade," *American Educational Research Journal,* 1: 139–143; May, 1964.

Birch, Herbert G., and Lillian Belmont. "Auditory-Visual Integration, Intelligence, and Reading Ability in School Children," *Perceptual and Motor Skills,* 20: 295–305; February, 1965.

Dyer, Dorothy W., and E. R. Harcum. "Visual Perception of Binary Patterns of Preschool Children and by School Children," *Journal of Educational Psychology,* 52: 161–165; June, 1961.

Getman, G. N. *How to Develop Your Child's Intelligence.* Luverne, Minn.: Announcer Press, 1962.

Groff, Patrick J. "A Study of Handedness and Reading Achievement," *The Reading Teacher,* 16: 31–34; September, 1962.

Jones, J. Kenneth. "Colour As an Aid to Visual Perception in Early Reading," *British Journal of Educational Psychology,* 35: 21–27; February, 1965.

Keislar, Evan. "Conference on Perceptual and Linguistic Aspects of Reading," *The Reading Teacher,* 18: 43–49; October, 1964.

Kephart, Newell C. *The Slow Learner in the Classroom.* Columbus, Ohio: Charles E. Merrill Books, Inc., 1960.

Lackmann, Frank M. "Perceptual-Motor Development in Children Retarded in Reading Ability," *Journal of Consulting Psychology*, 24: 427–431; October, 1960.

Rice, Arthur E. "Rhythmic Training and Body Balancing," *The Nation's Schools*, 69: 72–81; February, 1962.

Robbins, Melvyn Paul. "The Delacato Interpretation of Neurological Organization," *Reading Research Quarterly*, 1: 57–78; Spring, 1966.

Santostefano, Sebastiano, Louis Rutledge, and David Randall. "Cognitive Styles and Reading Disability," *Psychology in the Schools*, 2: 57–62; January, 1965.

Smith, Henry P., and Emerald B. Dechant. *Psychology in Teaching Reading.* Englewood Cliffs, N. J.: Prentice-Hall, Inc., 1961. Chapter 2.

Taylor, S. E. "Sensation and Perception: The Complexity of Word Perception," *Journal of Developmental Reading*, 6: 187–206; Spring, 1963.

Wechsler, David, and Rosa A. Hagin. "The Problem of Axial Rotation in Reading Disability," *Perceptual and Motor Skills*, 19: August, 1964.

12

Linguistics

Linguistics is *not* a method of teaching reading! It seems imperative to make this point perfectly clear, since there is a tendency to talk about "the linguistic method" as if it were a new way of teaching. Linguistics is the scientific study of language. It is hoped that the findings and insights of linguists will be helpful in improving methods of teaching reading, but these findings, in themselves, do not constitute a method. Instead, methods are derived from interpretive applications of linguistic findings. The findings that are interpreted and the ways in which they are applied will ultimately determine the reading achievement of our pupils.

There is little doubt that the increasing information about our language — about the nature of sounds as used in communication, about the structure of words, and about the general structure of language — can lead to refined procedures for teaching children how to read that language. Some linguistic principles support sound methods of teaching reading which have been used by good reading teachers for some time. One example is the understanding that the initial reading task of a child basically involves transforming printed symbols into a language that is already familiar to him. The child knows the word; the only thing he must determine initially is *which* of the words he knows is the one he sees printed on that page in his reader! Another example is the understanding of the relationship between meaning and context. The child is much better able to unlock and retain knowledge of word forms when they are introduced in context rather than in word lists.

Although no new knowledge is added in cases such as these, still the linguist is serving a very useful function. He is providing a scientific basis for procedures which have proved successful in the past but have not had the respectability that linguistic study now provides. His support for such procedures is also likely to increase their use by encouraging those who have not yet adopted them to try them out.

In the first selection in this chapter, Paul C. Burns presents a brief overview of linguistics. Although this summary is not related to any single area of instruction such as reading, it is valuable as an introduction to or review of the various terms linguists use to describe our language.

In the following selection, Emmett A. Betts discusses the values which may derive from using the best of what is known of reading research, linguistics, and psychology.

Next, Kenneth S. Goodman does an excellent job of showing how linguistics can contribute to improved reading instruction. In addition, he clarifies the dangers that may arise through the blanket acceptance of anything labeled *linguistics* — particularly the danger of a subsequent disillusionment with and rejection of all linguistic contributions — many of which may be truly valuable — on the basis of such an unthinking adoption.

In the last two selections Carl A. Lefevre and Charles Loyd Holt add dimensions to the contributions of linguists and suggest trends in the field which may prove valuable in improving reading instruction.

Linguistics: A Brief Guide for Principals ❖ PAUL C. BURNS

As early as 1925, the late Professor Leonard Bloomfield, founder of the Linguistic Society of America, wrote: "Our schools are conducted by persons who, from the professors of education down to teachers in the classroom, know nothing of the results of linguistic science, not even the relation of writing to speech, or of standard language to dialect. In short, they do not know what language is, and yet must teach it, and in consequence waste years of every child's life and reach a poor result."[1]

This was written at a time when there was little communication between the linguist and the educator. Fortunately, since that time the situation has changed. Educators have recognized that if the teaching of language arts is to be improved, one important source of help is the scholars who know most about the language itself — the linguists who have spent years studying language in general and the English language in particular. (It is important to note that the explanation of mere technicalities of language is not the greatest contribution of linguists. On the contrary, they have given society a mirror through which the culture of man in varying times and places and its relationship with language may be more clearly reflected.) At the same time, linguists have become more and more aware of the problems teachers face in developing in all children the literacy and understanding of language needed for life in this century.

A recent statement by Professor Charles Fries indicates the efforts being made by linguists to bring their knowledge to focus upon educational problems:

For many years I have held the view that, in order to achieve basically sound solutions to educational problems, we must in some way, learn how to bring to bear upon the pressing problems of education all the knowledge that has been won . . . I have firmly believed also that, in order to accomplish that end, some of us who have worked primarily in academic disciplines must struggle to understand sympathetically the work, the methods, and the language of those devoted to the professional study of education. We must achieve such an understanding as to make complete communication and thorough cooperation possible. The bridging of the gap between the academic scholar-teacher and the education specialist demands that kind of communication and that kind of cooperation.[2]

The growing interest in linguistics among educators and the efforts of linguists to understand the problems of teaching children have resulted in the gradual development of "that kind of communication and that kind of cooperation" between linguists and educators. This drawing together of those who

From *The National Elementary Principal,* 40: 37–42; September, 1965. Reprinted by permission. Paul C. Burns is Professor of Elementary Education, The University of Tennessee, Knoxville.

[1] Leonard Bloomfield, "Why a Linguistic Society?" *Language* 1: 5; 1925.

[2] Charles C. Fries, *Linguistics and Reading* (New York: Holt, Rinehart and Winston, 1963). Pp. vii-viii.

understand the teaching-learning process best and those who know most about the language to be taught provides a logical basis for improving instruction.

Communication between educators and linguists has been directed toward identifying the linguistic concepts which appear applicable to elementary education and to determining when and how they should be introduced into language arts instruction. The result has been a growing body of literature — in books, professional journals, and commercially published materials for children — interpreting the principles of linguistics, suggesting practical applications of linguistic concepts for classroom use, and describing "linguistically oriented" language programs.

What is meant by "linguistics" or a "linguistically oriented" approach to the language arts? What are some of the major concepts from linguistics which may help us to strengthen instruction in the language arts?

Basic Concepts

The linguistic point of view emphasizes the primacy of speech over writing. The linguist hopes that such characteristics of language as the following can be examined by elementary school pupils:

1. Language is a set or system of sounds (not symbols on a page), and the connection between the sounds and the objects they represent is purely arbitrary. For example, the animal called *the dog* in English is called *le chien* in French. There are many opportunities to develop this concept with pupils in the study of social studies and of a foreign language.

2. Language changes, yet remains durable. Old words may be given new meanings and new uses, and new words may be coined or adapted. "Change is an aspect of human language as regular and relentless as the birth and death of men. It asks no man's permission and waits on no man's approval."[3] Some examples of the ways language changes include:

(Meanings change): *nice* once meant "foolish" but today means "pleasing."
(Makeup of words changes): words are made into compounds, as *beforehand*; neologisms develop, as *edit* from *editor*; portmanteau words are devised, as *smog* from *smoke* and *fog*.
(New words are added): as *blitzkrieg, commando*.

3. There are many social variations in language, such as slang (*scram*), jargon (*knowing the ropes*), and cant (*sawbuck*).

To the linguist, creating interest in language among pupils is of urgent importance. One way to accomplish this in the elementary school language-arts program is to develop an understanding of the heritage of language. A number of tradebooks about language are available for children, teachers, and principals.[4]

---

[3] Donald J. Lloyd and Harry R. Warfel, *American English in Its Cultural Setting* (New York: Alfred A. Knopf, 1965), p. 7.

[4] One reference for children would be Helene Laird and Charlton Laird, *Tree of Language* (Cleveland, Ohio: World Publishing Co., 1957); and for Teachers, Charlton Laird, *The Miracle of Language* (New York: Fawcett World Library, 1957).

Language Structure

Years ago, grammarians superimposed the Latin grammar system on the English language, and the incompatibility of the two has caused teachers — and their pupils — unending problems. Modern linguists, recognizing the differences between the Latin and English languages, have developed new ways of looking at language, of sorting out the data, and of classifying the findings.

In brief, linguists state that a language is made up of basic units of sound called *phonemes*, such as the *s* in *sing*. Phonemes are the smallest usable units of speech sound.

Phonemes are built into *morphemes* which consist of phonemes used in sequence to form larger working units. Morphemes are indivisible language elements and are the basic meaning-bearing units of language. A free morpheme is a morpheme which can be used by itself. For example, *sing*. A bound-form morpheme, such as *er*, must always be bound to another morpheme. For example, *singer*.

Morphemes, in turn, are put together into patterns of *syntax*. Syntax refers to the patterning of morphemes into larger structural units.

In analyzing English structure, linguists emphasize *form class*, *intonation*, and *sentence pattern*.

A *form class* consists of all the words which are interchangeable in a construction. For example, since *works* and *sings* can be interchanged in "The boy works" and "The boy sings," the two words — *works* and *sings* — are said, in this instance, to belong to the same form class. There are four form classes in English: noun, verb, adjective, adverb.

Modern linguists do not define these form classes with the old, traditional definitions for the "parts of speech." They have developed an entirely new and more accurate way of describing language structure. For example, when a verb is defined as "a word that expresses action," such words as *arrival* and *operation* could well be classified as verbs. But since no one says, "He will arrival," *arrival* is not considered to be a verb — not because it does not somehow express action but because it does not occur in what is recognized as a verb structure.

Similarly, while the word *sings* in our previous example, "The boy sings," is a "word that expresses action," it may also be used in such a pattern as "Our family used to have Sunday evening sings." In this latter construction, the word *sings* is not considered to be a verb because it is not used in a verb structure.

Linguists suggest more functional definitions and tangible signals to distinguish one major class from another. Thus, in rejecting the statement that "a noun is the name of a person, place, or thing; if it is not a name, it is not a noun," they propose a definition such as "A word is a noun because it is used in a particular way in a particular sentence frame." Thus, a noun is a word that can fill the blank in "The . . . was lost"; or a noun is a word like *oogle* in such a statement as, "The *oogle* was lost." Or a noun takes an inflectional suffix as *s* (more than oneness) or *'s*. Or a noun, by position, comes after such signals ("determiners") as *the, an, a*; possessive pronouns such as *his, her, my*; or demonstratives such as *this, that*.

Some linguists refer to *structure words* — words that mark structural sentence elements — in the following sense:

Noun markers: *a, an, the, their, this, my, some*
Verb markers: *am, are, is, was, have, has, has been, done, did*
Phrase markers: *up, down, in, out, out of, below, above*
Clause markers: *if, because, although, even though, that, which*
Question markers: *who, why, how, when, where, what.*

In brief, words that pattern alike belong to the same word group or class.

It is true, of course, that definitions based solely on morphology (inflectional endings and the like) can lead to confusion. That is, if a noun were defined simply as "a word that forms a plural," then *chaos* could not be classified as a noun. A single signal in the structure, while helpful, is not infallible in our non-perfect language. The signals in our language are generally multiple — position, form (inflectional and derivational endings), and function, and probably in that order of importance.

Intonation is an important structural feature of our language. Intonation involves *stress, pitch,* and *juncture.*

Stress is a matter of the loudness or softness with which syllables are uttered. As an example, consider the word *anticipate.* There are four syllables to the word: an-tic-i-pate. They are not uttered with equal loudness. The second syllable *tic* is the loudest of the four. The weakest is the syllable *i.* Conventionally marked for stress, using the marks / ∧ \ ⌣ which indicate descending degrees of loudness, the word would appear àn tíc ĭ pâte.

Stress can help clear up ambiguity, as *the orderly róom* (a room that is neat) and *the órderly room* (a room for orderlies). And note the different types of question when any one of the component words is pitched higher and given more stress: Where is he going? (casual) *Where* is he going? Where *is* he going? Where is *he* going? Where is he *going?*

Pitch refers to the idea that if air is made to vibrate rapidly, we have a high pitch; if slowly, we have a low pitch. Various levels of pitch can be detected. For example, if the statement is made, "I am going," the listener will know that that utterance is finished; but if the statement, "I am going . . ." is made, the listener waits for the speaker to continue. The reason for the feeling of incompletion is not that less has been said, but that the two utterances have different characteristics. Sometimes numerals (1, very low; 2, normal; 3, high; and 4, very high) are assigned to mark pitch. Notice the changing of the statement to a question in the following:

²
The people who were here went ³away.¹ (Declarative sentence)

²
The people who were here went ³away?³ (Interrogative sentence)

Children's attention can be called to the way in which the voice signals a question or a statement. "When are you going home?" ends with a rising intonation, while the answer, "In a short time," ends with a falling intonation. The word *now* may be either a statement or a question, depending upon the pitch employed. Excitement can be indicated in such a situation as:

^{4 1}
He needs some money!

The need for punctuation is often revealed in the indicated pitch:

Knowing what he had to do^3 Bill didn't hesitate a moment.^{1}

At times pitch or the comma is the only signal which can give meaning to a sentence, as in the following:

The boys^3 without coats^3 were very cold.

or

The boys, without coats, were very cold.

Attention to such rhythmic patterns of speech will reduce problems of misplaced modifiers and questions about punctuation of nonrestrictive modifiers.

Juncture is the breaking off or interrupting of the speech according to the structure of the sentence — the breaks in the succession of sounds. These gaps are of specific types and come in specific places. One type of juncture enables the listener to distinguish between *announce* and *an ounce.* In *announce,* all the sounds are linked together without a break. But in *an ounce,* there is a break between the second and third sounds. The same phenomenon (called "open juncture") occurs in such pairs of words as *nitrates* and *night rates* and *I scream* and *ice cream.*

There are other kinds of juncture. "Level" juncture — so called because the voice usually resumes speech, after the gap, at the same level of pitch at which it broke off — can be illustrated: "Bill is waiting without, Paul" and "Bill is waiting, without Paul." The shift of juncture restructures the entire statement. Rising juncture, characterized by rising pitch, is commonly an end signal in an interrogation; falling juncture, characterized by falling pitch, is most commonly the end signal of a declarative sentence. Rising juncture inside an utterance usually separates the elements of a series as "Bill, Tom, Mary, and Jim . . ."

To summarize, an open or plus juncture ($+$) roughly indicates a word division, as *an $+$ ounce;* single bar juncture (/) roughly indicates word group or phrase divisions, as "The man / in the car / was laughing." The double bar juncture (//) marks a more pronounced interruption and is usually thought of as a comma juncture, as "My brother // who lives in Boston // came to see me." The double cross juncture ($\#$) marks a more pronounced interruption and is associated with terminal pitch patterns at the ends of sentences. "I am going home. $\#$ Are you going with me?" $\#$

In brief, the punctuation of writing symbolizes, though imperfectly, the intonation of speech.

Sentence order and pattern refers to the systematic, recurring patterns of words, put together in characteristic designs and composed of a great variety of appropriate fillers. Pupils are tuned to sentence order or patterns that are typical of the English language. "He brought his father a tie" would be accepted as a proper statement. If the sequence were "His father he a tie brought," pupils would instantly recognize it as not typical of the language pattern.

Basic intonational units called sentences tend to pattern themselves in recurring structures called "basic patterns" or types:

1. Father laughed. (Noun — verb or subject — verb)
2. The dog chased the cat. (Noun — verb — noun or subject — verb — object)
3. His dog is a monster. (Noun — linking verb — noun or subject — linking verb — predicate noun)
4. His dog is black. (Noun — linking verb — adjective or subject — linking verb — predicate adjective)
5. The boy laughed loudly. Mother is away. (Noun — verb — adverb or subject — verb — adverb)

Pupils can be asked to write sentences based on these patterns and to experiment with expanding these basic patterns through *elements of expansion* denoting object, time, and place. They can thus discover how meaning and emphasis are influenced by the position of these parts in the sentence. (For example, "The black dog chased the white cat down the street yesterday.") Without getting technical about prepositional phrases, infinitives, or participles, pupils can detect open points in the basic patterns where subordinate units can be inserted; where modifiers can be inserted before the subject, after the subject, before and after the verb.

Another way to show how sentences structure is through *transformations* such as:

> The cat was chased by the dog. (passive)
> Do dogs chase cats? (question — active)
> Dogs do chase cats. (emphatic)
> Dogs do not chase cats. (negative)
> Don't dogs chase cats? (Negative question)

Finally, pupils can learn to say things in different ways by *substitutions* and style, largely coordination and subordination, as, "The dog chased the cat, and father laughed."

Such an interest in manipulating words and sentences can be drawn upon to teach the process of constructing a compound or complex sentence from a series of simple ones. When confusion arises in the pupil's writing of a compound or complex sentence, he has at his command the ability to return to the basics of sentence pattern in order to clarify his thinking and reorganize the structure of the questionable sentence.[5]

Usage and the Dictionary

The linguist might say that *I done it* is correct, in the sense that it is correct in relation to the dialect, but that it is perhaps incorrect from a sociological point of view. This does not mean that teachers should neglect attempts to encourage pupils to use *I did it,* for pupils who continue to say *I done it* will be handicapped in their relationships with many people with whom they come

---

[5] An excellent reference for principals would be Ruth G. Strickland, "The Contribution of Structural Linguistics to the Teaching of Reading, Writing, and Grammar in the Elementary School," *Bulletin of the School of Education, Indiana University,* Vol. 40, No. 1, January, 1964.

in contact. In other words, the issue is not to be decided by *Websters's* but by people and situations. The linguist says, "This is what users of English do when they speak and write." The prescriptionist says, "Here is your rule. Obey it." The descriptive linguist's purpose is to supply data, not ethical judgments. *Right* to the linguist means that the element is clear, appropriate to context, and in accordance with contemporary practice of able speakers and writers. *Wrong* means just the opposite.[6]

When it comes to lexicography, the question is whether the dictionary makers should record English as it is actually used by educated people in both their writing and speech (that is, should it be *descriptive?*) or whether they should record it as some people think the language should be used (that is, should it be *prescriptive?*)

To the linguist, the dictionary is a scientific, unbiased, objective record of the English language as it has been in the past and is at the moment of preparing the dictionary. In elementary schools, the comparative study of dictionary status labels (slang, colloquial, dialect, substandard, nonstandard, etc.) will lead into the question of how dictionaries are developed. The linguistic approach views the dictionary as a guidebook, not as a rule book. It does not tell us how words *should* be used, but rather how they *are* used by educated people. It indicates not how words should be spelled, but how writers spell them. It suggests not what the compilers think words ought to mean, but what speakers and writers of the language use them to mean. It tells us not which expressions are elegant and which are inelegant, but which are used in elegant circles and which are not.

The urgings of the linguistic scholars for more knowledge about the language can be partly met through the dictionary. For example, through the study of the pronunciation key the pupil learns of the stability of the consonants and the variances of the vowels. He gains insight into the way the language grows and changes by detecting different spellings (as *taboos, tabus*); different pronunciations (as *tomato, either, economic*) acceptable in different parts of the country; different meanings of words (as *track*) depending upon context; and differences in parts of speech depending upon function in a sentence (as *spring*). There is no better source for the study of such ideas than the dictionary itself.

Semantics

The linguist is interested in the choice of words (in the responsible and humane use of words) as well as in increasing the number of words in a child's vocabulary.[7] Here attention would be given to words employed to convey attitudes and feelings even though these conditions are not in the words themselves at all. Students of semantics have sharpened and reinforced concern with meaning in a number of crucial ways — by stressing the need for identifying and limiting the referents that our words symbolize; by emphasizing the difficulties inherent in words at a high level of abstraction; by warning of sweeping general terms; and by pointing out how verbal labels prejudge responses.

---

[6] Two fine references for principals would be Robert A. Hall, Jr., *Linguistics and Your Language* (Garden City, N. Y.: Doubleday and Co., 1960), and Margaret M. Bryant, *Current American Usage* (New York: Funk and Wagnalls Co., 1962).

[7] Stuart Chase, *Power of Words* (New York: Harcourt, Brace and World, 1954).

Attention to the responsible use of language will benefit the pupil in many ways. It will help him become a more perceptive listener and reader. It will teach him the art of reading between the lines and the elementary distinction between what is said and what is meant. It will prepare him to look for the precise shade that a word has in its context, the subtle hint conveyed by a metaphor or a simile. It will help to protect him from the manipulators of language whose emotive language and connotative terms are found everywhere.

Spelling and Reading

To the linguist, a large number of English words are spelled in a regular manner; that is, the grapheme-phoneme correspondence is reliable.

To learn the symbol-sound correspondences rapidly and efficiently, linguists recommend that the pupil's first experiences with written words be with words which are regular in spelling (as *stop*). There should be one letter for one sound until it is learned. Semi-regularly spelled words (as *pay*) would come later; and highly irregular words (as *come*) would be encountered last. It is proposed that instead of controlling the words themselves, there should be control of introduction of sound and the graphic symbols for these sounds.

Such an approach would mean that pupils would turn from learning the spelling of each separate word. Instead, once a second-grade child has learned to spell *all,* he would be encouraged to discover that he can now spell many words — *ball, call, fall, hall, tall, halls, calling, called, taller, tallest.* Other patterns would serve to group words for instruction: for example, the short sounds of vowels (*met*); the long vowel-consonant-silent *e* pattern (*mete*); and the long sounds of the vowels. The regular consonants and the consonant blends and digraphs would be systematically and sequentially developed. Spellers that are "linguistically oriented" present words in groups to show similar features of spelling, emphasizing different ways of spelling the same sound (as the *f* sound spelled with *f, ph, gh*) and in different sounds of the same letter (as in *add, dollar* and *May*).[8]

Also the recognition in reading of many words built on the same pattern is advocated. Attention to similar word patterns has the advantage of giving extensive experience with a single pattern in order to establish the sound and spelling of each pattern. For further ideas, application, and an understanding of linguistic impact upon reading, principals are referred to two recent books of value.[9]

[8] An important reference for principals would be Robert A. Hall, Jr., *Sound and Spelling in English* (Philadelphia: Chilton Co., 1961).

[9] Charles C. Fries, *op. cit.;* also, Carl A. Lefevre, *Linguistics and the Teaching of Reading* (New York: McGraw-Hill Book Co., 1964).

A New Area: Reading and Linguistics

✤ EMMETT ALBERT BETTS

Another high pressure center has moved into the reading instruction area: linguistics. But this pressure system has been moving in for a long time — undetected, to be sure, by those concerned more with methods than with content.

While Barrows and Cordt's *The Teacher's Book of Phonetics,* published in 1926, has been superseded by Charles K. Thomas' *Phonetics of American English,* at least one course on the sounds of speech has been available to undergraduate and graduate students for more than a generation. Although Bloomfield's descriptive grammar and Chomsky's generative grammar have put Priestly's "traditional" grammar and Jesperson's historical grammar under at least a broken cloud cover, teachers of reading and writing have had access to courses on the structure of language for several generations.

Hence, the two major facets of linguistics — phonology and grammar — have been a high pressure center for serious students of reading instruction for a considerable time.

Neither linguistics nor the teaching of reading is a new area of concern in education. That "linguistics and reading" is viewed as a new interdisciplinary area provides evidence that the house of reading may be given stronger foundations.

American reading instruction has been plagued by perpetual emotion: the alphabet method, John Russell Webb's word method (1846), phonetic and phonic methods, a sight-word method for beginning reading, a three-group plan, individualized reading, and so on. Each exclusive method or plan offered a magic that failed. Each one equipped teachers and teachers of teachers more often with fashionable *words* rather than with fundamental *ideas.* Now, on this superstructure of progress (or of confusion), this so-called linguistic approach to reading instruction may be superimposed.

Linguistics

Reading and linguistics! What is reading? What is linguistics? "Reading and linguistics" is a mixture of hope and apprehension for some teachers, an illusory goal for a few who live on expectations, an invitation to broaden the base of reading instruction for others.

Reading is far more than a process of saying words — of relating letters of the alphabet to the sounds which they represent. Yet reading does require the automatic use of perception skills, because the reader has only one mind and, therefore, tends to give his attention either to word forms or to ideas. But,

Reprinted from the May, 1964, issue of *Education.* Copyright, 1964, by The Bobbs-Merrill Company, Inc., Indianapolis, Indiana. Emmett Albert Betts is Research Professor, University of Miami, Coral Gables, Florida. This article was originally presented as an address at a meeting of the National Council of Teachers of English. November 29, 1963, at San Francisco.

basically, reading is a thinking process — a process of reconstructing personal experiences symbolized by language. Because language itself has structure and because language, at the same time, represents structured experience, the reader learns to deal with a dyad of meaning: structural and referential.

Phonemics

Linguistics offers *content* — pedagogical oxygen for teachers of reading! — rather than *methods* of teaching reading or *plans* for differentiating instruction. Linguistics is a story with a purpose: it is much ado about something worthwhile.

In the first place, linguists have identified fairly large segments of speech sounds called phonemes. These phonemes are abstractions without meaning, but they are signals or distinguishers of meaning. For example, each of the spoken words *sat* and *sad* has three phonemes; two of these, *s* and *a,* are the same in each word, but the phonemes *t* of *sat* and *d* of *sad* — along with contextual aids — signal different meanings.

Of course, a number of phoneticians have studied speech sounds; therefore, differences of opinion regarding the identity of the phonemes and their organization are par for the course. But honest differences of opinion regarding the phonemic structure of language are to be ironed out by the linguists themselves. In the meantime, teachers of reading must recognize the plurality of linguistics.

In general, most people, including teachers, are not aware of the speech sounds they use. They learned to hear and to use most of these sounds long before being admitted to school; hence, they make automatic responses to them in both listening and speaking. However, a master teacher — such as phonetician Charles K. Thomas — can help qualified graduate students to acquire a working knowledge of phonemics in a three-semester-hour course.

A very substantial reduction in the time required for learning methods of teaching reading is made when prospective teachers have studied both the phonemic and grammatical structure of language as a pre-requisite. Today very few teachers have the opportunity to study either phonemics or a more comprehensive course in linguistics. No wonder there is so much despair in the air regarding the teaching of phonic skills.

Since word perception involves phoneme-grapheme relationships in perceptual settings, some linguists have concerned themselves not only with the study of phonemes but also with the letters used to represent them.

Moreover, they have gone further afield by prescribing the form of letters (e.g., all capital letters or all lower case letters for beginning reading) and methods of teaching these relationships (e.g., use of analogous spelling-phoneme patterns as in *hit-sit* and *hit-hip*.) They offer plausible but not necessarily painless method magic. Again, however, these linguists — as outsiders rather than insiders — offer widely diverse suggestions regarding methods and materials for teaching reading.

Furthermore, some linguists tend to stereotype plans regarding the programming of phonics in today's reading instruction: (1) the time at which phonic skills are introduced, (2) the sequential and cumulative development of skills. There are, of course, a diversity of *opinions* regarding these important matters and these different opinions are reflected in different types of phonic programs.

In a well-structured program, the teaching of phonics is done systematically:

First, the pupil is taught the sounds usually represented by letters; e.g., the *ch* sound represented by *ch* in *chair*.

Second, the pupil is taught that a sound may be represented by different letters; e.g., the *sh* sound by *sh* in *she*, *s* in *sure*, *c* or *t* before *i* in *vicious* and *nation*, *ch* in *Chicago*, etc.

Third, the child is taught that different sounds may be represented by the same letter (s); e.g., the letter *s* may represent *s* in *saw*, *z* in *was*, *sh* in *sure*, etc.

Some educators tend to under-emphasize the consistency of spelling patterns (e.g., *at-hat-sat*, *eat-heat-bleat*, *ate-date-mate*). On the other hand, some linguists tend to overemphasize the consistency of the relationships between sounds and the letters used to represent them.

Linguists have served as a balance wheel in the teaching of word perception skills. Beginning with Bloomfield, many of them have emphasized that pupils can talk or they could not be taught to read; hence, the purpose of phonics is to teach the child the relationships between the speech sounds he already uses and the alphabet used to represent them. But some educators persist in the belief that phonics embraces the "teaching of vowel and consonant sounds." This belief is a dangerous delusion and gives the teaching of reading an air of unreality.

Then, too, very few linguists are aware of crucial factors in perception, such as *need, grouping* of letters and sounds, *feedback* between a stimulus and previous learning, *closure* of likely whole words, *referential* as well as structural meaning, and so on. Hence, they are unaware of the need not only to teach a new skill but to insure its retention by application — of teaching a phonic skill by proceeding from the spoken word to its written form and of completing the feedback when the pupil relates the written form to the spoken word during his silent reading activity.

Grammar

In some schools, educators limit their discussions of "linguistics and reading" to phonemics. This limited view of linguistics tends to distort the confusion regarding the possible contributions of linguistics to reading instruction.

Linguistics does embrace the *phonemic* structure of language. But it also embraces the *grammatical* structure of language: morphology plus syntax (word formation and sentence structure). That is, language as codification includes the phonemic, morphemic, and syntactic structure. Phonemics contributes to word perception in reading; grammar, to the thinking facet of reading instruction.

Reading is thinking that results in comprehension or concept formation. It also is the use of skills for a specific purpose and a relationship with the author. But, equally important, reading is thinking in a language.

In grammar, as in phonemics, most people make automatic responses. That is, they are vaguely, if at all, aware of signals of structural meaning, e.g., word order, grammatical inflection, function words and intonation.

Bloomfield and his followers emphasize that phonemes "do not occur in isolation" or "are not uttered in isolation." With a few exceptions, such as the pronoun I (*I*), their statement appears to be true. These linguists imply that having the pupil hear the sound *a* in *at* or say the sound *a* as a part of a teaching procedure is "to create a difficulty."

Some linguists, however, have developed materials for beginning readers using *isolated* words, such as *can, Dan, fan,* to teach the "alphabetic principle." This procedure is impractical pragmatism because intonation contours are violated. That is, in ordinary speech each word is not given equal stress, but if each word is equally stressed, word-by-word reading is likely to result.

At the present time there is no substantial evidence that the study of either descriptive grammar or generative grammar increases the pupil's ability to write or to read. However, the possible contributions appear to be substantial:

1. An intonational, especially pitch and juncture, basis for understanding the use of punctuation and the structure of sentences
2. A grammatical basis for teaching an understanding of higher level structures, especially the sentence
3. A structural dimension for the study of context clues to words and ideas in reading situations; that is, structural as well as referential meaning
4. A psycholinguistic approach to the assessment of language development; e.g., the seven-year-old's control over language structure
5. A morphemic basis for teaching informative parts of words: roots and affixes.

Goals of Reading Instruction

Over the years a substantial amount of respectable research has been accumulated on three major goals of reading instruction:

1. The development of worthwhole *interests* which take the child to reading and which are satisfied through his increasingly effective reading-study skills — a facet of motivation
2. The learning of *word perception skills* to the point where they are used automatically
3. The maturing of *thinking* and related comprehension abilities needed to draw conclusions, to solve problems, etc., and to get genuine satisfaction from reading-study activities.

Guidance in the development of these attitudes, skills, and abilities begins in the kindergarten or first grade and continues as long as the individual is in school. These three "firsts" of reading instruction are indispensable and inseparable.

Other things being equal, the goals of reading instruction are achieved to the degree that each pupil is taught where he is — at his own achievement level in terms of his motivation, perception skills, and thinking abilities. But the program of systematic reading instruction rests on linguistics (the scientific study of language) and psychology (the scientific study of behavior). Interlacing these two sciences are semantics, logic, and a number of other disciplines.

In today's schools there are many classrooms of opportunity where teaching is done with vision — where there is "know why" as well as "know how." In these classrooms of quiet freedom, teachers have taken three essential steps:

First, they have estimated the independent and the instructional reading levels of their pupils and they keep this information current.

Second, they have experimented with plans for differentiating instruction at their own levels of professional competence — making optimum use of both group and individualized plans.

Third, they have managed to obtain instructional materials for a comprehensive program of differentiated instruction.

In terms of the above goals of reading instruction, it appears that linguistics does not embrace all of the essentials needed by the teacher for the improvement of reading instruction. In the first place, linguistics does not reduce the increasingly wide range of pupil achievement and needs at succeeding levels of instruction. A teacher with an excess of professional preparation in linguistics would still lack the necessary competence in the teaching of reading, especially for differentiating instruction.

In the second place, linguistics does not *per se* offer help on interest and other facets of motivation. There isn't a shred of evidence, for example, that Bloomfield's descriptive grammar or Chomsky's generative grammar has a stronger appeal to students than traditional grammar.

On the other hand, linguistics has contributed to two goals of reading instruction: word perception and thinking.

The identification of distinctive segments of speech sounds, or phonemes, has given an air of reality to the teaching of word perception skills and interpretation of pronunciation symbols in the dictionary. This shift of emphasis from a multiplicity of phonetic elements to approximately thirty-eight segmental phonemes has helped to move this facet of reading instruction to today, rather than yesterday.

Phonemics has made a significant difference in the development of dictionaries. This science has been applied, for example, in the G. & C. Merriam dictionaries for elementary (1956) and secondary school (1959) pupils. As a result, one symbol is used to represent one phoneme and each symbol is used consistently.

For example, one pronunciation symbol, the schwa, serves in place of nine different pronunciation symbols for this phoneme. The use of one symbol rather than nine symbols to represent one phoneme gives the pupil the right to be secure. Then, again, consistent use of symbols is made; e.g., the same symbol is used to represent the vowel sound in *few* and *use*.

Although the fruits of research in phonemics has been available for some time, most phonic systems of today are based on the syllabicated vocabulary entries in dictionaries rather than on the respelling. This fact alone produces disenchanted teachers and a profusion of confusion among the learners.

For example, the vocabulary entries in *Webster's New Secondary School Dictionary* (1959) includes items to show how to break words into syllables and respellings to show how to pronounce them. Accordingly, the respelling of each word shows how to say the word and serves as a basis for word perception skills.

Summary

Reading instruction is being moved forward today by two significant interdisciplinary approaches. The significance of these approaches stems from the promise they extend of fruitful future improvement.

First, linguists offer important concepts regarding the structure of language — the system of symbols with which thinking is done.

Second, psychologists offer important concepts regarding individual differences, motivation, perception and concept formation — which provide the basis for both differentiated instruction and methods of teaching.

Educators who share the responsibility for the improvement of reading instruction are not satisfied with the status quo. Instead, they are extending the cutting edges of progress by working closely with scholars in cognate disciplines: linguistics, semantics, psychology, sociology, etc. To serve as custodians of quality in reading instruction, educators are making systematic efforts today to understand the possible contributions which may be made by enlightened leaders in these important and relevant areas of learning.

The Linguistics of Reading

✣ KENNETH S. GOODMAN

To many who have labored long in the field of reading it must certainly appear that linguistics has literally burst on the reading horizon. Sessions are devoted to the subject at meetings of the International Reading Association and the National Council of Teachers of English. Books are appearing. Journal articles are multiplying. And publishers seem to be tripping over one another in a race to be the first out with a reading series that carries a linguistic label.

Linguists as well as educationists are showing grave signs of missing the essential significance that linguistics has for the teaching of reading. Reading materials, reading curriculum theory, and reading teaching have suffered from a lack of accurate knowledge of the language. This lack is not the fault of the workers in these fields. The lack is not confirmation of what the linguist suspects is poor scholarship in the field of education. Accurate, scientifically based knowledge about the English language simply has not been available. Linguists can provide this knowledge. Reading is language, and the teaching of reading must be based on the best available knowledge of language.

Educators need not come to the linguists hat in hand, but neither can educators justify ignoring the knowledge of language that the linguists are so rapidly producing. The knowledge that has been amassed in the field of reading is not bad knowledge. Psychological, sociological, physiological, and pedagogical generalizations about reading are not inaccurate. But old knowledge must be accommodated to new. And it is primarily the educator who must accomplish this assimilation of linguistic knowledge to the end of producing better teaching of reading.

The linguist is carrying on his proper function when he advances linguistic

From *The Elementary School Journal,* 64: 355–361; April, 1964. Reprinted from "The Linguistics of Reading," in *The Elementary School Journal* by Kenneth S. Goodman by permission of The University of Chicago Press. Copyright © 1964 by The University of Chicago. Kenneth S. Goodman is Associate Professor of Education, Wayne State University, Detroit, Michigan.

generalizations that he believes apply to the teaching of reading. He is also performing a fitting and useful function when he criticizes the teaching of reading from his linguistic vantage point. But he is not on firm ground when he produces reading programs that are based solely on linguistic criteria.

Educators who are self-conscious about their lack of linguistic knowledge would do well to consider linguistics as they have come to view psychology. Psychology has furnished many principles that are incorporated in reading programs. But a reading program cannot be built on a single psychological principle. Nor can we guarantee that a reading program that is psychologically valid will be a good reading program. Further, there are many schools of psychology as, indeed, there are of linguistics. Completely contrasting programs can have psychological or linguistic validity.

Teachers' Linguistic Sense

Good teachers, those with some sensitivity to what is happening to the children they teach, teachers who care whether their young charges are learning, have always instinctively used certain linguistic principles. Every time a teacher says to a child, "Read that the way you would say it to a friend on the playground," she is demonstrating that she senses the significance of natural intonation and its effect on comprehension. Teachers who encourage oral language expression, who build experience charts based on the child's own use of the language, who type stories dictated by children for use as reading material, may be totally ignorant of linguistic research, but these teachers have discovered for themselves some basic principles of linguistics as they have watched children striving to become literate.

Linguists, or others who have come lately to an interest in reading, should not overlook a number of important facts about reading: Most — almost all — children learn to read; in the elementary-school curriculum reading gets more time than any other subject (1); most teachers make use of the best knowledge and materials available to them; more research has been done on the teaching of reading than perhaps on any other area of the curriculum (2).

Phonemics, Phonetics, and Phonics

The concept of the phoneme is one important contribution that linguists have made to the understanding of language and how it communicates thoughts. Almost any variation of sound that a human being is able to produce can be significant in language. The number of these variations is almost infinite. But in any given language only a relatively few variations really do make a difference. These units of sound that make a difference are phonemes (3).

The way to differentiate *ramp* and *lamp* in English is by the initial phonemes. But in certain oriental languages these initial sounds are not separate phonemes. The mature native speaker of Japanese has trouble producing these sounds because he has great difficulty hearing the difference between them in speech. In his native language the difference has no significance.

A branch of linguistics called phonemics has developed. It is the most highly developed branch and the one in which there is the most agreement among linguists. Two other major branches are morphemics and syntax. If phonemes are the atoms of language, then morphemes are the molecules. A morpheme is the smallest unit of language that can bear meaning. It may be a word or a combining form (as *ed* added to a base morpheme to signal past tense). Syntax is the study of the structures in which morphemes fit together to produce language.

It is not surprising that linguists' first attempts at criticizing the teaching of reading were aimed at phonics and phonetics. Indeed, linguists found that these terms were used interchangeably and that the knowledge which supported "phonics" programs was highly unscientific and often without basis (4: 140–46). The linguists reacted as the early scientific astronomers must have reacted to astrology. The linguists fell into the trap of concluding that phonics programs did not work because they were unscientific; that is, they were not phonemic programs.

Bloomfield (5), and others who followed, advanced programs that were based on the same essential principle as phonics programs. According to this principle the child is introduced systematically to the written symbols that represent specific phonemes. In Bloomfield's approach learning is simplified because each phoneme is always represented by the same letter or digraph.

Some reading series that are now being rushed on the market are based on this essential principle, except that sound-symbol representations are always introduced in words. Fries's "linguistically sound approach" is another slight variant (4: 186–215). He stresses contrastive patterns of letters in words that function in consistent ways. Thus, he would teach children to contrast groups of words such as *man, Dan, ban* with *mane, Dane, bane* and *mean, dean, bean.*

These programs, which would more properly be labeled phonemic rather than linguistic, have been viewed by some educators as "just another kind of phonics." In a sense that is exactly what they are. They are based on phonemic insights — the best available knowledge of the sounds of the language — but they are not complete reading programs from either an educator's or a linguist's view.

Educators should be concerned, for example, that all these programs present groups of very similar words. Psychologists have long known that it is much harder for children to learn to differentiate things that are very similar than it is to learn to differentiate things that are quite different. Indeed, this is one basis on which intelligence tests are constructed.

Linguists should object to the isolation of words or parts of words from "living" language. Indeed, Fries instructs teachers never to say or have the child say anything in the program that is less than a word. But he then tells the teacher to pronounce each word *"in normal talking fashion"* (4: 203; italics his). His University of Michigan colleague Pike could hardly find this directive acceptable (6). Words pronounced out of language context cannot be pronounced in "normal talking fashion" because the speaker has no way of knowing what intonation (stress and pitch) to use.

One danger of phonemic reading programs is that their scientific base will give them great respectability and they will gain wide use before they have been sufficiently tried. There are two other dangers. One is that fuller application of linguistics to reading will be delayed. The other is that educators will reject linguistics while rejecting phonemic reading programs.

Primer-ese

Advocates of so-called new approaches to reading frequently exploit the public amusement with "those silly primers." "Oh, Oh, Look, Look" is always worth a laugh. The implication is that the alternate approach to teaching reading will not produce such silly stuff.

This is an irrelevant and unfair argument when used by any person who advocates any approach to reading teaching that involves using materials that are simplified according to any criteria. Whether the criterion for simplification is word count, sound-symbol representation, or sentence structure, what results (particularly in the beginning materials) is artificial language. Witness this sentence from Fries: "Pat a fat cat" (4: 203). Stratemeyer and Smith offer this gem: "Jump, Pud. Jump, Zip. Jump, jump" (7).

Pseudopsychology was the inevitable companion of psychology. Pseudolinguistics inevitably has accompanied the development of linguistics. We can expect that reading programs that have not the vaguest lingustic justification will be described as linguistically based. The word *linguistics* is already appearing in the promotional material of publishers of basal readers. Educators as well as linguists need to be on guard.

Contributions to Education

If we assume that linguistics has a great deal to offer education but that educators must make the application, it is important to consider carefully how linguistic knowledge can be applied in education. The following contributions deserve consideration:

1. Linguistics can provide education with an accurate description of the language.

2. Linguistics can provide techniques for language and reading research. Availability of new tools and concepts will necessitate the careful review of past research in reading. Much past research could be redone. For example, excellent research in eye movements in reading had a predominantly physiological base. But what do we know about the influence of syntactical structure on eye movements?

3. Linguistics can provide new criteria for judging the readability of reading material.

4. Linguistics and psycholinguistics can provide new insights into child language and describe more accurately how children learn languages.

5. Linguistics, together with psycholinguistics and communications theory, can give us clues on how language conveys meaning.

6. Linguistics can describe and explain the development of regional and social dialects of English.

7. Linguistics can provide sensitizing concepts that educationists and teachers can use. In this respect it is apparent that a field of applied linguistics must emerge in education — educational linguistics. The postwar developments in the teaching of foreign language in this country are the result of the use of linguistic-sensitizing concepts to improve language-teaching.

Educators will have to resist the linguists' excessive enthusiasm for their science, an enthusiasm that leads them to hope that one day every little first-grader will be an analytical linguist. There is an inconsistency here. Linguists and educationists have demonstrated that by the time a relatively normal child comes to school he has an excellent subconscious command of the syntax of the language as he hears it spoken, not to mention an immense vocabulary (8). Still, some linguists somehow see the need for teaching children about the language they already use with the facility of an expert. Teachers have learned, however, that improved use of the language does not depend on the child's ability to describe the language in technical terms.

Generalizations from Linguistics

I am not a linguist but an educationist. From linguistic resources I have gleaned a set of generalizations, the sensitizing concepts I referred to earlier, that I feel must be considered by those interested in the teaching of reading. Some of these concepts conflict with concepts currently in use in reading. Some conflict with other linguistic generalizations. But they must all be tried. They must be "plugged in" to current reading theory and practice to produce a new and higher synthesis in reading instruction (9). The generalizations follow:

1. The child comes to school with great control over his language. He derives meaning from a rapid stream of speech by responding to certain built-in cue systems such as pattern, inflectional changes, key function words, and intonations.

2. Virtually every child's language is adequate for his present needs in communication. All language is equally good.

3. Reading is an active aspect of communication. Just as the person who hears but does not comprehend is not listening, so the reader who calls words but does not comprehend is not reading.

4. The need to communicate plays a vital role in the child's language learning. His need to express his thoughts or desires and to understand the expression of others is the stimulus that causes him to develop language.

5. Language in and of itself has no meaning. It is a code, a system by which those who know the code may communicate meaning. Yet language has no existence except in association with meaning.

6. Reading materials must always say something to the child that is worth saying, in a language he can understand, involving concepts within the scope of his reach and interests.

7. If the child is to make the greatest use of built-in cue systems in language for deriving meaning, he cannot be made dependent on other systems and extraneous cues. This means that the role of pictures in early reading materials must be re-evaluated.

8. The basic units of speech are phonemes, but they have no existence outside of morphemes, the molecules of the language. Morphemes are the minimum units of language that can carry meaning, but they have no existence outside of syntactical structures. Syntactical structures, such as sentences, have reality only in the stream of language.

9. Words taken out of language context cannot be defined, pronounced, or

categorized. (Can you define *contract?* Can you pronounce *contract?* Can you classify *contract* as a noun or a verb? And if you could do any of these things, could you decide the proper stress and pitch to use when you said the word?) The common practice of using word lists in teaching reading must be reconsidered.

10. The tasks of teaching children to read and teaching them to speak a preferred dialect are separate and may be conflicting. This fact is well illustrated by the following incident:

A group of second-graders were reading in round-robin fashion. It was Jim's turn. "There was a lot of goats," he read. "There was black goats and white goats."

His teacher smiled encouragingly. "Would you repeat that, please, Jim," she said.

Somewhat puzzled, Jim reread: "There was a lot of goats. There was black goats and white goats."

Still smiling, his teacher stepped to the board. In excellent manuscript she wrote two words. "Do you see a difference in these words," she said.

"Yes, they have different endings," said Jim.

"Can you read these words?" the teacher asked.

"Was, were," Jim read. "Good," said his teacher. "This is *was,* and this is *were.* Now read again what you just read from the book."

"There was a lot of . . ." Jim began.

"No, no!" his teacher said with some annoyance. "It's *were* 'There were a lot of goats'. Now, please reread."

"There *were* a lot of goats. There was black goats and . . ."

The parable of the goats illustrates a common dilemma in reading teaching. The teacher, using an approach that emphasizes word recognition, assumes that Jim is confusing the words *was* and *were.* Jim, on the other hand, is demonstrating a high level of attainment in reading. He is reading his own speech off the page, subconsciously making corrections where the book is wrong in terms of his knowledge of the language.

Reading instruction has much to learn from linguistics. Important new knowledge about language, how it functions, and how it is learned has been produced. This knowledge must be assimilated into the reading curriculum. The process must be presided over by educators primarily, perhaps under the banner of educational linguistics. In any case, the raw material for building the linguistics of reading is now available.

References

1. Austin, Mary C., and Coleman Morrison. *The First R: The Harvard Report on Reading in Elementary School.* New York: Macmillan Company, 1963.
2. Gray, William S. "Reading," in the *Encyclopedia of Educational Research* (third ed.), ed. Chester W. Harris. New York: Macmillan Company, 1960. P. 1087.
3. Gleason, H. A. *An Introduction to Descriptive Linguistics.* New York: Holt, Rinehart and Winston, 1961.
4. Fries, Charles C. *Linguistics and Reading.* New York: Holt, Rinehart and Winston, 1963.

5. Bloomfield, Leonard, and Clarence Barnhart. *Let's Read.* Detroit: Wayne State University Press, 1962.
6. Pike, Kenneth L. *The Intonation of American English.* Ann Arbor, Mich.: University of Michigan Press, 1945.
7. Stratemeyer, Clara, and Henry Lee Smith. The Linguistic Science Readers, *Frog Fun* (first preprimer). New York: Harper and Row, 1963. P. 8.
8. Strickland, Ruth G. *The Language of Elementary School Children: Its Relationship to the Language of Reading Textbooks and the Quality of Reading of Selected Children.* Bulletin of the School of Education, Indiana University, Vol. 38, No. 4. Bloomington, Ind.: Bureau of Educational Studies and Testing, School of Education, Indiana University, 1962.
9. Goodman, Kenneth S. "A Communicative Theory of the Reading Curriculum," *Elementary English,* 290–98; March, 1963.

A Comprehensive Linguistic
Approach to Reading

❖ CARL A. LEFEVRE

1. Introduction: The Need for a Synthesis of Linguistic Approaches

We often hear such questions as these: What do you think of the linguistic approach to reading? Just what is the linguistic approach to reading anyhow?

Such questions are off point because at present no single linguistic approach merits the use of the noun marker or determiner *the,* which would signify the one and only. Bloomfield and Fries have given their names to spelling and word methods of teaching beginning reading, and despite all denials, reading teachers will consider both methods as part of phonic word analysis because both deal with relationships of sound and spelling; they do not even venture into *structural* word analysis. The veneration that these men have earned by their other work in linguistics hardly justifies the use of the exclusive term, "the linguistic approach," to designate their narrower methods. Possibly no single method ever will deserve it.

This is true for a number of reasons. Primarily, our present knowledge is so far from closed that it is commonly said to be exploding; this is true in linguistics as in other disciplines. Moreover, in no age has progress been achieved

From *Elementary English,* 42: 651–659; October, 1965. Reprinted with the permission of the National Council of Teachers of English and Carl A. Lefevre, Professor of Curriculum and Instruction, Temple University, Philadelphia, Pennsylvania. Copyright © 1965 by Carl A. Lefevre. This paper was presented on November 27, 1964, at the Fifty-Fourth Annual Meeting of the National Council of Teachers of English in Cleveland, Ohio.

through blind or myopic imitation of what has already been done. Quite the contrary. Modern linguistics is both a revolution in and a continuation of the study of language. When we break eggs to make our omelet, we do not lose the eggs.

What must inevitably come, in my opinion, is a synthesis of linguistic approaches to reading: a synthesis developed, controlled, and corrected by means of an interdisciplinary attack on reading problems, bringing to bear all pertinent knowledge; a synthesis in line with the best experience of teachers of reading and the English language arts, and in line with the best experimentation these teachers are capable of. Such a synthesis must move far beyond spelling and word attack and into reading processes at the sentence level even in beginning reading; eventually it should range into problems of reading extended discourse, not only of exposition but the many forms of literature. This is something of what is meant by "a comprehensive linguistic approach to reading."

2. Linguistic Phonics: Phonemes and Spelling

Leonard Bloomfield. If Leonard Bloomfield's son when he entered school had not encountered a "far-out" exponent of the kind of phonics Bloomfield derided as "the hiss and groan method" of teaching reading, the development of linguistics applied to reading might have been quite different. As it was, Bloomfield invented an approach to beginning reading that limits instruction during a long introductory period to a rigid alphabetical principle — single phoneme by single letter — applied to a language whose spelling is notoriously inconsistent with its phonemes. It is hard not to feel that Bloomfield's method was the result of an impassioned effort to straighten out some of the worst kinks of bonehead phonics. However it was, his introductory method featured such so-called sentences as "A man ran a tan van," and "Can a fat man pat a cat?"

Unfortunately, this kind of ingenious but un-English material not only bears the great name of Bloomfield, but it has been hailed as *the* linguistic method of teaching reading." Bloomfield's followers among linguists are too many to be counted; his work has been the source of numerous graduate theses; the imitative materials based upon it are too numerous to be cited. All this is a bit like "The Emperor's New Clothes."

C. C. Fries. Recently C. C. Fries, the present dean of American linguists, has presented an extension of the Bloomfield method of teaching beginning reading. If the Bloomfield method is a spelling approach at the level of single letters and phonemes — and it is — the Fries method is a spelling approach at the level of one-syllable words. Fries himself admits that it is a specialized word method; it generates such un-English sentences as these, presented all in capital letters: "PAT A FAT CAT" and "A CAT BATS AT A RAT." It is difficult to detect any qualitative differences between Bloomfield's "Can a fat man pat a cat?" and Fries' "A CAT BATS AT A RAT." It is the misfortune of both methods to present, among the very first lessons in reading, tongue twisters and jawbreakers far removed from the language of children.

I understand that Mrs. Rosemary Wilson and her associates, however, in consultation with Professor Fries, are making adaptations and additions in classroom experiments with these materials.

Some Important Distinctions. We seem to have been so blinded by our ritual thinking of handwriting and print as spelling that we have come almost to equate both writing and reading with spelling, though we know better. Correct spelling has become a shibboleth, even in the very beginning stages of teaching reading and writing: too many children have a traumatic fear of misspelling. (The elimination of this fear is no doubt an important reason for whatever successes may rightfully be claimed for i/t/a, along with the i/t/a emphasis on *writing*.)

Let us make some important comparisons and contrasts among the operations of *spelling, writing,* and *reading.* As linguistic operations, spelling and writing are active in a sense that reading is not. Spelling requires recognizing and producing single letters and single words; writing, however, requires the creation of meaning-bearing patterns of words, using the sentence as the basic building block of composition. Thus we see that writing, not spelling, is seriously concerned with communication. Now consider reading: reading involves no active production of letters, words, or sentences at all; what reading requires is recognition and interpretation of the graphic counterparts of entire spoken utterances as unitary meaning-bearing patterns; *this is reading comprehension.* These considerations may help us to evaluate the role of spelling in reading and in reading instruction.

Sooner or later all the letters in all the words, and all the words laid end to end, line after line, and page after page, must reach not from here to eternity in the child's eyes; all words must pattern themselves into sentences. The sentence is the fundamental unit both for written composition and for reading comprehension; with patience and skill, sentences may indeed be skillfully put together in interesting ways to compose all the larger language constructs — but not in the primary grades. The first lesson is that each sentence begins with a capital letter and usually ends with a period. Let the children take it from there, with no more initial emphasis on spelling than the reading process itself requires.

3. Reading in Terms of the Requirements of the English Language System

Reading as a Language-Related Process. Because our writing system ultimately represents the spoken language, any attempt at a *direct* interpretation of the graphic symbols laid out in neat rows on the printed page is not the best approach to reading. We must go first from writing to sound, and then from sound to message; even the most rapid reading probably involves both steps in virtually simultaneous succession. Written and printed communications not only can be read aloud, but when they are read visually, or "silently" as we say significantly, the mental ear still picks up, be it ever so fleetingly, the sound track of the same utterances in speech. It is this echo of the sound of speech, more than mere punctuation, that groups and orders English words into meaning-bearing patterns. When the pattern does not come off right, we go back and reread until it "sounds right."

The process of going from print to sound to meaning is rather more than what is often meant by so-called inner speech, suggesting stammering, inefficient comprehension. It involves the process of thought itself, "a silent flow of words," as Sapir phrased it. Or in Vigotsky's penetrating statement, remarkably pertinent to reading comprehension: "Thought is not expressed in words, but comes into existence through them." Thus, to approach visual reading as the direct interpretation of a set of graphic symbols, like the Morse code in print, would be quite superficial, and very seriously misleading. What is needed now in reading is an approach in depth, an approach to, and through, the basic language itself.

Since writing and print represent graphic counterparts of spoken language patterns, the natural and best way to read is precisely in those terms. English language patterns have been described by linguists as composed not only of the basic individual sounds — phonemes; not only of basic meaning units, words and word parts — morphemes; but normally of sentences, which in turn have components that may be arranged in an infinite variety of patterns and orders — syntax. Beyond this tri-level structure, the sounds of language, and this is true of English in a very significant way, include the over-all melodies and rhythms of patterns longer and more complex than words, phrases, and clauses. In beginning reading these patterns would be sentences predominantly.

Reading Sentence Patterns. Introductory treatments of descriptive and structural linguistics usually suggest common English kernel sentences, note some of the possibilities of expansions, substitutions, and inversions, and give an indication of passive and other transformations. In his method of "sector analysis," Robert Allen is developing an interesting approach to reading and writing sentences by analyzing out the important sentence parts. My own book, *Linguistics and the Teaching of Reading* (McGraw-Hill, 1964), is the first work to attempt a comprehensive application of linguistic data to reading and writing processes with primary emphasis on the sentence. This is an introductory book, of course, and makes no attempt to be comprehensive. *Writing by Patterns,* a collaboration of Helen and Carl Lefevre, is a work text that applies structural grammar to writing problems in Grades 11–14, depending on the students' needs; much of the material is applicable to reading, and the two are treated somewhat as cross-related. This book was published in April, 1965, by Alfred A. Knopf, Inc.

The great virtue of descriptive and structural grammar is its objectivity, its clear focus on the structure of the code as the means of carrying the message. This virtue is not found in the recent transformational and generative grammars, which, under the banner of "deep grammar," enter the subjective realm of the message. They also admittedly hark back to traditional grammar and school grammar. While these new-old grammars represent a legitimate effort to penetrate the relatively unknown area between language structure and psychological meaning, they will not necessarily help the native English speaker read and write his language. No one any longer defends the old grammars on these grounds.

Transformational or generative grammar attempts to formulate all the "rules" according to which it is assumed the native speaker can invent new sentences of his own and interpret new sentences invented by others. It is questionable whether these subjective, "internalized" rules will prove helpful in teaching native speakers to read and write, however, because teachers and pupils alike possess native linguistic intuition and intelligence enabling them to invent and interpret new sentences unconsciously, without recourse to rules for invention and interpretation. For teaching the skills of literacy, it hardly seems necessary to codify native linguistic intuition and intelligence. On the contrary, these invaluable traits should be exercised freely and creatively, rather than self-consciously analyzed. On the other hand, a clear, objective consciousness of the structural patterns themselves and their common transformations, available through study of structural grammar, can improve the pupil's understanding of his language as a code, and hence liberate his creative energies to develop his skills of literacy.

Reading Paragraphs and Extended Passages of Exposition. Up to now, linguistic analysis of reading problems has been largely confined to structures below the level of syntax: phonemes and morphemes. We have seen, however, that applications of syntactical data have already begun to yield some results, and it seems probable that similar and related data and principles can be extended into the analytical reading of longer passages. Making this extension is an important next stage in linguistics and in English linguistics applied to teaching the skills of literacy. Some work has already been done and more is in progress.

So far as I know, Zellig Harris was the first modern linguist to make a tentative entry into rigorous "discourse analysis"; his student and colleague, Noam Chomsky, has given some further consideration to this topic. Current applications of Kenneth Pike's "tagmemics" and experimental investigations by some of his students into extended language patterns and forms give promise of producing interesting new insights into the structure of both expository prose and literature. It seems possible that tagmemics may have the potential of relating language patterns to particle, wave, and field theories.

An obvious first consideration in analyzing the "organic" structure of well-written paragraphs is the use of structural joints and connective tissue not only *within* sentences, but *between* and *among* sentences. For example: simple pronoun references, both to the usual persons and to "things" and abstractions; similarly noun references; similarly by structural extension references by means of other word-form classes, such as verb cross-references by means of derivational prefixes and suffixes added to the same base.

Also, referring ahead or back to a noun, an adjective, or an adverb having the same base; parallel syntactical patterns including elliptical constructions that constitute structural references to each other; the use of all structure words, such as the coordinating conjunctions, *and, but, for, nor, or, yet, so;* and especially the subordinating conjunctions, such as *although, because, however, moreover, nevertheless, since* — the whole set; and the correlatives, such as *if . . . then, not only . . . but also, while . . . still,* and so on through the list. These are some of the syntactical devices that extend into paragraph construction and into longer passages of well-knit prose.

Reading Literature as a Syntax. Structural resources of English such as we have just been considering in expository passages also lend themselves admirably to imaginative writing. Creative writers are fertile in their production of structural inventions and manipulations of language patterns; an extended treatment would require detailed discussion of many points of linguistic interest in literature that can only be mentioned here, however.

For example: what I call structural puns, the unconventional substitution of a member of one word class for another, such as a noun for a verb, and then using grammatical inflections with the substituted word (Ciardi, Keats, Wordsworth); unusually long and involved sentence patterns running to many lines (Browning, Chaucer, Faulkner, Shelley, Steinbeck); extended syntactical patterns treated as sentences, but that are "fragments" according to school grammar (Blake, Coleridge, Dickens, Keats, Shelley, Whitman, Wordsworth); myriad special sentence patterns, apostrophes, commands, inversions, prayers, wishes, apposition, compounding of elements, ellipses, parallelism of ellipses, parallelism of certain word forms, or of word groups and clusters, phrases, clauses (writers far, far too numerous to mention).

The point in a discussion of reading is that to fully comprehend literary passages having unusual, or as often as not unique structure, the reader must absorb the entire meaning-bearing pattern as a whole. He may do this either by an automatic, unconscious, and intuitive process which is the fruit of long experience, or he may do it by means of a direct analysis of each author's peculiar and characteristic uses of language resources. Direct linguistic analysis is an excellent means of breaking an author's code and so involving pupils in an appreciative study of literature in their early and formative years. In time they should automatically respond to the meaning-bearing structures as wholes, each one having its overriding intonation pattern, or tune; in this respect, literary passages are comparable to the phrasing of music, building toward larger movements.

4. Reading in Terms of Intonation: Requirements and Options

Intonation in Visual, or Silent, Reading. The English graphic system partially represents the important sounds of the language system far beyond the representation of phonemes by graphemes, beyond the representation of morphemes by spellings, even beyond the representation of sentence patterns by capitalization, word order, and punctuation. The *part* in the term *partially* stands for intonation, both in single elements and in over-all patterns of the melodies and rhythms of English.

Merely to pronounce words having two or more syllables requires correct accent; in linguistic parlance, *accent* is called *stress* and is defined as "loudness"; stress is a very important grammatical and syntactical feature of intonation. "He puts the emphas'is on the wrong syllab'le" is a hoary linguistic joke that makes the point. Putting the emphas'is on the wrong syllab'le betrays the speaker as either non-native or a half-educated fool, the latter being a lot more fun.

The difference between *con'tract* and *con-tract'* distinguishes noun from verb in a whole set of contrasting pairs. This grammatically important distinction is not signaled by any specific feature of the writing system; only the distribution of such words in larger patterns gives the clue. And yet no literate native speaker of English misses the point. The same use of stress difference also distinguishes a set of pairs of nouns and verb-adverb groups, as in *set'up* and *set up';* and still another set, pairs of compound nouns and noun groups, as in *black'board* and *black board'.*

Many, though not all, punctuation marks correspond to decisive points of intonation in equivalent spoken language patterns. The period always, and the semicolon usually, are signals for a special way of dropping the voice, indicating that the preceding meaning-bearing pattern has been completed; conversely, the absence of a period normally indicates that the voice should *not* be allowed to drop in the end-signaling way between the opening capital letter and the closing semicolon or period. Persons who use this "fade-fall terminal" within sentences in oral reading are reading either by single words — word calling — or by fragmentary word groups that do not bear meaning. This kind of reading, all too common in the elementary school, destroys the unity of the unitary meaning-bearing pattern. It is a dangerous practice, because, unchecked, it may lead to a habitual intenalized word-and-fragment-seeing procedure in silent reading, deadly to reading comprehension.

The fade-fall terminal also occurs at the end of many questions in English, notwithstanding the popular falsehood, "A question always ends with a rising inflection." For example: *Who won the game? Where are the keys? Who was it?* A rising inflection on these questions changes their meaning completely, the point being that the difference between a fade-fall and a fade-rise terminal in such questions is the only structural signal we have for a qualitative difference of intent. There is no graphic symbol for it at all. The fade-fall terminal would be the high-frequency choice in such questions.

The rising inflection may be used to terminate other questions also: *Where did you say my notebook is? Did you tell me that this is your car?* The one hard rule for the fade-rise terminal to signal a question in English applies to statements converted to questions solely by this terminal. It is often used ironically in such questions as "You call this a ball game?" The rising inflection is the only spoken signal we have that this is a question rather than a statement.

A rising tone is commonly used within sentences where commas occur and usually in counting and in listing: *one, two, three, four, five; wood, glue, nails, cloth, paint.* The fade-fall is used only at the the end of the last item.

The foregoing comments are concerned only with gross obligatory features of English intonation, those features that native speakers normally produce with intuitive ease and that foreigners find extremely difficult to master. In primary teaching of reading to children who are native speakers, all we have to do is see to it that they read orally (in order to hear silently with the mental ear) intonation patterns that are indigenous to their speech communities. This is all we have to do about intonation — but it is exceedingly important that we do it unfailingly and very well.

Intonation in Oral Reading and Interpretation. Many linguists designate all that we call "tone of voice" as *paralanguage;* it includes such effects as whining, laughing or crying while talking, or talking with overtones suggestive of these; talking with relish or gusto; talking with distaste or disgust; using rasping, whispering, oversoft, or overloud tones; and all like effects. Paralanguage is often referred to as an "overlay" of subjective interpretive characteristics on the basic code pattern required for communication; the point is that every speaker must use the required features of the language code, but he may exercise various intonational options as well. His options must never violate the code, however, except for a deliberate communicative purpose.

Some linguists designate as *kïnesïcs* all those non-lingual actions that accompany speech, often more important in communication than all that could possibly be communicated by the bare linguistic structures themselves. *Kïnesïcs* includes all bodily gestures, nudges, nods; finger, hand, and arm signals; shrugs and facial gestures such as winks, smiles, sneers, and leers — the whole gamut of expressive actions, so important in acting and interpretation.

All these rich resources of human communication should be brought to bear on the oral reading of literature, for the sheer joy of it, but also in order to develop associations that may carry over into the individual pupil's visual or silent reading of literature.

Oral reading "with expression" is interpretive reading that builds upon but far outreaches obligatory intonation features and patterns; with sufficient practice oral reading can develop into a fine art, closely allied with acting. So long as the interpreter observes the requirements of the intonation system, he is limited only by the dictates of good taste and judgment. Keen interest in both written composition and in silent reading can be stimulated by the teacher's skillful involvement of the children's imagination and vivacity in oral interpretation.

Reading Literature as Language and Form. Sensitivity to the nuances of language, appreciation of dialects, access to poetry, responsiveness to the forms of literature — all can best be cultivated on the basis of *the whole sound of the piece* when well read aloud. Not every reader need be an artist in oral interpretation — a producer; every child has his own potential, however, worthy of a little classroom attention. Surely every child should have many opportunities to hear and attend to good oral interpretations of literature — to be a consumer. If the child has the authentic sound in his ear, his eye then in silent reading can help his mental ear tune in on the mnemonic sound track by association with other pieces; but if he has never had the authentic sound in his ear, his mental ear will be deaf to the graphic presentation, no matter how beautifully done.

Professional readings and movie, television, and radio presentations are all excellent sources of enrichment, but the audio-visual device of choice is the classroom teacher, or a parent, in everyday, seemingly casual interpretive readings. No one loves literature because he was assigned to love it; no one can possibly feel in his heart that it is great, just on his teacher's say-so. The best approach, not only to drama and fiction, but above all to poetry, is to hear it live and flowing sweetly on the tongue. A parent at home or a teacher in your schoolroom is not an artist way off on a high pedestal somewhere, but someone you know and can touch.

The arbitrary division of poems into lines, and rigid notions of meter, present problems that often baffle and finally discourage the young hopeful trying to appreciate poetry. The line of verse is a visual rather than an auditory unit; even when an elaborate rhyme scheme is followed, the echoing of the rhyme is contained within meaning-bearing structures. Stanzas and other verse forms are overlaid, often very skillfully, on patterns of English syntax. In poetry as in prose the good old sentence is still the basic building block of English. Nothing is more destructive of good verse than a ding-dong metrical reading, line by line, with a fade-fall terminal at the end of every line. (A mechanically repeated fade-rise terminal would be no better.) Every sentence should be read as a sentence, with syntactical terminals where they belong according to English syntax — not according to lines, or to rhymes.

Any attempt to read English poems with a uniform two-stress meter is foredoomed and absolutely fatal to poetry, because English is a four-stress language. This four-stress system itself is a structural part of the language system as a whole, not an interpretive option of the speaker or oral reader; the interpreter does have options but his options fall within the English four-stress system. This stress system and the meter of any poem can be reconciled if the presumed two stresses of the meter are regarded as relative rather than absolute stresses. That is, certain stresses are regularly heavier than the others, but the heavy stresses are not equally heavy.

For an example, let's take a look at Stevenson's "Requiem," a simple poem in two stanzas, having an *a a a b, c c c b* rhyme scheme. The *a* and *c* lines have four beats, or heavy stresses, each; they begin and end with a beat. The *b* lines begin with two weak stresses (the equivalent in certain respects of one heavy stress or beat) and then have three more beats. Taking fade-fall terminals as the chief clues, the poem is written in four sentences: (1) lines 1–2; (2) lines 3–4; (3) lines 5–6; (4) lines 7–8. Visually, the second stanza is punctuated as a single sentence with a colon at the end of the first line.

Below, the poem is presented twice: first marked for a uniform two-stress metrical rendition; second, marked with suggestions for a reading that observes the meter, but follows the four-stress system. The stress notations are: ′ for heavy stress; ∧ for medium stress; ‵ for light stress; ˘ for weak stress. Instead of two stresses, one strong and one weak, we use heavy, medium, and light for strong, reserving the weak stress of the four-stress system for the weak stress in the two-stress metrical reading. Thus we preserve the contrasts of the meter without killing the poem.

REQUIEM

Under the wide and starry sky
Dig the grave and let me lie.
Glad did I live and gladly die,
And I laid me down with a will.
This be the verse you grave for me:
Here he lies where he longed to be:
Home is the sailor, home from the sea
And the hunter home from the hill.

REQUIEM

Under the wide and starry sky
Dig the grave and let me lie.
Glad did I live and gladly die,
And I laid me down with a will.
This be the verse you grave for me:
Here he lies where he longed to be:
Home is the sailor, home from the sea
And the hunter home from the hill.

The mistaken effort to achieve equality of beat and uniformity of meter throughout this or any poem cannot help producing a metronomic, rocking-horse effect. The deadly soporiferous sequel is too well known. Children don't naturally hate poetry; they love it. But given too much poetry read in a rocking-horse jog, they will either learn to ignore it if they are normal, or kill it with kindness if they are teacher's pets. A few will go to college and major in English in spite of all.

A final point. Longer language constructs, such as poems, essays, sonnets, short stories — especially those literary forms that can be read at one sitting, as Poe suggested for the proper length for a short story — probably have over-all melodic and rhythmic contours, embracing all components into an organic form so as to create a sense of completion when the piece has run its course. That is, the various forms of writing, particularly creative writing, are not static forms, but intricate linguistic processes, events patterned through time. The graphic form of these processes or events is the permanently organized embodiment of the writer's original creative experience: this I take to be the essence of literary form. In performing the piece, as it were, either silently or orally, the reader recreates for himself the writer's experience in the form he has shaped to it, but with appropriate nuances and overtones of the reader's own.

In all this, literary forms resemble songs or sonatas; longer works may well resemble concertos, symphonies, operas. This is not mere imagery. Musical notation and all the forms of music have developed within cultures of men who speak; the analogies and interrelationships of speech and song, of language and longer forms of music, make a fascinating subject for study.

A Linguistic Approach to Reading

✤ CHARLES LOYD HOLT

You are reading now. With an agility approaching virtuosity, you are some-how translating these comfortable orthographic symbols on the page in front of you into the noises you make when you open your mouth to order a tank of gas, propose to the girl across the street, or bid four spades vulnerable. Reading, in other words, is a kind of talking — or at least good reading is.

The bad reader is busy elsewhere. Groping feverishly among the alleged sounds of traditional orthography, he clears his throat, grimaces, and produces a series of staccato grunts intended to represent in careful order the words of language. His difficulties are several. Pronouncing sounds in blatant series is no more language than the clicking of an IBM machine is language. Sounds in

From *The National Elementary Principal*, 42: 7–11; February, 1963. Copyright ©
1963, Department of Elementary School Principals, National Education Association.
All rights reserved. Reprinted by permission. Charles Loyd Holt is Assistant Professor of English, Kingsborough College, the City University of New York.

morphemic, or meaningful, sequence in English are inevitably relative one to the other in pitch, loudness, and degree of separation or termination.

Moreover, the bad reader's concern with words and their "proper" oral rendition one — after — the — other has practically nothing to do with speech. We don't talk words — groups of words, yes, but never "words" in splendid etymological isolation. Both sounds and words in English are significant only in utterance context.

If you want to teach a child to read, teach him how sounds fall into morphemic sequence, how words fall into measurable order within the utterance. If you want to teach a child to read, teach him that reading in a very important sense is a way of talking to oneself.

There are some thirty-three meaningful segments or slices of sound used by English speakers, or so the descriptive linguists remind us: twenty-one consonant phonemes, or tension restricted sounds; nine simple vowel phonemes, or comparatively unrestricted sounds; and three semi-vowel phonemes, meaningful sound categories that in production show the characteristics of both consonants and vowels. The only significant differences between /pin/ and /pen/, between /sit/ and /bit/, between /slip/ and /sliyp/ are differences of single sound classes. These differences involve a meaning change and are therefore phonemic. Simple phonic exercises based in graded drill will introduce the six-year-old native speaker of English to the curious curlicues on the printed page that regularly correspond to, say, the voice velar stop (the /g/ sound in *go*) or the voiceless alveopalatal affricate (the /č/ sounds of *church*). The irregularities of English spelling need be brought up only when the child is ready for them.

Were educators generally to fret less about the irregularities of English orthography and spend more time categorizing the broad areas of perfectly regular sound-symbol correspondence within that orthography, children would grasp at least part of the dialect of American English known as reading almost as rapidly and completely as their teachers argue confusion.

Obviously, the letters of the English alphabet do not stand for sounds; *dough, ought, enough,* and *slough* illustrate the occasional vagaries of English spelling. At the same time, one has only to be familiar with the diachronic existence of language, with the sound and spelling changes of Old through Middle through Early Modern English, with the studies of the vigorously inept folk etymologists of the English Renaissance and the so-called Enlightenment of the eighteenth century — in short, one has only to be familiar with the total English language in order to realize that English spelling is not only basically regular but also completely teachable if the teacher has the patience to categorize and to describe what is in front of him.

Stress Phonemes

Take a deep breath now and do something you have done perfectly well since you were about six years old — speak English. Say the name of your country. Give it the full dimensionalization of that remarkable system of quantitative and qualitative sound that is our language. If you are an American, you probably said, "The United States of America." And if you are an American, you almost certainly said the name in a predictably complex but measurable way. In addition to the twenty-eight or more slices of sound you used to make the utterance (depending, of course, on the phonemic peculiarities of your speech community), you pronounced three of the syllables louder than the other seven syllables (although none of the three syllables was sounded with the same degree of loudness); your voice started on a normal pitch level, went up one level on the second syllable of *America* and went down two levels through the penultimate and ultimate syllables of the word; you separated slightly the words *The* and *United, United* and *States,* and *States* and *of;* and at the end of *America* your voice "trailed off" phonemically to indicate that you were finished with what you had to say.

Each of the intonational phenomena listed in the preceding paragraph is a phonemic or meaning phenomenon. Certainly, different stress patterns change meaning in English: per-VERT is identified immediately by an English speaker as a verb; PER-vert is an English noun. HE hit him (I didn't); he HIT him (he didn't pat him); he hit HIM (he doesn't strike ladies). Obviously, primary stress in an English utterance may be shifted from word to word depending on the desired emphasis. Each of these emphases is accomplished because stress in English is phonemic.

Since capitalizing syllables will not accurately differentiate among the four separate meaningful degrees of stress in our language, linguists have devised a convenient method of indicating these relative degrees of loudness: / ˊ / signals the loudest sound or groups of sounds in a given phonological phrase; / ∧ / is second loudest; / ＼ / is tertiary or third loudest; and / ⌣ / (or nothing at all) signals the weakest stress. The utterance "elevator operator" permits us to hear the four degrees of loudness functioning within easily contained limits. Whether we say élĕvàtŏr ôpĕràtŏr" as opposed to someone who operates a trolley car or "êlĕvàtŏr ópĕràtŏr" in contradistinction to the fellow who merely washes the thing, the four relative degrees of stress are operative within the phonological phrase and should be thoughtfully categorized as such.

In the designation "The United States of America," the second syllable of *America* usually receives primary stress in the mouth of an American, *States* regularly is secondary, and the second syllable of *United* is tertiary.

Making use now of comparatively familiar phonemic symbols to suggest the segmental phonemes (the slices of sound), I can indicate as well the stress phonemes of the utterance "The United States of America":

$$/ðĭ+yŭwnàytĭd\ stêyts\ əvăméhrĭkə/.$$

(It is possible, of course, to vary the stress contour of this cluster of words according to the number of phonological phrases involved in the speaker's production. If I may, however, I shall reserve discussion of these variations to a later paragraph.)

As regards pitch (or rate of vocal-fold vibration), there are also four distinct meaning levels for the speaker of American English. How many different "melodies" can you meaningfully pattern with the following words?

What are we having for dinner, Mother?

A typical production of this sentence would probably involve first a normal pitch level, a rise to a second higher level on the first syllable of *dinner,* a single level drop on the second syllable of the same word, a slight pause, a reintroduction of the same pitch level on the first syllable of *mother,* and a full level lift on the second syllable. Suppose, however, I had dropped two full levels within the word *dinner,* let my voice fade away, and returned to a normal level of pitch for the first syllable of *mother* and made a full pitch level rise on the second syllable. You would, of course, deplore immediately my cannibalistic tendencies and realize that the only way to write the second utterance in traditional orthography would be

What are we having for dinner? Mother?

Regularly, the four levels of pitch are symbolized /4/, /3/, /2/, and /1/ (from very high through high and normal to low) or are linearly depicted on the page. I shall combine the two techniques in our incrementally patriotic repetition:

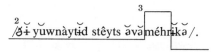

It is important to note that this 231 pitch contour is perhaps the most usual one in the English language. Many assertions and most questions whose answers involve more than a "yes" or a "no" arrange themselves within this contour.

Sound Junctures

If the relative pitch of sounds can have definite meaning in English, so can the separation of sounds or the terminal rendition of a sound have a distinct significance.

When I pause before the /s/ sound in /ayskriym/, I have said, "I scream." When, however, I pause gently *after* the /s/ sound, I've said "ice cream." There is no other phonemic distinction between the two utterances. The distinction is known as a plus juncture and is symbolized /+/.

For many Americans the utterances

He said, "Mary, the girl next door."

and

He said, "Marry the girl next door."

are precisely the same as far as sound slices, stress, and pitch go, but are obviously different in final production. A level juncture after the word *Mary* /mehriy/ in the first response signals that the remaining words are a nonrestrictive appositive of a girl's name. The absence of such a group juncture signals that the words following *marry* /mehriy/ are the object of an imperative verb. Level junctures in speech frequently correspond to commas in writing; certainly, this is the case in the contrasting of restrictive and nonrestrictive elements in the sentence. The level juncture is symbolized / → /.

Two other sound junctures / ⟋ / and / ⟍ /, the rising and falling terminals, occur at the end of syntactic units, whether single words, phrases, groups, clauses, or complete utterances. When I say

one / ⟋ / two / ⟋ / three / ⟋ /

and trail the sound off in an upward direction (normally not a full pitch level, but perceptibly) you recognize that I haven't finished counting as yet; but when I say

one / ⟋ / two / ⟋ / three / ⟍ /

and my voice fade-falls at the end, you know perfectly well that I have run out of things to count. Moreover, the rising terminal regularly signals a question whose answer is "yes" or "no." Compare "Are you going?" and "Where are you going?" Repeat the questions aloud. You will notice and be able to contrast immediately the two different terminal signals.

Finally, then, we are able to transcribe completely the way that most native Americans say the name of their country:

$$\underset{2}{\overset{\smile}{/\eth\dot{\imath}}} + \text{yŭwnàytĭd} + \text{stêyts} + \overset{\smile}{\text{ăvă}}\overset{3}{\overline{\text{méhr}}}\overset{\smile}{\text{ĭkă}} \quad \searrow /.$$

Had I or any native speaker decided to emphasize that our union is one and indissoluble, however, the second syllable of *United* could have received a primary stress as well; but in that case we would be dealing with two phonological phrases instead of one, and a level juncture would necessarily separate *States* and *of*. Every phonological phrase in English is separated from the other by one of the terminal junctures, / → /, / ⟋ /, or / ⟍ /. In other words, only one primary stress is possible within a phonological phrase. Reduce the number of terminals and you reduce the number of possible primary stresses. I could, for example, say simply, "The"; the transcription would be

/ð ĭy ⟍ /: one primary stress, one terminal.

Or I could say, "The United"

/ðĭ + yŭwnáytĭd ⟍ /: still only one primary stress, one terminal juncture.

Having shifted the original falling terminal to a plus juncture and having moved perforce the primary stress to another syllable, I necessarily give a weak stress to *The* and I change the phonemic shape of the word from a full glide /ð iy/ to the unstressed barred i /ðĭ/.

Professor Donald Lloyd, Wayne State University, has suggested a kind of hierarchy of these units of sound:

Terminals may override each other in relation to the speed of the utterance. A level or phrase-terminal replaces any lesser juncture as we speak more slowly and use more heavy stresses; a [rising] terminal can replace a level terminal or any lesser juncture; and, as we speak very deliberately, a [falling] terminal can replace any of the others. . . . The utterance divided into phonological phrases is something like a string of sausages stuffed by a careless hand — some large, some small, some long, some short, but each set off by a neat twist of the casing from the sausage before and after.[1]

In the same way that it isn't necessary to teach a third grader the complex terminology of articulatory phonetics in order to get him to hear the sounds he makes and to learn the orthographic symbols of those sounds, so he need not be burdened with the descriptive details of intonational phonemes.

But try him on this: write "I like girls" on the blackboard. Have him argue this friendly assertion aloud. He will undoubtedly stress the sentence "I like girls." Then in rapid succession ask him, "Who likes girls?" "How do you react to girls?" and "What is it you said you liked?" Each red-blooded American boy between San Diego and Oyster Bay who has outgrown the mud-throwing stage will inevitably stress the three words in respective and respectful order: "I like girls," "I like girls," and "I like girls."

Or if your students already have some command of the written dialect of American English, ask each of them to take out a piece of paper; then you write this sentence on the board:

John went fishing.

Don't ask them to say the words aloud this time. Rather, ask them to write the sentence and to hear and mark the different stress patterns that occur in the answers to the following four questions: (1) Who went fishing? (2) Where did John go? (3) Did John go hunting? and (4) When is John going to go fishing?

Developing Pitch Awareness

Pitch awareness (although one of the first things a language-learning baby has command of) is perhaps more difficult to teach children than stress patterns. Contrasted questions and assertions, identical assertions whose only meaning difference is in pitch — How many ways are there in which to say "yes"? — an actual attempt to "sing" the melody of a given assertion — these are possible exercises in helping a child to understand that an awareness of pitch contour is a meaningful guide to better reading.

Too, since relative pitch is finally the common denominator of all intonational phonemes, perhaps exercises leading students to a complete awareness of the stress and juncture differentiations among utterances comparable to the following examples will prove to be most valuable in the end.

[1] Although I have generally avoided documentation in this paper, I ought to point out here that my obligation to Donald Lloyd does not end with this brief quotation from a paper presented originally to the International Reading Association (1962). Most of the basic concepts delineated in these paragraphs are ultimately his. I hasten to point out, however, that he is in no way responsible for strained understanding on my part or awkward application. A full treatment of *Linguistics and the Teaching of Reading* by Dr. Lloyd and Professor Carl Lefevre has recently been published. The phonemic notation system employed in these pages is that of Trager and Smith, excepting the symbolization of terminal junctures which has been promulgated by H. A. Gleason. The examples used in the final paragraphs of this essay are in part from an unpublished student paper by Hugh W. Black.

For Juncture

The sun's rays meet.	(The rays of the sun meet.)	The+sun's+rays→meet
The sons raise meat.	(They're in the meat business.)	The+sons→raise+meat
This bear's watching.	(A bear is watching.)	This+bear→'s+watching
This bears watching.	(Keeping your eye on this.)	This→bears+watching

For Stress and Juncture

a lighthouse keeper	(keeper of a lighthouse)	líghthoùse→kêepĕr
a light housekeeper	(a skinny housewife)	lîght→hoúsekêepĕr
the green house	(a house painted green)	grêen→hoúse
the Greene house	(Mr. Greene's house)	Gréene→hôuse
the greenhouse	(where they grow flowers)	gréenhoùse
a blackbird's nest	(nest of a blackbird)	blâckbìrd's→nést
a black bird's nest	(the nest is black)	blâck→bírd'snèst
a black bird's nest	(the bird is black but not a blackbird)	blâck+bîrd's→nést

Syntactic Construction

The remarkable complexity of an English utterance is not limited to phonemes in morphemic sequence; sounds combine, separate, and take their relative positions in larger performance as well. Words, groups, phrases, clusters, and clauses assume for the good reader immediate comparative significance one to the other within that handy-dandy meaning generator known traditionally as the sentence.

Probably the simplest approach to the syntactic mechanisms of Modern English is a historical approach, a diachronic evaluation of synchronic probabilities.

When Alfred's scribes at the end of the ninth century laboriously rendered the Latin of Boethius or Bede into the West Saxon dialect of Old English, they were translating into an English best described as synthetic and inflectional — which is to say that Old English syntax depended in great measure on inflectional additions to words in order to signal case, person, gender, number, and tense. Old English word order, like the word order of Latin, was primarily stylistic or conventionalized.

The period of Middle English (1100–1500) was a period of syncretized inflections; endings blended one into the other, and, in an effort to compensate for waning inflectional signals, English developed a much more rigid word order and gave prepositions and other structure words the task of signalling the syntactic relations formerly accomplished by inflectional affixations.

Although still an inflectional language, Modern English is much more analytic than synthetic. Word order reigns supreme. But a note of caution here. In present-day teaching, too great an emphasis has been placed on "words" in order and on their relative "part-of-speech" definition. It isn't the word that is important, really, nor its "part" of speech. What matters syntactically is the function area of the utterance in which the word occurs.

Thus, in the sentence

Gertrude, who has a gold tooth in front, loves taffy pulls

neither the beautifying dependent clause nor its adjectival modification of the noun-subject has anything to do with the basic sentence functions of the declaration. Both Gertrude and her gold tooth serve as N-subject to the verb function in this assertion in the same way that two nouns, one modifying the other (*not* an adjective and a noun) function as N-object; the function pattern of the sentence, in other words, is N V N.

Indeed, if we were to measure out the function patterns of English declarative utterances in general, these several patterns would all be implicit in a basic pattern, $A N V N N A$. Obviously, N V (I gave), NVN (I gave my all), and N V N N (Mary gave mother a hotfoot) are all variations within the adverbial confines of the basic pattern. Adverbial modification of an English utterance normally precedes or follows a syntactic unit, excepting adverbs of frequency and occasional single-word adverbs which serve as a part of the verb-group function.

Given these function patterns, it is of primary importance to point out that the noun functions in any of these sequences may be fully maintained by what traditional grammarians call verbs or adjectives or adverbs as well as nouns, by a "group" of words (any one of these "parts of speech" with pre-modification), by a "cluster" of words (any of these "parts of speech" with pre- and post-modification), by a prepositional phrase, or by a clause.

In the same way, the verb function can be fulfilled by a single verb, an analytic verb group, or by an adverb plus a verb or a verb group. The adverb functions are accomplished by single-word adverbs, adverbial groups, adverbial phrases, or adverbial clauses. In other words, *conversion* (the shifting of function of a "part of speech") and *reduction* (the making use of groups, phrases, clusters, and clauses as single sentence functions) characterize the English we speak today as much as does word order. Why not make these characteristics, then, at least part of the syntactic basis of our teaching of reading?

If youngsters are made aware that the long dependent clauses and the seemingly complicated noun and verb clusters that stare back at them from the printed page serve only a single sentence function and that the significant words within these complexes are carefully signalled in speech by normal intonational contours, their reading capabilities must necessarily improve.

But that's the parents' problem and the teachers'; and you have finished reading now.

Further Reading for Chapter 12

Allen, Robert. "Better Reading Through the Recognition of Grammatical Relations," *The Reading Teacher,* 18: 194–198; December, 1964.

Bateman, Barbara, and Janis Wetherell. "A Critique of Bloomfield's Approach to the Teaching of Reading," *The Reading Teacher,* 18: 98–104; November, 1964.

Bormuth, John R. "Readability: A New Approach," *Reading Research Quarterly,* 1: 79–132; Spring, 1966.

Botel, Morton. "What Linguists Say to This Teacher of Reading and Spelling," *The Reading Teacher,* 18: 188–193; December, 1964.

Cain, R. Donald. "What Do We Mean By Linguistics?" *English Journal,* 54: 399–404; May, 1965.

Cammarota, Gloria. "Word Groups in Speech and Reading," *The Reading Teacher,* 18: 94–97; November, 1964.

Durkin, Dolores. "Linguistics and the Teaching of Reading," *The Reading Teacher,* 16: 342–346; March, 1963.

Edward, Sister Mary. "A Modified Linguistic Versus a Composite Basal Reading Program," *The Reading Teacher,* 17: 511–515, 527; April, 1964.

Everetts, Eldonna. "Influence of Linguistics," *Educational Leadership,* 22: 404–408; March, 1965.

Fries, Charles C. *Linguistics and Reading.* New York: Holt, Rinehart & Winston, Inc., 1963.

————. "Linguistics and the Teaching of Reading," *The Reading Teacher,* 17: 594–598; May, 1964.

Goodman, Kenneth S. "A Communicative Theory of the Reading Curriculum," *Elementary English,* 40: 290–298; March, 1963.

————. "A Linguistic Study of Cues and Miscues in Reading," *Elementary English,* 42: 639–643; October, 1965.

Hildreth, Gertrude. "Linguistic Factors in Early Reading Instruction," *The Reading Teacher,* 18: 172–177; December, 1964.

Lefevre, Carl A. "The Contribution of Linguistics," *The Instructor,* 74: 77, 103–105; March, 1965.

————. *Linguistics and the Teaching of Reading.* New York: McGraw-Hill Book Co., Inc., 1964.

Lloyd, Donald. "Intonation and Reading," *Education,* 84: 538–541; May, 1964.

Marquardt, William F. "Language Interference in Reading," *The Reading Teacher,* 18: 214–218; December, 1964.

Owen, George H. "Linguistics, An Overview," *Elementary English,* 39: 421–425; May, 1962.

Spache, George D. *Reading in the Elementary School.* Boston: Allyn and Bacon, Inc., 1964. Chapter 5.

Tyler, Priscilla. "Sound Patterns and Sense," *Education,* 83: 527–531; May, 1963.

13

Evaluating Reading

The best materials and the wisest methods lose their effectiveness when we know too little about the reading of our pupils to determine the appropriate levels at which to teach them. If we operate with materials and skills below the children's levels, at best they merely tolerate us or come to view school as a place in which they can learn nothing. If we operate above the children's levels, we can expect frustration and rebellion, but very little learning.

Our initial evaluation of our students must include at least an estimate of the levels at which they can read. If we use basic readers, this information will direct us to the appropriate readers for grouping; if we use an individualized-reading approach, it will help us to direct children to the kinds of books they can read independently. At upper-grade levels, where content books such as social-studies texts are used, our evaluation will also help us to decide whether supplementary content materials designed for students at other grade levels must be relied upon. Specific suggestions for obtaining such an evaluation are offered in the selections in this chapter.

Beyond this gross kind of information, however, we must have more refined assessments of the strengths and weaknesses of each pupil in our classroom. Many elementary-school teachers have had the experience of receiving students in their rooms who have "been through" the children's readers at previous grade levels but who have not yet been taught the skills normally learned at those levels. One frequent reason for this situation, among many others, is the unwise pressure to force children through the grade-level materials before they are ready for them. A child who learns more slowly than many of his classmates, then, may spend most of his time memorizing words so he can finish the reader at his grade level, while the development of needed skills and abilities is neglected.

Thus the most efficient reading instruction demands that the teacher know as precisely as possible the exact skills and abilities in which children need instruction or additional practice. For example, it is not enough to know that a pupil is reading below grade level; we need to know the general skill area in which he is weak. If word attack is one such area, we should determine the specific weaknesses within that area. Does the child know letter-sound associations? Can he apply the knowledge that he has? Which specific letter-sound associations require additional instruction or practice?

We may not always be able to evaluate precisely the strengths and weaknesses of each child, but our instruction can become more efficient as we become more adept at pinpointing them.

In the lead article for this chapter, Gus P. Plessas reviews and summarizes a number of studies which have compared children's scores on standardized reading-achievement tests with their instructional levels in basic readers. He presents reasons for the wide disparities which are often found and recommends the use of informal classroom inventories as a needed supplement to these test scores.

The other two selections present specific suggestions for making and interpreting such classroom inventories. In the second selection, Mary C. Austin and Mildred H. Huebner describe both group and individual inventories in detail. In the third, Marjorie Seddon Johnson adds suggestions that can be adapted for use in any classroom.

Another Look at the Reading

Score ✢ Gus P. Plessas

In schools today the use of standardized reading tests has become increasingly important. A modern program for appraising students' reading status and needs includes formalized measurement.

Formerly few teachers made systematic use of standardized reading tests. In recent times, however, classroom teachers administer formal reading tests to identify the range of differences in reading abilities within their classes and to determine the achievement level of each class member. Reading specialists use diagnostic reading tests to analyze precisely a pupil's strong and weak areas. Moreover, school administrators give survey tests to evaluate pupils' progress in reading. These are among the most significant uses of standardized reading tests in administering an effective appraisal program.

The Problem

The purpose of this article is to explore the reliability of a single test score as a precise measure of an individual's instructional reading level.

Recently a new teacher expressed a personal concern over her apparent misinterpretation of standardized test scores in reading. She discovered a consistent disparity between her students' reading scores as indicated on a standardized test and the level at which instruction proved effective. Her problem became increasingly clear after she placed students in reading groups according to their scores on a standardized reading measure.

She found, for example, that a few fourth-graders who scored at the grade level were unable to perform satisfactorily in a fourth reader. These students had difficulty distinguishing main ideas from related details. Many were unable to draw inferences from selected passages.

Furthermore, her poor readers, rated on the average at third-grade level, read with many inaccuracies in material at this reader level. Their reading performances characteristically included many word-analysis difficulties. This serious weakness made it highly improbable that the youngsters could develop in and through reading materials chosen on the basis of scores obtained by a standardized reading measure.

According to this teacher, the number of reading problems seemed disproportionately high in relation to the students' measures of achievement in reading. For instance, instead of finding the basal readers appropriate and challenging, most children found themselves frustrated in using the materials. Since special care was taken to place children in reading groups based on the standardized test scores, why, asked the observant teacher, didn't her pupils respond successfully to instruction at these levels?

Why does this common disparity occur? Is it the result of poor or inexperi-

Reprinted from the April, 1966, issue of *Education.* Copyright, 1966, by The Bobbs-Merrill Company, Inc., Indianapolis, Indiana. Gus P. Plessas is Professor of Education, Sacramento State College, Sacramento, California.

enced judgment? Does it reflect inadequate teaching? These questions are real possibilities. Accordingly, what does research say on this matter?

Research Findings

The misuses of standardized reading tests were outlined by Betts (1). He claimed that these tests frequently rate children from one to four grades above their actual achievement level. He also cautioned against using standardized measures as the sole criterion for assessing a particular pupil's reading level.

Perhaps the earliest study relating to this problem was completed by Killgallon (2). He concluded that the scores on standardized reading-achievement tests placed children an average of one grade above their instructional level as determined by the use of a reading inventory. In support of the foregoing views, Sister Mary Julitta (3) reported that scores obtained from silent-reading tests often rank children higher than their instructional level.

In his investigation of the relationship between the standardized and informal estimate of reading levels among fourteen hundred pupils in Grades 2 through 6, Botel (4) found:

1. In Grade 2, 85 per cent of the pupils are overrated by the standardized test from one to five levels. Eleven per cent of the pupils are rated properly, 4 per cent are underrated one or two levels.

2. In Grade 3, 68 per cent of the pupils are overrated by the standardized test from one to five levels. Seventeen per cent of the pupils are rated properly, 15 per cent are underrated from one to three levels.

3. In the intermediate grades, on the average, about one-third of the pupils are overrated from one to five levels, one-third rated properly, and one-third underrated by the standardized test.

Botel claimed evidence to support his view that there is little justification for using grade scores from standardized reading tests to place students in basal readers. He pointed out the complex relationship between a score on a test and the instructional level of a pupil. It is not a simple matter of adding or subtracting a constant figure from a pupil's reading score to arrive at the instructional reader level. "As we have seen, pupils who achieve the same standardized test score may vary as much as eight reader levels."

In a similar study using only fifty-six sixth-graders, however, McCracken (5) concluded that the standardized reading test scores were significantly higher than their reading performances as determined by an informal reading inventory.

On the other hand, Chall (6) challenged the practice of placing students in readers on a level below the grade scores as indicated on standardized reading tests. She believed that "This may not always be wise, since for many children, especially those who lack confidence or have an unusually slow rate of reading, the standardized test scores may give a minimal estimate of performance. Such children can actually benefit more from a higher level of material."

Harris's (7) view approached the middle ground; he asserted that formal reading test scores do not discriminate among the various reading levels. However, he stated that, in most instances, standardized scores generally reflect the instructional level, but he also pointed out that the reading performance of pupils who find the test materials too difficult, or who mostly guess on a standardized test, may yield a score indicating their frustration level in reading.

A Possible Explanation

If a large percentage of students are overrated by standardized reading instruments, there may be reasons which in some measure explain why a score on a formal test reflects a pupil's frustration reading level. To theorize why this is so, let us consider some of the conditions which may contribute to this disparity.

First, a careful examination of standardized reading tests reveals that most of them are extremely limited and indiscriminate. According to Dolch (8), present reading tests measure a variety of reading skills without precisely identifying the particular skills being measured. He explained that when a pupil achieves a certain reading score, one cannot determine whether this score represents a sight vocabulary, word analysis, or comprehension abilities.

Furthermore, most reading tests do not evaluate adequately the higher creative reading processes involving thoughtful reactions and appreciative responses to the printed ideas. The majority of existing tests emphasize the measurement of word meanings and limited comprehension skills such as reading to note supporting details or main ideas (9).

However important the above skills are to the reader, their mastery does not necessarily reflect the reader's ability to apply higher interpretive skills in his reading. Consequently, if the level of instruction challenges the pupil to *think* critically about the ideas presented in his reading, his score on a standardized reading measure would not likely indicate his true instructional level.

Second, a standardized achievement test does not necessarily encourage a pupil to discern freely and independently his personal responses in reading. Most survey reading tests consist of vocabulary and comprehension sections in which the subject usually defines words by selecting appropriate synonyms from a group or reads graded passages to answer questions from a list of choices. The arrangement for selecting answers in such comprehension tests may unintentionally aid the subject in advancing his reading achievement score beyond his actual instructional level.

True reading experiences typically demand that the reader associate words with their meanings or react to ideas *without* reference to carefully worded choices. In other words, his responses to the reading situation should be self-determined and unconditional. This is not the case with formal measures in reading.

Third, the limited time allowed for a pupil to take most standardized reading tests can prompt him to perform in a manner unlike that required in normal reading activities. That is, he is forced to apply unnatural vigor to his reading effort to gain rapid responses in the testing situation. Such a forced rate could not be sustained in reading longer passages.

This difference is analogous to a track athlete who may run the one-hundred-yard dash in ten seconds, but he would find it difficult to maintain that speed and run four hundred yards in forty seconds. It seems important, therefore, for a pupil to read material at a reader level in which the pupil feels comfortable and free from unnecessary tension. If he is to grow in all reading dimensions, he needs to have material that will be challenging but easy enough for him to think clearly about the ideas presented.

Implications

The foregoing comments described several conceivable reasons why teachers should take "another look" at children's reading scores on standardized tests. Classroom teachers should consider perhaps less formal measures for assessing pupils' reading strengths and weaknesses to supplement the findings of formal tests. Teacher-made tests can easily be constructed to determine the student's level for successful reading instruction. In this manner, an informal reading inventory based upon graded selections can be a useful adjunct to the use of standardized measurements for appraisal purposes.

References

1. Betts, Emmett A. *Foundations of Reading Instruction*. New York: American Book Company, 1954. P. 441.
2. Killgallon, Pat A. "A Study of Relationships Among Certain Pupil Adjustments in Reading Situations," unpublished doctoral dissertation, Pennsylvania State College, State College, Pennsylvania, 1942.
3. Sister Mary Julitta. "Selection and Use of Standardized Reading Tests," in *Education in Reading*, Supplementary Educational Monographs, No. 88. Chicago: University of Chicago Press, 1957. P. 122.
4. Botel, Morton. "Newer Techniques in the Supervision of Reading Instruction," in *Frontiers of Elementary Education*. Syracuse, N.Y.: Syracuse University Press, 1957. Pp. 25–39.
5. McCracken, Robert A. "Standardized Reading Tests and Informal Reading Inventories, *Education*, February, 1962, p. 368.
6. Chall, Jeanne S. "Interpretation of Results of Standardized Reading Tests," in *Evaluation in Reading, op. cit.,* p. 135.
7. Harris, Albert J. *How to Increase Reading Ability* (3rd ed.). New York: Longmans, Green & Co., 1956. P. 153.
8. Dolch, Edward W. "Do Reading Tests Test Reading?" *Elementary English*, April, 1964, p. 202.
9. Davis, Frederick B. "What Do Reading Tests Really Measure?" *English Journal*, April, 1944, pp. 180–187.

Evaluating Progress in Reading Through Informal Procedures

❖ Mary C. Austin and Mildred H. Huebner

Educators today recognize that growth in reading is a continuous process which should be measured periodically. They know that pupils and teachers benefit from evaluations of reading progress which indicate what has been accomplished and what skills, methods, and materials should be presented next in the developmental sequence to assure further growth. They are aware also that their evaluations should combine the findings both of formal and of informal appraisal procedures.

In their efforts to provide better reading instruction for all children, teachers ask: What are the values of informal measures? Which types have been most useful? How can these procedures be used to greater advantage in the classroom?

Values of Informal Measures

Informal appraisals can assist teachers in a number of ways. The results of such procedures supply evidence regarding pupil reading levels, including pupil strengths and weaknesses. This information is useful in forming reading groups based upon instructional levels or special needs. It is helpful also in selecting appropriate materials for these purposes, as well as for independent reading activities.

When used in conjunction with other appraisal techniques, informal procedures assist teachers and pupils in assessing pupil growth over a period of time, thereby pointing to the possible need for reviewing and reteaching certain reading skills before the introduction of new ones. In other words, when informal appraisals are conducted skillfully, and when the results are interpreted accurately, they enable teachers to *program* reading instruction more effectively.

Types of Informal Appraisals

Whenever teachers note a pupil's reading ability or deficiency for planning purposes, they are using informal evaluation procedures. They observe pupil behavior for signs of inadequate sight recognition vocabulary, poor methods of word attack, vocalization during silent reading, unusual reading posture, comprehension problems. They discover the ease with which a pupil locates information in a card catalog and in reference books. They use teacher-made tests to determine a reader's depth of understanding and his ability to read critically.

From *The Reading Teacher*, 15: 338–343; March, 1962. Reprinted with permission of Mary C. Austin and Mildred H. Huebner and the International Reading Association. Mary C. Austin is Professor of Education, Western Reserve University, Cleveland, Ohio, and Mildred H. Huebner is Director of the Reading Center and Professor of Education, Southern Connecticut State College, New Haven.

Teachers also devise inventories, questionnaires, and checklists for additional data about pupil reading interests and abilities. Interest inventories, for example, may be developed by preparing statements to be completed by students, such as, "If I had three wishes . . . ," "During my free time I like to . . . ," and "My favorite book is . . . ." Study skills may be ascertained by informal small-group discussions of previously planned items, such as "I study best . . . ," "When I want to learn more about a topic, I . . . ."

A pupil's instructional level can be estimated quickly by means of a checklist which samples the vocabulary from several graded textbooks in reading, social studies, science, or other areas. The checklist may include from ten to fifteen words from the primary-grade texts and twenty words or more from the upper-grade texts. Words from several levels, both above and below the pupil's grade level, may be presented for flash recogniton by means of a hand tachistoscope or by the teacher's manipulation of two small cards in such a manner that a single word is exposed rapidly. Usually the failure to recognize one or more words at a grade level will indicate the necessity for choosing easier materials for instructional purposes. Vocabulary checklists, then, can be helpful on several occasions: to test a pupil's mastery of words from previous reading levels, to form a tentative judgment of his independent and instructional levels, to provide reading materials with which he can succeed until further information is available about his ability, and to estimate the starting level for the administration of an informal reading inventory.

Because teachers frequently ask about informal reading inventories, two types are described somewhat in detail in the following sections of this paper.

Group Inventories

As a first step toward the selection of appropriate materials for each pupil at the beginning of the year, teachers usually refer to the information about pupil achievement to be found on cumulative records and on reading progress sheets. In referring to these data, teachers recognize that changes probably have occurred in the pupil's reading status during the months following the last recorded items. They therefore plan to give a vocabulary checklist, similar to the one mentioned above. By using the results of the checklist, the scores from the most recently administered standardized tests, and the information of the student's completed reading list of the preceding year teachers can estimate the present reading levels of their pupils. Materials for developmental and independent reading, as well as for the content areas, can then be assembled.

During the first week or two of the school year, many teachers seek more reliable evidence of their pupils' reading levels by giving inventories based upon the reading materials tentatively selected. If, for example, a teacher has decided that a fifth-grade basic reader is appropriate for a number of her pupils, she can "try out" the new book by inviting four or five pupils to read orally at sight from a representative story. As each child presents a passage from the story, the teacher may note special characteristics of his ability to read with fluency, comprehension, and accuracy. Following his oral reading, each pupil can be asked a series of questions prepared by the teacher to determine the extent of his comprehension and his grasp of word meanings. The passage and questions below serve as an illustration:

It was close to sunset in the woodlands of the Adirondack Mountains. Joseph Brant, the young leader of a group of Mohawk Indian boys, halted. The hunting trail that they had been following all day led into a small open space in the forest. Under a great tree, a spring of clear water trickled over mossy stones.

The leader raised his arm as a signal for his band to halt. "We will camp here for the night," he said. "It is a good place."

"Joseph Brant is very careful," said the boy next in line. "If I were leader of this hunting party, we would walk on until nightfall."

Joseph half turned. He began to answer sharply, but stopped. He knew that a leader must not let himself become angry. He was a sachem's son and must handle his men well.

1. Who was Joseph Brant?
2. What had the boys been doing all day?
3. What did the leader decide to do?
4. What did the next boy think about this decision?
5. Why didn't Joseph give the boy a sharp answer?
6. What do you think a sachem is?

Oral: (140 words), p. 116
Fifth Reader (3)

Should the pupil make more than one word recognition error for every twenty words in the selection he has read, and should there be an obvious lack of story comprehension, the material probably is not suitable for him. In this way the results of the group reading inventory show the teacher immediately for which pupils the material is not appropriate for instructional purposes, either because of its difficulty for the less able reader or because of its lack of sufficient challenge for the more able one. On subsequent days she may regroup her pupils for an inventory based on more advanced reading for those whose achievement is at a higher level, and, similarly, she may present easier books to those who appear to need them. In a relatively short time the teacher is able to appraise the present reading levels of her pupils, to re-evaluate the suitability of the materials she has selected for their use, to form groups within her classroom, and to make plans for individualized work.

The above techniques are equally helpful in assessing reading levels in the content areas, particularly in social studies and science throughout the entire school program.

Individual Inventories

While teachers would like to analyze the reading performance of each student by means of an individual inventory, class size may make such a procedure impractical. It will be especially helpful, however, for evaluating the ability of those pupils who do poorly on a group inventory and of those transfer pupils who enter during the year with incomplete records. In situations such as these, the individual inventory is an effective tool for the reading specialist and the classroom teacher to use in determining a pupil's specific strengths and weaknesses, as well as his readiness for reading at a higher level.

The informal inventory is typically a compilation of graded reading selections with questions prepared in advance to test the reader's comprehension. Graded textbooks in reading, or in the content areas, may provide the material for the inventory. At least two samples are chosen from each book. The length of each sample will vary from under one hundred words at the primary levels to more than one hundred at the intermediate and upper grade levels. One passage at each level is read orally without previous preparation by the pupil, and a second passage is read silently.

The starting level on the inventory may be estimated by the teacher through the use of a vocabulary checklist. As the pupil reads aloud, the teacher carefully notes the child's errors on a separate oral reading checklist or on a transparent paper placed over the page of her book. If the latter technique is used, the teacher will have prepared transparent sheets beforehand to correspond to the pages of the story, so they can be realigned easily for her appraisal at another time. Having a tape recording of the pupil's oral reading, if this can be arranged, is of great value for an accurate analysis of the pupil's reading performance.

The items listed below are illustrative of those which might be incorporated into an oral reading checklist. If the teacher places a mark after the errors as they occur, and writes an example, whenever possible, she will have a graphic picture of the pupil's performance.

1. Word recognition errors
   a. Mispronunciations
   b. Omissions
   c. Substitutions
   d. Words pronounced for the pupil (after a five-second hesitation)
2. Fluency
   a. Word-by-word reading
   b. Inadequate phrasing
   c. Punctuation ignored
   d. Repetitions
3. Observations
   a. Finger pointing
   b. Strained, high-pitched voice
   c. Marked insecurity
   d. Tension movements
   e. Poor posture
   f. Head movements
   g. Lack of interest
   h. Holding book too close

Detailed oral reading checklists both for sight reading and for prepared reading may be found in *Reading Evaluation* (1).

Following both oral and silent reading, the pupil's comprehension should be checked by asking previously determined questions orally and by having the child respond in a like manner. The number of questions usually will range from five to eight, the lower number accompanying the selections at the primary-grade levels. In formulating these questions, certain guides are helpful (4):

1. Questions should be based upon the reading material rather than on experiences the child may have had.
2. "Catch" questions should be avoided.
3. The language of the questions should be geared to the level of the material.

4. Unaided recall-type questions should be used.

5. Questions should be stated so that the exact wording of the story is not necessary.

Whenever possible, four types of questions should be included in the comprehension check: (a) factual — those dealing with the child's ability to recall specifics in the story; (b) inferential — those measuring the child's ability to draw inferences or make judgments based on events or implied occurrences in the story but which are not directly stated; (c) vocabulary — those attempting to measure the pupil's knowledge of words used but not defined in the selection, and (d) use of context clues — those attempting to measure the child's ability to use context clues to gain the meaning of presumably unknown words (4).

In evaluating the results of an informal reading inventory, teachers should clearly understand the differences between the pupil's *independent reading level* and his *instructional level*. In the first place, the child's independent reading level is somewhat lower than the one at which the teacher plans to carry on developmental reading instruction. Usually, the independent level is indicated by the pupil's ability to read orally without making more than one word-recognition error per one hundred words, to understand at least 90 per cent of what he reads, and to read without such symptoms as finger pointing, head movements, and poor phrasing. His *instructional level* is reached when he can read orally with no more than one word-recognition error per twenty words, with at least 75 per cent comprehension and recall of the material he has read, and when symptoms of difficulty are absent. Betts (2) discusses these levels in detail, and he provides instructions for constructing and administering individual and group reading inventories.

Sources of Informal Inventories

Informal reading inventories may be developed by classroom teachers individually or by a school system for its own use, as has been done in Lakewood, Ohio, and in the Bucks County, Pennsylvania, Public Schools.

Several inventories have been published and may be examined for their content: (a) M. Austin, C. Bush, and M. Huebner, *Reading Evaluation* (New York: Ronald Press, 1961), pages 235–246; includes an inventory based upon the Sheldon Basic Readers for Grades 1–8, published by Allyn and Bacon, Inc., 1957. (b) E. Betts, *Handbook on Corrective Reading* (Chicago: Wheeler Publishing Company, 1956), pages 20–35; includes an inventory based upon the graded American Adventure Series. (c) N. B. Smith, *Graded Selections for Informal Reading: Diagnosis for Grades 1 through 3* (New York: New York University Press, 1959); an inventory for the primary grades. (d) R. Strang and D. K. Bracken, *Making Better Readers* (Boston: D. C. Heath, 1957); includes examples of teacher-made tests in the content areas.

Concluding Statement

The wide range of reading achievement at every academic level is an accepted fact today. Awareness of this situation, and of the importance of adapting instruction to individual accomplishments, focuses attention upon two related instructional needs: (a) accurate appraisal of each pupil's level of reading achievement, and (b) the use of such information as a basis for the selection of suitable reading methods and materials.

Teachers who give more than "lip service" to providing for individual differences in the reading program recognize the valuable contributions of informal procedures in their evaluation of pupil progress. During the next decade they will use an even greater variety of approaches than in the past to assist them in meeting the needs of all pupils in their classes.

References

1. Austin, M. C., C. L. Bush, and M. H. Huebner. *Reading Evaluation.* New York: Ronald Press, 1961. Pp. 10–11.
2. Betts, Emmett A. *Foundations of Reading Instruction.* New York: American Book, 1957. Pp. 438–485.
3. *Sheldon Basic Reading Series.* Boston: Allyn and Bacon, 1957.
4. Sipay, Edward R. "A Comparison of Standardized Reading Achievement Test Scores and Functional Reading Levels," unpublished doctor's dissertation, University of Connecticut, Storrs, Conn., 1961. Pp. 81, 83.

Reading Inventories for Classroom

Use ❖ MARJORIE SEDDON JOHNSON

Good teaching is dependent on understanding of those to be taught. Planning for reading instruction is, therefore, impossible without thorough investigation of each pupil's present level of achievement, his capacity for achievement, and his specific strengths and weaknesses. The classroom teacher must make an evaluation, in all of these areas, of each pupil in his group. He can accomplish this task most efficiently through the use of informal inventories.

Nature of Informal Inventories

Standardized tests rate an individual's performance as compared to the performance of others. By contrast, an informal inventory appraises the individual's level of competence on a particular job without reference to what others do. It is designed to determine how well *he* can do the job. Materials of known difficulty are used to find out if he can or cannot read them adequately. Inventories can be administered on an individual or a group basis. For general classroom use the group inventory is most desirable, except for those pupils whose status cannot be appraised adequately without a complete clinical inventory.

From *The Reading Teacher,* 14: 9–13; September, 1960. Reprinted with permission of Marjorie Seddon Johnson and the International Reading Association. Marjorie Seddon Johnson is Associate Professor of Psychology and Associate Director of the Reading Clinic, Temple University, Philadelphia, Pennsylvania.

For them, the evaluation may depend on an individual word-recognition test and reading inventory.

In either case, the child reads material at known levels and responds to questions designed to measure his understanding of what he has read. When group procedures are used, material at one level only is usually employed for each test. When an individual inventory is administered, materials at successively higher levels are read until the pupil reaches the point at which he can no longer function adequately. In both cases specific abilities can be evaluated at the same time that information is obtained on the appropriate difficulty level of materials for independent reading, instruction, and listening activities. Getting all this information through group inventory techniques may require a number of sessions with reading at various levels. However, with either procedure the teacher has an opportunity to determine levels and needs in the only logical way — by seeing how the pupil functions in an actual reading situation.

Purposes

If instruction has the object of helping the child improve his performance, it must begin at his present functioning level. The first purpose of the inventory, therefore, is to find the correct level for instruction. Does the particular pupil need to begin work at primer, third-reader, or sixth-[reader] level? Where is the point at which he has needs which require instructional help and at which he can profit from it?

Not all work which the child does should be dependent on instructional aid. He should have opportunities to apply the abilities he has acquired, to function under his own direction, and to practice so that he can develop a more facile performance. All of this must be done at a level where he can achieve virtual perfection without assistance. A second purpose of the inventory, then, is to determine the highest level at which the individual can read well on his own, his independent level.

Reading ability is not an entity, but rather a composite of a large number of specific abilities. Improvements in reading performance, therefore, can be brought about only as the individual gains greater grasp of needed abilities. Before plans can be made to help a pupil, the teacher must determine what causes him trouble, etc. A third purpose of the inventory is to get this information on each child's specific assets and liabilities in the total picture of his reading ability.

Many factors, in addition to the language and thinking abilities, influence the child's performance in reading. How well is he able to attend and concentrate? What does he expect to get from reading? How does he respond to ideas presented by others? How much background of information and experience does he have to bring to the reading? How efficiently does he use his background? A fourth purpose of the inventory is to find answers to these and other related questions.

Procedures

For evaluating in group situations, the first step is to make an estimate of the possible instructional level of each child. Many kinds of data can be gotten from cumulative records, former teachers, and observations of daily performance. From these sources comes the information on which the hypothesis about instructional levels is made. Perhaps in a sixth-grade class, for instance, a teacher decides tentatively that he may have one group ready for instruction at fourth level, another at fifth, a third at sixth, and a fourth somewhere above sixth. In addition, he feels that four of his pupils are quite far below the others in achievement, but is uncertain about definite levels.

He might proceed by selecting a good piece of reading material at sixth level and preparing himself thoroughly for using it as an inventory. This preparation would include all of the attention to vocabulary, word recognition problems, thinking abilities, etc., which would be given to a piece of material to be used for an instructional reading activity. When hs preparation is complete, he is ready to begin the inventory for those whose instructional levels are approximately at sixth reader.

When this group is assembled for the inventory, the over-all plan for the activity will vary little from that for any good instructional reading activity. The differences lie in matters of emphasis. The objective is not to teach, but rather to find out if this material would be suitable for teaching. The basic question to be answered for each pupil is this: "Can he profit from instruction in this material?" Each phase of the reading activity, therefore, must be slanted toward evaluation. Actual teaching would be done only to see how well various individuals can respond to instruction given at this level. Thus any instruction given in the inventory situations is actually for purposes of further evaluation.

During the readiness or preparatory period of the group inventory the teacher may use a variety of techniques and materials. His objectives are the following: to evaluate the pupils' background of relevant experiences and their ability to use these experiences, to see how many relevant concepts they have at their disposal, to determine whether or not they have a grasp of the vocabulary used in this material to express essential concepts, to evaluate their ability to perform whatever thinking processes are involved in understanding the selection, and to determine the degree of interest they show. These same objectives guide the evaluative phase of an instructional directed reading activity. In both inventory and instructional activity these objectives will be achieved only if the teacher allows freedom for the pupils to reveal themselves — their interests, concepts, vocabulary, experiences, thinking abilities, attention, etc. As the teacher guides the activity he must not become the dispenser of information, the judge of ideas presented. He may stimulate group discussion through use of what he knows about the children's backgrounds, materials read previously, pictures accompanying the material to be read currently, concrete objects rich in stimulus value, or countless other things related to the chosen material.

In the inventory no attempt would be made to fill all the discovered gaps. For some of the pupils taking the inventory, deficiencies in experience, vocabulary, concepts, or thinking abilities, for instance, might be so severe that instruction in this material would be impossible. For them the essential question has already been answered — sixth reader is too high for instruction. Depending on the total classroom situation at the moment, they might be dropped from the reading inventory to go on with some other activity or continue in it even though no more evaluation of their performance at this level is necessary. If they continue, the teacher is obligated to see that it is not a frustrating experience for them and that their inability to function is not evident to all to a debilitating degree.

For those pupils who seem able to proceed with the material the preparatory phase would continue with some developmental work. Clarification or development of concepts, introduction of essential vocabulary, guidance in thinking processes, etc., might be undertaken. Students would be guided toward the establishment of purposes for reading. All this would be done to further the evaluation — to see how well they can profit from this help and apply it during the rest of the reading activity.

Once the preparation has been completed and purposes for reading established, the second phase of the activity begins. Pupils read the material silently to satisfy the purposes they set up. Now the teacher has an opportunity to observe their performance. Some may proceed with no difficulty — reading at an acceptable rate, reflecting their understanding in their expressions, stopping when they have achieved what they set out to do. Others may exhibit various symptoms of difficulty — frowning, lip movement, finger-pointing, requesting frequent help, and many others. Some may take an inordinate amount of time as they struggle along. All the things the teacher sees and hears during this silent reading period will become part of the data on which he bases his final evaluation. If pupils want to ask questions, he will be available. From the questions they ask and the comments they make to him he may discover a great deal about the strengths and weaknesses in their performance.

When the silent reading has been completed, group discussion will focus on the purposes established for reading. Here the teacher will have an opportunity to discover how well various individuals satisfied these purposes. Rereading, both oral and silent, may occur spontaneously or be done on request. Appraisal can be made of oral reading performance, ability to locate information, ability to determine relevancy of ideas, etc. Questions other than those raised in the original purposes can be asked to allow for more nearly complete evaluation of each individual's understanding of the material and his handling of the word recognition problems.

By the time the preparatory phase, silent reading, discussion, and rereading have been completed, the teacher should have clear evidence of each child's ability or inability to profit from instruction at this level. About those who can function adequately with his instructional aid, he should have a great deal of additional information. He may have noted that one had difficulty getting meaning from a context clue expressed in an appositional phrase. Another may have needed help with handling the *ti* element in words like *partial*. A third may have had trouble with two vowels together when they are in two separate syllables. A fourth may have trouble with a sequence based on order of importance. In other words, the teacher may have discovered a great deal about the specific needs of these pupils he is going to instruct at sixth level. At the same time, he undoubtedly learned much on the positive side as he observed the things they were able to do well and the readiness they had for additional learnings.

About those who handled everything independently, spontaneously, and virtually perfectly at sixth level, the teacher may know only that he must check them at a higher level. He has not seen their needs because they are not evident at the independent level. About those for whom this material was much too difficult, he may know little more than that he must check them at a lower level. He could not appraise their skills and abilities because they were in so much trouble that they were unable to apply even those they had. Evaluation of specific needs would have to wait for the inventory at the instructional level.

During succeeding periods the same procedures would be followed with other groups and other materials. Those for whom sixth-reader materials had been too difficult might become part of groups being checked at fourth or fifth. Those for whom sixth had been too easy might be checked at seventh or eighth. Even after all the group inventories are completed, additional information might be needed on some pupils. It would be to these that individual inventories would be administered. This might well mean making special arrangements outside the classroom setting.

Materials

For both group and individual inventories materials must be ones of known difficulty level. Each piece of material should be a meaningful unit, not a disjointed portion of a longer selection. It should offer the possibility of evaluating important skills and abilities. It should not be material with which the pupil is already familiar.

Many types of material can be used. Selections from basal readers, graded texts in the content areas, "news papers" designed for pupil use — all these and many others are among the choices. For the group inventory in the classroom one might well use selections from the very texts being considered for use. In this way a direct answer can be gotten to the immediate question — "Is *this book* suitable instructional material for *this child?*"

If a science teacher wants to determine his pupils' instructional levels for science work, he needs good science material for his inventory. The question, however, might be this: "What level should this child be using for his light, recreational reading?" In that case, the inventory should be done with story-type material. In other words, the material must be pertinent to the purpose for which the evaluation is being made.

Summary

Reading needs can be diagnosed only through observation of reading performance. Instruction can be planned effectively only on the basis of such diagnostic study. Through group reading activities conducted with the stress on evaluation the good classroom teacher can determine appropriate levels for independent and instructional work. Having found the right level for instruction, he can appraise each child's strengths and weaknesses and plan to meet his needs. All this can be accomplished with classroom materials by any alert, sensitive teacher who knows his pupils, knows a reading program, and knows his materials for the informal inventory.

Further Reading for Chapter 13

Artley, A. Sterl. "Evaluation of Reading," *The Instructor*, 74: 89, 110; March, 1965.

Austin, Mary C. "Evaluating Reading Progress," *The Journal of the Reading Specialist*, 4: 20–23; December, 1964.

Berry, Althea. "Schools Report to Parents," *The Reading Teacher*, 18: 639–644; May, 1965.

Bond, Guy L., and Eva Bond Wagner. *Teaching the Child to Read*. New York: The Macmillan Co., 1966. Chapter 14.

Dawson, Mildred A., and Henry A. Bamman. *Fundamentals of Basic Reading Instruction*. New York: David McKay Co., Inc., 1963. Chapter 16.

Della-Piana, Gabriel. "Analysis of Oral Reading Errors," *The Reading Teacher*, 15: 254–257; January, 1962.

Dressel, Paul. "The Evaluation of Reading," *The Reading Teacher*, 15: 361–365; March, 1962.

Gray, Lillian. *Teaching Children to Read*. New York: The Ronald Press Company, 1963. Chapter 15.

Harris, Albert J. *How to Increase Reading Ability*. New York: David McKay Co., Inc., 1961. Chapters 7 and 8.

Hester, Kathleen B. *Teaching Every Child to Read*. New York: Harper & Row, Publishers, 1964. Chapters 25 and 26.

McDonald, Arthur S. "Some Pitfalls in Evaluating Progress in Reading Instruction," *Phi Delta Kappan*, 45: 336–338; April, 1964.

McKim, Margaret G., and Helen Caskey. *Guiding Growth in Reading in the Modern Elementary School*. New York: The Macmillan Co., 1963. Chapter 13.

Smith, Nila Banton. *Reading Instruction for Today's Children*. Englewood Cliffs, N.J.: Prentice-Hall, Inc., 1963. Chapter 16.

Spache, George D. *Reading in the Elementary School*. Boston: Allyn and Bacon, Inc., 1964. Chapter 10.

Tinker, Miles A., and Constance M. McCullough. *Teaching Elementary Reading*. New York: Appleton-Century-Crofts, Inc., 1962. Chapter 16.

Witty, Paul A., Alma Moore Freeland, and Edith H. Grotberg. *The Teaching of Reading: A Developmental Process*. Boston: D. C. Heath and Company, 1966. Chapter 17.

❖ *14* *❖*

Reading Disorders

Despite continued advances in materials, methodology, and our knowledge of children, and despite evidence that today's pupils read better than yesterday's, there are still many children who should read better than they do. Since we must admit that our schools are not perfect, we must also admit that some of the causes of reading disabilities are educational in nature.

In fact, many who specialize in methods of teaching reading contend that most of our reading disabilities are caused primarily by ineffective education — by inadequately trained teachers, overcrowded classrooms, a lack of funds to obtain essential reading materials, etc.

The problems of a child who is not reading as well as he should because of *ineffective* teaching can be prevented or cured by *effective* teaching. If his disabilities have become unusually severe, however, it may be necessary to refer him to a remedial-reading teacher, who can give him the kind of prolonged, individualized attention that a regular classroom teacher cannot provide. It is probable, however, that the majority of our disabled readers can be taught to read effectively in regular classrooms by competent teachers when classes are not too large and good materials are available.

What can we do for such students? There are probably as many answers to this question as there are reading specialists, but there are at least two essential steps that can be agreed upon by all. First, we must know the child as thoroughly as possible — his potential ability, his achievement, his specific reading strengths and weaknesses, his interests. Second, on the basis of this information, we must provide interesting reading and skill-development activities at a level at which he can succeed. Chapter 13 has suggested some procedures for implementing the first step. This chapter will present suggestions for the second step.

The first three selections deal with methodological procedures for working in a regular classroom with children whose reading achievement is below their potential. These are the pupils who have no deep-seated mental, emotional, or physical blocks to learning but who can be helped in the regular classroom by perceptive teachers. In the first of these selections, Riva R. Reich notes some characteristics of such children and cites some general principles which must be followed if we are to be successful in teaching them to read.

In the next two articles, a number of specific suggestions are given for working with these pupils. A. Sterl Artley concentrates on finding and treating reading problems as soon as they begin, and Virginia Graff and Shirley Feldman report the kinds of activities which were successful in a club situation for intermediate grade boys. Any of these activities could be easily adapted for use in most classrooms.

Although many believe that the majority of reading-disability cases are primarily the result of inappropriate education and can be alleviated through better instruction, no one contends that all of them fall into this category. There are many possible causes for poor reading that are simply beyond the jurisdiction of the classroom teacher. The last two selections in this chapter deal with a variety of factors.

N. Dale Bryant's article, which merits special attention, may be better understood if we first clarify the reading specialist's distinction between *causes* and *types* of reading disability. Causes are generally the factors which have led to specific reading weaknesses, such as inadequate instruction, emotional immaturity, poor eyesight, and brain damage. Types of reading disabilities generally consist of specific weaknesses in reading, such as poor comprehension, inadequate word memory, and ineffectiveness in word attack. As Dr. Bryant describes dyslexia, then, it would most likely be classified by the reading specialists as a type of difficulty — difficulty in word recognition — rather than a cause of reading disability. Dr. Bryant indicates that a neurological disorder — a causal factor — may be *associated* with dyslexia, but that in *most* cases, this is merely inferred. It is interesting to note the similarities between this article and the articles in Chapter 11 on perception.

In the final selection, Ursula M. Anderson explores a number of factors which may be direct or indirect causes of reading disability. Although these factors must be assessed by a physician, the good teacher should know how they can influence the reading success of his pupils.

More Than Remedial Reading

✤ RIVA R. REICH

Just as there is no "typical" or "normal" third-grader, just as we cannot speak of a typical or normal situation in any phase of classroom or small-group work — so there is no "typical" or "normal" remedial reading "case" or remedial-reading situation. And yet, those of us who have watched how they function, or do not function, in their classrooms, do find that there are certain characteristics or attitudes common to all or to most.

Poor Reader Is Discouraged

A child who comes for remedial help is a discouraged child. He has failed in an area that he can conceal neither from himself nor from his parents, and worst of all, not from his peers. He has failed in an area that, in our culture, has tremendous status-giving power, and the lack of reading, by the same token, results in serious feelings of inadequacy. In our society everybody is expected to know how to read — this is the burden that is carried into the school by every child who enters first grade. You have only to see the apprehensive look in the eyes of first graders — a look that often says, "I'm glad to be in First Grade. I'm going to learn to read." Just as often that look says, "Will I learn to read? Will I be able to please my mother? She expects me to learn to read. What if I fail?" This burden and this fear of failure becomes aggravated as the child grows older, so that our third-grader or fifth-grader who comes to us for help has been carrying this emotional load for years.

A child who comes for remedial help is a frustrated child. He has tried to learn to read; his teacher has tried to teach him; his mother (sometimes also father, grandmother, and the "aunt who teaches") has pressured him and he has not learned. He is bored with the "easy" books. He says he "doesn't like to read," or "hates books" or "school." Many times he feels he's just "dumb" and will never learn, so what's the use?

Poor Reader Is Frustrated

A child who comes for remedial help is a child who has lost his self-respect. He has lost status with his peers, with his parents, and last, but not least, with himself.

It is our job, then, to restore confidence, to build up self-esteem just as much as to teach these children to read. Scars will remain; we cannot remove them. But we can so build the child's acceptance of and belief in himself that he can begin to learn and meet success.

Our first duty is to face the child with his problem, not to minimize it. Thus, to a younger child we might say, "Yes, you have a hard time with reading,

From *Elementary English*, 39: 216–219, 236; March, 1962. Reprinted with the permission of the National Council of Teachers of English and Riva R. Reich, Lecturer and Advisor to Student Teachers, Bank Street College of Education, New York City.

but now that I've heard you read, I can tell what's wrong. It's my job to help children like you and I've been able to help many, many children. I'd like to help you, too."

Or, to an older child we might say, "Yes, you have a reading difficulty, but I think I can help you. I know others have tried, but perhaps you weren't ready to be helped at that time." Often, with a little encouragement and friendly interest, the older child will be able to analyze his own reading problem. "I don't know how to sound out big words," or "I can read and I know all the words, but I don't know what I'm reading." Sometimes a child's own diagnosis is even more revealing: "I can read here for you, but when I read in class in my reading group, I stumble over the words." Enlisting the child's help in verbalizing his problem is often a good beginning. An eighth-grader said, after one session with the remedial-reading teacher, "I never read so well in my life." What he is really saying to us is, "I now have hope. There is someone who cares and wants to help me."

Inform Child of Progress

Informing the child of the diagnosis of his reading difficulty seems to have real value in most cases. Even second-graders seem to gain assurance from knowing that they point with their fingers too much, or do not move smoothly enough from line to line, or do not know their consonant or vowel sounds. This is even truer of older children, who seem to find relief from knowing that they need work on word-attack skills, or that their phrasing is poor, or that syllabication is weak. You almost hear the sigh of relief, as if they were saying to themselves, "Whew! So that's all it is! And I thought there was something wrong with me, that I was stupid, that I was just a failure at reading, and would never learn."

Materials of instruction need to be selected wisely and subtly. Finding the right book is not always easy. Sometimes it seems almost impossible: a book about a veterinarian for a sixth-grade boy who is reading on second-grade level; or a book on nursing for the fifth-grade girl whose reading ability is third grade. Even the First-Book-Of series is too difficult, and some of the I-Want-To-Be series are too juvenile and therefore insulting to the child. Here the teacher's judgment, and, better still, intuition is the best guide. If the child can wait, then a substitute book can be found which the child will accept as "next best" until the "best" turns up. If the need seems urgent, then the teacher and child together can write a book of their own, hunt for pictures together or make their own illustrations. This book may be dictated to the teacher, may be written by the child, bound and decorated and "dedicated," too. For her book on nursing, the fifth-grader interviewed her pediatrician and his nurse and made a visit to the local hospital where she collected pictures, folders, and valuable information.

"What if the child wants a book that is too easy or too hard?" the perplexed teacher often asks. Again, we must try to find out what this choice means to the child. Why does he want a book that is "too hard" or "too easy"? If it seems very important psychologically, then perhaps the "hard book" can be read through quickly with the teacher's help. Here a bargain, an honest legitimate bargain, can be made: "The next book will be one I recommend to you," says the teacher, and the pact is sealed. There should be no feeling of condescension in granting permission to the child to read an "easy" book. It is more honest and realistic, not just comforting to the child to say, "I know how you feel. Once in a while I like to read an easy book" (or relax with a crossword puzzle). Again a bargain between friendly, understanding partners is easily understood and honored, and the next time the child will accept the teacher's suggestion easily and gracefully.

An accepting attitude on the part of the adult breaks down the resistance and creates a good give-and-take relationship. The child becomes more amenable to suggestions and begins to feel that the teacher is working for and with rather than against him. A simple, concrete illustration sometimes helps a child who refuses to face his weakness or inadequacy in reading and persists in choosing work that is beyond him. Elicit from the child an answer to the question: "If you were going to build a house, where would you start?" Depending on the age and experience background of the child, the answers may be "from the ground," "from the bottom," "from the basement," or "first you dig a foundation." Then you ask, "After you have the bottom or basement what would you build?" The answer always is "The first floor." "If you were going to build a tall building, with many floors, could you build the fifth floor after the first one?" The child never fails to see the humor and the impracticability of this suggestion. "It's the same way," the teacher says, "with reading. I cannot start with you from the fifth floor or the sixth floor — we must start with a good foundation and build up. And I'm sure you'll get to the top floor in good time."

Poor Reader Is Easily Bored

The child who comes for remedial help is easily bored and has a short span of attention. To meet this, there must be a variety of materials, a flexibility in approach, and a sensitivity to children's moods. Attractive books (not necessarily those on the "latest list"), games, puzzles, are indispensable. In addition, paper, oak tag, crayons (and what would we do without the Magic Marker?) should be available so that materials for drill can be made by the teacher and/or child which answer an immediate need. One boy worked out an ingenious chart for suffixes and prefixes by backing these with magnets and then matching them to his "base" words on a chart. This chart later was put up in his classroom, and the recognition he received helped greatly in giving him the status he sorely needed.

Over every remedial-reading case hovers an anxious parent. At times this is a kindly, overprotective attitude. More often it is charged with deep feelings of disappointment, failure, and guilt. Whether expressed or not, these feelings come through to the child, and he reacts either with resistance or rebellion and flatly refuses to read and says so; or he resists inwardly and blocks himself so that it looks as if he "just can't read." Parents try to help him but in their anxiety and frustration they become impatient and strike out at the child, wounding him in his most vulnerable area. "Why don't you remember that word? You had it on the other page." Or, "How many times have I told you the difference between *went* and *want?*" Also, "Why do you bring home such baby books? When I was your age, I was reading the classics." Or, worse still, "You have to read with me every day for half an hour, even if it means giving up play or TV."

To help this situation, a close relationship must exist between the parent and the remedial-reading teacher. The parent should be advised about the nature of the difficulty. If possible, the parent should observe so that the attitude, methods, and materials can be explained and demonstrated. Parents must have a role, but they should have a clear conception of what that role is. An arrangement like this has proven effective. Say to the parent, "Yes, methods and materials have changed since your school-days, so why not leave the teaching to us? We are especially trained and prepared. We will look after the phonics, speed, etc. You read with your child and make it a mutually enjoyable experience. If he stumbles or hesitates over a word, tell it to him, and let him go on. Perhaps you can read a page and have your child read one to you." Thus reading becomes a happily shared experience. The parent ceases to be the censor, the child is gradually freed from this feeling of pressure, and both parent and child become more relaxed. In turn, reading is helped.

Cross Grade Lines

Crossing grade lines in planning remedial reading groups has many advantages. It gives an older child an opportunity to help a younger one. For the older child this is often the first time he has been called on to help another child. It is an agreeable change of roles for him. In his own group he was always in the "third" group, the lowest, or among the nameless ones who are not even part of a group. Someone has always been assigned to help him with reading, with arithmetic. Here, for the first time, he is in a position where he can help another. "I feel like a teacher," was the way a sixth-grader articulated his obvious pleasure. Perry, a fifth-grader, asks if he can listen to Elliot, who is very anxious to finish *Something New at the Zoo*. The teacher, who is busy with someone else, nods assent. About ten minutes later both boys run over and announce proudly (together), "He's finished the book!" "I've finished the book!" Both boys have accomplished something. "Can I help him find another book?" asks Perry, for whom this is an entirely new experience. After some deliberation and selection, Perry is heard to advise, "Elliot, take *Nobody Listens to Andrew*. Is it ever funny! It's about this boy who says there's a — no, I won't tell you any more, because I'll give away the whole story." We have no way of measuring quantitatively the positive effects these situations have on our Perrys and Elliots, but the change in attitude towards work and self are sufficient proof.

Teacher Cooperation Necessary

A close relationship must exist, too, between the remedial teacher and the classroom teacher. It is important sometimes for the remedial teacher to watch the child in his classroom. It can also benefit the classroom teacher to see how he functions in the remedial situation. The classroom teacher can be helpful by supplying information about background and general behavior, relationship to peers; the remedial-reading teacher is often in a better position to contribute personal, intimate remarks and attitudes which the small group or one-to-one relationship can foster. When there is mutual understanding and trust, the remedial-reading person can offer suggestions as to materials, procedures, and so on. A classroom teacher with twenty-five or thirty children, with a reading range of five years or more, beset with all kinds of problems, plus extra duties such as collecting Red Cross money and putting on a play for Christmas and participating on a panel for PTA — cannot always find the time to help a child who does not fit in any group.

"I have never written a book report," confides the sixth-grader to the remedial-reading teacher. "My class is studying the American Revolutionary period," announces a fifth-grader, "but I can't make a report because all the books are too hard." In the first case, it was easier for the remedial-reading teacher to help this boy find the right book and help him write a book report — a small accomplishment, perhaps, but a step towards making the boy feel a part of the group. In the second case, the remedial-reading teacher helped the classroom teacher find some books relating to that period in American history on the first and second reading level, so that all the children could participate and contribute something. When there is easy, trustful communication between all the parties concerned, these things will happen. But before they can happen, the child, the remedial-reading teacher, the classroom teacher, the parent must be able to speak to each other.

Last, but not least, the child must be able to observe his own progress. Assurance from the teacher that he "is reading better" is necessary, but not enough. The child who has met failure over a long period is not convinced. He'd like to believe it, but he's not sure. He needs concrete proof, proof in terms that he can see and measure. Playing a recording of the child's reading made early in the year and comparing it with a later recording; comparing a "before-and-after" score of the same type of reading test — these are concrete proof. Plotting a day-by-day graph of reading speed or reading success; keeping a list of words "I Do Not Know" and seeing them checked off; using short, timed paragraphs — these proofs the child can follow, analyze, and evaluate himself.

Younger children, for example, seem to thrive on this simple, word-learning device: Any word that is missed during the reading session is written on a small piece of paper (2 x 4). If the child knows the word at the next session, the teacher or the child puts a small star in pencil on the corner of the paper. If the child knows the word at the second session, he gets another star. On the third day, if he knows the word (that insures repetition) he may throw it in the basket. It is both revealing and amusing to watch the variety of ways in which this paper goes to its last resting place. Some crumple it fiercely, some first tear it to bits almost with venom, others hurl it with great passion into the waste-basket. A picturesque name was given to this whole operation by a third-grader who came back after summer vacation and said, "Why don't we play that good game where you can throw words in the garbage?"

In summing up what "more than remedial reading" implies, perhaps the best that can be said was uttered by Gerhart, a fourth-grade boy who, after a year of remedial reading, poked his head in the door and said, "I'm not coming here any more. I don't need you any more. Thank you!" That was indeed a compliment!

Classroom Help for Children With Beginning Reading Problems

✤ A. STERL ARTLEY

For the sake of our discussion in this paper, we are placing children and youth with reading handicaps in categories, depending on the nature and complexity of their problems.

In the first group are those whose reading problem is only one of a constellation of problems. Usually it is deep-seated, multi-causal, and multi-faceted. Related problems may be neurological, physical, sensory, social, or emotional. Where facilities are available it is not uncommon for several specialists to become involved in both the diagnosis and remediation of the problem. Fortunately, in terms of the total number of retarded readers, the number of children in this group is relatively small.

A somewhat larger group is made up of children whose reading problem, though of varying degrees of severity, is unencumbered with the related problems found in the first classification, or at least stands out as the primary problem. Frequently these are children whose individual instructional needs have been unmet over a prolonged period. Not only has reading growth been at a virtual standstill, but family pressures and the effects of frustration have added complications. These children may be referred to a reading center or to a specially trained reading teacher for diagnosis. Remediation may be carried out in special classes or in summer remedial programs where the services of a specially trained remedial teacher are required.

Reading Difficulties Begin

A third group, a still larger one, is made up of children in the regular classroom who, in terms of specific skill areas, are failing to achieve as well as they should. These are children whose problem is just beginning and who will find themselves eventually in the second group which we have just described unless their needs are met through a planned program of instruction. These children and their problems are the responsibility of the regular classroom teacher. It is this group with whom we shall be concerned in this paper.

For the sake of clarification, let us describe a few of the children comprising this group. Tom has completed his first-grade readiness program but still shows limited ability to detect rhyming words and to indicate other words beginning with a given sound. Helen has been absent from school for a week with an illness and has missed the sequential instruction on several important reading skills. Mark fails to "catch on" to the application of an essential word-attack skill. Jane has a persistent confusion between four groups of similar words.

From *The Reading Teacher*, 15: 439–442; May, 1965. Reprinted with permission of A. Sterl Artley and the International Reading Association. A. Sterl Artley is Professor of Education, University of Missouri, Columbia.

Pat runs roughshod over material he is reading orally, getting the meaning through context rather than through accurate recognition of words. Marie's oral reading is accurate, but her voice is high-pitched and she gives little thought to the interpretation of the story. Cathy is a fifth-grade transfer pupil who is unable to use the dictionary to get the meaning or pronunciation of words.

One will observe that each child has a particular reading need — we can hardly call it a problem — which on the surface appears quite innocuous, or at the most only annoying. However, these innocuous difficulties have a way of combining and snowballing until we have a major problem which may require specialized services for both diagnosis and remediation. From our clinical experience we have found that the majority of cases referred for diagnosis are not those caused by some obscure emotional problem, an uncorrected visual defect, or an involved neurological problem. Basically, they are an accumulation of unmet reading needs.

Detecting Beginning Problems

To detect and diagnose these incipient problems is one of the primary responsibilities of the teacher. It is at this point that the prevention of major difficulties begins. She must be on constant watch for the child whose reading performance is alerting her to a possible problem.

One of the situations that lends itself to an assessment of needs is the directed reading lesson itself. In fact, every reading lesson should be a diagnostic lesson. It is here that the teacher may observe the application of skills that have been taught. Inability to recognize certain high-frequency words, to read for meaning, to use a familiar sight word to unlock an unknown one, to interpret implied ideas, or to apply a principle of syllabication are symptomatic of a lack of understanding or skill mastery. Both silent and oral reading situations will give the teacher clues to areas where instruction should be modified or adapted to particular children in the group.

Possibly one of the best diagnostic devices that the teacher has available is the practice or workbook. One of the functions of the workbook is to give the child opportunity to practice independently a particular learning or skill that has been taught in the directed reading lesson. Consequently, it will give the teacher an idea as to how effective that instruction has been and the kinds of additional help that a given child may need. If, on a fifteen-item page dealing with the short sounds of vowel letters, a child shows a preponderance of errors, the evidence is quite clear that additional teaching and practice are in order.

If the workbook is to be used to its maximum advantage, every page should be checked by the teacher or by a pupil-helper. If by a teacher, she may give needed reteaching help as the pages are being checked. If a pupil-helper checks the pages from a key supplied by the teacher, only those items indicating incorrect responses need to be marked, so that in a free moment the teacher may note pupils who need more help.

The "unit" tests supplied by the publisher of the reading series are designed chiefly as diagnostic instruments. They give an objective measure of each child's readiness for the succeeding level and indicate areas where special guidance is needed. Administering and interpreting the test as recommended by its authors will give an indication regarding the effectiveness of the basic instruction and the adequacy of the day-by-day corrective help.

The personal reading record of each child may also be a means of indicating areas where special guidance is needed. Through individual and group discussions with the children the teacher will be able to get answers to questions such as these: What is the quality of the content being selected for personal reading? Has the child made the discovery that books and magazines are a source of information and pleasure? What is the quality of insight into the motives and behavior of story characters? What types of reactions does he freely make? What is the level of comprehension for main ideas and supporting details? Is the child being frustrated by persistent errors of word attack?

Providing Special Help

Assuming that the teacher is able to identify the specific problem, what action follows? With problems of the type we have been discussing the child seldom needs more than additional teaching or reteaching, directed specifically to the problem at hand. Tom, the boy who needed more work in ear training before introducing the sounds of initial consonants, can profit from activities similar to those that have been suggested in the guidebook of the readiness program. Jane, who was confusing groups of words, needs to be shown in one group at a time the features that differentiate one word from the other. This should be followed by practice sentences where the context calls for careful choices between the confused words.

Seldom will it be necessary to use reteaching techniques requiring special training. Excellent suggestions for reteaching and practice will be found in the teacher's manual. In addition, teaching activities and suggestions of materials that may be constructed for practice purposes may be found in such sources as Russell and Karp's *Reading Aids Through the Grades;* Durrell's *Improving Reading Instruction;* and Harris' *How to Increase Reading Ability.*

Pages from workbooks of other series dealing with the skill on which one is working may be used to good advantage in particular instances. If the problem is one of word attack, selected pages from prepared workbooks such as Meighan, Pratt, and Halvorsen's *Phonics We Use* may be useful. Frequently the guidebook to the reading series will suggest activities to be used with children with special needs.

Organizing Special Help Groups

The question of organizing the class or group for additional help is one to be considered. Time is precious to any teacher and she seems never to have enough to do all the things that need to be done. Yet this is not the problem that it appears to be if one organizes special "help" groups made up of those children who require more help. In fact, the meeting of individual needs through "help" groups will provide the opportunity for the teacher to do some of her most effective and rewarding teaching. These groups are made up of the children who evidence the same need; they are designed only with one specific problem, and as soon as that problem is resolved the need for the group no longer exists. Hence, it is temporary in nature.

To be more specific, let us assume that in the directed-reading lesson we find two children who need reteaching and additional practice in attacking words where the vowel-digraph principle applies. These two children might be called aside for help at a time during the day when the other children are engaged in independent work. Quite possibly one, or at the most several, short sessions are all that will be necessary to help these children over their hurdle.

In many cases the teacher may find that the problem is one that the children may work on together without her direct supervision. For example, several of the children may be having trouble recalling certain sight words. After each child identifies those particular ones that give him trouble, either he or the teacher should write or type the words on halves of 3x5 index cards. Meeting in pairs, each child "flashes" to the other his trouble words.

In cases where a problem is more persistent, the teacher may need to keep a special group intact over a longer period of time. This may be the case where several children have been absent or where transfers show the need for the development of a particular ability.

Summary

A high percentage of the reading problems that one finds in a typical classroom are the result of the failure of instruction to provide adequately for individual needs. Unless these problems are identified early and individual or small-group help provided, many of these children will experience serious retardation. The time to care most effectively for these cases is when the problem first appears, rather than later when special services may be required for diagnosis and remediation.

Boys' Club for Middle Readers

❧ Virginia Graff and Shirley Feldmann

We hear much about the troubles that sometimes beset the middle child in the family. In our work in remedial reading we see many boys and girls who are middle pupils in reading achievement and in remediation.

In large-city school systems where many children come from underprivileged homes, reading retardation is generally recognized as a serious problem. The children often bring to their school life a background characterized by impoverished environment and, especially, by language and communication deficiencies. This type of background can jeopardize children's prospects for achievement in reading. When children lack the basic tool of reading, the ground is prepared for continuing cycles of frustration and failure, and sometimes for delinquency.

To help children in reading, two courses of action have been taken by the Institute for Developmental Studies at the New York Medical College. One course is preventive, one remedial.

Early enrichment programs for very young children are coming to be viewed as the single most important and most economical preventive measure. Specific remediation is the second approach. But the number of children in need of this kind of help is unfortunately far greater than the number for whom it can be obtained.

The possibility of a third — a middle — approach has recently been explored by the staff of the Reading Center of the Institute. We noted that many of the children not usually included in remedial programs had reading troubles that were only a little less acute than those of some of the children referred for treatment. The children who were not in remedial programs were not able to make full use of school instruction because they did not have the necessary background, especially in language and communication. We reasoned that a program which succeeded in helping these children even moderately might be a step toward better individual adjustment and social economy.

We decided to try out a boys' club with a program centered on reading. Of the measures we considered, this plan seemed most likely to provide timely and economical assistance. The club might also point up directions that enrich-

From *The Elementary School Journal*, 64: 131–136; December, 1963. Reprinted from "Boys' Club for Middle Readers," in *The Elementary School Journal* by Virginia Graff and Shirley Feldmann by permission of The University of Chicago Press. Copyright © 1963 by The University of Chicago. Virginia Graff is Remedial Clinician and Reading Therapist, Children's Aid Society, New York Infirmary Reading Clinic, New York City, and Shirley Feldmann is Assistant Professor of Education, The City College of the City University of New York. The project reported here was carried on as one aspect of the work of the Institute for Developmental Studies, Department of Psychiatry, New York Medical College, where reading disabilities of underprivileged children are being studied and treated. The data reported were collected as part of a program on "Verbal Enrichment and Social Achievement in Lower Socio-Economic Groups," which is supported in part by a grant from the Taconic Foundation.

ment and preventive procedures for children above the primary level might eventually take.

Spontaneous inquiries from interested adults in the neighborhood suggested that there was a need for extending our services. One child who had heard about the reading program dropped in at regular intervals to assure us that he wanted to "belong to the club." Welcoming this interest, we carried out our plan to form a boys' club to explore the possibilities offered by small groups oriented toward reading (1).

We decided that the emphasis in the club groups would be different from the emphasis in our tutoring groups. Children in the tutoring groups were usually reading on a level somewhat lower than the children in the club were. The more severely affected children required specific and intensive methods of treatment. In tutoring, therefore, we provided as much individual and supportive attention as possible.

But through the club program, we felt it might be possible, in a group situation, with moderate expenditure of time and effort, to improve the boys' attitudes toward learning and toward the whole academic process.

Plans for club activities were shaped by limitations of space and staff, and by our conviction that it would be wise to proceed cautiously in this new venture. We decided to begin with twelve to fifteen boys, expecting that this group would settle down to a core of about eight boys who would come fairly regularly. Our guess proved accurate.

Members were selected from applicants recommended by the public schools of the area. The boys, like those in tutored groups, were fourth-, fifth-, and sixth-graders, from nine to eleven years of age. Boys and their mothers were interviewed before admission, but neither a specific level of reading performance nor formal test scores were used as a condition of admission.

As we have noted, the reading level of the club group — as indicated by school reports, testing, and staff observation — was higher than the reading level of the tutored groups seen at the institute. Yet most club members were boys whose school performance was no more than passable. Like the retarded readers, members came from homes and schools in underprivileged neighborhoods; they were markedly deficient in cultural background, in experience, and in communication skills. Some of the boys came from homes where little or no English was spoken.

The goals set for the boys' club were modest. If membership came to be regarded as a privilege, the club could provide an atmosphere different from that of home or school, but conducive to bridging the two. It was agreed, therefore, that the club should not resemble or duplicate school experience. We planned to use interesting activities based on reading to challenge the boys and to narrow the formidable gap between their achievement and school expectations.

Staff for the undertaking was drawn from the reading tutors. One able volunteer also gave us a good deal of assistance. Two adults were regularly in charge of meetings, which were held once a week, from 3:15 P.M. to 4:45 P.M., from November through May. In keeping with the atmosphere that we wished to prevail, the adults did not take a narrowly instructional role, but one that combined the roles of friend and teacher.

Serious thought was given to dividing club time in a way that would be most likely to effect the ends in view. At first we decided to divide the session into two parts, one devoted to activities for individuals or small groups of children and the other to projects involving the whole group. Actually, in the early phase of the club's existence the program for the whole group was the more popular; later the individual or small-group activities were preferred. But both programs were continued throughout the year.

Through the individual activities, we hoped to open up new areas of interest and ability, to increase concentration span, and to establish an inclination to work on one project for a reasonable length of time. We had observed that children often flitted restlessly from task to task, not staying with any activity long enough to give it shape and meaning. Because the children could not devote themselves to a task, they lost out on a sense of accomplishment.

We noted a lack of consistent application when the children worked alone. We also felt that form and structure needed emphasis in the co-operative efforts. The boys' past experiences at home, on the street, and in school had certainly included many group activities. But we surmised that these experiences had too frequently been dictated by expedience. Group efforts might often — and unavoidably — have been geared to adult convenience rather than to children's best learning interests. So it appeared wise to stress communication skills and their social implications in such loosely structured learning situations as the club could foster.

Some of the activities we tried lent themselves readily to individual participation, while others were more advantageously used with the whole group. Some activities enjoyed steady popularity throughout many sessions; others were doomed to prompt and unlamented obsolescence.

Staff members were in for many surprises at the reception children gave certain projects. We expected that the boys would enjoy plays and puppets. But these activities, along with writing stories, got a cool reception. An adapted quiz program, which we thought might be too academic for their taste, was successful. We came to the tentative conclusion that the boys were uneasy with demands for the kind of creativity required in story- and play-writing. But the competition of a quiz program tailored to their capacities was an exciting challenge.

The easy give and take of conversation seemed to have much appeal for them. Talk was always an important feature of the sessions, especially during the period devoted to activities for the whole group.

The discussions grew out of various sources: reading materials and projects, experiences of everyday life at home and in school, and current happenings. Just before historic birthdays a spirited discussion could be set off simply by asking, "Who can tell us one thing about the life of ———?" Facts — and sometimes mis-facts — piled up.

Space and space explorations were favorite topics. One lively discussion got under way through a reference to a flying horse. From this subject the boys promptly took off to dragons and mermaids. Sometimes staff members could give a discussion a boost by asking about a television program or characters in comics. The quality of the talk varied a good deal, even with continuous effort to channel it into useful directions.

At the end of the year one boy said that he had liked "just the talk" best of all. His comment was one indication of the need the discussions satisfied.

In accordance with our aim of developing abilities in self-expression, large blocks of time were assigned to activities concerned with extending the children's awareness of words and usage. The staff devised many simple procedures and games. In one game the children guessed the opposites of given words — *large, full, dark.* In another game the boys were asked for synonyms of given words — *pretty, quick, happy.*

One popular guessing game we dubbed "Categories — Which One Doesn't Belong?" The adult might say: "Orange, apple, milk, plum"; or "Pen, magazine, book, newspaper." This word play sometimes led to talk to determine how well the child could support his choice.

A quiz called "Definitions" was popular. Here are several definitions we used: "Who knows what we call the stairs you ride to go up and down in a big building? The instrument that shows whether you have a fever? The thing you look at to see what day of the week the Fourth of July comes on?"

Riddles were always popular and good for promoting conversation. Here is one favorite: "What is the biggest jewel in the world?" Answer: "A baseball diamond." After the response was guessed or supplied, the adult would ask: "What word makes the riddle? Why?" When the children had finished working over this question, the talk could be guided to bring out meanings of the word *diamond.*

Proverbs, folk sayings, and similes came in for attention. One day we used a color theme, drawing out as many spontaneous contributions as possible, then supplementing them and elaborating on them. The expressions included: "brown as a berry," "in a black mood," "was his face red?" Or the talk might center on meanings of sayings concerned with parts of the body: "pain in the neck," "sticks out like a sore thumb." Or we might use insects or animals as a theme: "snug as a bug in a rug," "bold as a lion."

The boys were asked: "What do you mean when you say 'quick as a wink'? Why? Can you say this same thing in other words?" "What is a 'fly in the ointment'?" "How do you feel when you 'walk on air'?" "Did you ever hear of 'splitting hairs'? What are you doing when you split a hair?" "How slow is molasses in winter? Why molasses?"

"Scrambled Words" was another activity the boys liked. The letters were written on cards four inches by six inches. The words varied in difficulty. There were easy words like *c l p a (clap), a h n d (hand), l e s p l (spell)*; and harder ones like *y h i l a d o (holiday), h o l o s c (school).* It amused the adults to note how often average or poor readers came up with the right answer for such favorite "core-vocabulary" words as *c o t a l h o c e (chocolate)* and *v e i s n t o e l i (television).*

Definitions and scrambled letters were sometimes combined. The card might read:

> This means go fast. *r h r y u*
> This is something you use when you eat. *n o p o s*

"Scrambled Words" afforded some opportunity for incidental reading instruction. Double vowels, double consonants, and blends could be treated as units or could be separated. The discussion leader could point out such clues as the possibility that two identical consonants, separated by other letters, might belong together.

During the individual-activities part of a typical meeting, the Reading Room might look something like this: David and Carlo are competing fiercely at checkers. Our lone wolf Milton is poring over a comic book. Roberto is hunched at the typewriter over a homework assignment. Philip and José are laboriously putting the big United States puzzle together. Roger is agitating for someone to provide him with more Roman numerals so that he can get on with his practice of this newly learned skill.

Obviously the two adults present were kept hopping. But since all the children never needed attention at the same time, they could usually manage by circulating among the members. Milton, our reader of comics, might decline any offer of help and indicate that he wanted to get on without interruption. (But on another day Milton might ask for the tutor's help in figuring out a word.) If Roberto seemed to be battling with the typewriter, the adult might point out a typing gimmick or two; and her help with the assignment might be welcomed. If Philip and José bogged down over a particular section of the United States puzzle, the tutor might help them locate the elusive piece and, if the opportunity seemed favorable, call attention to a geographical fact — for instance that the part they were inserting was one of the southwestern states.

How useful was the program? This was the question the Institute Reading staff asked at the end of May. We feel that programs of enrichment that provide early and specific help are the best approach for young children who lack a background for reading. For limited numbers of older children specific remediation of deficiencies meets a need.

But between these two approaches another territory stretches — extensive and, for the most part, empty. Modest reading-club programs could be a third, a "middle," treatment, another kind of enrichment to meet the needs of many older children. These programs could stress not reading instruction specifically, but many aspects of communication and language-arts skills. One or two hour-long sessions a week over the school year or in summer might serve these children well. Such programs could be independently organized, or they could be an adjunct to school programs. They could be organized within already existing and more comprehensive programs set up by libraries, churches, camps, community houses.

The need for specialized personnel is not a prime consideration. If a modest quota of supervision could be assured, intelligent and interested, though unskilled, persons could be used to advantage. Some of the criteria for screening, as well as some of the generalizations and procedures outlined earlier, might prove useful in setting up other ventures of this sort.

Our brief experience with the club showed that it was a constructive project for the boys and useful to the staff as a pilot to explore the possibilities of such undertakings. We feel that the club demonstrated a place and a function for similar groups.

This assumption was recently confirmed by the sudden appearance of one of the club members in our Reading Room about 3:30 one afternoon long after the club's demise. We talked for a few minutes, and then he volunteered the information that he missed the meetings: "On Monday afternoons after school I turn down this street before I remember," he finished wistfully.

Characteristics of Dyslexia and Their Remedial Implications

✣ N. DALE BRYANT

Remedial procedures for dyslexia are implicit in the general characteristics of the reading disability as those characteristics are revealed through diagnostic measurements, including errors made in reading and difficulty in accomplishing certain simple learning. Dyslexia is not a simple entity since there is considerable variability in degree and nature of the impairment. However, much of this variability arises from associated and secondary factors, and there are certain common characteristics that form the core of the disability. This paper will attempt to outline some of these characteristics and point out a few remedial cues to be gained from them.

Dyslexia must be differentiated from other reading difficulties, such as problems of reading comprehension, lack of adequate reading instruction, attentional problems, or "emotional blocking," even though in some cases these may also be present, thus complicating the symptom picture. Dyslexia is concerned with word recognition, and the term "word-blindness" used by some neurologists to popularly identify the dysfunctioning is descriptive of the extreme difficulty in learning to recognize words. The term *dyslexia* implies a neurological dysfunctioning if only because of its similarity to the neurological condition alexia, which represents a loss of ability to read resulting from damage to the association areas and connections in and around the angular gyrus of the dominant cerebral hemisphere. However, while alexia is a traumatic disruption of existing skills and memories, dyslexia represents a developmental inefficiency in functioning that handicaps learning. Certainly, in some cases, damage, prenatal complications, or genetic factors have been causally associated with dyslexia. In most cases, however, a neurological disorder is merely inferred from the nature of the dysfunctioning and associated symptoms. In many cases, it is also apparent that emotional and educational factors are contributing to the learning problems of the child, regardless of whether or not neurological factors are primary.

Associated Characteristics

Dyslexia first becomes evident as a child reaches kindergarten and first grade, though it is often not recognized until much later and, indeed, is frequently never recognized for what it is.

The child is usually a boy although the reason for this is not unquestionably established. Explanations include: (a) greater vulnerability of males to prenatal and other sources of brain damage; (b) sex-linked or sex-influenced

From *Exceptional Children*, 31: 195–199; December, 1965. Reprinted by permission. N. Dale Bryant is Executive Director, Study Center for Learning Disabilities, State University of New York, Albany.

genetic factors; (c) slower maturation of males; (d) different social expectations and activity levels for males. It is probable that, at least in some cases, each of these factors contributes individually or in combination to the higher frequency of dyslexia in males.

Dyslexia is not a broad defect in general intelligence; I.Q.s tend to be in the normal range and occasionally reflect very superior ability. However, certain indices of intellectual performance are usually found to be relatively low, e.g., the Coding subtest of the Wechsler Intelligence Scale for Children.

Primary Characteristics

While the primary symptoms are not apparent until school age, many associated symptoms occur with much greater frequency than in the normal population. Usually associated with reading difficulties is confusion when quickly identifying left or right. There is a good chance that the dyslexic boy has some confusion about months, seasons, and judgment of time, direction, distance, and size. On a test of motor development and coordination, he is likely to score low, frequently below the norms for his age. He is much more likely than a normal child to have had speech difficulties and some difficulties may still remain. Similarly, he may have poor auditory discrimination in spite of his adequate auditory acuity. He is more likely than the normal child to have male relatives with similar difficulties in learning to read, and he is also more likely to have been premature or to have survived some complication of pregnancy. The dyslexic child will probably not show gross defects on a neurological examination and will not necessarily appear immature on pediatric examination, although both of these conditions are not infrequent. As in all cases of children with difficulties, he is likely to feel inadequate, stupid, and guilty because of his disability and his repeated failures.

With the exposure to reading instruction, the primary characteristics of the disability become apparent. In spite of learning to recognize some words, he has extreme difficulty in associating the sounds with the visual symbols of letters. This disability is apparent in the confusion of letter sounds, particularly the vowels which have several interfering sounds. Even in the simplest situation of remedial instruction, the stability of sound association in word recognition is many times more difficult to establish than for the normal child. In the classroom situation, children are expected to abstract the common sound elements associated with letters when words containing different letters and sounds are presented. For the dyslexic child this compounds the associational problems. Either because of interference between the various associational pairs or because of a defect in the ability to abstract in this area, the dyslexic child has great difficulty in learning sound associations as they are commonly taught in the classroom. This is a key point in designing remedial instruction for dyslexia. Remediation is almost doomed to failure if it merely repeats the classroom procedure requiring the child to abstract and associate common visual and sound elements when several associations are to be learned at once.

A second primary characteristic of the dyslexic reader is his tendency to ignore the details within words and, instead, to base word recognition on initial letter, length of word, and a few other insufficient cues. This is not due to a simple defect in visual discrimination since adequate discrimination can be made when two words are presented together; rather, the defect comes in the utilization of memory of word shape wherein the details and sequences of letters within the word are often undifferentiated. Thus, a dyslexic boy is likely to accept the word *postal* and even, in an extreme case, a letter combination such as *peistad* as being the word *pasted*. No other memory difficulties may be apparent though the inadequacies of most memory batteries make this very hard to determine. Lack of sound association may contribute to the dyslexic's inadequate use of details in word recognition since sound association helps identify and sequence a perception of separate letters within a word. However, the converse may also be true and poor differentiation of details in the visual memory of words may contribute to the difficulty in learning to associate sounds with the letters in those visual memory images. It is evident that classroom or remedial procedures which do not focus attention on the details within words are unlikely to overcome this disability.

A third primary characteristic is a spatial confusion most obvious in the child's inability to consistently differentiate between reverse images such as letter pairs like *b* and *d*. Sometimes, up and down reversals add *p* to the *b-d* confusion. Since this confusion of reversed images is often associated with confusion of the child's own left and right and, because proper differentiation depends entirely upon subjective cues, not merely greater discrimination of shape variations, this is one of the confusions most resistant to remediation. Since the subjective cues of left and right are based upon kinesthetic experience, remedial procedures need to use kinesthetic factors.

These three primary characteristics are probably manifestations of basic defects in neurological functioning. However, for purposes of describing the consistent symptoms of dyslexia, these characteristics may be adequate even if not all-inclusive. These same characteristics are normally seen in children just beginning to read but they are rapidly overcome without special help. The dyslexic child persists in these characteristics as he grows older. It is as if dyslexia represents a massive unreadiness for reading. The maturational process that, in conjunction with experience, produces reading readiness in beginning readers seems to lag for dyslexic youngsters even though there is some slow improvement apparent as the child grows older. Improvement with age in a dyslexic boy who had not been helped by years of remediation may reflect maturation. However, in addition, it may also reflect the fact that remedial procedures often confuse and obscure the very learning they are attempting to bring about. As he grows older, a child with moderate dyslexia may develop considerable reading ability, even though he is still far behind his age-mates. His recognition of familiar words increases, but his errors in reading are likely to reflect the same characteristics described. While his reading may be at fourth-grade level, most of his errors are likely to be simple ones, more typical of the reading performance of a child reading at first- or second-grade level. Simple words are correctly identified in one sentence and incorrectly recognized in a later one because of poor differentiation of details within the words. Vowel sounds are inconsistent if the word is the least bit unfamiliar, and reversals of letters (and sometimes words or word parts) are still frequent.

Remedial Implications

First of all, it is essential to understand that the dyslexic child's inability to abstract when several associations are presented together makes it necessary to simplify tasks that he is asked to perform so that only one new discrimination or association is made at a time. Furthermore, this discrimination or association must be made repeatedly until it is automatic for the child. Thus, if a child confuses the letters *m* and *n*, he needs to differentiate them alone. Once this is done, differentiation should be made in words where no other discriminations or associations are required, e.g., when he knows that one of the two words shown him will be *map* or *nap, man* or *tan.* Correct differentiation of perhaps a dozen trials for each pair of words would prepare the child for correct differentiation of *m* and *n* in pairs and then groups of words of gradually increasing complexity until the child is recognizing the *m* and *n* in words he knows but doesn't expect to be presented. In this way, a dyslexic child may learn to discriminate *m* and *n* in a matter of fifteen minutes and may never have trouble with that discrimination again. The same child might go for years having his *m* and *n* errors pointed out to him without learning to correctly and consistently differentiate between them because there were too many other discriminations and associations that he was attending to at the same time.

Similarly, the dyslexic child will probably never learn vowel sounds when they are thrown at him all together. However, practice with a single vowel and a single sound for that vowel (preferably the more common short sound) when no other discriminations or associations are required is likely to establish an association that will become automatic. Later, when another vowel or another sound for the previously learned vowel is introduced, the automatic association is likely to be retained without either interfering with the new learning or causing a loss of established association.

Thus, an essential procedure in remedial instruction for dyslexia is to simplify a confusing task to a single discrimination or association that can be correctly made by the child and then to practice it in recognition tasks of increasing complexity until it is well established as an automatic response. In this manner, the dyslexic's inability to abstract from a complex situation can be circumvented. Identifying letter-sound associations that the child confuses and working in the manner described helps overcome the difficulties in associating symbols and sounds.

There are several procedures suggested by the primary characteristic of ignoring details within words. Obviously, the child's attention needs to be called to the details. The usual teaching by the "whole-word method," which is adequate for the normal child who will attend to details on his own, is not adequate for the dyslexic child. Writing a word is useful, not only because of kinesthetic feed-back, but because each letter must be remembered and reproduced even when the child has to look at a copy of the word immediately before he writes it. If he cannot write it, tracing it and copying it can prepare him for writing it. Filling in missing letters in a word is another way of forcing attention to the details and, perhaps, sharpening the visual memory image. Regardless of the procedure used to call attention to the details of each word learned, once the word is learned, it should be differentiated from other words with which it is likely to be confused. For example, if a child learns the word *then,* he should practice differentiating it from *thin, there, their, than,* etc., even though he may not be able to identify the other words except that they are not *then,* which he has just learned. This child, dyslexic though he may be, is unlikely to confuse these words later but without such discrimination practice, he would be almost certain to confuse some of them.

Confusion of reversed images as in *b* and *d* particularly needs to be approached in as simple a task as possible because of the great difficulty in overcoming this confusion. If the child is also confused about his own left and right, this should be worked on, perhaps by using a ring, watch, or bracelet on the dominant hand and by providing kinesthetic practice for the dominant side. An important procedure in kinesthetic practice is writing or tracing one of the confused letters. Each day a large letter (e.g., *b*) should be traced and "words" such as *bab* pronounced as it is traced. (A tracing poster on the door of the child's room at home can encourage frequent practice.) The letter should be traced or copied in various sizes on blackboard, paper, and in the air. Variations of this practice should proceed until the child can differentiate *b* from *d* when the letters are presented alone. Subsequently the same procedures can be followed that are described above for overcoming confusion between *m* and *n;* that is, from *b* and *d,* presented alone, a child can go on to practice with pages of words like *dog* and *hog.* These more complex words should be gradually introduced, with the child tracing each of the *b*'s on a page and saying the word. As he establishes correct differentiation of the letter *b,* he can begin to trace the letter *d,* always saying words containing that letter. The steps in increasing the complexity of the task should be so small that he is never allowed to make a mistake because a few errors can disrupt a great deal of previous learning and re-institute confusion. Thus, the characteristic of letter reversals suggests a procedure for using kinesthetic practice and discriminating tasks of gradually increasing difficulty. Experience suggests short practice periods separate from other remedial work, very gradual steps when increasing difficulty, and massive distributed practice.

Summary

Dyslexia is a complex syndrome with considerable variability in degree of reading disability and nature of associated characteristics. Secondary factors, as well as emotional and educational factors, increase the apparent complexity of the disorder. However, there are at least three characteristics that are so consistent as to be considered primary to the disability. These are: (a) difficulty in simple learning of associations between letter symbols and letter sounds (particularly multisound vowels). This difficulty is related to trouble in abstracting common elements from complex experiences; (b) use of insufficient word recognition cues by attending primarily to initial letter, length, and general shape while tending to ignore cues of details within words; (c) confusion of left-right reversals in letters of similar shape (e.g., *b* and *d*).

These primary characteristics suggest procedures that might help overcome the disability. Each discrimination or association problem that causes repeated errors in material even below the child's reading level should be worked with by itself until the difficulty is overcome. The simplest and most basic discriminations or associations should be established first. Each new word should be taught by some procedure involving writing the word or filling in missing letters so that attention is directed to details within the word. In addition, it is essential to provide discrimination training between each new word and words of similar shape. Confusion in left and right reversals of letters requires distributed kinesthetic practice and discrimination training with materials of gradually increasing difficulty. No other discriminations should be required during the practice in discriminating left-right reversals. In contrast with the standard, but relatively ineffectual, remedial procedure (of having a dyslexic child read "at his level" with correction of errors), the above procedures consistently work to improve the dyslexic's reading ability because they help overcome disability characteristics.

References

Bryant, N. D. "Reading Disability: Part of a Syndrome of Neurological Dysfunctioning," in J. A. Figurel (ed.), *Challenge and Experiment in Reading,* 1962 Yearbook of the International Reading Association. New York: Scholastic Magazine Press, 1962. Pp. 7, 139–143.

————. "Learning Disabilities in Reading," in J. A. Figurel (ed.), *Reading as an Intellectual Activity,* 1963 Yearbook of the International Reading Association. New York: Scholastic Magazine Press, 1963. Pp. 8, 142–146.

————. "Some Principles for Remedial Instruction for Dyslexia," *Reading Teacher.* (In press [at the time this article was first published].)

Hermann, K. *Reading Disability.* Springfield, Ill.: Charles C Thomas, 1959.

Money, J. (ed.). *Reading Disability.* Baltimore: Johns Hopkins Press, 1962.

Pasamanick, B., and H. Knobloch. "Epidemiologic Studies on the Complications of Pregnancies and the Birth Process," in G. Kaplan (ed.), *Prevention of Mental Disorders in Children.* New York: Basic Books, 1961. Pp. 74–94.

Rabinovitch, R. "Reading and Learning Disabilities," in Sylvano Arieti (ed.), *American Handbook of Psychiatry.* New York: Basic Books, 1959. Pp. 857–869.

Reading Disability: What Should the School Physician Look for in Determining Its Causation?

❖ Ursula M. Anderson

In our society, the acquisition of knowledge depends to a tremendous degree on the ability of the individual to read. However humble the individual's niche may be, society demands for his gainful employment a modicum of knowledge, and this in turn depends to a great extent on the ability to read and write. Any condition, therefore, that interferes with the ability to read, seriously handicaps the individual so affected. The fact that a reading disability is not as readily apparent, as for example, a congenital hip or a congenital heart,

From *The Journal of School Health,* 35: 145–153; April, 1965. Reprinted by permission. Ursula M. Anderson is Director of Child Health, Erie County Health Department, Buffalo, New York.

causes it to be too often neglected for too long a time. It would also seem that even when a reading disability is recognized, an attitude of hopelessness is brought to bear on its treatment, for what otherwise would be the reason for the host of "socially promoted" children in our schools other than perhaps lack of adequate facilities to cope with them? A child with an uncorrected defect harbors the beginnings of further deviations, particularly in the sphere of emotional and behavioral problems. Therefore, in terms of the prevention of some of the later effects of a reading disability, the early recognition and appropriate treatment of such a basic defect assumes obvious importance. It is axiomatic to say that to recognize the abnormal, one must first know the normal. In regard to the ability to read, this axiom remains true. However, from experience, I believe it is equally true to say that while this disability itself may be recognized, it is seldom that a child with a reading disability is put through a systematic examination of the factors involved in the normal process of learning to read. The following is a review of these factors together with a review of the major factors that may impede this process. The factors involved in the normal process of learning to read may be categorized as those associated with (a) vision; (b) hearing; (c) the precise association of major portions of the cerebral cortex; and (d) individual variation in developmental attainment.

The following exercise will illustrate better than any amount of verbal description, just precisely how the first three factors itemized above are simultaneously involved in the process of reading. Read the following sentence out loud, and then pause for a moment to examine what happens in this process:

The Cat is on The Mat.

Seeing these words gives meaning to them, hearing them gives meaning to them, and the seeing and the hearing combined gives rise to a definite mental image. On closer examination of what took place, it will become apparent that use of either vision or hearing was dominant in terms of the mental imagery produced. In this regard it is well to recognize the fact that even when we read silently, we "speak" words to ourselves thereby making "silent" use of our auditory pathways by interpretation of the phonetic qualities of the words. Thus the stimulation of hearing by sounds that convey meaning, and the stimulation of vision by symbols that convey meaning, gives rise to a process whereby these sounds and symbols are integrated into meaningful imagery. It is this constant interaction and integration of the peripheral functions of vision and hearing, and their cortical interpretation, a fact that is related to Gestalt (1, 2, 3, 4) that enables us to communicate through the medium of the written and the spoken word. A reading disability will result if any one of these three major factors is deficient, or if there is a deviation in the developmental pattern of attainment of visual, auditory, or cerebral skills.

The Role of Vision and Visual Handicaps

The power of visual discrimination is not only a matter of refraction and retinal images, but is also a matter of the competency of the nervous elements, from the eye to the visual cortex, to transmit proper stimuli to the brain for proper interpretation of the images formed thereon (5). With regard to visual defects, the more easily detected ones, such as defective visual acuity, are the least offenders in relation to reading disabilities. Most school systems have vision-testing programs in which these defects are picked up at a relatively early age. However, it should be fully appreciated that vision testing has for its purpose *only* an analysis of the integrity of form sense and it is this quantity only that is measured when the Snellen Chart and/or the orthorater are used (6). The examination of a child's vision cannot be considered complete until evaluation of visual acuity has been complemented by an examination of the child's eyes by the school medical examiner, the observations of the teacher, and the school nurse.

Astigmatism and defects in the fusion of images are probably more common causes of difficulty in learning to read than we presently think. One wonders how often these defects are present in the mind of the medical examiner as a cause of a child's failure in the classroom, for it is usually only when symptoms directly referable to these conditions, e.g., headache, distorted imagery, etc., become severe enough for the child to complain, that he is referred to the opthalmologist.

Cross-eyed or squinting children present a special problem, for while the defect per se may not interfere with the learning process, the resultant amblyopia as well as the behavioral problems associated with the aesthetic effects of the defect may very well do so. Early detection and treatment of all strabismi should be instituted in the early years of life, to quote from Worth's treatise on squint, "If there is a squint, the child pays with its sight for every day's delay."

The defects associated with the transmission of imagery to the cerebral cortex and its subsequent interpretation will be discussed later under visual agnosia and visual aphasia. However, it might be well to point out here that with the almost universal employment of the "Look-and-Say Method" of teaching children to read and the emphasis this places on the use of vision and the visual pathways, a child with a defect of same is at an obvious disadvantage. However, as noted already, the rule, indeed the basis of all learning, is the interaction of all factors involved; and in the case of a defect of one of the senses a compensatory emphasis is placed on the use of the intact pathways.

The Role of Hearing and Auditory Defects

The role of hearing and the part it plays in the process of learning to read is a fascinating field of inquiry. To understand the effects of deafness on the learning process, it is first imperative to understand the role that hearing plays in the normal development of speech, for speech is the medium through which teacher and pupils communicate. The first important point to understand is that sounds are not necessarily understood merely because they are heard. Two mechanisms are involved — a peripheral one in the cochlea of the ear where the sounds are received, and a central one in the auditory centres of the cerebral cortex of the brain where the sounds are recognized. The ability to distinguish between different sounds is known as auditory discrimination. This auditory discrimination is something which has to be learned, and the learning is a slow process which goes on unconsciously during the early years of life. During the first three years of a child's life, it is easy for him to learn it — after this it becomes increasingly difficult. Speech, the most complex system of sounds which he has to learn from this process, is the last to be mastered. Understanding of speech always precedes production of speech and the child can understand and obey simple instructions before he can produce speech himself. The period between the ages of twelve to eighteen months has been called the period of "readiness to speak." It is, however, much more important to realize that it is preceded by a period of "readiness to listen" during the first year of life (7).

These facts concerning the assimiliation of speech sounds and their interpretation assume tremendous importance in regard to the child with a defect of hearing. In the first place, if the stage of "readiness to listen" which continues throughout the whole of the first year of life is passed without the defect being detected, the child's ability to store the memory of sounds gets less and less from then on. Since, as we have already noted, the understanding of speech *always* precedes the production of speech, it can readily be seen what disastrous results this will have, not only on the child's ability to talk, but on the totality of the learning process. If this is so, and there are indications pointing to the fact that it is (8), then one might ask the question that logically follows, "Why are we not concentrating our efforts at detection of the deaf child in the early years of life, rather than in the school years and the years immediately preceding entrance to school?" While school hearing screening programs are admirable, the *early detection* of deafness, with all that this implies in terms of prevention, is perhaps a vast field of little tapped endeavour in the field of pediatrics.

The effects of deafness on the child's learning ability will depend, of course, on the degree of the hearing loss. The following is a categorization of hearing loss (9), together with an indication of how each subgroup should be managed:

Slight Hearing Loss. Children in this group acquire speech spontaneously. The child can be managed by placing him in a favorable position in class, i.e., second or third row center.

Moderate Hearing Loss. In this group the hearing loss is such that the conversational voice cannot be heard at twenty feet. Children in this group will acquire speech spontaneously although slight to moderately severe defects of speech may be present. Some of these children will require a hearing aid and special help and follow-up by the otologist and their teacher in order that they may learn to get proper value from the use of it. Speech therapy may also be indicated.

Severe Hearing Loss. Many children, when the deafness is congenital, acquire speech spontaneously, although it will be very defective and often delayed. Hearing for conversation varies from eighteen inches to three feet. Early detection of these children is most important. If adequate auditory training[1] is started in infancy, these children should be able to acquire correct speech and to hold their own with hearing children in regular schools; if not, they will surely show learning problems, particularly in the field of reading, which require special school placement.

---

[1] Auditory training may be defined as that process whereby the child is taught (a) to listen to sound, (b) to recognize the differences between sounds, and (c) to associate sounds with their meaning.

Subtotal Deafness. Children in this group fail to develop speech spontaneously, in which case they will have presented symptoms long before reaching school. At initial testing, these children may show no response to sound, for it is meaningless to them and may, therefore, be classified as totally deaf. Subsequent testing after adequate auditory training will show the presence of hearing, so that they must now be classified as having a subtotal deafness. Nearly all children in this group will be transferred to the previous group, i.e., severe hearing loss, as after adequate training, they will be able to talk and to comprehend speech in others. Only when this is accomplished can we begin to teach them to read.

Total Deafness. Very few children suffer from total deafness. Many children who suffer from a subtotal deafness and fail to comprehend speech are regarded as suffering from a total deafness, and the opportunity to use their hearing in the acquisition of speech is denied to them. Those who really are totally deaf will require to learn speech through lipreading alone.

Because we live in a hearing environment, it is obvious from what has been said that regardless of the method of teaching used, the child with a hearing loss will be at a disadvantage in the learning process — unless of course his defect is detected and managed as indicated above.

The Role of the Cerebral Cortex and Defects of Cortical Function

This heading concerns itself with those functions whereby the brain meaningfully interprets and uses the information which is presented to it by the senses. In this regard, another simple example will illustrate what is involved. When one takes a dime, or for that matter any object in one's hand, one knows from the feel of it that it is a dime. This particular sensory perception is known as stereognosis and the nerve pathways involved are the tactile pathways, i.e., the sensory nerve endings in the fingers — the afferent neurons to the spinal cord and the network of neurons that proceed from the spinal cord to the sensory area of the cortex of the brain. From the sensory area of the cortex other neurons arise which distribute themselves to other areas of the brain — these are called association tracts (10), and their function is to integrate the messages they receive so that in the example cited, one recognizes the nature of the object in one's hand. With regard to language function and the ability to communicate, of which the capacity to read is an integral part, a similar type of integration results from the use of association tracts concerned with language function. As already noted, the sensory modalities of vision and hearing are involved and so it is presumed that association tracts run from the visual and auditory areas of the cortex to that part of the cortex where the messages received are meaningfully interpreted by a process of abstract conceptualization into language components.

In regard to language function, the brain of man has the unique capacity to formulate symbols that substitute for sensory configurations. Elaboration of symbolic substitutes for the sensory configurations of sight and sound constitutes the fabric of written and spoken language (11). It is the inadequacy of the brain to do just this that constitutes the group of disorders considered under this heading. Why the brain should be unable to do this is a subject for further research, but it may result from a disturbance or blocking of function of the association tracts described above, or it may result from direct damage to the cortical areas concerned with each of the sensory modalities involved. These disorders may be classified according to whether they are (a) agnosias or (b) aphasias.

An agnosia denotes a disturbance in the identification and recognition of sensory perceptions at the cortical level, whereas aphasia refers more to the comprehension and understanding of the meaning of total sense data. The difference between the two is really a quantitative one, but the term *aphasia* is only properly used when there is a disturbance in abstraction and conceptualization of sensory perceptions into complex symbolic language.

Visual Verbal Agnosia. This is a failure to identify and recognize symbols by vision. It is not a peripheral failure of vision, but a failure of the cortex to interpret the symbols seen. In view of the common usage of the "Look-and-Say Method" of teaching, the handicap of the child with this defect is obvious. It is a relatively simple matter to ascertain whether or not a child with a reading disability has this defect. Providing there are no over-all defects, such as mental retardation (differentiation of which can be made by clinical psychological evaluation), the presentation of words or individual letters will mean little or nothing to the child. In older children with basically normal intelligence who have this defect, I have observed that there very often occurs a compensation of the defect through the subconscious use of hearing and the cortical centers associated with the interpretation of sounds. What happens is that in a sense these children teach themselves to read and write by learning to interpret what they hear phonetically, and they subsequently somehow relate this with written symbols. I have observed in certain instances that if the child is asked to write a sentence that has definite phonetic qualities such as, "The sun is shining brightly," he will usually write it thus: "The son is (or si) shining britly (or britlee)." The reproduction is, of course, completely phonetic. If the examiner now writes this sentence correctly and requests the child to read it, he will show difficulty in doing so. However, by his ability to reproduce the phonetic qualities, he demonstrates that not only does he have intact auditory pathways and cortical interpretative function, but also that his brain was able to by-pass his basic defect by vigorous use of other pathways, particularly those associated with hearing. These children then, it would seem, are able to reproduce what they hear with a great deal more ease than they can read the same material in the written form. This demonstrates not only the compensatory mechanisms that take place when there is a defect of one sense (either at the peripheral or central level), but also illustrates the totality of function, peripheral and central, involved in the reading and learning process. The obvious advantage of teaching these children phonetically will be apparent.

Visual Aphasia or Alexia. Described by such terms as mind blindness, psychic blindness, word blindness, etc., this disorder consists essentially in an inability to read written or printed material. Hinshelwood (12, 13) described the alexia of congenital origin as congenital word blindness. Orton (14), however, who made extensive studies of this disorder, named it strephosymbolia. He stated that hemispheric rivalry might play a part in the genesis of this condition, and the reader is referred to his work for a more detailed description of this. (Crossed laterality has long been associated in people's minds with reading disorders.) Special mention is made of this because of the confusion that arises as a result of the relative frequency of use of the terms *word blindness, aphasia, strepho-symbolia,* etc., as applied to this condition. Attention is also drawn to the fact that it is very difficult to differentiate a visual agnosia from true alexia. The former is often accompanied by other defects, such as disturbances of body image and spatial defects, while the latter often occurs in pure form in children. However, children with visual agnosia and visual aphasia form the hard core of children with specific reading disabilities. The association of this disability with normal intelligence is nothing less than tragic if left without help. It is estimated that of the 10 per cent of children with reading disabilities about 1 per cent are true dyslexics or alexics. (15) The management of these children belongs to the teacher of remedial reading and emphasis should be placed on the use of the auditory, and if necessary, the tactile pathways.

Auditory Agnosia and Aphasia. It is extremely difficult to separate an acoustic agnosia from an acoustic aphasia, because in man, sounds are closely linked to meaning. (16) However, the term auditory agnosia would relate to a defect in the identification and recognition of sounds. Auditory aphasia, however, relates more to the comprehension and understanding of sounds, and this in turn would be related to other cerebral functions, such as the relation of sounds to written symbols — a process that must be intact for the child to be able to read. Children with either of these defects are likely to be late vocalizers, but the child with auditory aphasia is more likely to show severe difficulty in integrative cerebral function when the reading process is presented to him on account of his difficulty in relating sounds to their written symbols. These children find greater ease in interpretation of sensory stimuli through use of their visual pathways; therefore, emphasis should be placed on the "Look-and-Say" method of teaching. Their management definitely belongs to the remedial reading class and the continued efforts of the remedial reading teacher.

Tactile Agnosia. In this condition, the tactile sensory pathways at the cortical level are defective. Mention is made of this disorder only on account of the importance of the integrity of these pathways when the visual and auditory pathways and their respective functions are involved in one or the other of the defects described above. If a child has defects of both his visual and auditory perception at either the peripheral or cortical level, then if his sensory pathways are intact, use may be made of these in order to teach him to read by the kinesthetic method. Children who need to be taught by this method obviously need the help of a teacher well versed and experienced in the field of remedial reading.

Individual Variation in Developmental Patterns

Development is an orderly process with, however, a broad spectrum of variation in the time taken to reach certain milestones. While it is usual, for example, for children to walk by the time they are one year of age, not all children who are completely normal do so, nor do all children talk by the age of two. As has already been pointed out, the period of readiness to talk precedes the act of talking and the period of readiness to listen precedes them both. The same developmental pattern pertains to reading. It is extremely important to realize that there is a period of readiness to read and until this stage is reached, attempts to teach the child will meet with failure. Most children reach this development level by the time they are six years of age, but some do not. Pressuring the child beyond his development level can only lead to frustration for him and the establishment of an atmosphere of failure which will hardly be conducive to his learning. Reading-readiness tests should be given to any child showing slowness in learning, and if he is clearly not ready to learn, then other skills should be fostered until his developmental level catches up. The fact that he is slow in beginning does not mean that he will continue to be slow. Many an experienced teacher can testify to the slow beginner who finally outstrips his initially more precocious peers.

All of the conditions enumerated can and do, for the most part, occur in children who have normal basic intelligence. The idea that the backward reader must in some way be cerebrally defective has too long influenced educator's conceptions. (17) The same may be true of the physician's attitude, and the examiner's own realization of this bias is an important fact for him to bear in mind when he examines a child referred for learning failure or reading disability. Unfortunately, too many of these children progress to the point where they become behavior problems before referral is made, and their difficulty, and the examiner's, is thus compounded in terms of diagnosis and management. It would be an interesting exercise to delineate how many children referred for psychiatric treatment do in fact have a reading disability due to one or another or a combination, of the above defects. Eisenberg states that most cases are brought to a physician's attention, not as reading problems per se, but as scholastic failures or behavior disorders. (18)

All of the four major factors cited may be considered a primary cause of reading disability. These primary factors, may, however, be intact and yet the child may be handicapped in his ability to read by various exogenous factors, e.g. anxiety, depression, emotional blocking, and limited schooling opportunity. (19) These exogenous factors may then be regarded as secondary causes of reading disability. Mental retardation may also be considered as a secondary cause, though it should be borne in mind that the primary causes of reading disability may also be operative in these instances.

Summary

A review of the primary and secondary factors involved in reading disability readily demonstrates that such a defect is not a distinct clinical entity, but merely a symptom of many different conditions. It is imperative that every child with a reading disability be given an examination that will screen for the following: (a) defects of vision — acuity, astigmatism, fusion, etc.; (b) defects of hearing; (c) defects of cortical function, mixed dominance, visual agnosia, and auditory agnosia; and (d) defects of emotional adjustment or intellectual capacity.

In cases where screening procedures indicate that further evaluation is necessary, the child should be referred for pediatric, opthalmological, audiological and otological, and neurological consultation. The examination of a child with a reading disability cannot be considered adequate until all of these factors have been thoroughly screened and, if necessary, further investigated.

The present and the future role of the physician caring for children will be concerned more and more with the management of children with long term disabilities, the effects of which, if left unmitigated, can be devastating to the child, his family, and society. Particularly will this be so in the content of those areas of disability that conflict with the demands that society places upon the individual. In few spheres will more dynamic prevention be practiced than in that of a child with a reading disability, the unmitigated effects of which can lead to the mildest and the severest behavioral problems.

Bibliography

1. Katy, D. *Gestalt Psychology*. London: Methuen, 1951.
2. Koffher, U. *Principles of Gestalt Psychology*. New York: Harcourt & Brace, 1953.
3. de Hirsch, K. *Journal of Gestalt Psychology*, 102: 277–297; 1963.
4. *Reading Disability: Progress and Research Needs in Dyslexia*, ed. John Money. Baltimore: The Johns Hopkins Press, 1962.
5. Lanciano, Ralph. *Clinical Pediatrics*, 1, 3: 160.
6. *Ibid.*
7. Whetnall, Edith. *The Practioner*, 174: 375; London, 1955.
8. Stinchfield, S. N., and E. H. Young. *Children with Delayed and Defective Speech*. London: 1938.
9. Whetnall, E. *Journal of Larynology and Otology*, 70, 11: 644–645; London, 1956.
10. Johnston, T. B. *A Synopsis of Regional Anatomy*. London: J. A. Churchill, 1945.
11. Steegman, A. T. *Examination of the Nervous System*. Chicago: Yearbook Medical Publishers, Inc., 1962.
12. Hinshelwood, J. 1900 Lancet, 1506.
13. ———. 1917, Conference on Word Blindness, London.
14. Orton, S. T. *Studies in Language Function*, Proceedings of the Association for Research in Neurological and Mental Diseases, 13: 614–633; 1932.
15. MacDonald, Critchley. Proceedings of the Royal Society of Medicine, 56: 3; March, 1963.
16. Steegman, A. T. *Examination of the Nervous System*. Chicago: Yearbook Medical Publishers, Inc., 1962.
17. Schonell, F. J. *Backwardness in the Basic Subjects*, 4th ed. Edinburgh: 1948.
18. Eisenberg, L. *Pediatrics*, 23: 997; May, 1959.
19. Rabinovitch, R. D., in S. Arieti, *American Handbook of Psychiatry*, Vol. I. New York: Basic Books, Inc., 1959.

Further Reading for Chapter 14

Adler, Sol. *The Non-Verbal Child*. Springfield, Ill.: Charles C. Thomas, 1964.

Bateman, Barbara. "Learning Disabilities — Yesterday, Today, and Tomorrow," *Exceptional Children*, 31: 167–177; December, 1964.

Bing, Lois B. "Vision and Reading," *The Reading Teacher*, 14: 241–244; March, 1961.

Bryant, N. Dale. "Some Principles of Remedial Instruction for Dyslexia," *The Reading Teacher*, 18: 567–572; April, 1965.

Capobianco, R. J. "Diagnostic Methods Used with Learning Disability Cases," *Exceptional Children*, 31: 187–193; December, 1964.

Cohn, Robert. "The Neurological Study of Children with Learning Disabilities," *Exceptional Children*, 31: 179–185; December, 1964.

Criscuolo, N. P. "Let's Stimulate Our Reluctant Readers," *Peabody Journal of Education*, 42: 157–162; November, 1964.

Deverell, A. F. "Specific Dyslexia: Nature and Treatment," *Canadian Education Research Digest*, 4: 279–290; December, 1964.

Dolan, G. K. "Effects of Individual Counseling on Selected Test Scores for Delayed Readers," *Personnel and Guidance Journal*, 42: 914–919; May, 1964.

Eames, Thomas H. "Physical Factors in Reading," *The Reading Teacher*, 15: 427–432; May, 1962.

Frostig, Marianne. "Corrective Reading in the Classroom," *The Reading Teacher*, 18: 573–580; April, 1965.

Gray, Lillian. *Teaching Children to Read*. New York: The Ronald Press Company, 1963. Chapter 14.

Harris, Albert J. *How to Increase Reading Ability*. New York: David McKay Co., Inc., 1961. Chapters 9, 10, 11, and 14.

Heilman, Arthur W. *Principles and Practices of Teaching Reading*. Columbus, Ohio: Charles E. Merrill Books, Inc., 1961. Chapters 12 and 13.

Hewett, Frank M. "A Hierarchy of Educational Tasks for Children with Learning Disorders," *Exceptional Children*, 31: 207–213; December, 1964.

Ketchum, E. Gillet. "Neurological and Psychological Trends in Reading Diagnosis," *The Reading Teacher*, 17: 589–593; May, 1964.

Lovell, K., and M. E. Woosley. "Reading Disability, Non-Verbal Reasoning and Social Class," *Educational Research*, 6: 226–229; June, 1964.

McCarthy, William, and Joan Oliver. "Some Tactile-Kinesthetic Procedures for Teaching Reading to Slow-Learning Children," *Exceptional Children*, 31: 419–421; April, 1965.

McKim, Margaret G., and Helen Caskey. *Guiding Growth in Reading in the Modern Elementary School*. New York: The Macmillan Company, 1963. Chapter 14.

Money, John (ed). *Reading Disability: Progress and Research Needs in Dyslexia*. Baltimore: The Johns Hopkins Press, 1962.

Ofman, William O., and Morton Skaevitz. "The Kinesthetic Method in Remedial Reading," *The Journal of Experimental Education*, 31: 317–320; March, 1963.

Otto, Wayne, and Richard A. McMenemy. *Corrective and Remedial Teaching: Principles and Practices*. Boston: Houghton Mifflin Company, 1966. Chapters 1–7.

Pollack, M. F. W., and Josephine A. Pierkarz. *Reading Problems and Problem Readers*. New York: David McKay Co., Inc., 1963.

Robeck, Mildred C. "Readers Who Lacked Word Analysis Skills: A Group Diagnosis," *Journal of Educational Research*, 56: 432–434; April, 1963.

Robinson, Helen M., and Helen K. Smith. "Rate Problems in the Reading Clinic," *The Reading Teacher*, 15: 421–426; May, 1962.

Roswell, Florence, and Gladys Natchez. *Reading Disability: Diagnosis and Treatment*. New York: Basic Books, Inc., 1964.

Sawyer, Rita I. "Does the Wechsler Intelligence Scale for Children Discriminate Between Mildly Disabled and Severely Disabled Readers?" *The Elementary School Journal*, 66: 97–103; November, 1965.

Smith, Henry P., and Emerald V. Dechant. *Psychology in Teaching Reading.* Englewood Cliffs, N.J.: Prentice-Hall, Inc., 1961. Chapters 5, 6, and 15.

Tinker, Miles A., and Constance M. McCullough. *Teaching Elementary Reading.* New York: Appleton-Century-Crofts, Inc., 1962. Chapter 25.

Walters, Richard H., and Helen Doan. "Perceptual and Cognitive Functioning of Retarded Readers," *Journal of Consulting Psychology*, 26: 355–361; August, 1962.

Witty, Paul A., Alma Moore Freeland, and Edith H. Grotberg. *The Teaching of Reading: A Developmental Process.* Boston: D. C. Heath and Company, 1966. Chapters 13 and 14.

Zimmerman, I. L., and G. N. Allebrand. "Personality Characteristics and Attitudes Toward Achievement of Good and Poor Readers," *Journal of Educational Research*, 59: 28–30; September, 1965.

LB1050 .D85   010101 000
Durr, William Kirtley, 19
Reading instruction; dimension

0 2002 0045748 5
YORK COLLEGE OF PENNSYLVANIA 17403